Networked Applications:

A Guide to the New
Computing Infractructure

The Morgan Kaufmann Series in Networking
Series Editor, David Clark

Networked Applications: A Guide to the New Computing Infrastructure
David G. Messerschmitt

Modern Cable Television Technology: Video, Voice, and Data Communications
Walter Ciciora, James Farmer, and David Large

Wide Area Network Design: Concepts and Tools for Optimization
Robert S. Cahn

Optical Networks: A Practical Perspective
Rajiv Ramaswami and Kumar Sivarajan

Practical Computer Network Analysis and Design
James D. McCabe

Frame Relay Applications: Business and Technology Case Studies
James P. Cavanagh

High-Performance Communication Networks
Jean Walrand and Pravin Varaiya

Computer Networks: A Systems Approach
Larry L. Peterson and Bruce S. Davie

Networked Applications:
A Guide to the New Computing Infractructure

David G. Messerschmitt
University of California, Berkeley

Morgan Kaufmann Publishers, Inc.
San Francisco, California

Senior Editor	Jennifer Mann
Director of Production and Manufacturing	Yonie Overton
Production Editors	Julie Pabst, Elisabeth Beller
Copyeditor	Judith Brown
Proofreader	Jennifer McClain
Illustration	Lineworks, Inc.
Composition	Nancy Logan
Text and Cover Design	Ross Carron Design
Cover Photo	Erich Lessing/Art Resource, NY
Indexer	Steve Rath
Printer	Courier Corporation

Designations used by companies to distinguish their products are often claimed as trademarks or registered trademarks. In all instances where Morgan Kaufmann Publishers, Inc. is aware of a claim, the product names appear in initial capital or all capital letters. Readers, however, should contact the appropriate companies for more complete information regarding trademarks and registration.

Morgan Kaufmann Publishers, Inc.
Editorial and Sales Office
340 Pine Street, Sixth Floor
San Francisco, CA 94104-3205
USA
Telephone   415/392-2665
Facsimile   415/982-2665
Email   mkp@mkp.com
WWW   http://www.mkp.com

Library of Congress Cataloging-in-Publication Data
Messerschmitt, David G.
     Networked applications : a guide to the new computing infrastructure /
David G. Messerschmitt.
             p.   cm.
     Includes bibliographical references.
     ISBN 1-55860-536-3
     1. Internet programming. 2. Computer networks.   I. Title
QA76.625.M47   1999   98-52772
005.2'76—dc21   CIP

To Dody and Laura

Contents

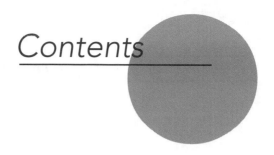

viii   Contents

Preface

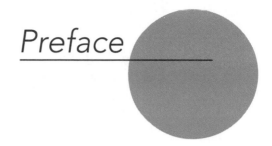

When computers are networked, two industries—computing and communications—converge, and the result is vastly more than the sum of the parts. Social computer applications—those that support groups of users and even groups of organizations rather than individual users—become available. Management of information and knowledge, previously the purview of an individual or an isolated organization, becomes a global activity. Suddenly computing applications become available for business-to-business coordination and commerce and for small as well as large organizations. The global Internet creates a public place without geographic boundaries—called cyberspace—where ordinary citizens can interact, publish their ideas, and engage in the purchase and sale of goods and services. Publications assume new multimedia forms, combining text, images, audio, and video. In short, the impact of both computing and communications on our society and organizational structures is greatly magnified.

This book presents the core concepts and terminology of the converged computing and communications technology and industry. It takes an application perspective, addressing these questions:

- How do the uses of computers change when they are networked? What new applications become possible, and what old applications are irrevocably changed?

- What possibilities and limitations are imposed on applications by the technology and infrastructure of networked computing?

- What business, economic, and government policy issues most strongly impact the applications of networked computing and the evolution of the technologies and infrastructure that enable them?

The goal of this book is to empower you to participate fully in generating new ideas for using these exciting technologies and to work effectively with implementers to bring these ideas to fruition.

Who Should Read This Book

Do you want to utilize networked computing to your personal and professional benefit? Would you like to understand the existing applications of networked computers? Would you like to understand the underlying technologies well enough to be in a position to appreciate what new applications may be possible or unlikely or impossible? Do you want to understand how the industries that support these applications and technologies work so that you can be a better customer and better anticipate the future evolution of the systems and applications? If your answer to any of these questions is yes, then this book is for you.

More specifically, this book is targeted at two audiences. The first includes those who have considerable education and experience with information technology and want to appreciate the unique application opportunities afforded by the networking of computers as well as the technologies and infrastructure that underlie those technologies. These readers may also want to enhance their knowledge of the industry and government issues that affect networked computing and its applications.

The second audience includes those who don't yet have expertise in information technology—and may not even be interested in getting deeply involved in it—but have observed its growing importance in all aspects of industry and society and feel the need to learn more about it. Because networking moves computing into the realm of the general society's discourse and interaction—for individual users and organizations of all types—it participates in many activities previously not affected so deeply by information technology. As a result, a broad range of citizens, from corporate managers and executives to economists, intellectual property attorneys, venture capitalists, investment bankers, and many others, will benefit from an understanding of both the constituent technologies and how they are applied to a broad range of applications.

To accommodate this second audience, prior knowledge of networked computing or the supporting industries is not presumed. The book does presume a working familiarity with personal computers and their applications, which today is almost universal among students and working professionals. Chapters 3 through 5 in particular provide a preparatory working knowledge of information technology and its industry necessary for appreciating the later chapters so may be read selectively by readers already well versed in information technology.

A Conceptual Approach

This book presents the big picture and also offers a number of features especially designed to meet the needs of those already versed in information technology as well as the needs of those who are not:

- *Application perspective:* Everything is presented from the perspective of the application. The topics, and the depth and breadth of coverage of these topics, have been chosen with their relevance to applications in mind.

- *Basic concepts rather than an alphabet soup:* Computing and networking technologies and applications change so quickly, it is easy to get drawn into giving descriptions of current products and approaches littered with arcane terminology and an alphabet soup of acronyms. This book concentrates instead on long-lasting core concepts and terminology and minimizes technical detail except where deemed necessary. The book does provide numerous topical examples to relate these concepts and terminology to the real world, empowering you to successfully track ongoing industry and technology developments.

- *Top-down, general to specific:* Rather than beginning with bytes, megaflops, objects, and transactions before understanding how the technology is used, this book *begins* with applications, imparting the usefulness and impact of networked computing on your personal or work life. It then proceeds to develop an understanding of the specification, development, and deployment of networked applications, followed by the supporting technology and infrastructure. At each stage, you will be motivated by an understanding of context and the importance of the topic at hand. Since each chapter is organized similarly, details can be skipped without sacrificing coherence or perspective.

- *Plentiful analogies:* Illuminating analogies from everyday life are used liberally. They make concepts easy to understand and give them depth. They also illustrate that there is nothing unique about networked computing. Most challenges are also encountered elsewhere, in a different (and usually recognizable) form.

- *Industrial and policy context:* To appreciate networked computing and its applications, the book conveys a working knowledge of the industry that supports the suite of networked computing technologies—so you can be an effective customer—and an understanding of the social and political context. The economics and structure of the industry affect the future of the applications as much as the technology. Networked computing introduces a host of difficult social issues, such as privacy, globalization, security, etc., and the societal response to these issues in turn impacts the technology and its uses.

- *No programming:* This is not a book on computing or programming skills. Rather, it is about the applications of networked computers and the fundamental ideas, concepts, and related terminology that support them. The goal is to empower you to conceptualize new applications, not implement them. Many readers are already facile with implementation issues, but this isn't necessary to effectively conceptualize new applications and bring them to fruition, working with the aid of professional programmers.

- *References:* Those seeking more detailed and specialized knowledge will find recommended references at the end of each chapter.

Other Resources

Supplementary resources, such as Web links relevant to each chapter and errata, are available on the book's home page at *http://www.mkp.com/netapps.*

The home page describes what chapters and sections can be skipped without loss of continuity and includes downloadable presentation slides.

This book can be used in the classroom and is particularly well suited to short courses and executive training seminars. A textbook version aimed at university courses will be published by Morgan Kaufmann Publishers in the summer of 1999. It will include more in-depth treatment of many topics in Chapters 4 through 12 and other resources, such as discussion topics, exercises, Web explorations, and classroom presentation slides.

Acknowledgments

The origins of this book can be traced to Hal Varian, Dean of the University of California at Berkeley School of Information Management and Systems, who not only suggested that I develop a course in the applications of networked computing for the new SIMS curriculum but also helped me develop and teach it.

My editor at Morgan Kaufmann, Jennifer Mann, and the consulting editor David Clark, of the Massachusetts Institute of Technology Laboratory for Computer Science, have been enormously helpful in keeping my attention focused on accuracy, excellence, and the market. Karyn Johnson conscientiously sought out excellent reviewers, and in the end brought in all the reviews.

The reviewers of the original proposal for this book provided numerous excellent suggestions for retargeting and reorganization. They include Thomas Badgett of Synergy South, Michael Borrus of the Berkeley Roundtable on International Economics, Chris Dellarocas of the Sloan School of Management at MIT, Gordy Dhatt of Goodale & Barbieri Companies, Paul Resnick of the University of Michigan School of Information, Pamela Samuelson of Berkeley, Thomas Uslaender of Fraunhofer-Institute for Information and Data

Processing (Germany), Michael Vitale of the University of Melbourne (Australia) Department of Information Systems, James Ware of the Berkeley Haas School of Business, Robert Wilensky of the Berkeley Computer Science Division, and Janet Wilson of the Mutual Insurance Corporation of Arizona. The full manuscript of this book was reviewed and commented on in detail by Al Erisman of the Boeing Company, Brian Jaffe of *PC Week,* Bart Stuck of Business Strategies LLC, Matt Tavis of Sapient Corporation, and Janet Wilson of the Mutual Insurance Corporation of Arizona. Overall, these reviewers provided invaluable insights from a number of perspectives and especially the industrial application of information technologies. My student William Li, my wife Dorothy and daughter Laura, and Chung-Sheng Li of the IBM Watson Research Laboratory provided helpful suggestions.

Special thanks go to Hal Varian and Paul Resnick. In co-teaching parts of this material with Hal, I have learned much about the economics and policy issues, and he greatly influenced this aspect of the book. Paul provided numerous substantive comments on both technical and policy issues, and those thoughtful suggestions particularly impacted the organization and content of Chapter 2.

I am especially indebted to the students in the Berkeley Information Systems 206 class who endured—with enthusiasm and good humor—an early attempt to convey this material, and whose suggestions, questions, and innocent misconceptions influenced my approach in many substantive ways.

Finally, I appreciate the support and patience of my wife Dorothy during the lengthy process of preparing these materials and writing this book.

Introduction

The networking of computers—a technology more than twenty years old—is substantially impacting individuals, organizations, and business. The global public Internet now interconnects a significant portion of the world's computers, allowing them to communicate freely to realize shared applications. No longer is computing confined to serving isolated individuals or organizations. Networked computing supports groups of users (or organizations or enterprises) jointly participating in applications as well as the citizenry at large. This is a watershed in the history of computing.

Two previous technologies profoundly affected social and cultural institutions: mass transportation and telecommunications. Modern transportation transformed the urban landscape, leading to suburban growth, often at the expense of central cities. The telephone and television irrevocably affected politics and government; the free flow of ideas and a direct window into other societies have impacted political thought. Together, transportation and telecommunications led to a globalization of many communities, organizations, and institutions. They enabled and empowered the multinational corporation and the global superpower nation.

Networked computing is a seminal addition to this technical infrastructure. Like its predecessors, it will have a substantial and lasting impact on individual lives as well as business, social, and cultural institutions. It will facilitate the dissemination of information and knowledge, collaboration among individuals, business processes spanning geographically dispersed organizations, and commerce (among businesses and with consumers). Unlike telecommunications (which has emphasized voice and facsimile media), networked computing supports virtually all forms of information, such as data, images, and video, as well as money, and allows them to be integrated in innovative ways. Beyond information transport, networked computing supports software-defined storage and manipulation of information, and automates many knowledge-intensive tasks.

We have entered an information age, for which the key technological enablers are the network, the computer, and its software applications. This book is a guide to the possibilities of this information age, the technologies, and the supporting industry. It will position you to make best use of these far-reaching new technologies in your own area of expertise. The book will give you an appreciation of the possibilities of networked computing as well as the limitations. It will also position you to work effectively with professional programmers to implement your ideas and equip you with enough understanding of the industry to be an informed customer. Armed with this knowledge, go out and change the world!

1.1 A Historical Perspective

Networked computing is a collection of related technologies that support a broad range of geographically distributed computer applications. (It is distinct from a similar term in current vogue—the *network computer*, or NC—which describes one computing technology.) The *computing* portion of networked computing enables the storage, retrieval, and processing of tremendous amounts of information and also serves as an interface to users. A *network* enables computers to interact and share information, much like the telephone allows people to talk. A computing *application* is a software program that provides direct and specific value to a user or an organization, and a *networked application* distributes programs across two or more computers, which then collaborate in realizing the application. *Users* are the people leveraging the application for their job, to interact or collaborate with other users, or merely to have fun.

Computing technology has changed and expanded over the years, resulting in an expanding range of applications. As originally conceived in the 1930s, the computer performed massive calculations. Due to electronics advances, its computational capability continues to expand rapidly. Later, mass storage media (such as magnetic disks) extended applications to encompass the storage, retrieval, and manipulation of massive quantities of information. The relatively recent addition of networking allows computers to communicate and interact.

1.1.1 Technology View

When running an organization, your first impulse, if you want to become more flexible and responsive, is to decentralize. Then you discover there isn't enough coordination, so you establish hierarchical management structures, hold meetings, and generate memos and reports to improve internal communications. In consonance with technological advances, the computer industry has undergone precisely the same transitions, resulting in the major phases of computing technology shown in Table 1.1.

These phases are not mutually exclusive. Centralized mainframes still flourish—as the repositories of mission-critical corporate information—and are integrated into networked computing applications. Time-sharing still exists, in the sense that departmental-level computers support multiple users at their desktop computers. The isolated computer *is* a thing of the past; virtually all computers are networked today.

The most important enabling technology for networked computing is the network itself, which builds on data communications media (especially fiber optics) and the advances in electronics (which also made much faster and cheaper computers possible). Networked computing results in the convergence of two industries—computing and communications—irrevocably changing each.

1.1.2 User and Organization View

Each phase of computing brought expanded opportunities and challenges. Until the early 1990s, mainframes formed the information core of major organizations' work processes. However, centralized and time-shared computing—in part because their applications

Table 1.1 Four major phases of computing.

Phase	Characteristics	Typical applications
Centralized computing (a few computers for a whole organization)	A relatively few *mainframe* computers were physically large and expensive, affordable only to large organizations.	Automate major business functions, such as payroll and accounting, and manage enterprise information resources, such as customer lists or inventories.
Time-shared computing (a few computers shared by a large number of users)	Terminals were added to allow a large number of workers to directly access applications on a centralized computer.	Workers could directly interact with the centralized applications to input data, initiate transactions, and extract information. Users could participate in shared applications.
Decentralized computing (a computer for every department and every user)	Less expensive centralized computers could be deployed at the departmental level. Inexpensive personal computers could be dedicated to a single user, supplementing the centralized computers.	Personal productivity was enhanced by word processing, spreadsheet, and small data management applications. Home users and students could benefit from similar applications, as well as others dedicated to personal finances, education, or entertainment.
Networked computing (computers can communicate and interact with one another)	All computers are connected by networks, allowing them to participate in geographically distributed applications on a global basis. Desktop computers can provide access to information in centralized computers. Networked computing is distinct from the "network computer (NC)" discussed in Chapter 3.	Networked applications not only benefit from more sophisticated user interfaces (graphics, pointing device, etc.) supported by the personal computers, but also access the processing power and massive data residing on servers and mainframes. Groups of users can participate in applications that enable collective communication and collaboration.

were provided by a centralized information technology (IT) organization—were comparatively unresponsive to the needs of departments and workers. Decentralized computing empowered users by allowing them to add their own applications and process data in personalized ways, but the downside was the organizational chaos resulting from inconsistent solutions. Looking at the transition to decentralized computing in retrospect offers the following insights:

- The users benefited from greater innovation by independent application suppliers. Users had greater computing power at their disposal, enabling, for example, user interfaces based on graphical user interfaces.

- Organizations had to adjust their information technology organizations to a new technological reality. Many organizational problems are still with us, such as high cost of administering a diversity of computers and fragmentation of the organization's information assets.

- For computer suppliers, the old strategy of proprietary turnkey applications became obsolete. The premier firms of the centralized computer industry didn't adapt fast enough (such as IBM, DEC, and Data General). Today, they have recovered, but many companies at the pinnacle of the industry were formed in response to decentralized computing.

- Desktop computers unleashed computing into every walk of life and have impacted the everyday lives of many citizens. Today, yearly sales of home computers exceeds television sets in the United States, and computing as a part of education, every occupation and job, and many avocations is increasingly accepted.

This gives an optimistic view, but these trends also have negative ramifications. There is an increased administrative overhead associated with decentralized computing, including the greater involvement of individual users in maintaining and upgrading their desktop computers.

While desktop computing had widespread ramifications, the impact of networking is even greater. In the mid-1990s, networked computing founded on networked microprocessor-based computers made significant inroads into applications previously the domain of mainframes, as the networked computers became sufficiently reliable and offered a path to new and reorganized work processes and greater customer satisfaction. Some of the implications of networked computing include

- The transition from centralized applications that performed hidden "back-office" functions, to the expectation that most computing applications will intimately involve users, is complete.

- Networked applications empower computer-mediated interaction and collaboration.

- Applications can span organizational boundaries, opening up many opportunities in commerce (the buying and selling of goods and services, and their coordination).

- Networked computing is a basic infrastructure for the society. As evident from the increasing attention from legislative, regulatory, and judicial authorities, networked computing has substantive impact on society and its citizens.

From an individual's perspective, computing has followed a trajectory from an invisible back-office function (centralized computing), to a tool for enhancing personal productivity and entertainment (decentralized computing), to an expanded role in accessing vast global information resources, and in interacting and collaborating with others.

1.1.3 Unrelenting Change

Progress in the underlying technologies of computing (processing, storage, data communications) has been dramatic and unrelenting for several decades. Likewise, driven by the rapidly decreasing costs of these technologies and better ideas of how to exploit them, the applications of computing have seen dramatic expansion and change. The computing industry is distinctly different from most others in this dramatic rate of change.

Applications implemented in the technology of yesterday are called *legacy applications*. One result of rapid change in the industry is an expanding set of legacy applications. Unfortunately, any application using today's most modern technology will be tomorrow's legacy application. History has seen—and this is likely to remain so for the foreseeable future—a continual evolution from today's to tomorrow's technology, while having to maintain and integrate legacy applications. One implication is the importance of a forward-looking rather than retrospective view of technology when conceptualizing applications—a view, I hope, that will be aided by the understanding imparted in this book.

1.2 Computing in the Future

The history of computing (and technology more generally) illustrates that progress is far from steady. Technology makes big leaps—from centralized to decentralized, from decentralized to networked—that take a while to be assimilated within the industry and the applications. Can future leaps be anticipated? Probably some can—those listed in Table 1.2—because they are well under way. A quick summary of the table is that computing will be *anywhere*, *everywhere*, and *within*. If you find this alarming, take heart in the observation that computing will put on a much different face. Replacing the big boxes that clutter our homes and offices will be smaller, less obvious, and less obtrusive computers [Wei93]

Computing is not the first technology to follow a similar evolution. A century ago, electrification (analogous to networking) had as its major applications light and mechanical power. Both light and power followed a clear evolution to mobility (battery-operated flashlights and power tools), ubiquity (electric outlets and appliances in every room), and embeddedness (small electric motors within many products). The greatest lesson from electrification—and also one evident in computing—is that the first step is retrofitting a new technology into the existing ways of doing things. Eventually, however, people figure out new ways to use the unique capabilities of the technology, and only then substantial gains become evident (see the sidebar "Electrification: Lessons from an Earlier Technological Advance" for a historical observation).

The same will be true with computing. You can tell that the technology and its applications have matured when computing is incorporated in everyday life in natural and unobtrusive ways, when computing makes things easier, more efficient, and more pleasurable, and when computing doesn't get in the way. This isn't quite true today, but it is forthcoming.

Electrification: Lessons from an Earlier Technological Advance

Electrification had its greatest impact on productivity and standards of living only after ways were found to exploit its unique characteristics. Computing will follow the same course.

In part, the industrial revolution substituted machinery and water or steam power for human labor. For a single factory, water or steam power from a central source (analogous to centralized computing) was distributed throughout a factory using cumbersome drive belts. The factory was organized around the distribution of power, with compact, multistory factories. Electric power initially had little impact because large electric motors were simply substituted for water or steam sources—nothing else was changed. It took decades to recognize that smaller electric motors powering individual machines (analogous to decentralized computing) enabled the reorganization of the factory around the needs of the work process (linear assembly lines) rather than power distribution, with dramatic improvements in efficiency and quality.

The electric motor also has a parallel to embedded com-

Table 1.2 Future trends beyond networked computing.

Trend	Description	Comments
Mobility (computing anywhere)	Networked computers can be taken anywhere and still benefit from full network services.	Laptop computers and personal digital assistants are the precursors. Mobility requires ubiquitous networking access analogous to the cellular telephone.
Ubiquity (computing everywhere)	Networked computers are unobtrusively sprinkled throughout the physical environment.	Information kiosks, mobile phones with Web browsers, and personal digital assistants are steps in this direction. In the future, as computers gain a similar size and resolution to paper, magazines, and books, computers should become as ubiquitous as the printed word is today.
Embedding (computing within)	Networked computers are embedded in most everyday products.	This is already common: Automobiles, consumer electronics, toys, and appliances have computing within. In the future, many more products—even as mundane as light switches and lightbulbs—will not only have computing within but also network connections.

Computing embedded in a plethora of products (such as automobiles and appliances) is "embedded computing in the small," and represents only the tip of the iceberg. Arguably even more important is "embedded networked computing in the large," which focuses on networked computing within many essential systems supporting society and the economy.

For some time networked computing has been embedded within (and crucial to the operation of) much of the infrastructure. It has been the controlling element for telecommunications and electric power networks and many aspects of the transportation system, such as air traffic control and train control. The world's financial systems, including the flow of money and financial markets, depend on a networked computing infrastructure.

Today networked computing is being integrated into a broader range of large systems. Large companies are automating many of their repetitive business processes, controlling the flow of material, finished goods, and money within their organizations. Increasingly, business-to-business relationships with customers and suppliers are automated by *electronic commerce* applications using networked computing. Even consumers are joining the fray, conducting a small (but rapidly growing) fraction of their financial and commercial transactions over the Internet.

A less tangible (but no less real) impact of networked computing is its application to the interaction and discourse among individual citizens on a global basis, utilizing Internet applications such as email, chatrooms, and newsgroups. This is important because the interactions among citizens (as well as social compacts) most clearly distinguish a society from a collection of individuals.

What is distinctive about computing embedded within these large systems is that computers, networks, and software are only a *part* of a system, which also includes citizens and workers, procedures, policies, and laws, the flow of material and finished goods, and many other aspects. To be most effective, technology cannot simply replace and automate existing functions (this is also illustrated by the historical example in the sidebar "Electrification: Lessons from an Earlier Technological Advance"). The design of organizational processes should create a holistic combination of workers and technology, determining what is best delegated to technology, and to people, and defining the interface between the two.

puting. Today, the electric motor isn't a separate consumer product, but is embedded in many products. Like computing, electric motors passed through a "personal motor with accessories" phase, until they became small and inexpensive.

1.3 Bits: The Atoms of the Information Economy

The *industrial economy* is giving way (in relative terms) to the *information economy*. The former focuses on the manufacturing of physical goods and the latter on the creation, access, and manipulation of information and knowledge.

E X A M P L E :   *The entertainment and software industries exemplify the information economy. An increasing fraction of the economy is "services," many of which are information based (accounting, law, education, etc.).*

Any Information Can Be Represented by Bits

A *bit* (short for "binary digit") is a number that assumes one of two values: "0" (zero) or "1" (one). Text such as you're reading now can be represented as bits by associating each character in the English language with a set of seven bits. By representation, it is meant that the original text can be recovered from the bits.

E X A M P L E : *Unique sequences of seven bits can be assigned to each of the letters in the English alphabet, as for example:*

a $\leftrightarrow$ 0000000,
b $\leftrightarrow$ 0000001,
c $\leftrightarrow$ 0000010, etc.

Altogether, 128 characters could be represented this way, more than enough for the 26 letters of the alphabet and punctuation marks.

In a similar manner, bits can be used to represent all written languages, including those based on ideographs (such as Chinese). Because written language is formed of characters (in English or Arabic) or ideographs (in Asian languages), it is *discrete*. This means that it is represented by characters drawn from a finite alphabet. The alphabet

"Information" in this context includes text and numbers as well as other media such as art, video entertainment, games, money and financial instruments, and many other goods and services that don't have a physical presence. "Knowledge" means understanding and judgement based on large amounts of information and represents an intangible but essential asset of most organizations. Just as transportation and machinery form the technological foundation of the industrial economy, networks and computers are the technological foundation of the information economy.

Physical goods, broken down into their most fundamental and indivisible elements, are composed of atoms. Similarly, the fundamental and indivisible elements that represent information (as it is represented in networks and computers) are *bits*. Atoms are the building blocks of the physical world, and bits are the building blocks of computer-mediated information [Neg96]. Not all information is in the form of bits—for example, when you listen to the radio, the sound reaching your ears is not bits—but it is possible to *represent* any information (including sound) by bits (see the sidebar "Any Information Can Be Represented by Bits").

Bits are an appropriate building block for the information economy because they can easily be stored, communicated, and manipulated. The simplicity and universality of bits make possible computers, equipment, and software that can flexibly manipulate different types of information and also combine different types of information as necessary. This last point is important because older technologies (books or newspapers) lack this capability. In effect, bits are a *universal alphabet* for representing and manipulating all forms of information.

In the remaining chapters, analogies between the physical world and the information world will frequently be used to enhance your understanding of both.

1.4 Road Map to the Book

This book covers three main topics. The first is *applications* of networked computing; the second is the *industry* that supplies computing, networking, and software products and services; and the third is the basic concepts and terminology that underlie the *infra-structure* and *technology* of networked computing, from an applica-tion perspective. These topics are covered in roughly that order, although the goal is to emphasize their mutual influences. How do economic, legal, and policy issues impact the nature of the supplier industry and the infrastructure? What characteristics of the infra-structure impact the applications? What characteristics of the tech-nology are ripest for exploitation in innovative new ways? What are the limitations of the technology that restrict the application possi-bilities? How are performance characteristics necessary for many large-scale applications obtained, and particularly, how do perfor-mance requirements impact the design of applications?

The first topic (covered in Chapter 2) is the applications of net-worked computing. These are divided into specific categories: social applications (that support the activities of groups of users), information management, education, and business. Each applica-tion area is broken down and classified—and numerous application examples described—with the goal of understanding the value and functionality the application affords to the user or organization. This is the most important chapter in the book and should not be skipped. It is only by addressing the goals and characteristics of applications that the technological and industry requirements can be inferred.

You doubtless have experience in using personal productivity appli-cations on a desktop computer and thus understand what the moni-tor, graphical user interfaces, keyboard and mouse, etc., do for you. By comparison, you may know relatively little about the arcane ter-minology underlying *networked* computing (for example, mes-sages, concurrency, packets, middleware, distributed objects, and transactions). Therefore, beginning in Chapter 3 and continuing in Chapter 9 (middleware), Chapter 11 (networking), and Chapter 12 (communications), the book describes the infrastructure and tech-nologies that support networked applications. The goal is not an understanding of all the details, but rather an appreciation of the opportunities for and limitations on applications imposed by tech-nology. This is imparted through the most significant underlying

can be small, as in English, or as large as the vocabulary, as in ideographs. Anything dis-crete can be represented as bits by simply associating an appropriate number of bits with each member of the alphabet.

Less obviously, a sequence of bits can also represent audio (such as a voice or music recording), images (such as pictures taken by a camera), and video. Unlike written lan-guage, these media are *ana-log* (meaning continuous, not discrete, in amplitude and time), but they can be approx-imated by bits with sufficient accuracy that a human cannot tell the difference.

The representation of infor-mation by bits is a special case of a *digital* representa-tion, meaning a representa-tion in terms of numbers. A bit is just a digit with a base of two, but any other base (such as base ten) would be equally effective.

concepts and terminology, supplemented by numerous topical examples.

Beginning in Chapter 4, and especially in Chapter 5, the economic laws, the structure of the supplier industry, and government involvement are discussed. These are arguably as important as the technology in determining the evolution of products and applications. Also, in Chapter 3 the life cycle of an application is discussed, and Chapter 6 describes modern software technology suitable for developing new applications. Together, the coverage of the industry, underlying technologies, and the application life cycle will position you to work effectively with vendors, contractors, and implementers in bringing new application ideas to fruition.

Further Reading

Books that cover general areas of technology and social issues encompassed within this book are recommended at the end of each chapter. There are two other general classes of books that can be recommended: those that convey computer literacy, of which [Bir96, Oak96] are examples, and those that discuss the societal and business impacts of networking and computing, including [Cai97, Haw96, Mit96, Ros97].

The Applications

2

The global Internet liberates many activities from geographical constraints. It joins mass transportation and telecommunications in giving people and organizations considerably more freedom in geographical location while they continue their essential functions. Only a century ago the essence of an organization was centralization—to enhance internal communication—while today, organizations are largely freed from this constraint [Cai97]. An enterprise can be global in extent: A university need not be confined to a campus, a library no longer needs a building, and a community no longer presumes a geographical boundary. All this presumes appropriate applications supporting the necessary activities.

The word "virtual" is often used in conjunction with these applications. A dictionary defines virtual as "being such in essential character." What the Internet—and its close cousins, modern transportation and telecommunications—portends is enterprises, organizations, and communities that are freed of geographical boundaries but are virtual in that they *appear* to have many desirable properties of geographical centralization.

2.1 Users, Organizations, and Applications

A computing *application* performs some function on our behalf involving computation, manipulation of information, or communication. It does our work, enlightens us, entertains us, or connects us to other users. A *networked* application is partitioned across two or more computers, leveraging the network for communication among application elements.

Two fundamental types of networked applications are those that empower *users* (people using computers) and those that empower *organizations* (collections of users with a common mission) and enterprises (organizations with a business mission). There is commonality, in that users may be supporting an organizational mission.

2.1.1 Before Networking

Centralized, time-shared, and decentralized phases of computing have emphasized solitary user-oriented applications. These *personal productivity* applications enhance the speed or effectiveness of users.

EXAMPLE: *The word processor helps users author documents; the spreadsheet automates otherwise tedious computations, allowing many what-if scenarios. Drawing editors turn users into draftspersons (although probably not graphic artists). Speech recognition automates dictation, previously available only to professionals with support staffs.*

In organizations, the centralized and decentralized computing eras have been marked by departmental applications. These compartmentalized, hierarchical departments have a specific mission (such as inventory or payroll or purchasing). Prior to networked computing, computing applications were typically retrofitted into the existing departmental structure, serving to extend the capability, improve the productivity, or enhance the quality of its work (much as a personal productivity application extends an individual user).

EXAMPLE: *Generating payroll or keeping track of inventory or customers and generating mailing lists are examples of departmental applications.*

In contrast to personal productivity applications, the emphasis of departmental applications is often the worker serving the application (rather than the application serving the worker).

EXAMPLE: *In inventory tracking, workers may input data, such as informing the application when material arrives to join the inventory.*

2.1.2 After Networking

The transition to networked computing shifts the emphasis in user-oriented applications from personal productivity toward *social applications*, which serve a group of users with a shared mission in some collaborative or communicative activity. In addition, networked computing provides the same capabilities to users who are traveling (called *nomadic* users). The network supports communication among these users, and networked applications also serve to coordinate their activities. The network also supports virtual interest groups of users sharing common concerns and creates a new public place without geographic boundaries, called *cyberspace*.

Networked computing is also ideal for creating, accessing, and manipulating information. In *information management* applications, the network not only enables a single user to globally access vast information resources but also enables information updated in one place to become immediately available everywhere.

Educational applications mix the social aspect (teacher and students) with information access. *Business* applications serve to coordinate the myriad resources and activities required to produce a product or service and support the communication among workers and managers. Increasingly, business applications extend outside the enterprise, to support and coordinate suppliers and customer relationships—as well as to sell to and support individual consumers—in *electronic commerce*.

To some extent, both social and business applications predated networked computing. It is feasible to centralize the informational needs of a business process in a single computer, although this has serious disadvantages, including administration (Chapter 3) and scalability (Chapter 10). A time-shared computer can support social applications, as the users sharing that computer can communicate and coordinate. These possibilities are, however, quite limiting.

In contrast, the global Internet supports communication among all users and all organizations. This removes the computing capacity and administrative boundary limitations of previous phases of computing and enables social applications across organizational, geographical, and political boundaries. The biggest revolution is the *virtual interest group* or *virtual organization*. In the virtual interest group, users opportunistically coalesce around a cause or issue. It need not be formally organized or officially recognized (which is why it is called virtual) nor abide by any limitations imposed by geography.

EXAMPLE: *Active virtual interest groups have coalesced around issues relevant to the Internet, such as the trade-offs between free expression and limiting children's access to objectionable material, or the trade-off between unfettered electronic commerce and individual privacy. Groups have access to discussion forums and Web pages that link to one another, among other assets that enhance their interest group.*

The global network allows any individual or organization to publish information, which is immediately accessible to all citizens with network access. Educational resources can be accessed by all, with fewer geographic limitations.

In business, the Internet allows smaller firms to band together to form *virtual enterprises* for developing and marketing new products. The virtual enterprise offers many advantages previously afforded large vertically integrated firms, while benefiting from specialized and nimble small firms.

2.2 Application Building Blocks

The building blocks of networked computing applications include physical elements (user, computer, network, etc.) and logical and informational elements (data, infrastructure and application software, etc.). The physical elements are illustrated in Figure 2.1 and briefly described in Table 2.1.

Information is the basic commodity of computing applications. Computers and networks are able to store, manipulate, and communicate digital information (see Section 1.3 on page 9). This information can assume many forms depending on application needs, including

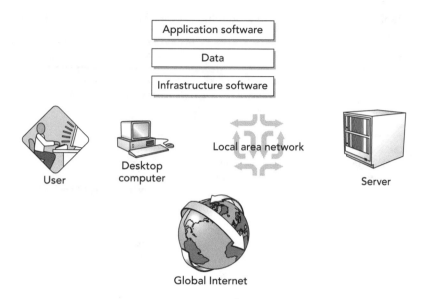

Figure 2.1 The building blocks of networked computing applications.

- *Numerical values and text.*

- *Images:* pictures captured by photographic cameras, and their three-dimensional counterpart, virtual reality.

- *Graphics:* an artificially generated image created by a computer program.

- *Audio:* sound captured by a microphone.

- *Synthesized audio:* artificially generated by a computer program.

- *Video:* a sequence of images representing time as well as space.

- *Animation:* video artificially created by a computer program.

Applications also manipulate information in ways that combine these media. A premier example is the *document*—often used to archive or communicate human knowledge—which can combine text, images, and graphics in various ways. Computer-mediated documents can be *multimedia*, meaning they combine the usual features of paper documents with audio, video, animations, etc. All these forms of information, including audio and video and multimedia documents, can be communicated over the network.

Table 2.1 Description of the building blocks shown in Figure 2.1.

Building block	Description	Typical function
User	Person who interacts with and derives benefit from a networked computing application.	Enters, retrieves, or manipulates information, or performs calculations.
Desktop computer (or personal computer or client computer)	A computer directly accessed by the user that acts as an interface between user and application.	Its screen displays windows, menus, graphics, graphs, etc., and its keyboard, pointing device, camera, and microphone accept input from the user (Chapter 3).
Server computer	A computer not directly associated with a user, usually missing a display, keyboard, or pointing device (except perhaps for administrative purposes). Often has substantial computing power and storage capacity and peripherals.	Stores, accesses, and manipulates large repositories of data, and realizes the logic of how the data is manipulated in light of user directives (Chapter 3).
Application software	The programs running on the clients and servers realizing application functionality.	Embodies the unique functionality of the application (Chapters 4 and 6).
Data	The collection of bits representing—within the computer and network—the information manipulated by the application.	The form in which information is stored, processed, and communicated (Chapter 6).
Infrastructure software	The programs running on the computers and providing many common needs for all applications.	Provides communications support (Chapter 7) and manages resources (e.g., storage and memory—see Chapter 10).
Network	The communication infrastructure connecting the computers running an application. This may be a local area network (LAN) or a wide area network (WAN) such as the global Internet.	Allows the programs running on the different computers to communicate data (Chapter 11).

The major categories of applications supported by networked computing can be divided into general classes, including social, information management, educational, and business applications.

2.3 Social Applications

Social applications focus on supporting activities of groups of users, whether or not a group is associated with an organization or enterprise. They are sometimes called "collaborative applications." although collaboration is only one of numerous activities supported. You are no doubt familiar with many of these applications, including telephony (two users holding a conversation), email and voicemail, newsgroups, and chatrooms. The possibilities are much richer than suggested by these early successful examples. Social applications can be categorized not only by the characteristics of the group of users participating but also by what the group is attempting to accomplish.

2.3.1 Characteristics of User Groups

Before considering many representative networked applications, it is helpful to classify groups of users according to their characteristics. The most pertinent group attributes include

- *Number of users:* A group served by a social application can range from two users to the entire population of users with network access.

- *Narrowness of purpose:* Some groups form for the purpose of accomplishing a specific task (like scheduling a meeting), while other groups are very unfocused (like those coalescing around a discussion on some topic).

- *Duration:* Some groups only exist for a short period of time (like two users participating in a telephone call), while others can be very long lasting (like the coauthors of a book).

- *Social relationships:* In some groups—particularly small ones—all the users know who the other users are and may well know them personally. In very large groups, each user will typically not even be aware of who the other users are, let alone know them. In the latter, there may be subgroups who are mutually familiar or friendly, or social relationships may be more diffuse.

With these group characteristics in mind, a classification of the types of groups supported by social applications is shown in Table 2.2. The terminology defined in this table will be used in the remainder of this chapter.

As implied in Table 2.2, these types of groups actually have a structural relationship like that of Figure 2.2. The citizenry includes a very large group of users, subsets of which form ongoing interest groups. The number and composition of these interest groups

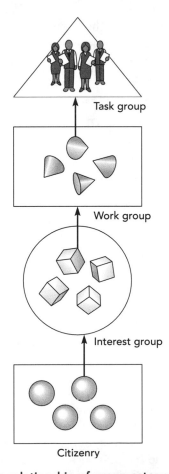

Figure 2.2 The inclusive relationship of group categories.

Table 2.2 A classification of groups using a social application.

Category of user group	Description	Examples
Individual	A solitary user working to accomplish some goal. This is the limiting case of no group. Computer applications are meant to enhance quality and productivity.	A user writes a single-author memorandum; a user adds an appointment to his personal calendar; a user accesses stock prices using the Web.
Task group	A *task* is a short-term effort directed at an immediate goal. Members of a task group *interact* with one another to complete a task. This interaction may require the undivided attention of all users.	One user telephones another to make a lunch date; a group of workers holds a meeting to evaluate a competitive bid or plan the next step in a project.
Work group	A *project* is a longer-term effort directed at a challenging goal. Members of a work group *collaborate* to complete the project. A project may spin off short-duration tasks addressed by constituent task groups.	Employees from the marketing, sales, engineering, and finance departments develop a product plan; scientists write a joint-authored paper; members and staff of a legislative committee work on a new computer security bill.
Interest group	An *interest* is a topic, profession, hobby, or goal that is ongoing and open-ended. An interest group (occasionally called a *community*) pursues an interest through common discussion, study, or collective action. Interest groups typically form constituent work groups to collaborate on projects related to the group interest.	Historians share a common interest in World War II; world's coin collectors pursue an interest in coin sale and valuation; employees of General Motors Corporation pursue an interest in building and marketing automobiles; users concerned about network privacy pursue an interest in policies and laws.
Citizenry	A large group of users without a specific organized purpose. Typically subsets of the citizenry form ongoing interest groups around topical issues.	Citizens of San Francisco, California; all the users with Internet access or telephones.

change with time, but on a timescale of weeks or months. Similarly, interest groups break off to form sporadic work groups to pursue particular projects (such as the design of a product or the organization of an international conference). In turn, a work group may require sporadic task groups that interact on short-term tasks, interspersed with the individual effort of members of the task group.

EXAMPLE: *American business is a citizenry, and an interest group within is the employees of General Motors (GM). When GM designs a new car, it forms a team (work group) that collaborates on the design project. That collaboration consists, in part, of numerous short-term tasks that are addressed through interaction in a meeting or conference call. A typical project is to develop a marketing plan—involving marketing, sales, development, manufacturing and distribution, etc.—with a detailed planning document as the outcome. This may take several months, during which there could be task groups formed to interact on particular issues (such as developing a schedule and coordination plan for the next month).*

Table 2.3 lists typical characteristics of these categories of groups (for the three largest groups). Although each user likely participates in at most one task group at a time and gives it her undivided attention, she may participate in multiple work groups and interest groups and split her time and attention among them.

2.3.2 Styles of Social Applications

Having categorized the groups participating in social applications, the next step is to appreciate the characteristics of the applications themselves. Examining current and emerging applications, there are two major styles (which will subsequently be broken down further):

- *Communication:* Any group effort requires the communication of information among group members. This may take the form of a discussion or the circulation of draft documents.

- *Coordination:* To accomplish its goals efficiently and effectively, the different activities of a group must be coordinated. Often, certain tasks or projects depend on the outcome of other tasks

Table 2.3 Typical characteristics for different categories of groups.

Group category	Work group	Interest group	Citizenry
Number of users	Small, typically from two to ten or twenty.	Large, typically from hundreds to tens of thousands.	Everybody.
Narrowness of purpose	Typically pursues a specific near-term project goal with a defined outcome.	Although constituent interactions and collaborations are focused around the mutual interest, they may take the group in many different directions (even simultaneously).	No specific common purpose or interest.
Duration	Typically days to months.	Indeterminate, as there is no predefined goal.	Forever.
Social relationships	Each user typically knows who the other group members are and may personally know many of them.	Each user typically knows only a small subset of the other group members.	Each user knows a tiny fraction of the other group members.

or projects or individual efforts, so the proper ordering must be coordinated. The group may require common resources requiring coordination, such as preventing conflicts in the joint editing of a document. In addition, communication opportunities must also be coordinated, for example, scheduling the time of a meeting.

Together, communication and coordination are what distinguish social and isolated activities, and the objective of social applications is to improve and enhance both dimensions—even for a group that is geographically or administratively dispersed. Both styles are now examined further.

Communication Style

The communication style of social applications can be further divided into four substyles, as shown (with example applications) in Table 2.4. One style dimension accommodates the degree of knowledge that one user has of other users:

Table 2.4 Examples of communication applications in each of four substyles. Applications in each row are immediate and deferred variations.

Social application styles	Immediate (users participate simultaneously)	Deferred (users need not participate simultaneously)
Direct (users know precisely which other users are participating)	*Telephony* and *video conferencing* simulate "face-to-face" interactions of users (a meeting).	*Electronic mail* (email), *voicemail*, and *facsimile* allow one user to originate a communication and another user to access it later.
Publication (users do not know other participating users)	*Broadcast video* (analogous to broadcast television) allows one user to simultaneously address many other users for seminar viewing or distance learning.	*Video on demand* (analogous to the video rental store) allows one user to store a video presentation on a server and other users to view that video at a time of their choosing.
	Information push (analogous to a newspaper) allows one user to publish volatile information (like stock quotes) to be viewed immediately by other users.	World Wide Web (an example of a more general category *information pull*) allows any user to publish information to be viewed later by other users.

- *Direct style:* In the task group and work group, users typically know the other users in the group. This admits a direct style in which users communicate directly with other users.

- *Publication style:* In the interest group and citizenry, direct communication may not be possible—because the users don't know one another—except of course when the group forms smaller work groups or task groups. In spite of these loose or nonexistent social relationships, communication within the group is valuable, for example, to disseminate ideas or form work groups. In the publication style, one user (or small group) makes information available in a form that can be accessed by any other user. By its nature, a publication benefits the group as a whole, not specific users. Each user makes his or her own decision to access the information, and typically some do and many do not. The user publishing the information cannot anticipate who will eventually access it.

ANALOGY: *The direct style is analogous to how the telephone network is used, or a memorandum in business with a specific distribution list (an important tool for work groups). Scholarly journals (an important tool for scholarly interest groups) and newspapers (an important tool for the citizenry) illustrate the publication style.*

The direct style of communication distributes information to a known set of recipients (possibly a single recipient), while the publication style distributes it to an unknown set of recipients. The direct style is most appropriate for task groups and work groups, while publication serves interest groups and the citizenry.

The other style dimension for communication applications makes a distinction based on whether users participate simultaneously or not:

- *Immediate style (sometimes called synchronous):* In this style, users participate in the application at the same time. This is practical for a task group, where the number of users is small and they know one another. It is not practical for the citizenry, because it would be impossible to schedule them to interact at the same time, and there would be too many participants for this to be effective.

- *Deferred style (sometimes called asynchronous):* This style removes the constraint that users participate simultaneously. This eases scheduling difficulties, reduces the invasiveness of the communication to the individual user, and increases the size of the group for which communication is feasible.

ANALOGY: *A mother phoning her daughter to wish her happy birthday is the immediate style, while sending a birthday card in the mail is deferred.*

Coordination Style

Group activities create dependencies among users and other resources. For example, the very viability of immediate applications makes the users dependent: They have to participate at the same time. Often, deferred communication applications create similar dependencies. For example, users collaboratively editing a document have to work on it in a particular order, they have to avoid making conflicting changes, etc. Coordination style applications manage these dependencies, expediting the completion of a task or project. This style of application can be further broken down into two substyles, as listed in Table 2.5.

Coordination applications particularly aid work group project management and allow workers to minimize disruptions caused by conflicts or delays in receiving necessary resources.

How do these application styles relate specifically to the needs of groups? The following subsections (and sidebars) describe a num-

Table 2.5 Two styles of coordination application.

Style	Description	Examples
Resource allocation and scheduling	The members of a group share resources, which must be managed for efficiency and to avoid conflicts. One aspect of resource allocation is the scheduling of a shared resource so that it can be used by different users or groups at different times.	A meeting room must be scheduled so that only one meeting occurs at a time. In the collaborative authoring of a document, the additions or changes of different users must not conflict. Members of a task group participating in an immediate application must be scheduled. Auctions or other economic mechanisms can be used to allocate consumable resources (see the discussion of electronic commerce later in the chapter).
Monitoring and notification	Monitoring (sometimes called *awareness*) applications allow group members to benefit from information about some remote resource or user. Notification provides an alert that some condition has occurred.	One user can monitor the availability of another worker for a direct/immediate interaction (like a telephone call). A work group member can request notification when a conference room becomes free. The productivity of workers can be monitored (this raises privacy concerns—see [Gar89]).

ber of social applications, in each case relating them to the group categories and application styles. Collectively, these applications illustrate the wealth of valuable networked applications. They are meant to give you the sense that the space of possible applications is very rich, with many unexplored possibilities.

2.3.3 Remote Conferencing with Shared Workspace

Without networked computing, a task group or work group might find a conference room to conduct their collaboration. In that conference room, they would hold a meeting—with face-to-face discussions—and also locate any work items to be examined and modified (such as documents being collaboratively edited). The team would likely also use a visual aid such as a whiteboard to share ideas.

Such an interaction or collaboration can also be conducted over a large geographical area by using a social application called *remote conferencing with shared workspace*. This direct application serves task groups or work groups. The direct-immediate form of this application attempts to reproduce all the facets of a physical conference room, including

- *Telephony:* Speech is the most basic form of human communication, and thus telephony (holding a conversation at a distance using speech) is the most successful communications application. Telephony is provided by the telephone network but can be provided in a networked computing infrastructure as well.

- *Video:* Humans also communicate through facial expressions and gestures, and thus a video presentation of remote users can lend a feeling of presence, proximity, and trust that contributes to the quality of the interaction. *Video conferencing* is a combination of telephony and video and can be enhanced by other media, such as those listed next. (However, many feel that video is the least important element of a conference.)

Collaborative Authoring

The most basic function of a collaborative authoring application is allowing any user to view and edit a group document. Because of possible conflicts when two or more users edit the same document, the application also coordinates the users in several ways, for example:

- *Access control* and *locking* limit who can edit and who can read documents. Access can be restricted to particular users or temporarily precluded while a document is edited.

- *Version control* keeps track of current and past versions of the document. For example, anyone can see who made what changes, see what those changes were, undo them, etc.

- *Annotation* of the document allows one user to pass comments to another user (without editing the document itself). Comments can be attached to the precise location where they apply and can be multimedia (for example, voice rather than text).

- *Replication* and *reconciliation* are sophisticated capabilities. Normally, editing a given document would be restricted to one user at a time, slowing the authoring process. Replication creates two or more

- *Presentation graphics:* It is common in meetings to use visual aids like slides and transparencies. Since they are prepared in electronic form, they can be projected to remote users.

- *Collaborative authoring of a shared document:* A document that is being collaboratively authored can be stored somewhere and the group members allowed to view and edit it (see the sidebar "Collaborative Authoring").

- *Hand drawings and doodles:* Participants in a meeting frequently communicate ideas or designs through hand drawings on a whiteboard or blackboard. These drawings can be captured and communicated to remote users, as they are drawn, using a *liveboard*. Alternatively, a *shared whiteboard* application uses a mouse or tablet to draw, with the result displayed remotely.

EXAMPLE: *The screen capture shown in Figure 2.3 shows the visual aspect of a remote conference. Shown are standard applications developed for the* multicast backbone (Mbone), *which is an Internet capability for sending audio and video media from one source to many destinations (see Chapter 7).*

2.3.4 Groupware

Remote conferencing is primarily intended as a direct-immediate application serving a task group, where users work directly together, at the same time, and the collaboration may have their undivided attention. Unfortunately, this style becomes ineffective when a group becomes too large. For example, this makes it difficult to capture and display video of everyone, along with whiteboards, on a small screen. Too many participants also reduce the quality of the interaction (as is starting to happen in Figure 2.3 as the screen gets cluttered).

ANALOGY: *Consider the quality of the interaction when a dozen, a hundred, and a thousand people meet face-to-face. A dozen people can have an effective meeting, allowing everyone to participate and interact. On the other hand, a hundred or a thousand people cannot effectively hold an interactive meeting. It takes too long to hear from everyone on any particular point—the number of inputs is beyond the point of diminishing returns—and it becomes difficult*

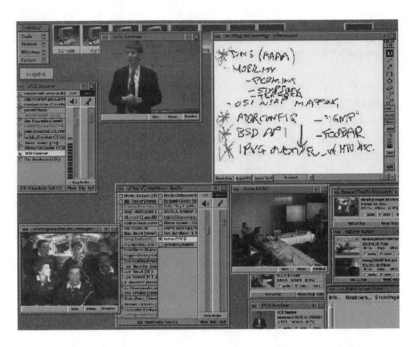

Figure 2.3 Example of several collaborative tools for the Mbone: vic (video), vat (audio), and wb (whiteboard) from [McC95]. *Source:* this image depicts experimental collaborative applications developed by the MASH Research Group at the University of California, Berkeley. See *http://www-mash.cs.berkeley.edu/mash* for more information on the MASH Project.

identical replicas of the document that can be independently edited. The problem, of course, is merging the changes back into a single version, which is reconciliation. Reconciliation is relatively simple if changes are made in independent places and more complicated if common sections are modified.

As you can see, collaborative authoring applications mix communication and coordination. The users communicate through the document itself as well as through annotations, but the application also coordinates the shared access to the document.

to fairly allocate talking time without hearing the same points over and over.

These problems can be avoided by a deferred version of the remote conferencing application, called *groupware*. Because it is deferred—allowing group members to participate when they choose—and also because it can aid larger groups, groupware is appropriate for work groups.

EXAMPLE: *The major suppliers of groupware are Lotus (a division of IBM), Microsoft, and Novell, and each sells complementary client and server software (Lotus Notes and Domino, Microsoft Outlook and Exchange, Novell WebAccess and GroupWise). These products began with deferred work group and document management*

*but increasingly incorporate immediate conferencing capabilities
as well. An example is* real-time messaging, *in which a message
appears immediately on group members' screens.*

Collaborative authoring—discussed in the previous section and the
sidebar "Collaborative Authoring"—is a pillar of groupware. The
joint editing and coordination functions associated with document
authoring don't depend on the users participating simultaneously—
they can easily be deferred as well as immediate.

Groupware has to reproduce—in a deferred style—the communication facilities afforded by remote conferencing (see the previous
section). It also has added coordination challenges, since the users
themselves perform many needed coordination functions when
they are interacting directly and immediately.

The most basic capability in groupware is messaging. Users can
send one another a *message*—a package of information that one
user wants to pass to one or more other users.

ANALOGY: *In the physical world, when one person is unable to telephone another, she might use a postal letter, which is a form of
message. The letter encloses in an envelope whatever information
the sender wishes to convey to the recipient. The letter could
include not only text but also pictures or audio or video (stored on
magnetic tape).*

Like the postal letter, a groupware message can include multimedia
information, such as text, an audio recording for playback, pictures,
graphics, etc. A message can even include an entire formatted document. The recipient can read the text, play back the audio or
video, look at the pictures, and read the document. A message is a
form of direct-deferred communication between users: The recipient need not participate at the same time as the sender but can
look at the message at the time of his choosing. The message
replaces the direct interaction via audio, video, images, etc., in
remote conferencing.

EXAMPLE: *The most basic messaging service is* electronic mail *(or*
email). *A sender of an email message can designate one or more
recipients for that message. Each user has an* inbox *where mes-*

sages arrive and await access by that user. Although only text messages were supported originally, increasingly, email applications allow multimedia messages. Email is an almost direct analogy to the postal service in the physical world, including notification of a nonexistent recipient or notification of delivery and access by the recipient.

As illustrated by email, a message can be designated for a single recipient or multiple designated recipients. Since a given user can receive messages from many senders, a message system must merge these messages. Message applications can add a number of other features, such as

- *Priority:* Senders can attach priorities to messages, so that recipients can access high-priority messages first.

- *Filtering:* A fundamental issue with message systems is that a recipient has no control over who can send him a message. This may result in wasted time sifting through many uninteresting messages. A message filter can discard messages that don't meet criteria specified by the user (negative filtering) or, alternatively, only allow messages that do meet specified criteria (positive filtering). These criteria might include the sender's identity or be related to the subject or content of the message.

- *Authentication:* It might be possible for an imposter to send a message; authentication verifies the identity of the sender.

- *Integrity:* A message might be modified somewhere between the time it is sent and it is read, either accidently or for some nefarious purpose. A message with integrity is assured to be exactly as composed by the sender.

- *Confidentiality:* Some messages contain sensitive information that should be available only to the recipient. Confidentiality ensures that only the recipient can read it.

The first two features add coordination functions, and the latter three enhance the utility of the communication (and can just as easily be incorporated in remote conferencing as well).

Aside from collaborative authoring and messaging, groupware also includes coordination capabilities. Even in a work group, messaging

Calendar and Scheduling

Calendar and scheduling applications manage the personal calendar of each user and also schedule users for task groups (meetings, remote conferencing, telephone calls, etc.). They can schedule auxiliary resources (such as meeting rooms or video conference facilities). A user must publish his or her personal calendar for the application—minimally, times available for task group interactions, or more information if automatic rescheduling is desired. The more willing the user is to relinquish personal control, the more automated and effective scheduling can be.

Calendar and scheduling illustrates the tension between automation and privacy. Without the personal involvement of the user, it may become too easy to schedule interactions of marginal value. For the future, ways are needed for users to describe priorities and automate interaction possibilities. Otherwise, users may be reluctant to cede total control to a faceless application.

is rarely sufficient for communications. Sporadic remote conferences and face-to-face meetings are valued, especially for establishing mutual trust and dealing with complex issues or negotiations. Since remote conferencing is an immediate application, it has to be scheduled at a time mutually suitable to members of the task group, and they may even have to rearrange schedules to make an immediate interaction feasible.

EXAMPLE: *You have encountered the endless round of voicemail messages often required to talk to someone (called telephone tag) or the time consumed in coordinating and juggling everybody's schedule for a meeting (accentuated in the global economy, where time zones reduce the feasible times). These problems reduce the viability of direct-immediate applications, in spite of their compelling advantages for task groups.*

Calendar and scheduling is a groupware application that eases these logistics by making the calendars of individual users available to a scheduling application, which can access and manipulate them to coordinate schedules (see the sidebar "Calendar and Scheduling"). It illustrates a publication-deferred application, since each user in the group publishes his or her calendar for the benefit of anybody in the group.

2.3.5 Discussion Forums

Typically task group interactions are scheduled with forethought to a specific purpose and agenda. This is fine for well-defined outcomes with clear steps to get there. On the other hand, discussion and creative brainstorming have no predefined outcome or stopping point. They can be performed by a task group but often are more effective in a deferred style. Performing brainstorming over a longer period of time—interspersed with other activities—is often less intimidating to participants and more conducive to new ideas. Brainstorming is supported by the *discussion forum*, where any group member can propose ideas or comment on ideas previously proposed.

The remote conference is a direct-immediate style of discussion forum that serves task groups. The discussion forum is an even more important tool for interest groups—for which direct applications like the remote conference are not feasible because users often don't know other users in the group—because it is typically realized in a publication style. That is, a discussion forum works by one user publishing an idea in the forum (by sending a message to the forum application, rather than directly to other users) where it becomes available for any user in the group to access or not access at his or her option. Thus, the discussion forum illustrates that a messaging application need not be direct: A message can be sent to an unknown set of recipients. It is also possible for discussion forums to be *anonymous*—the sender's identity is not revealed. There are typically many simultaneous discussion forums on different topics, serving different interest groups.

Like most social applications, the discussion forum comes in deferred and immediate styles. A deferred style of discussion forum is the *newsgroup* (see the sidebar "Newsgroups"). A discussion is started by one user sending a message (called a *posting*) to a common repository of messages (called a *newsgroup*) that is published for the benefit of the group.

ANALOGY: *As China loosened political control, there emerged a "democracy wall" devoted to discussion of political freedom. This was a physical wall in Beijing, where anybody could post thoughts on paper, and anybody else could read them and post responses.*

Chatroom

Since a newsgroup is deferred, the immediacy of a face-to-face interaction is lost. A remote conference—being a direct style of application—is not a suitable replacement for a newsgroup. This motivates the *chatroom*—a publication-immediate style of discussion forum.

ANALOGY: *The chatroom is analogous to a continuously running town meeting. Any member of the interest group can join the discussion in a town meeting at any time. Unlike a remote conference, the other participants are not known in advance.*

Newsgroups

A publication-deferred application, newsgroups associate a topic of discussion with a specific subject heading and are particularly targeted at interest groups. Any user can *post* a message relevant to that topic, and any other interested user can read previous postings and post responses. Typically, each message posted on a given subject stimulates responses from other group members. Those responses are posted under the same subject heading, and that group of messages forms a *thread*. The users joining a thread are a working group that collaborate on that specific subject. Note that the thread forms opportunistically about that subject—the user initiating the thread does not have to anticipate which other users may be interested in participating.

The newsgroup has mechanisms for hiding unwanted messages. For example, previously read messages can be hidden, and threads are collapsed under a single heading, with the individual messages visible only if desired. A newsgroup may also have a *moderator*—a user with special authority to determine which postings are allowed, to change the sub-

Any user can join an ongoing discussion by reading and posting messages to other users who happen to be simultaneously participating. It works like a remote conference associated with a named topic. Users participate by "entering" the chatroom, after which they see all postings immediately as they occur. Anybody with something to say on the topic can post a message, which other participants see immediately. A posting may engender an immediate response from others—hence the spontaneity and immediacy—leading to a "conversation" that can be viewed by all.

EXAMPLE: *The group of customers (and potential customers) of a company is an interest group. Chatrooms are used for customer service, allowing customers to communicate with service agents and one another. Acuity Corporation and Business Solutions Inc. are two providers of chatroom applications.*

The chatroom can be viewed as either an immediate variation on a newsgroup or as a publication variation on a remote conference. Like other messaging applications, messages in both newsgroups and chatrooms can be multimedia (incorporating audio, video, whiteboard, etc.).

Listserver

With a newsgroup, each user must make a conscious effort to periodically check postings, and a chatroom requires a user's undivided attention to derive full benefit. This does not work well for extremely busy people, or interest groups with infrequent postings. A *listserver* is a publication-deferred variation on the discussion forum that eliminates the published repository of messages and follows a *subscription* model, in which the user doesn't ask for specific information, but rather all available information on a specific subject or topic. Subscription is an important mechanism for information access, discussed in Section 2.4 on page 38.

ANALOGY: *A special-interest magazine serves an interest group. Each group member subscribes to the magazine, and each issue thereafter appears in that member's mailbox.*

A user wishing to join a topic subscribes by providing his or her email address to the listserver application. Any user can post a message to that topic, and each posting is automatically emailed to all subscribers, who therefore do not have to consciously access the postings. A user can also cancel the subscription and leave the interest group.

The email messaging system incorporated into the listserver application merges the messages coming from other users and other listservers. A disadvantage is that a subscriber's mailbox may be inundated with messages—especially as the interest group grows large. Because some users might want to "listen in" without posting, or avoid a large number of messages, a listserver can also maintain an archive of past postings.

2.3.6 Cyberspace Applications

Societies have always had public places, like the town square or public park. The Internet has created a new virtual public place, popularly called *cyberspace*. Citizens can go there to interact with others, share ideas and criticize government, or just hang out. Like a public park, crimes can be committed there, or privacy violated, or misleading or inflammatory information distributed. Cyberspace is global and hence not subject to the ordinary geographically based jurisdiction of governments.

Cyberspace citizens form short-term task groups (for example, to find a suitable date for dinner), form work groups to collaborate on a project (for example, to organize a neighborhood crime watch committee), and form interest groups (for example, to run a Boy Scout troop or rally around some cause). Thus, the social applications described earlier apply to the citizenry as well. Like an interest group—but even more so—communication frequently occurs among citizens who may not know one another in advance.

What applications specifically support the citizenry? Thus far, they mostly mirror the physical world.

ject heading of a thread to make it more transparent, etc. The moderator's job is to ensure order and organization (rather than anarchy and chaos) and keep the discussion on track. A newsgroup may also have *searching* capability, allowing it to look for threads whose subjects contain specific keywords.

Broadcasting

As mentioned in Section 2.2 on page 16, the information communicated through the network can be multimedia: It can include and mix text, documents, audio, video, pictures, etc. Cyberspace broadcasting—similar to radio and television broadcasting—similarly sends audio and video through the network to any citizen wishing to listen or watch. The radio spectrum limits the number of different radio and television stations; for example, broadcasters using the radio spectrum must be coordinated (by government licensing) to avoid mutual interference, and the number of licensees is severely limited. On the Internet, no government license is required (at least in most countries), and the restrictions are few (although there are issues such as protecting children—see Chapter 5). One can imagine, for example, all the broadcasts occurring anywhere in the world to be available to any citizen in cyberspace. As the Internet advances, it will accommodate many more broadcasters and many more specialized options.

Mass Publication

In the physical world, citizens are informed about current events by the mass media, including newspapers and magazines. The publication-deferred application supporting mass publication in cyberspace is the Web (see the sidebar "World Wide Web"). Many of the same publications available in the physical world are also published on the Web. Web publication can be multimedia in applications called *audio-on-demand* and *video-on-demand*, which are analogous to the video rental store. Broadcasting is a publication-immediate application, and mass publication is a deferred variation. There are variations that mix these styles—called information push—discussed in Section 2.4 on page 38.

In cyberspace, publication and broadcasting are inexpensive, making it possible for ordinary citizens to take advantage of them. All that is required to publish a Web page worldwide is Internet access and a desktop computer. Although cyberspace is increasingly populated by large corporations and commercial activity, this in no way precludes any individual from using the medium to express her or his views. Also, while conventional publishing and broadcasting is predominantly a one-way medium, cyberspace is more democrati-

Figure 2.4 A window from a Web browser, showing a typical page with hyperlinks.

cally two-way. It allows various forms of interactive publishing and broadcasting.

Information Retrieval

An overriding issue of cyberspace is, since citizens don't know one another and the volume of information available is huge, how do citizens find useful information or narrow down information to that which is useful? Similarly, how do citizens find and join interest groups?

There are a number of possibilities. The Web supports a *hypertext* model, which allows users to interactively navigate through large volumes of information by following links from one document to another. There are also *search engines* that look for information on particular topics. As in libraries and bookstores in the physical world, information *indexes* are available. In the commercial realm, *advertising* is an important mechanism for alerting consumers. These and many other possibilities are described in Section 2.4.

World Wide Web

The Web is a publication-deferred application (that has become almost synonymous with the Internet) offering rich possibilities for the publication of multimedia information. A user accesses the Web using a *Web browser* and sees various text, image, audio, and video pages (see a typical page in Figure 2.4). The browser can pull information from many *Web servers* holding a variety of information. Initiated by a user, the browser requests a *page* of information from the server, which is displayed by the browser. Each page can include hyperlinks, which allow immediate access to a related page (by merely clicking on the highlighted hyperlink).

The Web allows any user to publish information in cyberspace, and any other user to access it. The Web also serves an archival function, since published information remains accessible (as long as the publisher chooses).

Consumer Electronic Commerce

In the physical world, citizens go to a merchant's store to buy goods. Similarly, goods can be purchased in cyberspace from merchants who set up "storefronts" there. The Web has evolved into an application that supports consumer electronic commerce as well as information retrieval. If information goods are purchased, they can be delivered in cyberspace as well; otherwise, they may be delivered by the transportation system. Electronic commerce is discussed in Section 2.6 on page 52.

Recommendation Sharing

One way of identifying useful information, products, or interest groups is *recommendation sharing*. A *recommender system* is a communication publication-deferred style of application that collects recommendations from many users and makes them available to any interested user (see Section 2.4).

2.3.7 Back to the Big Picture

The specific social applications are listed in Table 2.6 by category of group they serve. Also listed are some analogous mechanisms in the physical world.

2.4 Information Management

One major category of networked application is the storage, manipulation, and retrieval of information. In the physical world, this is the domain of libraries and bookstores, which house vast information resources and offer ways to identify useful or targeted information. However, as the volume of information grows, libraries exhaust their physical space. The physical shelves of the library can be replaced by digital information repositories (residing in computer storage), in which information is represented by data (a collection of bits—see the sidebar "Any Information Can Be Represented by Bits" on page 10). The manipulation and searching of information can be performed by networked computers that have access to those repositories over the network, often guided interactively by users or librarians.

Table 2.6 Social applications organized by target group category.

Group category	Social applications	Physical-world analogy
Individual	Word processing; spreadsheet	Pencil and paper; electronic calculator
Task group	Email and voicemail; telephony and video conferencing; whiteboard	Postal letters; telephone; facsimile
Work group	Remote conferencing with shared workspace; calendar and scheduling; collaborative authoring; monitoring and notification	Face-to-face meeting; administrative assistant
Interest group	Discussion forum: newsgroup, listserver, chatroom	Town meeting; special-interest magazine
Citizenry	Publication: broadcast, Web; consumer electronic commerce; recommendation sharing	Television and radio; newspaper; news magazine; catalog shopping

Compared to the physical alternative, networked computing has some compelling advantages in its ability to store and manage information:

- It is especially effective in accessing *volatile* information—that which changes frequently (e.g., stock prices). Those changes—entered in one place—can be reflected immediately on the network, in contrast to the relatively slow dissemination in the physical world.

- One user can modify stored information, and other users on the network immediately see those modifications. For example, this can enhance the value of information as a tool for collaboration among users or organizations.

- The total information stored in the millions of computers on the Internet vastly exceeds what could fit in a personal computer's limited affordable storage capacity.

- The computers can process information in intensive ways, for example, to seek out more targeted or useful information.

- Computer-mediated information broadens the media from the printed page to include multimedia. The desktop computer's high-resolution screen is suitable for presentation, the computer can capture, store, and play back audio and video, and these media can be transported through the network. For example, the RealAudio and RealVideo media players allow audio and video content to be transported through the network and displayed on a desktop computer screen. A video media player is shown in Figure 2.5.

2.4.1 Finding Useful Information

Just capturing and storing large repositories of information doesn't directly meet a user's or organization's needs. Typically, an information repository is too large to be of value *as a whole*, but rather, users are interested in a targeted subset of the available information. Narrowing down information to a useful subset is a major function of information management, which the physical library addresses with information classification schemes, card catalogs, and reference librarians. Networked computing will eventually be much more effective at this, leveraging a computer's ability to process vast amounts of data.

User-Directed Access

The most straightforward way for a user to narrow down useful information is to question or interact with an application that has access to a large repository of information. There are three basic tactics listed in Table 2.7. The *search* exploits the computer's ability to systematically examine large volumes of data, if only the user can pose the right question. *Browsing* and *navigating*, on the other hand, allow the user to *interactively* guide the examination of the information, eventually honing in on useful information. The search is most useful in answering a specific question, whereas browsing and navigation are most useful when the user is curious or unsure of precisely what she seeks.

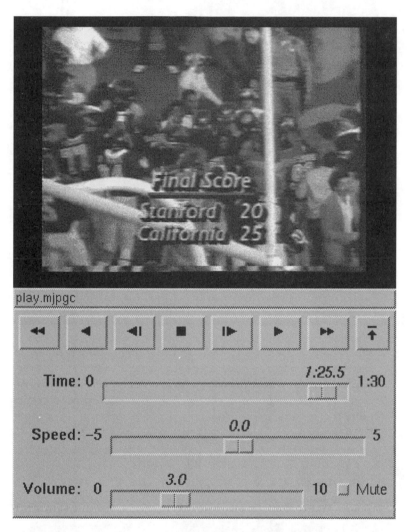

Figure 2.5 The continuous-media player allows viewing and control of a video/audio playback (from [Row92]). *Source:* the Berkeley Continuous Media Toolkit, a research project of the Berkeley Multimedia Research Center. Copyright © 1990–1998 by the Regents of the University of California. All rights reserved.

ANALOGY: *An item search is like inquiring at the library about the availability of a specific book (title, author, and edition), and a topic search is like inquiring about the availability of any book on a*

Table 2.7 Tactics for finding useful information.

Type of information retrieval	Definition	Example
Search	Pose a question, and information relevant to answering that question is returned. *Item search*: A narrow question with a precise answer. *Topic search*: A broader question about information on a broader topic.	Find articles in the medical literature containing the words "Parkinson's disease." The Web has search engines, such as AltaVista, that return pages containing specified keywords.
Browse	Examine a variety of repositories, hoping to opportunistically uncover interesting or useful information.	Follow a set of interesting Web hyperlinks. The Web hyperlink directly supports browsing (see the sidebar "World Wide Web" on page 37).
Navigate	Follow a map or similar navigational aid to arrive directly at the desired information and possibly related information.	Many Web sites have a site map that shows a complete tree of hyperlinks and subject headings.

specific topic (like cooking Mexican cuisine). Browsing is similar to wandering around a new town, at each corner heading in the direction that looks more interesting and promising. Navigating is like choosing a destination on the town map and working out an exact route to get there, perhaps noting alternative routes in case of traffic congestion.

E X A M P L E : *You may be familiar with some specific capabilities of Web browsers and servers supporting each of these four tactics (see the sidebar "World Wide Web" on page 37):*

- *Many Web sites specialize in answering queries, such as the latest selling price of a stock.*
- *The Web has a number of search engines that return Web content containing supplied keywords. Examples include AltaVista, HotBot, and Lycos.*
- *The Web hyperlink supports browsing. By adding hyperlinks, authors help users to find useful related information. The Web consists of a vast number of pages with hyperlinks among them.*
- *Web browsers make a history of accessed pages available on a menu, thus supporting a primitive form of navigation by allowing the user to backtrack to previously accessed pages.*

There is wide recognition that more sophisticated searching, brows-ing, and navigation mechanisms are needed, and this is the focus of research. Some techniques being explored include

- Searching will be based on an understanding of context of the information. Keyword searches may uncover information from distinct domains that can only be distinguished from the context (for example, "china" may apply to porcelain or a country).

- In the future, applications should automatically broaden a search to account for variations in terminology across organizations, fields, or nationalities, and may also perform automatic language translation. Simple keyword searches are complicated by differ-ent terminology used for the same concept (for example, a car "bonnet" in England is the same as a car "hood" in the United States).

- Browsing and navigation aids based on three-dimensional repre-sentations—exploiting users' ability to visualize information in three dimensions—will become commonplace.

Assistance from the Author or Publisher

The author and publisher can do much to assist the user in finding useful information, including several aids shown in Table 2.8.

As the world moves toward multimedia information, finding useful information is even more challenging. Indexing and metadata attached to audio, images, and video are particularly important, because inferring the content is difficult to automate (although this is being researched).

EXAMPLE: *The user may want a picture of a brown Chihuahua from a database with images of dogs. With current technology, automati-cally distinguishing a picture of a Chihuahua from an Australian Kelpie is impractical (although it is more feasible to automatically recognize pictures of dogs). An index or metadata allows the dog's breed to be included in a search.*

The idea of metadata is particularly useful for conveying other infor-mation about a document that requires human judgement and can-not easily be inferred from the document's content.

Table 2.8 Several ways an author can help the user find information.

Navigation aid	Description	Examples
Hyperlink	Link or reference from one document to another related document to assist in browsing and navigation.	Web hyperlinks lead browser to related pages (see the sidebar "World Wide Web" on page 37). References in this book lead you to related articles and books.
Index	A list of terms or subjects with hyperlinks or references to information about them.	Table of contents and index. Yahoo! provides an organized index to the Web.
Metadata	Think of metadata as "data about data." In the context of a document or unit of information, metadata is a description of the content (or possibly other attributes, such as quality, date of generation, etc.).	A short description of this book on the back cover summarizes its content. Other examples are the abstract of a paper, the title of a figure or table, or the textual description of image content.

EXAMPLE: *The World Wide Web Consortium is standardizing a Platform for Internet Content Selection (PICS), which adds a form of metadata known as labels to Web pages [Res97b]. Unlike keyword searches, these labels can convey other attributes requiring human judgement, such as whether content is judged humorous, or offensive, or suitable for viewing by children.*

Third-Party or Collective Recommendations

While assistance from an author or publisher of information is quite helpful, it does presume a relationship of confidence and trust between the publisher and user. It is useless in determining the authenticity or authority of information, or in conveying possibly unstated motives of the author or publisher (such as commercial gain, for example). Often, the judgement of other users or third-party authorities is helpful in overcoming these difficulties.

EXAMPLE: *Consumers often depend on independent reviews of books, music CDs, and movies in a newspaper or magazine. They may rely on the collective judgement of other consumers, as represented, for example, by the appearance of a book or movie on a best-seller list. Or they may rely on informal word-of-mouth judge-*

ments from their friends or the advice of others in a newsgroup or chatroom.

Information access over the network offers many opportunities to formalize and extend these mechanisms for identifying valued information. Computer-mediated systems that assist and augment the natural social process of exploiting a collective judgement are called *recommender systems* (or sometimes *collaborative filtering*) [Res97a]. In a sense, they are a hybrid between an information access and social application (as mentioned in "Recommendation Sharing" on page 38).

E X A M P L E :   *The on-line bookseller amazon.com provides recommendations on other books customers might consider buying (of course, in the interest of selling more books). One technique they use is to examine a database of books purchased by other customers. When the customer orders one book, amazon.com examines all the purchases of other customers who have purchased that same book. Written reviews submitted by other customers are also available.*

Recommender systems are an area of research and commercial activity and will become increasingly common and sophisticated.

Third-Party Organization and Indexing: Digital Libraries

The Web is a large and growing repository of information, but it is also chaotic and disorganized. Its allows anybody to publish information that can be easily accessed by others, but its weaknesses include lack of control over what is published and the fact that there are many uncoordinated publishers. The Web supports browsing well, but search engines are of limited value because there is no structured representation of the data or organized indexing or metadata. Similar problems are addressed in a physical library by adding organization and indexing to a large body of published work emanating from many (otherwise uncoordinated) publishers. This is done by a third-party librarian, largely independent of the publication process.

If the structure and organization of a library are combined with representation and access in a networked computing infrastructure, the result is called a *digital library* [Les97a, Les97b]. Subsets of the Web can be turned into digital libraries by adding indexing and navigation features.

EXAMPLE: *Yahoo! is a rudimentary digital library that indexes a subset of the Web by subject. Many scholars maintain an organized index to the most important papers in their field and publish them for other scholars.*

While some say that a vast collection of digital libraries will replace traditional paper-based libraries, this will take a very long time (if it happens at all). Many materials exist only on paper and would be time consuming and expensive to digitize. However, the digital library as a supplement to traditional libraries, particularly for newly minted information, is an idea whose time has come. For newly authored and published information, the digital library offers considerable cost savings by avoiding printing, physical distribution, and the geographic duplication of library materials. A digital library can also represent volatile and multimedia information and can be highly interactive.

There are several steps between author and information consumer, as listed in Table 2.9. None of these important functions evaporates with digital libraries—they all continue to add value. In digital form, they assume a different form, use a different medium, and may be more automated.

EXAMPLE: *Various personal productivity applications assist in authoring, such as word processors, draw and paint programs, and music composition programs. Many print publishers are expanding to the Web as a publication medium. Yahoo! and others index the content of the Web. Many Web sites have site maps and search engines that provide navigational aids similar to (but far less capable than) the services of a reference librarian.*

While technology can automate some of these functions, people will continue to add value. Keyword searches will identify pages relevant to a particular topic, but the difficult problem remains of information authenticity and reliability, which requires human judge-

Table 2.9 Steps from creation to consumption of information [Sch95].

Actor	Role	Examples
Author or performer	Creates information content.	Writes a book, performs a symphony, makes a music video.
Publisher	Verifies and improves quality, makes the work available for access or sale, controls use of its trademark.	Book publisher, record company, or movie studio.
Indexer	Classifies information and works.	Publisher of thesaurus, telephone yellow pages, library card catalog.
Librarian	Assists and guides user to appropriate content.	Reference librarian at the local library.

ment. A publisher also requires judgement to check an author's credentials, review information for accuracy, and invoke other quality-control measures. There is no complete substitute for a reference librarian, even for a digital library. The librarian can formulate more sophisticated searches after discussing user objectives and can often formulate better strategies for finding useful information.

2.4.2 Autonomous Information Sources

The user can determine what information is accessed, and when it is accessed, as discussed in the previous section. The broadcast is an extreme example of a diametrically opposite approach, in which the publisher determines what information is provided to the user and also when (see the section "Broadcasting" on page 36). The broadcast illustrates the extreme of an *autonomous* information source. In practice, many information access applications fall somewhere between user directed (sometimes called *information pull*) and autonomous source (sometimes called *information push*). There are different approaches, based primarily on three attributes of the application, as listed in Table 2.10. Most applications choose a mixture of these attributes and thus mix the pull and push models.

Table 2.10 Characteristics of information pull and push.

Characteristic	Pull extreme	Push extreme
Control	User requests specific, targeted information.	User subscribes to information on general topics.
Notification	User submits a specific standing question, which the publisher answers as appropriate.	Publisher provides appropriate notifications of useful information it thinks the user may want. The user can choose whether to access that information.
Timing	Information is provided at a time directed by the user (either immediately or at a scheduled time).	Publisher provides information at a time of its choosing. User may look at information as it is provided (direct style) or later (deferred style).

User Control: Subscriptions

The information-on-demand model is illustrated by the Web, where the user determines what pages to access and display. In the opposite subscription model, the publisher partitions information into what it believes to be natural categories or topics, each of which is called a *channel*. What information is actually delivered to each channel is under the control of the publisher. The user determines what channel(s) he or she wishes to receive and then makes a request (called a *subscription*) for the subsequent delivery of those channels.

ANALOGY: *Broadcast radio and television, newspapers, and magazines—each representing a channel—are obtained by subscription. Each publisher differentiates the information content of its channels so as to attract the most subscribers.*

EXAMPLE: *PointCast is a push application that provides a standard set of channels on topics such as the stock price for a particular company, business news, or sports news. The user subscribes to the channels of interest, and thereafter they are presented on the screen as a screen saver. A screen of PointCast is illustrated in Figure 2.6, where (A) is where the user chooses the channel, (B) is a menu of articles for that channel, (C) is an advertising window (which supports this free service), and (D) is the article. The presen-*

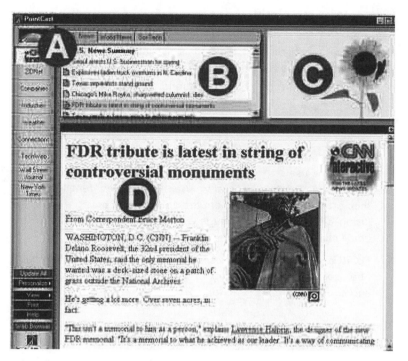

Figure 2.6 Illustration of PointCast screen. *Source:* **reprinted from** *PC Computing Online,* **August 1997. Copyright © 1997 ZD, Inc.**

tation is similar to a Web browser, except the provider chooses the content of each channel on behalf of the subscriber.

Subscriptions are particularly useful with volatile information, such as news reports or stock prices, since they remove the burden from the user of consciously requesting delivery. Further, if there is nothing interesting to report, the user is not bothered.

EXAMPLE: *If a user subscribes to a channel carrying weather bulletins, information is provided only when the weather bureau issues a bulletin, so users do not have to remember to check periodically for bulletins. This is a coordination-monitoring application (see Table 2.5 on page 26).*

User Awareness: Notifications

Rather than provide a stream of information, an alternative is to make users aware of what content is available and leave it up to them to determine what they wish to access. This approach is based on indexing the information in a channel and periodically pushing only the index—but not the indexed information—to the subscriber.

EXAMPLE: *Many publishers of volatile information on the Web encourage users to subscribe to notifications of new content by email. These notifications alert users to new content, attracting their attention and giving them the option of accessing the content (using a Web browser, through a hyperlink embedded within the email message).*

PointCast (see Figure 2.6) uses primarily a notification approach. The user is provided an index of stories available on each channel and chooses which ones to look at.

Timing

Users may or may not have control over the timing of subscribed information or notifications. If they do not have control, the information or notifications may still be stored for access at a time of their choosing.

EXAMPLE: *PointCast (see Figure 2.6) controls when its information is provided to the user's screen, but the user chooses when to look at the stories.*

An immediate form of information pull is appropriate for timely, volatile information, such as notification of a stock market crash or extreme weather event.

Push and Pull in Social Applications

The push/pull distinction arises in social as well as information access applications (see Section 2.3 on page 19), where the distinction is between one user initiating or responding to a request for interaction (or work group).

EXAMPLE: *Email is a push application, because one user "pushes" a message at another. A newsgroup is a pull application, since a user must consciously go to the newsgroup to "pull" a message from another user. In fact, the email and newsgroup applications can be viewed as push and pull variations of messaging.*

In the context of social applications, each model has its strengths and weaknesses:

- Push is invasive, since a user never has total control over what is "pushed" at her. Excessive reliance on push can make a user's life unnecessarily cluttered and stressful.

- Pull requires a user to consciously initiate the interaction with another user or an information source. It does not alert the user to the need for an interaction and thus requires more attention and conscious activity on her part.

In most contexts it is best to combine push and pull (see the sidebar "Role of Push and Pull in Work Groups" for an example).

2.5 Education and Training

One promising networked application is education and training. Occasional predictions to the contrary notwithstanding, it is unlikely that networked computing will ever displace entirely the classroom or campus, as face-to-face interaction and socialization are important, particularly for younger students. It does offer considerable value as a supplement to the classroom and may replace it in some contexts (such as some corporate training and lifelong learning). It may also result in significant shifts in instructional techniques.

Several areas where networked applications offer obvious value include

- *Remote learning:* Networked computing empowers a student to work from home or office in a *virtual classroom*. This would benefit from all the remote conferencing capabilities and groupware discussed in Sections 2.3.3 and 2.3.4.

- *Multimedia educational materials:* A textbook equivalent offered on-line can use multimedia to supplement text and images. This offers not only direct value (for example, the ability to see the events of history rather than just read about them) but also excitement and interest (and dare we say entertainment?). This exploits the applications discussed in Section 2.4 on page 38.

Role of Push and Pull in Work Groups

Combining push and pull in a work group can minimize the burden on users while ensuring their appropriate involvement. Generally it can be said that

- Email (push) should be avoided for discussions and brainstorming, because it forces every group member to deal with every topic. Also, discussions are mixed with more time-critical interactions in the user's mailbox. The newsgroup allows each user to better control which topics she joins in as well as when she chooses to participate.

- Newsgroups and the Web (pull) cannot be relied on exclusively, because users can easily forget or ignore them. Users may be unaware that a topic of interest is being discussed and feel disenfranchised when they discover that they didn't participate in decisions.

The best modality for collaboration mixes the pull and push models:

- Any documents in a work group should be posted on the Web rather than sent in an email message (proprietary information can be protected using

(continued)

restricted access). This pull model allows users to control which documents to read at what time, and they always access the latest version.

- Brainstorming and discussions should also use pull, that is, a discussion forum application.

- The attention of users in the work group can be solicited by push, such as email. Typically, users should be informed by email when a new discussion topic is initiated or a new document is posted on the Web. Ideally, such informational messages should be sent only occasionally, aggregating discussions and documents.

As the number of people using social applications increases, using them properly becomes ever more critical. This is largely a matter of proper education of users.

- *Just-in-time (JIT) training:* For corporate workers, immediate applications such as the virtual classroom are increasingly ruled out by scheduling and travel constraints. At the same time, because of rapid change, deferred forms of education and training that empower people to learn opportunistically—at the time of need—are increasingly valuable.

EXAMPLE: *DigitalThink is a successful start-up company providing training courses using the Web and also collaborative tools like chatrooms to allow students to interact with an instructor at a time of their choosing.*

No doubt, radically new models of education and training will arise using combinations of immediate and deferred, and pull and push, applications. Education combines, in part, knowledge acquisition with the assistance of a teacher to offer assistance, explanation, and guidance. It is natural to combine networked access to self-learning materials together with tools for collaboration with a teacher and other students and trainees. This application area is ripe for innovation.

2.6 Business Applications

It is not an exaggeration to assert that networked computing is transforming the nature of business itself. There are numerous aspects to this transformation:

- *Work groups:* Social applications directly assist workers and managers in their jobs. Their immediate impact is in relaxing geographical constraints, allowing greater interaction with field personnel, and flattening the organizational hierarchy. They also increase the attractiveness of modern organizational techniques such as ad hoc task forces across functional departments, as they assist collaboration among busy, geographically dispersed workers.

- *Operations:* Business requires the movement of goods, information, and money within enterprises and among businesses. Increasingly, networked applications are replacing paper and the transportation system in the flow of information and money, allowing better coordination (internally and externally) and reducing delay, administrative overhead, and errors.

- *Electronic commerce:* The transaction costs of firms dealing with one another and with consumers are being dramatically reduced, affecting firm boundaries and industry organization.

- *Decision support:* Managers and workers must make daily tactical and strategic decisions on what products to design and market, which suppliers to use, when and where to invest capital, etc. Networked computing can enhance the quantity and quality of information available to influence those decisions.

- *Information management:* Information and knowledge management applications allow enterprises to more widely distribute information internally and externally.

- *Mass customization:* The networked computing technologies enable greater customization of products and services sold to individual consumers.

- *Consumer relationships:* The rapid spread of the Internet enhances relationships between sellers and consumers, providing better customer support and new ways of selling.

All is not glorious, however. Networked computing as a means for cost cutting can make business relationships more impersonal and anonymous. It can automate the tedious and repetitive but can also eliminate low-skill jobs and reduce the autonomy of workers. Reliance on networked computing also introduces troubling vulnerabilities, as discussed in Chapter 8.

The evolution of these *business applications* parallels that of computing itself (see Section 1.1 on page 2) with four overlapping and coexisting phases listed in Table 2.11.

2.6.1 Departmental Applications

The typical enterprise is divided into specialized functional departments (accounting, manufacturing, purchasing, development, marketing, sales, etc.). The first business applications managed data within those departments, often replacing paper records.

Table 2.11 Four stages in the evolution of business applications.

Scope	Descriptive terms	Characteristics
Departmental	Client/server computing; enterprise databases; personal productivity applications	Move enterprise data from paper to electronic form, managed by mainframe databases.; add applications that exploit these databases and support workers, often on departmental servers; add decision-support functions and the ability of workers to access and manipulate data on their client PCs.
Enterprise	Business process reengineering; enterprise resource planning; data warehousing; data mining; groupware	Integration of databases is used to reengineer and automate business processes across the enterprise; data is consolidated for decision making.
Cross-enterprise	Electronic data interchange; electronic commerce; electronic business; supply-chain management	Data integration and business processes are extended to include other firms (both suppliers and customers); decision making is enhanced by real-time input; the Internet enables smaller companies to participate.
Consumers	Consumer electronic commerce	Provide shareholders and public with information about the company; provide consumers with marketing information; sell products and services and provide product support over the Internet.

EXAMPLE: *Typical department-level applications would include human resources (tracking employees, doing payroll), accounting and finance, and managing manufacturing inventories.*

A major application is *on-line transaction processing* (OLTP), which supports service agents who deal with customers, for example, to take orders, make reservations, take service or repair requests, or help customers make deposits or withdrawals. The large amount of data representing the information managed by these applications resides in a *database management system* (DBMS) (described further in Chapter 3). A DBMS excels at managing the type of data common in business applications, which includes numbers (bank accounts, employee ages, etc.) and character strings (employee and customer names, etc.). Many data management functions in OLTP and other applications are commonplace across different business applications, and hence the DBMS has emerged as a separate software product category.

Departmental applications were originally developed and are managed by *information systems* (IS) *organizations* on mainframes. Since they are mission critical—the business cannot function without them—they must often run twenty-four hours a day, seven days a week (known as 24 by seven) and must be highly secure and reliable (see Chapter 8). The mainframe provides this secure, reliable centrally managed environment. On the other hand, such centralized systems and their associated IS organizations are, by themselves, rather inflexible [Wat95]:

- Workers and managers wanting customized information have to submit special requests, resulting in the infamous "IS backlog."

- Mainframes require large and expensive support staffs that tend to perpetuate the status quo.

- Since the IS organization serves the entire enterprise and imposes a uniform solution, individual departments have little ability to streamline or increase their own efficiency.

Decentralized computing addressed some of these issues by allowing workers to manipulate data in ad hoc and customized ways on their desktop personal computers (PCs)—especially using spreadsheets—without the assistance of an IS organization. The networking of PCs allowed workers to retrieve data from mainframe OLTP systems for this purpose. A primary factor in the success of the PC was its empowerment of individual workers, unleashing them from some constraints of the IS organization.

Decentralized computing also enabled individual departments to set up and operate applications themselves, based on relatively inexpensive microprocessor-based computers called *servers*. This led to *client/server computing* at the departmental level, where workers' PCs (called *clients*) could store, access, and manipulate data stored in departmental servers or mainframes. Installing and managing applications within the departments added flexibility, and local control resulted in greater efficiency and streamlining. Client/server computing is discussed further in Chapter 3.

Client/server computing unfortunately also allows a proliferation of incompatible systems and applications across the enterprise. The computing environment became more heterogeneous, increasing maintenance and operational difficulties, and placing obstacles in the way of enterprise applications, as discussed next.

2.6.2 Enterprise Applications

The bottom line of the enterprise—the production and sales of products and services—requires the cooperation and coordination of departments across an enterprise.

EXAMPLE: *Manufacturing requires a flow of parts from suppliers, which in turn requires purchasing to order the parts and accounting to pay suppliers. Further, manufacturing must coordinate with sales to forecast demand and maintain manageable inventories, which in turn affects purchasing.*

Organizational theory defines the *business process* as a stream of related activities starting with the acquisition of resources (people, capital, supplies, etc.) and resulting in a product or service in the hands of customers [Dav93]. A key term in this definition is *stream*, which indicates that the constituent activities are repetitive. This distinguishes them from the social and information management applications discussed earlier, which tend to be ad hoc: Each inter-action or collaboration is different.

The structure of a business process is illustrated in Figure 2.7. It takes resources and services from suppliers and ultimately provides products or services to customers. The process requires coordi-nated activities within different functional departments, as well as the flow of material, finished goods, and information among them. It focuses on the activities to be coordinated and the pattern of information and material flows. The design of a business process

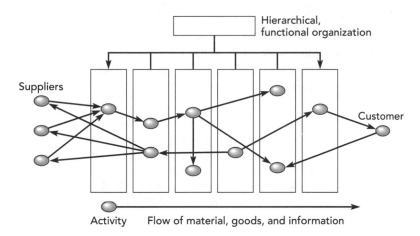

Figure 2.7 Illustration of a business process, which horizontally spans a typical vertical functional organization.

asks how the operation of the business can be made more efficient and effective by somehow modifying both activities and flows, finding a better partitioning of functions among workers and networked computing, and a better interface between workers and technology.

While networked computing cannot contribute directly to the flow of people, material, or finished goods in a business process, it is ideal for controlling that flow and the manipulation of information supporting its coordination. A business process application is similar to social applications in that it enables the communication among and coordination of departmental organizations, instead of users (see Section 2.3.2 on page 22).

EXAMPLE: *In manufacturing, networked computing can support the flow of requests for material and parts from manufacturing to purchasing (so that suppliers can be notified), from receiving to accounting (so that suppliers can be paid), and from sales and distribution to manufacturing (forecasting the volume of production needed), among others. It can also coordinate their actions, such as matching manufacturing volume to sales forecasts.*

Workflow

Where an application primarily supports a group of workers cooperating on repetitive tasks, a business process is often called *workflow*. It is another class of social application, in which the tasks are ongoing and repetitive.

E X A M P L E :   *In a customer service application, telephone agents typically interact with customers to ascertain their problems, and support technicians solve them. Each validated problem results in a trouble ticket, which flows from telephone agent to a group of support technicians. Within the group, each trouble ticket is routed to an appropriate and available technician. The solution is reported to the telephone agents to inform the customer.*

Business Process Reengineering

Because a business process involves repetitive activities, it can be planned and optimized in advance. This is termed the *engineering* of the business process, the goals of which include

- Minimize operational *cost* (personnel costs, inventory and transaction costs, etc.).

- Reduce *delays* required from inputs to customer, allowing the process to respond more quickly to customers and to changes in the marketplace.

- Better quantify and minimize the costs associated with the *overall* process (as opposed to costs at the department level).

- Provide improved and more timely information to support business decisions.

- Make the process flexible, so products can easily be changed in response to marketplace needs, or even customized to individual customer's needs (called *mass customization*).

Used effectively, networked computing can provide considerable value in each of these areas. However, most existing processes were designed years ago—or arose in an incremental and ad hoc manner—and fail to make the most effective use of computing.

It is popular to take a fresh approach to the design of a business process in a way that uses networked computing effectively. Called *business process reengineering* (BPR) [Dav93], where done effectively, this has resulted in major savings and competitive advantage. (The term *BPR* has lost some of its appeal because of its association with mass layoffs. A term used more recently is *business transformation*.) Business process reengineering is not only about networked computing but also accounts for all aspects of the process, including the contribution and organization of workers and the flow of material, supplies, and finished goods. An essential issue in the design of a business process is what people do particularly well, what networked computing does particularly well, and how the two can work effectively together. Simply automating an existing process is rarely the most effective use of networked computing (see the sidebar "Electrification: Lessons from an Earlier Technological Advance" on page 8 for a useful analogy).

The phases of a BPR project consist of

- An *analysis* of business requirements and costs.

- A *design* that structures the individual activities and the flow of materials and information among these activities.

- A *development* of the management and worker organizational systems, as well as computer systems and software.

- The *deployment* of the application, which includes worker training and installing and testing the information systems.

- The *operation* of the application supporting the production, sales, and distribution of goods and services.

The design phase brings managers (who understand the business goals and the organizational and human resource challenges) and technologists (who understand the capabilities and limitations of the information technologies) together, but it benefits greatly from participants who understand both the management and the technology challenges. This book will prepare you to participate in this. The design and deployment of new applications is discussed further in Chapter 3.

SAP: Largest ERP Vendor

SAP (Systems, Applications, and Products in Data Processing), headquartered in Walldorf, Germany, is the largest ERP vendor. Others are PeopleSoft, Baan, and Oracle.

SAP's most recent product offering is called R/3. It incorporates many of the software technologies described in Chapter 6 (frameworks, components, cross-platform object communication). SAP's most successful products support manufacturing, accounting, logistics, and human resources. In 1998 it is in the process of expanding its applications to the extended enterprise with supply-chain management.

Enterprise Resource Planning

The computing component of many business processes was designed and implemented by an IS department working with business units, often utilizing the services of outside consultants and professional services companies. Some of this custom design and implementation is unnecessary because—while there are always local differences—there is much commonality among the processes in different companies.

EXAMPLE: *Accounting systems have a common purpose and operate under the same accounting rules. Human resource management (payroll, benefits, taxes, etc.) is reasonably standardized across companies.*

It may be reasonable to purchase, rather than develop from scratch, an application to support a given business process. *Enterprise resource planning* (ERP) applications supply a major piece of an application, with sophisticated configuration tools to customize to local needs. (The software methodologies making this possible are described further in Chapter 6.) ERP products are available for business processes that are fairly standardized across different companies, such as the following:

- *Sales-force automation* supports the field sales force with automated order entry, availability, and delivery and pricing information, for example.

- *Document management* supports the massive documentation of designs, parts catalogs, etc.

- *Customer service and support* coordinates telephone agents and technicians supporting customers.

- *Manufacturing logistics* provides logistical support for the flow of materials and finished goods, inventory control, purchasing and payments to suppliers, etc.

- *Accounting* allows the company to keep track of cash flow, assets, profits and losses, etc.

- *Human resources* tracks employee history, salary and benefits, tax payments, etc.

- *Supply-chain management* coordinates with suppliers and customers, for example, in the supply relationships that support a finished-goods manufacturer.

A key to ERP is *data integration*—meaning that data associated with the application in question and previously closely held within departments must be integrated into a single application. (Given the heterogeneity of computers and software in most enterprises, this is a severe challenge, discussed further in Chapter 3.) In effect, an ERP application serves as a framework that allows information to flow automatically among department-level systems. ERP also provides several related functions:

- *Forecast and planning:* Effective operations dictate that many resources (such as real estate and worker head count) be planned well in advance, and suppliers may need considerable lead time to manufacture and ship needed supplies. The ERP application can support these functions by providing historical data and future projections.

- *Control:* Efficiency can be improved by actively controlling the flow of goods to minimize inventory and manage accounts receivable and cash. ERP can provide feedback through the chain of activities in the process to control and coordinate them.

- *Real-time monitoring:* The ERP application can observe the business process as it is happening and present summary performance information. It can also highlight problems—such as weather-related transportation delays—allowing managers to react.

The downside of ERP applications is that they require an enterprise to adapt its processes to the software, whereas ideally it would be the other way around. Also, planning and deployment typically utilize experienced but expensive consultants (often accounting firms that have entered this business).

Data Warehouses and Data Mining

Data warehousing and data mining are two applications tailored to decision support, addressing some limitations of OLTP applications. Decisions should take into account not only where things are now but also how they got that way, and use an enterprise-wide picture. A *data warehouse* is a very large nonoperational database (managed by a DBMS) that systematically captures information from a number of operational OLTP databases. It provides two major decision-support benefits:

- *History:* OLTP systems represent the present, but the day-to-day operational needs usually do not require maintaining a well-structured operational history. A *data warehouse* systematically captures the past. It is not updated on a transaction-by-transaction basis as in OLTP, but rather by periodically capturing snapshots of data from OLTP databases.

- *Consolidation:* OLTP applications typically don't present the total picture, because relevant data may be spread across major databases. Day-to-day operational needs may require only information for a single department or

Integrating Multiple Applications

As discussed in Section 1.2, a networked application is frequently embedded in a large-scale system, of which networked computing is only an element. Business applications illustrate this well, since any business process involves workers and materials, and often customers and suppliers, as well as computing systems. Frequently, more than one application is involved in a business process, and any given department has to deal with multiple processes and applications.

E X A M P L E : *A manufacturing process necessarily involves financial, inventory management, supply-chain, and shipping processes, among others. The manufacturing department is affected by all these processes, and data residing there may be manipulated by them all.*

Decision Support

ERP forecasting and monitoring illustrate the important role of networked computing in not only operations but also support of managerial decisions. Networked computing offers capabilities of particular benefit to this decision support:

- *Timely information:* The networking portion of networked computing communicates data around the world with negligible delay (seconds or fractions of a second). As a result, data that supports decisions is available almost "as it happens."

- *Data reduction and presentation:* In a typical business application, far too much data flows for a person to absorb in raw form. The computing portion of networked computing allows this raw data to be aggregated and summarized.

- *Knowledge acquisition and management:* Computers are increasingly capable of aiding workers in acquiring knowledge from massive amounts of organized information.

Data warehouses and data mining are applications directed at decision support (see the sidebar "Data Warehouses and Data Mining").

Knowledge Management

A working definition of *knowledge* in computing is large amounts of information suitably organized and indexed to make it more useful to people. Knowledge is especially crucial to good decision making and is also a key competitive asset of a modern enterprise. Historically, the acquisition and management of this knowledge was very informal. Most knowledge resided in the heads of managers and workers, or in large repositories of paper documents, and knowledge was shared among employees on an ad hoc basis. Modern trends such as downsizing and layoffs, higher turnover, and geographical dispersion of workers point to the need for more formal and structured approaches to knowledge management [Ole98]. Networked computing can aid the *acquisition* of knowledge by allowing workers access to large information repositories that can be systematically searched or navigated, and, with the aid of the network, knowledge can be widely dispersed throughout an enterprise. Recognizing the increasing importance of knowledge management, by 1998, 40 percent of the Fortune 1,000 corporations had put knowledge management on a similar plane with the management of technology, money, real estate, and other corporate assets by creating a "chief knowledge officer" responsible for creating the infrastructure and culture of knowledge sharing and management [Ole98].

EXAMPLE: *Consider a customer service organization in which service agents encounter and solve customer problems and enter this into a knowledge base. This acquired knowledge is immediately available to all service agents, increasing responsiveness and efficiency in solving similar problems. This knowledge—made immediately available to the manufacturing and product development—can be used to discover flaws in manufacturing processes or to improve designs.*

Knowledge warehouses are databases (again managed by a DBMS) storing qualitative rather than quantitative information—work manuals, documentation, proposals, employee information, directories, newsletters, etc.—previously stored on paper. Increasingly, the Web browser is used as the interface to a knowledge base, allowing knowledge to be geographically dispersed across different a single business process. A data warehouse consolidates information from multiple databases to gain an overall picture of the business operation.

Overall, the goal of a data warehouse is to present a consistent and correct historical image of an entire business, or at least a business process.

Data mining is an application that looks for unexpected patterns in large amounts of data. Unlike database queries, data mining does not require the user to ask a question, but rather tries to identify what questions *should* have been asked. Its emphasis is predicting future trends in a business by uncovering patterns within the massive data in a data warehouse. In a limited way, data mining attempts to extract knowledge from the information residing in a business process.

EXAMPLE: *Data mining is put to a number of uses [OHE96a], such as finding which medical treatments are most effective, uncovering the relationship of personal characteristics to voting patterns for courtroom jurists, relating credit card customer characteristics to the likelihood of default, finding risky behavior patterns for insurance companies, and performing technical analysis of stock prices.*

repositories and made readily accessible to managers and workers. The knowledge warehouse is essentially a digital library applied to a business application (see "Third-Party Organization and Indexing: Digital Libraries" on page 45).

2.6.3 Cross-Enterprise Applications: Electronic Commerce

Once business processes *within* an enterprise employ networked computing, and decision-support tools are in place, there remains a major opportunity. A primary operational function of any enterprise—selling goods and services to other enterprises and to individual consumers—can also exploit networked computing, particularly with the growing ubiquity of the Internet. The selling of goods and services among enterprises comes under the general heading of commerce, and when supported by networked applications, it is called *electronic commerce*. Electronic commerce provides many of the same benefits for groups of enterprises and individual consumers as business process reengineering within the enterprise, including reducing costs (administrative and overhead), delay, and errors. Electronic commerce also opens up entirely new channels, such as selling goods and services directly to consumers over the Internet, and improves management decisions by providing more timely, complete, and accurate information [Kee97].

Any commercial transaction involves three basic steps shown in Table 2.12. Each of these steps—if completed over the network—presents its own challenges. The matching of buyers and sellers is an information management challenge, the negotiation of terms is a social application, and the consummation raises issues of how payments are rendered and information goods delivered securely over the network.

Electronic commerce invokes many similar operational needs as enterprise applications but presents many more constraints and obstacles:

- Firms must maintain a hands-off business relationship, and thus the information flowing must be restricted and controlled. Inad-

Table 2.12 Three steps in a typical electronic commerce transaction.

Stage	Description	Typical mechanisms
Matching buyers and sellers	The seller makes the buyer aware of what is available for sale. This is largely an information management problem (see Section 2.4 on page 38).	The seller has to make the buyer aware of goods available, through mechanisms such as advertising, on-line catalog, recommender system (see "Third-Party or Collective Recommendations" on page 44).
Negotiating terms	The buyer and seller reach terms and conditions on the sale, including price, delivery schedule, etc.	Negotiations are supported by work group applications (see Section 2.3.4 on page 28). If multiple buyers and sellers are involved, this may include an *auction*.
Consummation	The agreed sale is completed by transfer of goods and payment.	Key steps are *order*: buyer places order with seller (in a form that cannot be repudiated); *fulfillment*: seller conveys goods to buyer (in a form that cannot be denied); *escrow*: ensure delivery of goods by putting payment in escrow with a trusted third party; *payment*: buyer pays seller for goods (in a form that can be proven).

vertent disclosure of proprietary information is a serious security breach.

- Commercial relationships always have associated payments, which is often not a requirement of an enterprise application.

- Commercial relationships are often not conducted at fixed pre-agreed prices, but there may be a market involving competitive bidding, negotiation of terms, etc.

Particularly interesting are the possibilities for real-time marketplaces that work similarly to the stock market, something that is not too practical in ordinary retailing.

EXAMPLE: *The FastParts Trading Exchange is a Web-based electronic marketplace that allows manufacturers, contract assemblers,*

Legacy Applications and the Year 2000 Problem

Once applications are installed, they're often around a long time. Illustrating this is the Year 2000 (Y2K) problem. Many programmers in the 1950s and 1960s didn't anticipate that their applications would still be operational forty years later, and they saved memory and storage (precious commodities at the time) by truncating years to the last two digits (assuming the first two are always 19). As "January 1, 2000" is misconstrued as "January 1, 1900," havoc may result. These programs are written in old computer languages, and the original programmers have long since retired, so it is difficult to find and repair all instances.

The extent of Y2K points to the surprising number of *legacy applications*—those using obsolete technology but still in operation. Replacing a legacy application is time consuming and expensive and involves difficult logistical challenges. More sobering is the thought that new applications deployed today may have long operational lifetimes. On the positive side, Y2K has itself stimulated many replacements of legacy applications. Bypassing Y2K is one by-product of installing an ERP application, for example.

component manufacturers, and franchised distributors to sell electronic components to one another. Companies with surplus components offer them for sale in an electronic marketplace with real-time negotiation. FastParts handles the payment and shipping of the parts and certifies sellers to ensure quality. FastParts ensures the negotiation and transaction are anonymous, so companies cannot communicate competitive information.

eBay is an on-line auction targeted at individuals. Contrary to Fast-Parts, it is completely public. Sellers and bidders are known to each other. Each bidder typically negotiates terms (delivery, payment method, etc.) with the seller before bidding and can inquire about the goods offered for sale by email. Buyers and sellers can rate one another, and these ratings and other details of each auction are available on the site.

Cross-enterprise applications also introduce administrative and technical challenges, because coordination and control is difficult across administrative boundaries. While enterprises can form bilateral coordination agreements with suppliers and customers, each supplier has its own customers and suppliers desiring similar coordination. The market is a complicated web of suppliers and customers, and since each enterprise can't afford a proliferation of systems, achieving the full potential of cross-enterprise applications requires that *all* enterprises adopt compatible solutions. This is a major technical challenge, especially in light of heterogeneous legacy systems.

EXAMPLE: *The U.S. automobile companies (General Motors, Ford, and Chrysler) have been among the most aggressive in adopting electronic commerce. They have formed the Automotive Network Exchange (ANX) connecting the automobile companies and suppliers. Members can use the network for electronic commerce even if the automobile companies are not involved. The reach of the automobile company suppliers is great, so ANX could form the basis for a much broader electronic commerce interest group [Jon97].*

The elements of electronic commerce listed in Table 2.12 have come together gradually and incrementally—only recently have commercial transactions been conducted in totality over the network. Cross-enterprise electronic commerce has passed through three increasingly ambitious phases: electronic data interchange, electronic money management, and electronic business logistics [Kee97]. Each of these phases expanded the role of networked computing. Technical challenges in business-to-consumer electronic commerce are discussed in Chapters 8 and 10 (see "Consumer Electronic Commerce" on page 38).

Electronic Data Interchange

Electronic data interchange (EDI)—the exchange of business messages in industry-specific standard forms—is a longtime electronic commerce application. EDI replaces paper supply/customer documentation, such as purchase orders and invoices, with electronic messages. Although it has been available for many years, it is usually associated with private communication links between the largest firms. The public Internet and the Web make EDI accessible to small companies. In addition, the interactive Web allows EDI to transcend computer-to-computer links and allow workers in one company to access supporting systems in another company.

E X A M P L E : *Boeing's Part Analysis and Requirements Tracking (PART) system uses the Web to extend EDI to their small-airline customers. It streamlines Boeing's organization by allowing customers to perform searches for obscure parts without help from Boeing workers. Significantly, PART also allows an airline's mechanics and other frontline workers to directly search for and order parts without help from purchasing.*

Electronic Money Management

Terms of sale must be negotiated and goods and services must be paid for. The second phase of electronic commerce—addressing the payments—is *electronic money management*, which is evolving from the province of large companies exchanging payments using banks as intermediaries (called financial EDI, or FEDI), to empowering smaller firms and even individual consumers to electronically manage payments. FEDI authorizes electronic funds transfers between bank accounts.

A major goal is the reduction of transaction costs, making electronic money management practical for smaller payments among small firms and from individual consumers. Even payments of a thou-

Dell Computer and Mass Customization

Dell Computer has eliminated traditional distribution channels, thus reducing costs in direct and indirect ways. Customers access the Dell Web site to view a product catalog and custom configure a computer to their budget and requirements and obtain an immediate price quote. Once an order is input, it generates immediate feedback to various internal business processes—such as manufacturing and purchasing—and directly to parts suppliers. Illustrating mass customization, a computer is manufactured to specification *after* it is ordered, rather than retrofitted by a retailer, distributor, or customer.

sandth of a cent (called a millicent) may be needed for selling individual snippets of information on the Web. While FEDI deals strictly in the transfer of money between bank accounts, credit card payments and cash allow direct payment from buyer to seller (although credit cards require later involvement of financial institutions). There needs to be the cyberspace equivalent of these payment mechanisms. However, where individual consumers and the Internet are involved, security and privacy are major concerns: Consumers are concerned that credit card numbers may be stolen or purchases may be tracked.

EXAMPLE: *Secure Electronic Transactions (SET)—an initiative of Visa International and Mastercard—enables consumers to more securely make credit card purchases over the network or in person. SET ensures the consumer is the legitimate card holder (called authentication), precludes the merchant selling the goods from seeing credit card numbers or other financial information, and precludes financial institutions from tracking purchases.*

Chapter 8 discusses secure electronic payments suitable for individual consumers, including credit card transactions and digital cash (the electronic equivalent of the cash you carry in your wallet).

Business Logistics

The third and final stage of electronic commerce is *integrated business logistics* [Kee97]. Logistics encompasses a broad swath of processes—transcending buying and selling—including coordination of material flows, finished goods, services, and people. It obtains efficiency, speed, accuracy improvements, and cost savings, not simply by automating existing paper-based processes, but by changing the very nature of business—reorganizing it around networked computing technologies and particularly the public Internet. An example of the possibilities is mass customization (see the sidebar "Dell Computer and Mass Customization"). Logistics extends the business process to the business-to-business processes in the customer-supplier relationship, reducing organizational barriers and flattening organizations, lowering barriers to those customers and suppliers, and integrating internal operations with suppliers and business partners. Logistics is heightening customer expectations for speed, accuracy, customization, and cost.

EXAMPLE: *Dell's business model has many advantages. Manufactur-*
ing immediately builds and ships a customer's computer, requiring
no inventory of finished goods. A procurement process can
respond quickly by transmitting orders to suppliers, minimizing
inventory costs. When new pricing or product strategies are intro-
duced, marketing obtains immediate feedback on their success
[SAP97].

ERP vendors are embracing *supply-chain management* (see "Enter-prise Resource Planning" on page 60). This class of cross-enterprise application extends ERP to controlling and monitoring the flow of materials, goods, services, and money through a supply chain. In its most extreme form, supply-chain management can create *virtual enterprises* [Gre96]. In this model of business, firms aren't tempted to accumulate all the specialties necessary for the manufacturing and marketing of products. Each individual product is designed, manufactured, and marketed by opportunistically pulling together (and later disbanding) an alliance of firms. In theory, virtual enter-prises can react more quickly to market opportunities, and competi-tively chosen partners can deliver high quality, responsiveness, and low cost (compared to an internal supplier). The impact of net-worked computing on the boundaries among firms is discussed fur-ther in Chapter 5.

2.6.4 Consumer Applications

Consumer applications allow enterprises to interact with individual shareholders and consumers and provide a major new channel for marketing and selling goods and services to consumers. Unlike cross-enterprise applications, where proprietary data networks are an option, before the Internet, it was difficult to reach consumers electronically for marketing, sales, and post-sale support. Such capabilities have been available using the telephone for many years—for example, catalog sales—but the Internet offers a richer interaction, the tailoring of sales techniques and pricing to individ-ual consumers (see the sidebar "amazon.com: On-Line Merchant" for an example), and lower transaction costs.

amazon.com: On-Line Merchant

A successful merchant that molded itself around consumer electronic commerce is the bookseller amazon.com (even its name reflects an exclusive on-line presence). Like any retailer, amazon.com is an intermediary between distributors and customers, but since its customers browse on-line, amazon.com need not maintain an inventory. Rather, it passes orders directly to distributors, in an illustration of supply-chain management.

Amazon.com also illustrates that on-line retailing can offer new features and services. For example, each book the customer considers is accompanied by reviews from other customers (a recommender system), and additional sales are encouraged by listing related titles (based on both topic sales and customer behavior). The interests and behavior of customers can be monitored and presentations tailored accordingly. The customer can request email notification of books in categories of interest (an information push application).

2.7 Similarity of Social Systems and Networked Computing

This chapter has emphasized that the unique applications of networked computing are intimately interwoven with social systems of all types: the citizenry, interest groups, and organizations pursuing business, education, and commerce. Although probably not evident yet, there are remarkable similarities between the types of issues addressed in this chapter—how networked applications serve users and organizations—and how networked applications are internally organized and implemented, which is the subject of much of the remainder of this book. Examples of this abound:

- Organizations and other social systems must delegate responsibilities to different people, and networked applications must delegate responsibilities to different computers.

- People must communicate and coordinate themselves to accomplish defined tasks and so must the pieces of a networked application.

- People must figure out how to avoid conflicts when they share a common task or resource and so must networked computers.

- Society must allocate finite resources efficiently—such as highways, water, electricity, etc.—and so must the network and the computers attached to it.

- Social systems must cope with breakdowns, natural disasters, criminal behavior, and such occurrences, and so must computer systems.

You are urged to reflect on these parallels throughout the remainder of the book. Many of the same issues arise in social contexts and in networked applications, and many of the solutions are directly analogous, or at least recognizable. This should help you navigate the many technical issues to be uncovered subsequently, and the book aids this by providing numerous analogies. The ideas and concepts applied to the design of computer systems may also suggest similar concepts that can be exploited in the design of social systems, such as business organizations.

2.8 Open Issues

Applications raise a number of open issues: How are they invented? What impact do they have?

2.8.1 The Productivity Quandary

Economists find it difficult to discern productivity gains attributable to networked computing. Macroscopically, in the United States overall productivity growth has slowed the last couple of decades just as networked computing became more prevalent. Microscopically, correlations between the financial results of individual firms and networked computing investments are difficult to discern. While these circumstances seem counterintuitive, there are a few relevant observations:

- Networked computing has its biggest impact on the service sector, where productivity is notoriously difficult to measure.

- Much of the benefit is in quality, which is difficult to separate from productivity when measuring improvement. For example, networked computing empowers solitary users to produce higher-quality documents (but perhaps consuming more time) and run financial projections not previously possible (but also consuming time).

- Most importantly, automating existing processes is not where the major productivity gains are expected. Rather, both the processes and the social dimension of the organizations that incorporate them have to be reengineered to make most effective use of the technology [Wal89] (see the sidebar "Electrification: Lessons from an Earlier Technological Advance" on page 8 for a historical analogy).

So, the question is, "When will substantial and documented productivity gains from networked computing technologies appear?" Only time will tell.

2.8.2 How Are New Business Applications Invented and Developed?

Automation of existing processes does not fully realize the potential of networked computing. The biggest gains are achieved when application design is integral to the overall process design, including human resource and organizational design. Application design is thus not primarily a technical activity, and yet the technical issues of performance, cost-effectiveness, and flexibility are also important. Thus, the traditional gulf between nontechnical and technical workers, where the former rely on the latter to define the applications and infrastructure and the latter rely on the former to define the application context, cannot meet the challenge of seamless interworking of the organization and its enabling networked applications. Can a collaboration of management with information technologists continue to work, or is a new cadre of technically astute managers (or managerially astute technicians) needed?

2.8.3 The Glut of Information and Communications

Both communication and information access become so easy that many users find their biggest problem is *too much* information and *too much* communication. Networked computing can transmit and manipulate astounding amounts of information and thus can filter, search, and present it in helpful ways. Recommender systems can also be very helpful. Communications and collaboration are arguably more problematic, since human communication is inherently "push," performed invasively and consciously [Mes96b]. As the global networked citizenry expands, the demands of communication expand with it, consuming more of the user's time. In response—to avoid the constant interruptions and scheduling problems—more interaction becomes deferred (email, voicemail, etc.), which is less invasive but also less efficient for many purposes.

Increasingly, applications must incorporate sophisticated capabilities to improve the quality and limit the quantity of information, communications, etc. Nevertheless, the growth of information and communications seems to be exceeding the capability of these technological measures. Certainly more research and commercial activity are needed in this area.

2.8.4 Accommodating Change

An obvious attribute of modern business is continual change. Firms recast their businesses rapidly, the product birth and obsolescence cycle shortens, reorganization is endemic, and networked computing penetrates more deeply. The boundaries of firms change with relentless mergers, acquisitions, and divestitures. These environmental factors place severe stress on information systems, which would ideally ease the path to change rather than inhibit it. An important objective—but one not achieved with the current state of technology—is flexible applications that readily adapt to changing needs. This is a serious challenge, not only to the applications themselves but also to the infrastructure that supports them, and one that is arguably not met by today's business applications.

Further Reading

There are not yet other books covering social applications of networked computing that can be recommended. [Les97b] is a good treatment of information management (especially digital libraries), [Ole98] is a concise and readable introduction to knowledge management, and [Kee97] is a good introduction to electronic commerce, with an extensive glossary.

Computers, Networks, and Organizations

3

The major classes of networked applications discussed in Chapter 2 must be supported by an *infrastructure*—those things not specific to any application, but which support all applications. To conceptualize good applications, it helps immensely to have an appreciation for the capabilities and limitations of the infrastructure that supports them.

ANALOGY: *A new organization in the physical world would be supported by an infrastructure, including highways, postal and package delivery systems, banking, accountants and lawyers, etc. To establish the most successful organization, this infrastructure should be used most effectively, which requires understanding of what each provides and how they work in combination.*

A networked computing infrastructure includes computers (for computation, information processing, and user interface), a network for communication among these computers, and a lot of software. This equipment and software require administrative and operational support, and some of it is leased from and operated by service providers. The goal of this chapter is a deeper appreciation of how computers, networks, and organizations work together to support networked applications, including their development and deployment. The primary concern here is the physical infrastructure, whereas Chapter 4 describes the software infrastructure.

A networked computing infrastructure supports four important capabilities:

- *Communication across distance:* This is supported by the network (even within the same building), which allows computers to communicate data to one another.

- *Communication across time:* This is provided by computer storage. Deferred social and information management applications permit users to participate at times of their choosing, so they need to store information temporarily or permanently. Business applications typically capture and manage massive amounts of data.

- *Computation and logic:* These are defined by software programs. Most applications require internal logic governing how they react to user (or other) inputs, and many require numeric computations.

- *Human-computer interface:* Many applications (particularly social and information management) support users in their activity or job (including interaction, collaboration, information management, etc.). The application governs user interaction—called the *presentation*—by allowing the user to input data (through a keyboard, mouse, microphone, television camera, etc.) and extract information (graphics, video, audio, etc.).

The overall infrastructure and application are illustrated in Figure 3.1 for the simplest of situations: A single desktop computer providing the user interface and a second computer managing data. Any computer connected to a network is—from the network perspective—known as a *host*. The terminology originates from the observation that the computer "hosts" the software (both infrastructure and application). Since this book is concerned with networked computing, all computers of interest are hosts. (The term "host" was also used to connote a mainframe in the earlier days of centralized computing, leading to some terminology confusion.) The desktop computer is called a *client* host (or just client), and the computer managing the data is called the *server* host (or just server) (see Table 2.1 on page 18). The client and server hosts can communicate over the network. The preeminent public network—the Internet—is emphasized in this book. Together, the network and computers form the equipment (sometimes called hardware) por-

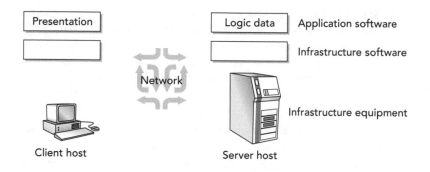

Figure 3.1 General structure of the infrastructure and application in the simplest case.

tion of the infrastructure. The software is equally important, including infrastructure software (Chapter 4) and application software (Chapter 6).

The partitioning of application software across hosts shown in Figure 3.1 is typical for a simple situation. The presentation—everything particular to the interaction with the user, including the human-computer interface—runs on the client host. Other aspects of the application, such as data management, computation, and logic, run in the server host. The portion of application software running on the client host is also called the client, and the portion running on the server host is also called the server. Scenarios involving more hosts are common and are discussed in Section 3.2.2.

3.1 Computing Systems

Any significant activity, such as a conference, business, or school, must be organized to be successful. Likewise, something as complex as a computing system also requires an internal organization to work properly (or to work at all). This organization takes the form of what engineers call a system. A *system* is a composition of subsystems that cooperate to accomplish some higher purpose. A *subsystem* is an element within the system that performs some narrower, well-defined function on behalf of the system and cannot be subdivided and still perform that function.

EXAMPLE: *A telephone system, consisting of switches, transmission systems, and telephones, is a system; these subsystems work together to provide telephone service. The government is a system consisting of executive, legislative, and judicial elements, and a bureaucracy, providing various services to the citizenry.*

In practice, no single person, group, or even organization can deal with the entire system as a whole. Thus, the purpose of decomposing the system into subsystems is to deal with the subsystems as individual units, independently of each other and independently of the system (insofar as practical).

3.1.1 The System Architecture

The *architecture* of a system encompasses its structure and organizing principles. An architecture has the three basic properties described in Table 3.1.

ANALOGY: *The architecture of a building is determined with its intended purpose (business, education, etc.) in mind. The subsystems are the rooms, halls, stairways, electricity, plumbing, etc. How these elements cooperate is determined partly by connections (the hallway has doors into each room, and the stairs connect the floors).*

Table 3.1 The basic elements of a system architecture.

Property	Description	Analogy
Decomposition	A partitioning of the system into individual subsystems that interact to realize the higher purposes of the system.	A government is partitioned into executive, legislative, and judicial branches.
Functionality	The specialized capabilities assigned to each subsystem supporting the overall system purposes.	The legislature makes laws, the executive branch enforces laws, and the judiciary determines the guilt or innocence of accused lawbreakers.
Interaction	How the subsystems communicate and cooperate to support the system purposes.	The executive branch informs the legislature of the need for new laws and brings accused lawbreakers before the judiciary.

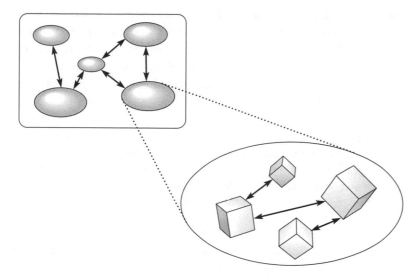

Figure 3.2 Illustration of hierarchical decomposition of a system into subsystems.

EXAMPLE: *A business process reengineering project (see "Business Process Reengineering" on page 58) defines an architecture. It is decomposed into activities, each activity with a specific functionality and a cooperation (flow of information and resources) among them.*

3.1.2 Decomposition of Systems

As illustrated in Figure 3.2, many systems have a *hierarchical* decomposition, meaning that subsystems are themselves systems with an internal decomposition into interacting subsystems.

EXAMPLE: *In the government system, each branch of government is a subsystem internally decomposed into its own subsystems (agencies, departments, etc.).*

A computing system follows this hierarchical model. At the top level, the subsystems include hosts, network, and application and infrastructure software, but each of these subsystems is itself decomposed into internal subsystems. For example—focusing on the equipment—the network includes switches and communication links, as will be discussed shortly. Each host has internal sub-systems—one or more microprocessors (single-chip processing units), memory, and storage—that cooperate to execute a program. Each of these is a subsystem; for example, a microprocessor's functionality (running program instructions) requires an internal decomposition into subsystems (e.g., transistors).

ANALOGY: *Biology displays a similar hierarchical system architecture. An organism is composed of cooperating organs, an organ is composed of cooperating cells, and a cell internally has a membrane, nucleus, etc. Similarly, organizations have a hierarchical decomposition, with divisions composed of departments, departments composed of groups, etc.*

This hierarchical organization is necessary to contain the inherent complexity of a computing system, and it also leads directly to an organization of computer suppliers in which the end-user assembles a system from subsystems, and in turn subsystem suppliers assemble their subsystems from subsystems they purchase from other suppliers (see Chapter 5). Eventually, this decomposition must terminate—an element in a subsystem can no longer be decomposed. In this case, the element is said to be *atomic*, meaning it can't be subdivided.

Subsystems and Components

There is a substantial difference between custom designing a subsystem as part of a system design and purchasing a subsystem as a product from another company. In the former, the system functionality and interaction can be chosen freely to match the precise system requirements, and in the latter the subsystem must be accepted as is and the system designed around it. A subsystem that is purchased as a product from an outside company is called a *component*.

EXAMPLE: *With rare exceptions, a networked application uses commodity computers, peripherals, and networking equipment from outside vendors. From the application perspective, these subsystems are components; the system is designed around them, accepting their functionality and interaction as is.*

The importance of components to both equipment and software suppliers is discussed in Chapters 5 and 6.

3.1.3 Hosts and the Network

For a given application, an architecture of the equipment supporting the application must be designed. The architecture includes subsystems (hosts and the network interconnecting them), an assignment of application functionality to each host, and an understanding of how those subsystems interact. These subsystems supporting networked applications were shown in Figure 2.1 on page 17 and in Figure 3.1 on page 77.

Client/Server Architecture

Two simple architectures supporting networked applications are shown in Figure 3.3 (more complicated scenarios are considered in Section 3.2.2 on page 92). In the client/server architecture, hosts come in two flavors: clients and servers. Clients are the hosts that directly support the user and are usually desktop computers (most often PCs or Macintoshes, but sometimes also UNIX workstations). Servers are hosts that do not interface directly to users but provide computation or logic to the networked application, or manage storage. It is typical for many users to access a single server (through their respective clients) remotely across a network, and a server often has higher performance than a client to serve those multiple users. It is also common for a single client to access two or more servers, often to run different applications.

The client/server architecture is suitable for information management applications, in which the server stores and manipulates information and the clients pass requests for information from users and display results for them. Many direct- and publication-deferred social applications also use this client/server architecture (Chapter 2 defined the application classification used here). A primary advantage of a network connection is that many servers can be accessed from a single client, either simultaneously or at different times.

EXAMPLE: *The Web (see the sidebar "World Wide Web" on page 37) assigns information management functions to a Web server residing in a server host, and the presentation to a Web browser*

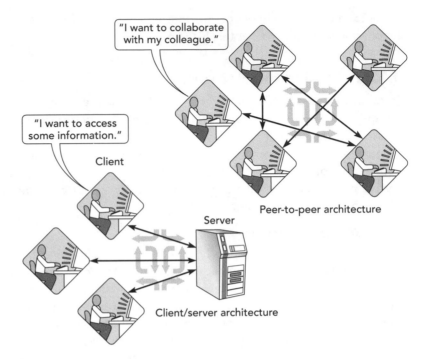

Figure 3.3 Two basic architectures for social and information manage-ment applications.

residing in the client host. The user uses a mouse to invoke hyper-links, and these invocations are communicated over the network to the server host, which returns the requested page for the browser to display. A Web browser can access many Web servers. When the user invokes a hyperlink (by clicking highlighted text), this may cause the browser to shift to an alternative server host.

In summary:

- The primary function of the client is to accept instructions from the user, make requests of the server, and display responses from the server for the user.

- The primary function of the server is to respond to such requests, typically from many clients.

This gives client/server an *asymmetry* of function, where the client makes requests and the server satisfies requests.

EXAMPLE: *In an airline reservation system, the travel agent is at a client, and the flight information is stored in a server, so the travel agent—through his client—can answer inquiries about flight times. When a bank customer visits an ATM to get cash, she is the user, the ATM is the client, and the bank's central mainframe is a server. The ATM accepts customers' requests for cash, clears them with the server, and then issues the cash.*

A server must be *available* at all times, waiting for requests from clients. Clients, however, can come and go, since they always initiate the interaction.

ANALOGY: *In a law practice, the customers are also called clients. The law office provides a service to multiple clients. A single person might be a client to both a lawyer and an accountant. A law office is always open for any potential client to request legal services, but the interaction is initiated by the client. Different clients may appear at different times.*

While the Web illustrates the client/server architecture for information management, it is also natural for direct-*deferred* social applications because there is a storage (communication across time) function naturally assigned to the server.

EXAMPLE: *Figure 3.4 illustrates an email application using a client/server architecture. The user can input her messages into an email client program on the client host, and the result is sent to the email server program on a server host. The server stores each message during the time that elapses between the originating user composing and sending a message and the recipient user reading the message, and it also routes the message to the intended recipient (not shown). The recipient user can retrieve and view the message using his own email client. An example of an email client is Eudora, and an example of an email server is a POP server ("POP" stands for "post office protocol").*

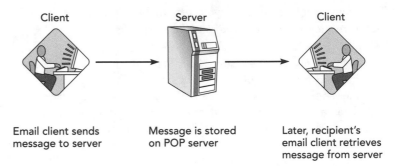

Client	Server	Client

Email client sends message to server

Message is stored on POP server

Later, recipient's email client retrieves message from server

Figure 3.4 Using a client/server architecture to support an email application.

Client/server is also appropriate for direct-*immediate* social applications, when there is application logic that naturally resides on a server, such as consolidation of information for many users.

EXAMPLE: *In a chatroom application illustrated in Figure 3.5, many users can participate at their respective clients. When a user types, each client sends the text to the chatroom server, which aggregates that typing and returns a single presentation to all clients. Each user can see everything typed by everyone.*

Peer-to-Peer Architecture

In the alternative peer-to-peer architecture of Figure 3.3, there is no server but only desktop computers—called *peer hosts* because of their similarity of function—supporting the application and users. This architecture is appropriate for direct-immediate social applications, in which there is no communication across time necessitating storage on a server and no centralized application logic is needed.

EXAMPLE: *Peer-to-peer architecture is natural for audio and video conferencing. Data representing the audio or video is simply communicated over the network directly from one peer to another.*

ANALOGY: *In the public telephone system, when two telephones are used to support a conversation, they are peers. However, when one telephone is used to access bank account information, then the telephone is a client and the bank's computer is a server.*

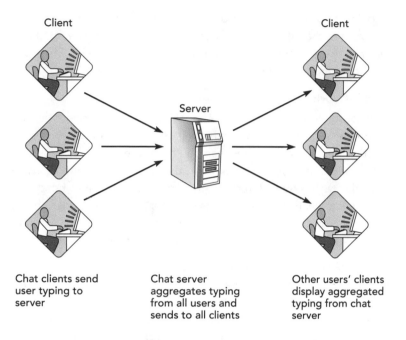

Chat clients send user typing to server

Chat server aggregates typing from all users and sends to all clients

Other users' clients display aggregated typing from chat server

Figure 3.5 A chatroom application using a client/server architecture.

A distinguishing characteristic of the peer-to-peer architecture is the symmetry of function—each peer provides essentially the same functionality—as contrasted to the asymmetry in client/server. Architectures can also mix client/server and peer-to-peer. For example, many direct-immediate social applications have an information management aspect and a multiuser interaction aspect. Their respective desktop computers may serve as both peers (to interact with other peers directly) and as clients (to access the information stored in a server).

EXAMPLE: *In remote conferencing (see Section 2.3.3 on page 27), each user's desktop computer might act as a client to the server that manages the document edits coming from multiple users, while simultaneously acting as a peer for the voice and video aspect.*

A given desktop computer can be a client or a peer; it is the software that defines the host's role in the application. There is no major distinction in the hardware between clients and servers, except as to the details of configuration (memory, storage, etc.) and performance and the requirement for user interface elements (display, keyboard, etc.) in the client.

The Network

A computer network is to hosts what the public telephone system is to people, allowing hosts to communicate data as necessary to support the application. Any host can communicate with any other host on that same network at any time. In the case of the world's largest network—the global Internet—this means that any host can communicate with tens of millions of other hosts. Each host on the Internet is assigned a *domain name* (for example, info.SIMS.Berkeley.EDU) that other hosts need in order to communicate with it.

Of course, limits must be placed to avoid chaos. One host requires *authorization* to communicate with another; it can't do whatever it pleases with another host without permission. Authorization must be accompanied by *authentication* that confirms the requesting host's identity. A host's owner controls which other hosts can access it and for what purposes. Techniques for authentication and authorization are discussed in Chapter 8.

ANALOGY: *The public streets enable Mary to travel anywhere in her car, including into her own garage. In principle, the streets allow any citizen to drive his car into Mary's garage, but only she is authorized to enter, and the garage door authenticates her by the key she carries.*

EXAMPLE: A public *Web server may authorize any host on the network to access its pages. On the other hand, access can be restricted, for example, to hosts in the same company. Another application running on the same host—one managing sensitive employee records—is only authorized to be accessed by the human resources department.*

The application pieces residing on different hosts may communicate by sending one another *messages* (very much like users in groupware—see Section 2.3.4 on page 28). A message is the smallest unit of data that makes sense to the sender and recipient; by assumption, a fragment of a message is useless to the application.

EXAMPLE: *In an email application, one user sends an email message to another (note the use of the term "message"). The email message is the smallest unit of information that is meaningful to the sender and recipient. Delivering half the message to the recipient isn't useful. In the Web application, when the user requests a page of information to be displayed, that page is a message communicated from the Web server to the Web browser.*

People use the telephone network by initiating a "call" and holding a "conversation," and typically a given telephone participates in only one conversation at a time. The Internet differs from the telephone network in that one host doesn't have to "call" another host: It can simply send a message to one or to multiple hosts (or receive them from multiple hosts). It is also possible to set up something analogous to a "call" and hold a "conversation"—an ongoing bidirectional exchange of messages—in a service called a *session*. These options are discussed in Chapter 7.

Switching

Architectures are often hierarchical (see Section 3.1.2 on page 79), and the network is no exception. To the communicating hosts, the network structure is not evident, but internally it is decomposed into subsystems—access links, switches, and backbone links. This internal architecture will now be described.

Consider the problem of carrying messages from one host to another. Although the application interprets the message as information, the network considers it data (a collection of bits). To communicate data in a message from one host to another requires physical interconnections called *communication links*.

ANALOGY: *The wire that connects a residence to the telephone's central office is a communication link. It carries the voice (using a telephone) and data (using a modem) from the residence to the telephone's central office and also in the reverse direction.*

The detailed characteristics of communication links are discussed in Chapter 12. For present purposes, a link simply carries messages from one geographic location to another. It is impractical to directly connect each host with every other host by a dedicated communication link. In the global Internet, for example, there are millions of hosts, and having millions of connections to each host is nonsensical. This full interconnection is avoided by requiring each message to traverse multiple communication links and by forwarding that message from one link to another using *switching*.

ANALOGY: *A city avoids having a dedicated street between each pair of garages by adding intersections (analogous to switches). Driving a car between two garages requires traversing multiple streets (analogous to communication links), and at each intersection, choosing one from among the (typically three) alternatives is analogous to switching.*

A simple switched network is shown in Figure 3.6. Each host is connected to a switch by a single dedicated communication link, and switches are in turn interconnected by communication links. A message can be communicated between any pair of hosts with only one link connected to each host. The network has two distinct types of communication links:

- Each host has a single *access link* (analogous to a driveway), which interconnects it with the first switch, called an *access switch*.

- Switches are interconnected by *backbone links*—defined as links not directly connected to hosts. Each switch is typically connected to at most a few other switches. The goal is to avoid—with switches as well as with hosts—an explosion of connected links as the number of hosts on the network grows.

There are also two distinct types of switches:

- An *access switch* forwards messages from an access link to the appropriate backbone link (and vice versa).

- *Backbone switches* forward messages from one backbone link to another.

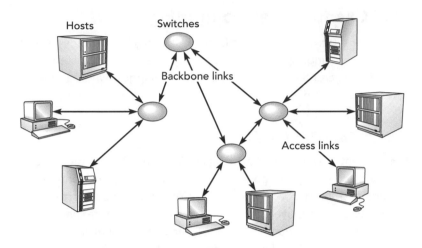

Figure 3.6 Introducing switches allows many hosts to be interconnected, with only one communication link per host.

The collection of backbone switches and backbone links is called the *backbone network*, and the access switches and access links are called the *access network*.

The particular pattern of interconnection of hosts and switches is called the *network topology*. The primary requirement is that from each host to all other hosts there must be at least one feasible *path*—consisting of switches and connecting links—that a message can traverse. As in the simple topology of Figure 3.6, there may be more than one such path, implying that switches must choose from among feasible alternatives. Each switch forwards a message to an appropriate output link, bringing it closer to the destination host, and switches must be coordinated so that the message eventually arrives at the intended recipient host (this function is called *routing* and is discussed in Chapter 11).

In practice, the network forwards not messages, but *packets*. A packet is typically a fragment of a message (a message may be composed of multiple packets), or a packet may be an entire message. For this reason, a computer network is called a *packet network*. The reason for the distinction between packets and messages is related to performance and is discussed in Chapter 10.

3.2 Client/Server Computing

The client/server architecture is popular today, particularly in business computing. However, nothing in the world of computers stands still, and the origins of client/server suggest where it may be heading.

3.2.1 Two-Tier Client/Server

In the centralized computing era (see Section 1.1 on page 2), applications commonly ran on a mainframe computer, and when users needed to interact with the application, this was supported by a terminal that displayed text (and only text). This terminal—called affectionately a "dumb" terminal—had no graphics, windows, menus, nor pointing device, but only a keyboard and text display. The dumb terminal was actually a major advance over *batch processing*, used in the 1960s and earlier, in which users submitted batch jobs using decks of punched cards. Multiple users—each at a dumb terminal—could simultaneously run their own applications on a single computer using *time-sharing*.

A N A L O G Y :   *Dropping your clothes off at a laundry and picking them up later is analogous to batch processing. A laundromat—where you share the available washing machines with others and wait for your clean clothes before leaving—is analogous to time-sharing.*

Dumb terminals, which were directly wired to a computer, allowed a user to interact with an application running on a centralized computer. Later, Ethernet (and other local area network (LAN) technologies) enabled one computer to communicate with other computers. In the networked computing era, the desktop computer supplanted the dumb terminal in support of the user interface and communicated with the mainframe using the LAN.

The arrival of the desktop computer and LAN evolved into the client/server architecture. Solitary applications such as word processing and spreadsheets could execute directly on the desktop computer, but users also wanted centralized capabilities previously supported by time-sharing. These included

- Social applications enabled by multiple users accessing a centralized computer.

- Ability to share information with other users without carrying physical media such as floppy disks. In addition, information stored on a central host allows collaborative authoring and sharing of volatile information.

- Centralized administration of widely used applications, which removes that burden from users.

These capabilities evolved in the client/server architecture without giving up the advantages of desktop computers. The server became the focus for the sharing and backup of information and centralized administration of applications, while users retained the ability to process information in personalized ways or install their own applications on desktop clients.

File System

One of the primary functions of the infrastructure is the storage of data on behalf of users and applications. For this purpose, hosts have storage media (such as disks, tapes, and CD-ROM) and also a *file system* provided by every computer operating system (see more discussion of operating systems in Chapter 4). The file system is very familiar to personal computer users, who use it to store documents or spreadsheets in *files*, which are in turn stored in *directories* or *folders*. A file is a collection of data managed by some application (such as a word processor or spreadsheet), and the file system stores and retrieves files in a collection of folders. Folders make it easier for the application or user to keep track of related files, by grouping them under a single name.

Both the client and the server have a file system. However, it is particularly important in the server, which is often where most files reside. By centralizing files in the server, systematic backup of data (by making copies on tape) prevents its loss due to equipment failure. Also, this allows data to be shared by multiple users, at their multiple clients. File systems are sometimes *distributed*, meaning there is a single hierarchical structure of files physically stored in different computers and accessed over the network. A file system does not know or care about what data is stored in the files—that is managed by applications.

3.2.2 Three-Tier Client/Server

The *two-tier client/server* architecture has been described, in which the first tier is the client and the second tier is the server. The combination of desktop computers and relatively inexpensive microprocessor-based servers enabled individual departments to operate their own applications (see Section 2.6.1 on page 53).

However, businesses also rely heavily on enterprise databases supporting mission-critical OLTP applications on mainframe computers. The data residing in these databases is useful for departmental applications and decision support (see "Decision Support" on page 62)—and so should be available to servers and desktop computers—but that data and the OLTP applications it supports are also mission critical. For reasons of security and reliability, these mainframes are not suitable as servers for general user access or running other client/server applications (see Chapter 8).

There emerged a three-tier architecture that distinguishes three distinct functions in enterprise applications, as illustrated in Figure 3.7 and listed in Table 3.2. The essence of the architecture is to define two types of more specialized servers—shared data and application logic.

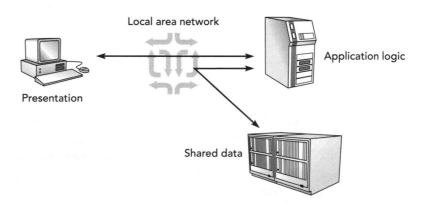

Figure 3.7 Three-tier client server.

Table 3.2 The partitioning of functionality in three-tier client/server computing.

Tier	Description	Analogy
Shared data	Enterprise mission-critical data shared by multiple applications; a server (often, but not necessarily, a mainframe) satisfies data queries from the application logic.	In a restaurant, the refrigerators store the ingredients (analogous to data). The kitchen prepares meals (analogous to information) on request from the waiters.
Application logic	Embodies the unique behavior and functionality of an application; runs in an application server (frequently more than one application server per shared data server).	Operation of the restaurant requires offering the customer (analogous to user) choices, eliciting his order, satisfying requests. The waiter (frequently more than one per kitchen) serves the customer.
Presentation	Displays information to the user by vision and sound; receives user input and requests by voice, keyboard, or mouse.	The table service (dishes, plates, glasses) present the meal to the customer, who uses silverware to eat it. The customer verbally makes requests of the waiter.

The application logic, which mediates between shared data and presentation, manipulates the shared data. It also takes inputs and requests from the presentation, decides what needs to be done, decides what shared data should be accessed or must be updated, manipulates that data appropriately, and responds to the presentation. The shared data answers queries from the application logic, and the application logic determines what data is stored and what queries are needed.

EXAMPLE: *A Web-based bookseller (see the sidebar "amazon.com: On-Line Merchant" on page 70) might have mission-critical shared data, including inventory, the status of active orders and back orders, customer information, etc., stored in a database server. A separate application server runs the application logic and Web server that interact with the presentation—the Web browser supporting the customer. The application logic is responsible for determining what is presented on customer screens and what database queries are necessary to generate those screens. It also accepts customer input and updates the database.*

There are several reasons to divide things this way:

- The presentation—dedicated to a single user—is natural to assign to the client for better interactivity.

- The application logic supports multiple users and thus is naturally assigned to a server. As the number of users increases, more application servers can be added, all accessing a common shared data server.

- The shared data server may support multiple applications and by dedicating a host can support more application users. It can also have a protected administrative environment for security and reliability (see Chapter 8).

- Keeping application logic out of the client is natural for applications accessed by the citizenry (such as consumer electronic commerce) because it avoids installation of special software.

The three-tier client/server architecture has a many-to-one (or at least few-to-one) relationship at each level: There are many clients per application server and potentially multiple application servers per shared data server.

Shared Data Tier: Database Management

The third tier—shared data—is usually supported by an off-the-shelf server product called a *database management system* (DBMS) purchased from a specialized vendor (such as Oracle, Sybase, Informix, or IBM). A DBMS assumes a specific *structure* for the data—one that is appropriate for the application.

> EXAMPLE: *In business applications, data often takes the form of numbers and character strings (see Section 2.6 on page 52). A character is a single letter in the alphabet, and a character string is a collection of such characters, for example, "San Francisco". Thus, employee or customer information would include character strings for name, address, city, etc., and numbers for telephone number, age, salary, etc. Another example of structured data is a document, which has headings and subheadings, paragraphs, figures, etc.*

A *database* is a file containing interrelated data with a specific predefined structure. Specifically, a *data element* is a digital encoding of a character string or number, such as a customer name or telephone number in the previous example. Each customer has the same set of data elements, although the *value* of the data elements will be different for different customers. The set of data elements corresponding to a customer is called a *record*, and a database might consist of a collection of records, one for each customer.

EXAMPLE: *An application that accesses stock prices might provide the most recent bid and asking price of a stock. It would likely use a DBMS to manage a large set of current and historical stock prices. An application that manages sales records might use a DBMS to manage customer contact and historical sales information.*

An alternative to a DBMS is an application that directly manages data in a file with a structure of its choosing. The DBMS offers compelling advantages when large amounts of structure data are managed:

- The DBMS can isolate the application from changes in computer systems. In many situations the data itself (for example, the customer data of a company) needs to survive the replacement of a computer system.

- The DBMS can provide many standard operations on data needed by many applications. Premier among these is the *search* mentioned in Section 2.4.1 on page 40, which in the case of a database is called a *query*.

- Often a common data repository must be accessed by multiple users and applications, and thus it is appropriate to separate the database and its management from those applications. That way, applications can be added or removed without affecting the data. Also, the DBMS can take care of many complications arising when different applications try to access the same database at the same time.

- Frequently data is a fundamental asset of an organization, and its safety and integrity are important. The DBMS provides many features that enhance the integrity of data. For example, it can prevent the loss of critical data when a computer fails.

The most common modern databases are *relational*, which implies that they structure data in two-dimensional forms (with rows and columns) called *tables*. The table captures the relationship among different types of data. Although this model may seem limiting, it is not, because of the ability to store data in multiple columns and also in multiple tables. The application accesses the data in the database through the *query*.

EXAMPLE: *A relational table storing data about tourism in four cities is shown in Figure 3.8. This table indicates the number of tourists by accommodation and year. Each row corresponds to a set of attributes (year, city, and type of accommodation). A typical query might be "tell me how many tourists stay in resorts in all cities farther from San Francisco than Oakland." The application would recast this into the database query for the relational table in Figure 3.8 as "tell me how many tourists stay in resorts in Oakley and Albany." Since the database is not aware of the interpretation of the data, it cannot translate "farther from San Francisco than Oakland" into "Oakley and Albany," but that would be inferred by the application, perhaps by consulting a separate geographical database.*

Because all data is stored in relational tables, queries take standard forms that depend on this structure. Other types of databases are discussed in Chapter 6, and more advanced uses of databases are discussed in the sidebar "Data Warehouses and OLAP."

3.2.3 Thin and Ultrathin Clients

The amount of application functionality in the client is controversial. One extreme—called a *fat client*—contains a lot of functionality, and the opposite is called a *thin client*. The three-tier client/server architecture, by keeping application logic out of the client, results in a thin client.

There is increasing concern about the administrative costs associated with desktop computers—not the least of which is time users spend maintaining their own software. The thin client moves toward central administration and avoids separately administering and upgrading many desktop computers. This is one motivation for the

Year	City	Accommodation	Tourists
2002	Oakley	Bed & Breakfast	14
2002	Oakley	Resort	190
2002	Oakland	Bed & Breakfast	340
2002	Oakland	Resort	230
2002	Berkeley	Camping	120000
2002	Berkeley	Bed & Breakfast	3450
2002	Berkeley	Resort	390800
2002	Albany	Camping	8790
2002	Albany	Bed & Breakfast	3240
2003	Oakley	Bed & Breakfast	55
2003	Oakley	Resort	320
2003	Oakland	Bed & Breakfast	280
2003	Oakland	Resort	210
2003	Berkeley	Camping	115800
2003	Berkeley	Bed & Breakfast	4560
2003	Berkeley	Resort	419000
2003	Albany	Camping	7650
2003	Albany	Bed & Breakfast	6750

Figure 3.8 An example of a relational table.

network computer (NC)—a highly simplified desktop machine (see the sidebar "An Ultrathin Client: The Network Computer (NC)").

3.2.4 The Future of Client/Server

Three-tier client/server architecture is only one of many possibilities for partitioning application functionality among hosts. A generaliza-

Data Warehouses and OLAP

Often an organization will have multiple operational database management systems but need to develop a "big picture" of the overall operation, not only at the present time but also historically (see "Knowledge Management" on page 63). A data warehouse is a very large database accumulated by systematically capturing data from multiple databases. Data warehouses are best understood in the context of business applications.

A data warehouse can store huge amounts of data, but ways to analyze this massive data are needed. *On-line analytical processing* (OLAP) applications present multidimensional views of data stored in two-dimensional relational tables.

EXAMPLE: *A three-dimensional view of the data stored in the two-dimensional relational table in Figure 3.8 is shown in Figure 3.9. While this representation is equivalent in supporting queries, it is often better suited to the presentation of data to a human who wants to understand relationships or trends in the data.*

An Ultrathin Client: The Network Computer (NC)

Several approaches to the NC share a desire to simplify desktop computers and move users' data and applications to centralized servers with central administration. The hope is to reduce the life cycle costs of the desktop computer. At its most extreme, the NC is a graphic-display engine. In this ultrathin client, even the presentation is moved to a server, and there is no application-specific software running in the client. Generic graphic-display capabilities can be exploited by all applications.

Many NC proposals include a suite of standard Internet applications—especially a Web browser—resulting in a networked *information appliance* (an appliance is a terminal with a specific purpose, as discussed in Chapter 5). Another approach is to allow application-specific presentation or logic to reside in the client but to dynamically load it into the client when needed (using mobile code—see Chapter 9).

The thin-client architecture limits a user's ability to install applications, so it is most appropriate when using a limited set of standard applications (as in point-of-sale terminals, airline counters, and simple data entry). One

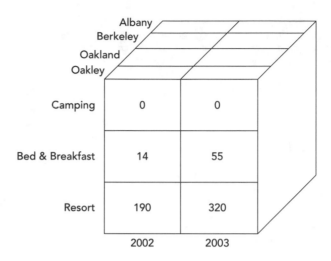

Figure 3.9 An example of an OLAP presentation of the data in Figure 3.8.

tion is *multitier client/server*, which structures the application in four or more tiers. The declining cost of servers based on microprocessor technology encourages approaches that trade more hosts for other benefits such as better performance or reduced administrative costs.

There are two major unmet needs that the current client/server architectures do not address sufficiently:

- Organizational needs change quickly, and it is also important to quickly deploy applications supporting new business opportunities. This implies an ability to build new applications faster than if they were built from scratch. New applications need to be designed, implemented, and deployed by mixing and matching existing components (databases, presentation, etc.). Client/server systems typically couple the tiers too closely to make this feasible, and one role of additional tier(s) is to mediate in a way that is more flexible.

- Enterprise and cross-enterprise applications require data integration across different departments and different enterprises (see Section 2.6.2 on page 56). Client/server computing has evolved primarily as a vehicle to support departmental applications and by itself does not supply the needed data integration.

Major vendors are addressing these issues, making their own proposals for architectures beyond client/server.

3.3 Internet, Intranet, Extranet

No, this isn't a children's rhyme. It's a special set of terminology used when the internet packet-switching technology is applied in several contexts. Following widespread use of local area networks, the internet technology was invented to create a wide area network by interconnecting preexisting LANs. An *internet* (lowercase) thus designates a "network of networks," including standard ways to interconnect networks as well as equipment and software implementing these standards. The *Internet* (uppercase) is a specific internet; namely, the large one that is global in extent, accessible to the citizenry, and subject to much attention in the news media.

3.3.1 Intranets

The same internet technologies are used to construct private networks—called *intranets*—for exclusive use within an enterprise. An intranet and its suite of applications are often used to improve internal communications and collaboration while protecting proprietary information. Other proprietary network technologies and applications can be used for this purpose; however, this is becoming less attractive as the internet technologies provide a suite of existing solutions.

E X A M P L E : *General Motors Corporation deployed a satellite-based intranet connecting over 9,000 locations, including all its dealerships. It replaces many volumes of paper-based manuals and daily service bulletins with remote interactive access to the same information. Later, the same intranet will allow customers to customize automobiles and receive delivery in just a few days, or summon help if stranded on the road [Pan98].*

Inevitably, intranet users want access to the Internet from their desktop computers, for example, to exchange email outside the

weakness of the desktop computer—security—is where the thin client or NC offers value. When many people may have physical access, restrictions on access to applications and data is easier with thin clients.

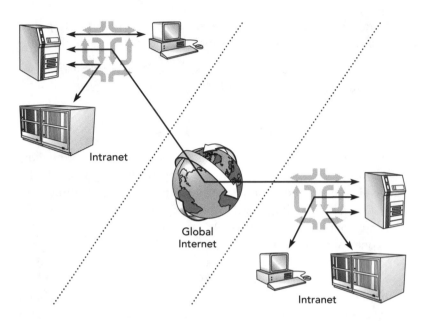

Figure 3.10 An extranet encompasses one or more intranets and the Internet.

organization or access the Web. For this purpose, the intranet is connected to the Internet in a way that does not compromise internal proprietary information, using a *firewall* (see Chapters 8 and 11). The firewall creates a protected enclave by enforcing restrictions on whether and how internal users can access the Internet and Internet citizenry can access the intranet. Figure 3.10 illustrates a pair of intranets and their connection to the Internet. The dotted lines denote the boundary between intranet and Internet, and all communication links traversing those dotted lines are firewall protected. An organization may also have internal firewalls to enforce restrictions on how employees in one department access resources in other departments.

3.3.2 Extranets

Frequently an organization has two or more locations—each with an intranet—that are geographically separated, and wants to join them in a single intranet. One option is private communication links among the locations, but this is relatively expensive. Another option is to connect the intranets through the Internet, as shown in Figure 3.10. This compromises the security of any messages traversing the Internet, because it's an unprotected domain outside the organization's administrative control. Confidentiality can be preserved using *encryption* (see Chapter 8), which can hide message content from anyone without a secret *key*.

ANALOGY: *A bank has vaults to store cash securely but must sometimes transport cash through public streets (analogous to the Internet) from one vault (analogous to an intranet) to another. For this purpose, the bank creates a mobile protected environment with an armored car and armed guards to prevent theft. Access to the armored car requires a key (analogous to an encryption key), possessed only by the trusted guards.*

An Internet incorporated into an intranet, as shown in Figure 3.10, is called an *extranet*. Similarly, when different companies use the Internet to interconnect intranets for cross-enterprise applications such as electronic commerce, this is also called an extranet.

EXAMPLE: *The Automotive Network Exchange (ANX) electronic commerce initiative from U.S. automobile companies (see Section 2.6.3 on page 64) is based on a large extranet. Designed by Electronic Data Systems (EDS), the network employs standard internet technologies. It offers numerous security and performance guarantees that ensure it is "business quality." Although the ANX network is separate from the public Internet, it does connect many firms' intranets securely [Jan97].*

An extranet also allows employees unfettered access to their company's intranet while traveling, as illustrated in Figure 3.11. Individual hosts are allowed intranet access through the Internet. An extranet also allows individual consumers limited and secure access to intranet resources—for example, in selling goods over the Internet—while preventing theft of confidential information (such as credit card numbers). For this purpose, Web browsers support limited extranet capabilities.

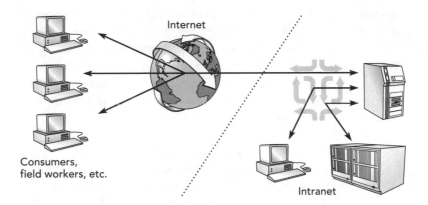

Consumers,
field workers, etc.

Figure 3.11 An extranet can extend an intranet to field workers and customers.

Nomadic and Mobile Access

As networked computing applications become widely used, network access becomes important not only at home and work but also while traveling. Access while traveling is called *nomadic access*. Access while actually moving—as in a car, bus, or train—is called *mobile access*.

> E X A M P L E : *Today's telephone system provides nomadic access with pay telephones and mobile access with cellular telephones. There are some nascent services providing nomadic and mobile access to the Internet, but for the most part this is an infrastructure waiting to be built.*

Nomadic and mobile users want the same suite of applications as fixed users. Radio communications technologies supporting mobile access are more limiting than the fiber-optic technologies supporting fixed access (see Chapter 12). A technical limitation on portable devices is battery technology, which limits the time of operation and processing power.

> E X A M P L E : *A sales force is naturally nomadic, while sales automation applications enable the representatives to demonstrate on-line catalogs, check inventory and delivery schedules, and place orders.*

The latter functions require access to mission-critical business processes, where security and confidentiality are important.

3.3.3 Internet Applications

While the internet is a "network of networks," it also provides a set of popular social and information management applications. When people in an organization speak of having an intranet, they often refer to these standard internet applications as well as using internet networking technologies. These applications include those discussed in Section 2.3 on page 19, such as email, newsgroups, chatrooms, listservers, the Web, etc.

The Web as the Presentation Tier

The Web was conceived as an information management application but has become the basis for a wider class of applications (see the sidebar "World Wide Web" on page 37). The Web browser includes capabilities useful for describing the presentation portion of almost any application, such as formatted text and graphics, and various ways to capture user input, including forms, dialog boxes, radio buttons, etc. Rather than reimplementing these capabilities, applications can simply incorporate a Web browser for presentation. (This is a thin-client architecture—see Section 3.2.3 on page 96.) A major advantage of incorporating the existing browser software is the reduction in development effort, but it also addresses a far more important practical problem. In an uncoordinated environment, such as individual consumer access to an intranet, getting application-specific programs installed on the client is logistically difficult and a deterrent to users.

3.4 Networked Computing and the Organization

In an organizational context, the networking of applications is integrally tied to the organizational structure. The life cycle of the application—its conception, fruition, and maintenance—is also integrally tied to the organizational mission.

3.4.1 Rationale for Networked Computing

Why should applications be networked rather than run on a single computer? Although networked computing has compelling advantages, the rationale is a bit complicated. Social applications, which require that every user has a desktop computer (client or peer) to support the human-computer interface and presentation, are inherently networked. What about other applications? Two important justifications are scalability and administration.

Scalability

Scalability is the ability of an application to support increasing levels of *activity* and *capability*. For example, information management or consumer electronic commerce should have no inherent limitation on the number of users or on the amount of information or goods and services for sale. A successful application should not self-limit because of some technological bottleneck. A single computer has limited capability and, as the level of activity increases, eventually exhausts some resource (processing power, storage capacity, etc.). Scalability requires at minimum multiple hosts.

> E X A M P L E :   *A Web server may initially use a single host, but as the number of users accessing the server increases, eventually the communications capability or processing power is exhausted. A second host (then a third, fourth, etc.) can accommodate more users.*

> A N A L O G Y :   *In principle, a company could hire a single employee, but as the company grows, eventually that employee can't keep up and it is necessary to hire more employees. Ways must be found to divide the work among those employees, and doubtless they will need to interact.*

Scalability also means the costs of the infrastructure grow no more quickly than key application activity and capability performance attributes (see Chapter 10).

Administration

Administration refers to the ownership and operation of an application; this requires workers to install, operate, and maintain it. Thus, the cost of the infrastructure—the emphasis of scalability—must be augmented by salary and other costs. Even where a single host may achieve the required performance, this may not be administratively desirable or cost effective: Some administrative justifications for networked computing are listed in Table 3.3.

Table 3.3 Administrative justifications for networked computing.

Issue	Description	Analogy
Administrative specialization	Each department finds it advantageous to administer its own dedicated infrastructure. Today, hardware is inexpensive in relation to salaries, so it makes sense to minimize administrative expenses by proliferating computers with more specialized functionality, if that reduces administrative costs.	An enterprise is broken down into specialized functional units (departments).
Administrative compartmen-talization	For cross-enterprise applications, it is not administratively practical to share computing resources. Each company owns and operates its own hosts, permitting them to interact by communicating over the network. This also makes it easier to allocate costs to each company.	Even when two companies need to cooperate, each hires its own workers rather than sharing them.
Locality	It is desirable to store information near where it is generated (administratively and geographically) and generate the presentation near where it is used (drawing upon multiple sources) (see Chapter 6).	A factory is located near transportation hubs and natural resources, but a retail outlet is located near customers.
Sharing	Certain information is needed by many users and applications. It should be maintained and updated in one place but made available to users and applications across the enterprise. Conversely, each user or department should access information maintained by multiple sources.	A firm may have many customers. A firm may have many suppliers.
Security	Information must be reliable, available, and protected against unauthorized access, while selected information is accessible on the outside. A single host can selectively make information or interaction available to other hosts. This is much more secure than sharing a host (see Chapter 8).	A firm wants its own dedicated building. Locating two firms in the same building is less secure.

In the centralized computer era—when computers were large and expensive—it was important to use computers efficiently, for example, by sharing them over many applications. Today, the cost of a substantial microprocessor-based server (including storage and peripherals) is comparable to a few months' loaded salary. Minimizing administrative costs is paramount, even if this means more hosts. Two administrators maintaining the same host—or worse, sharing a single host across two or more administrative units—introduces complications, so it often makes sense to dedicate servers to individual administrative units or even single applications. There can also be compelling reasons to centralize, such as an enterprise database that must be shared among applications. Thus, in practice there is often a mixture of centralization and distribution.

For cross-enterprise applications, the impact of the administrative boundaries on the partitioning of application and data becomes even more constraining. Compartmentalization—allowing access to data and applications by internal users while keeping out external users—is an overriding consideration.

3.4.2 The Application Life Cycle

The conceptualization, development, deployment, and maintenance of a business application must satisfy many stakeholders and (sometimes conflicting) objectives. In a business context, an application may be purchased off the shelf, developed internally, or developed under contract to a professional services firm (the considerations are discussed further in Chapters 5 and 6). The stakeholders whose influences and needs should be taken into account in application development include [BCK98]

- *Management within the application development organization:* Whether the development is internal or by a professional services company, managers will be concerned about the cost and time to completion.

- *End-users:* The users of the application and their management will be concerned about cost of acquisition, features, quality, administrative and operational costs, and flexibility to meet changing requirements (see Section 2.8.4 on page 73). There may also be different criteria applied by management and users.

- *Maintenance organization:* The staff maintaining the application, whether internal or external, is concerned about the maintenance costs and resilience to adding new features.

- *Suppliers and customers:* If a business application impacts suppliers and customers, they will be concerned about features, ease of use, etc.

Keeping in mind these stakeholders, the following subsections describe some phases in the application life cycle [Boo94, McC97]. Many large application developments ultimately fail—in the sense that they are never deployed—but avoiding this requires at minimum a well-thought-out and well-executed process. A caution is in order: The process is never as clean and linear as might be implied here; at minimum, these phases overlap, and they may even have to be repeated if the outcome of a later stage is not satisfactory.

Conceptualization

Conceptualization establishes the basic objectives. In a business application, this is an aspect of understanding and refining the business process or commerce, taking into account the organization of workers, the application functionality, and the interaction of workers and application. The conceptualization includes vision (what new function is to be accomplished?) and assumptions (what are fixed points that cannot be changed?). Typically, a business case has to be formulated to convince management that the investment in the development and deployment of the application is warranted. Important objectives include activity and capability performance parameters and how those parameters may evolve over time.

A useful validation tool is low-cost experiments. Using whatever means available, stitching together a prototype to validate basic ideas and assumptions is worthwhile. The human-computer interfaces to the application can be roughly prototyped and tried out on users. The earlier any major problems can be identified and addressed, the more likely the project will be successful. A prototype is also useful for selling the vision to top management.

Analysis

Once it is decided to move ahead, the next phase is the analysis of the application in its organizational context. The analysis is best described by its outcome, which is a description of what the application does in a form that can be reviewed by stakeholders, and in detail sufficient to allow them to make suggestions for change and judge whether development is advisable. It considers the application implementation details only to the extent necessary to validate the analysis; that is, establish that the behavior of the application meets reality.

A useful technique to use during analysis is *scenarios*. A scenario represents a typical usage of the application and specifies external events and the actions of both the people and the application in response to those events. The scenarios chosen should represent a reasonably complete set, so that no major objectives are neglected.

Analysis does not result in highly detailed specifications. That is best reserved for a process of "iterative refinement" during the design evolution phase. It is important to avoid moving ahead with architecture design before the analysis phase has reached sufficient maturity, or at least the analysis may have to be revisited after greater understanding is developed in the architecture.

A major requirement for modern business applications is flexibility to meet changing needs. The business environment will change as new products and services are introduced or organizations are split or merged. Thus, it is a mistake to overanalyze the near-term needs and ignore or compromise the needed flexibility. In the analysis and architecture phases, a major consideration should be trying to anticipate how application needs may change in the future.

Architecture Design

The application is a system performing the specific functions identified by analysis (see Section 3.1.1 on page 78). The system architecture phase requires the decomposition of the application into hardware and software subsystems, the functionality of those subsystems, and their interaction. Often, the application itself is only one subsystem embedded within a larger social or business system (see Section 1.2 on page 7). Often, this larger system context will include more than one networked application (see Section 2.6.2 on page 56).

Architecture is critical because it forms the basis of a divide-and-conquer strategy in the subsequent design evolution phase, where individual subsystems are farmed out to different programmers or groups of programmers. One goal is to make subtasks as independent as possible, avoiding excessive coordination. Insufficient attention to or poor design of the architecture is a frequent cause of project failure. At the other extreme, a poorly conceived architecture can constrain the programmers excessively, so the application cannot meet objectives or has insufficient flexibility.

An application architecture is primarily of concern to the implementers; it is not generally visible to or of concern to users. Its primary role is structuring the development process.

Development Evolution

Although not evident from the previous description, the outcome of architecture design is often a software program that is a very incomplete implementation of the system but incorporates major subsystems without details filled in. A major activity in the application development is programming, in which the nascent architectural description is successively refined into a prototype of the production system. Usually it is best to avoid going directly from architecture to production system, but rather to start with the architecture and incrementally add detailed capabilities through successive refinement.

Both the architecture and development evolution phases are described further in Chapter 6.

Testing

Testing an evolving implementation is crucial to uncover shortcomings and flaws [KFN93]. It does not await a complete production system, but rather is an integral part of the design evolution. With a well-conceived architecture, subsystems can be tested independently, with many problems uncovered and repaired. The merger of interacting subsystems—called *integration*—requires further testing of their successful interaction.

Once the first prototype of a production system is available, it can be tried out in an environment that approximates the intended usage, called an *alpha test*. Major problems needing repair are often identified at this stage, so it is "off-line" and users must be cooperative and tolerant. Once the problems are shaken out and repaired, it is typical to move to a second phase of testing called the *beta test* in an environment as close as possible to intended operational conditions. Ideally, beta testing is performed in a production context but, again, with cooperative and tolerant users. After completing beta testing, the application is ready for deployment.

Deployment

For a business application, the deployment phase includes the establishment of the human organization and the hardware infrastructure (network, hosts, and installation of software on the hosts) and user training. Not infrequently, deployment requires a conversion from some previous operational process and includes extensive planning to avoid major problems and outages, as well as special measures to convert and import relevant data to the new application. Deployment requires advance planning that is every bit as rigorous as design of the software, and total deployment costs frequently exceed the development cost.

Operations and Maintenance

Once successfully deployed, the application moves into the operations and maintenance phase. Operationally, vigilance of human administrators is necessary to take care of problems as they arise and, especially, to maintain security (see Chapter 8). In addition, an application requires continual maintenance by a group of programmers, for two reasons. First, no amount of testing can detect and repair all problems, but inevitably more arise in the operational phase, where conditions not anticipated in testing may arise. Evaluation in the operational phase may uncover fundamental problems, such as failure to meet all functional requirements or user needs. Further, the performance aspects of the application, as it grows to accommodate more users or transactions, are difficult to test fully. Problems must be repaired as they are observed. Second, the operational requirements typically evolve with time, and thus continual development is required to add new capabilities or change functionality to meet changing needs. One reason the architecture design is critical is that a well-conceived architecture is far easier to maintain (both repair and upgrade).

3.5 Open Issue: What Lies beyond Client/Server Computing?

The client/server architecture is not an endpoint in the evolution of computing, but a stepping stone. But a stepping stone to what? The origin—and the strength as well—of client/server computing is in allowing users on desktop computers to access legacy applications on mainframes or other servers. It was a logical and incremental progression and not a clean break with the past.

Much more radical departures from the past are discussed in Chapter 9, such as distributed object management. These suggest an amorphous architecture, in which applications can search for interesting subsystems from a wide variety of sources and configure themselves more dynamically. There may also be mobile subsystems (called agents) that actively roam the globe looking for interesting goods or information on the user's behalf. These architectures are analogous to the global commercial marketplace, where there are a multiplicity of buyers and sellers continually seeking opportunities and participating in opportunistic transactions that provide personal benefit. This vision will entail a sophisticated infrastructure that doesn't exist today, as the client/server architecture is too simplistic to support it.

Further Reading

[OHE96a] is an accessible and excellent source of additional detail on the client/server software technologies, including current industry activity. [Wat95] covers the same basic material in much less technical detail, with the needs of managers especially in mind. The process of developing new applications is discussed by [BCK98, McC97, Pre96, Boo94], where the latter served as the basis for the description here. Testing methodologies are covered in [KFN93].

Software Architecture
and Standardization

4

An elaborate software infrastructure joins the equipment emphasized in Chapter 3 in providing many capabilities benefiting all networked applications.

ANALOGY: *In creating a new business, much existing infrastructure—such as real estate and telephone and transportation—is available and analogous to the computer and network equipment. A services infrastructure analogous to the software infrastructure includes package delivery, legal and accounting firms, and real estate property management. Incorporating these existing capabilities rather than building them from scratch makes it much easier to build the business.*

Like the equipment emphasized in Chapter 3, the software infrastructure has an architecture, but one that is quite distinct from the equipment. This software infrastructure is based on layering, in which new capabilities are incrementally added to existing capabilities. Like the equipment infrastructure, the software infrastructure is typically integrated from components supplied by different vendors. This makes it necessary for vendors to get their software to work together properly, and this is the role of a business process called standardization.

4.1 What Makes a Good Architecture

The concept of an architecture was defined in Section 3.1.1 on page 78 and applied to the decomposition of a networked computing system into hosts and network in Chapter 3. Recall that an architecture decomposes a system into subsystems (where those subsystems may be components if they are purchased without modification from an outside vendor), with specific functionality and interaction among subsystems. A good architectural design requires an appreciation for what distinguishes "good" from "bad" architectures and the criteria used in determining what is "good." Architecture follows some well-established principles that aid in understanding the software infrastructure. Application software is deferred to Chapter 6.

A major challenge in software design is complexity. Because software is not constrained by physical limits, its complexity tends to expand to the limits of the designer's ability to cope (discussed further in Chapter 6). This problem is accentuated for infrastructure software, because its design and development is spread over multiple vendors. Artificial design constraints have to be established to contain complexity, and that is one role of architecture.

Architecture is one phase in the design of the software—both the infrastructure (considered here) and application (considered in Section 3.4.2 on page 106)—after analysis and before implementation. Important inputs are functionality and performance requirements, and an outcome is the specification of the architectural subsystems sufficiently detailed to set about their implementation.

ANALOGY: *The framers of the U.S. Constitution (who were the architects of the U.S. government) first decided on the roles and limitations of the federal government. Taking this "functionality" into account, they decomposed the government into executive, legislative, and judicial branches. Next, they determined the responsibilities and powers of each branch and their interactions.*

4.1.1 Decomposition and Modularity

Decomposition—the first and most important phase of architecture—is a divide-and-conquer strategy that allows subsystems to be implemented individually and, ideally, even autonomously. It allows individual firms to participate in the design, manufacture, and deployment of the infrastructure without excessive coordination,

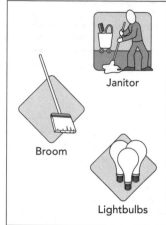

Loan department   Physical plant department

Figure 4.1 Partial decomposition of a bank.

and thus it affects the supplier industry organization as well as the technology.

The decomposition should be *modular*, which means the subsystems—called *modules*—have some special properties summarized in Table 4.1. The major property is *separation of concerns*; that is, the internal concerns of one module are mostly not of concern to other modules [Boo94]. This allows the modules to be designed and maintained relatively independently by different design groups or firms, with minimum interaction among them.

ANALOGY: *A bank is a system providing financial services to its customers. A partial decomposition of a bank is shown in Figure 4.1. It has departments with relatively little concern about the internal operation of others. The loan department focuses on managing its loan portfolio, underwriting (assessing the risk of a loan in the context of a portfolio), and issuing new loans, while the physical plant department maintains the buildings. There is interaction between departments, but it is less frequent and involved than activities within each department. For example, the loan department may report a dark room to the physical plant department but cares only*

Table 4.1 Some desirable characteristics of a modular architecture.

Property	Desirable characteristics	Analogy
Functionality	The modules are chosen as distinct functional groupings.	In government, establishing and enforcing laws and sitting in judgement of lawbreakers are distinct and well-defined functions.
Hierarchy	Each module can itself be a system, internally decomposed into modules (see Section 3.1.2 on page 79).	The executive branch of government is decomposed into agencies and departments, each of which has an internal modular structure.
Separation of concerns	The functional groupings incorporated within each module are strongly associated and weakly associated with functionality internal to other modules.	Law enforcement requires internal coordination, but its operations are of little concern to the legislature or judiciary.
Interoperability	Modules can successfully interact to realize the higher purposes of the system.	Law enforcement has well-defined procedures for bringing alleged lawbreakers before the judiciary, which results in their successful prosecution.
Reusability	Modules are defined, implemented, and documented independently of a specific system, so they can be reused in other systems.	Some modules of the U.S. government structure have been adopted by other countries, without the need to adopt them all.

that light is restored and not how this happens. The physical plant department concerns itself with details, such as diagnosing the problem.

EXAMPLE: *The architecture of a computer is an example of modularity. Figure 4.2 presents a simplified view, including major modules:*

- *A processor executes a program.*

- *The memory stores program instructions and data currently being used.*

- *The storage, such as magnetic disks, CD-ROMs, etc., keeps massive amounts of data, programs, etc.*

- *The network adapter connects the host to a network.*

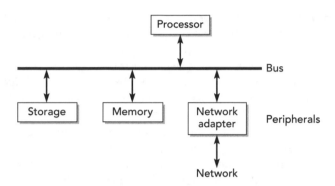

Figure 4.2 The simplified modularity in a computer system.

> *The storage and network adapter are called* peripherals, *because they assist the processor, and are connected to the processor by a bus (a very high speed connection shared by all the modules). Each of these modules has lots of internal activity, but their interaction with others is relatively straightforward. Modules can be designed and manufactured by different firms because of that well-defined and well-documented interaction; thus, these modules are components (see "Subsystems and Components" on page 80).*

4.1.2 Granularity and Hierarchy

Granularity determines the number of modules and the range of functionality of each. The architecture designer can choose a *fine* granularity, with many small modules, or a *coarse* granularity, with a few large modules. Hierarchy—meaning modules are themselves composed of internal modules—avoids defining a *single* granularity (see Section 3.1.2 on page 79). This "decomposition within modules" architecture allows the system to be viewed at different granularity, as appropriate.

ANALOGY: *In the bank organization of Figure 4.1, each of the two departmental modules has an internal decomposition into smaller modules. For example, the loan department is internally composed of a receptionist, an underwriter, a loan officer, etc. As there may be multiple underwriters and loan officers, there are finer-granularity modules associated with the loan officers (the "loan service* group") and all underwriters (the "risk management group"). At a coarser granularity, the bank is decomposed into "customer services" and "business management" divisions, in which the former groups modules dealing with customers (loans, withdrawals, deposits, etc.) and the latter encompasses internal functions (accounting, property management, physical plant, etc.).

EXAMPLE: *The single computer, whose internal composition into modules is shown in Figure 4.2, is itself a module (called a host) in the larger client/server architecture discussed in Chapter 3. The overall hardware architecture is thus a two-level hierarchy.*

4.1.3 Interfaces: The Module's Face to the World

Each module must interact with others to accomplish the higher purposes of the system. The architecture designer should be quite thoughtful about this interaction to ensure that the system operates correctly under all circumstances and is flexible enough to accommodate future change. This is assisted by defining an *interface* to each module. The interface is the view that one module presents to others, encompassing everything that other modules must know to interact with it. It has a second purpose, which is to guide the module implementers.

EXAMPLE: *In the bank example of Figure 4.3, the interface to the loan department expects certain standard actions, such as a request for a loan (from a customer) and the submission of a completed loan application (from the customer). Each request has predetermined responses, such as returning a blank loan application and responding yes or no to the loan request.*

More generally, each module typically has a standard "menu" of actions it will take, where each action has a set of *parameters* and *returns*. The interface description includes all actions a module is prepared to take, together with a definition of the parameters and returns of those actions.

A general approach to module interaction is shown at the bottom of Figure 4.3. That interaction includes a series of *invocations* of

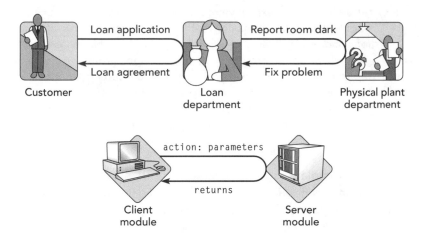

Figure 4.3 Examples of module interfaces in the bank example.

actions defined at the module interfaces (only one such invocation is shown). In each invocation, the module invoking the action is called the client module, and the module whose action is invoked is called the server module. (Note that the terminology was used to describe the role of hosts in Chapter 3.) Rarely does a module act exclusively as a client or server; at different times, it is each.

E X A M P L E :   *In Figure 4.3, when a customer makes a loan application ("invokes the loan application action"), she is a client of the bank, and the bank loan department is a server to her.*

4.1.4 Abstraction

People use *abstraction* to make complicated things easier to deal with. Its proper use in architecture design makes that architecture more transparent and flexible to future change.

Abstraction is concisely defined as "generalization; ignoring or hiding details." In the context of architecture, abstraction is used to simplify the perspective of a module as viewed through its interface, focusing on the important overall goals of the system and avoiding becoming mired in a clutter of unnecessary details (see the sidebar "Example of Abstraction: The Flora" for another example).

Example of Abstraction: The Flora

Physical and social scientists abstract complicated and interdependent natural and social systems. To make the study of complicated systems feasible, they focus on the aspects most relevant to the investigation at hand, ignoring other less germane details. This is not limited to scientists; for example, consider the following perspectives on the flora taken by different occupations:

- The botanist classifies plants based on evolutionary family dependencies.

- The master chef studies a plant's taste and smell, whether it is edible or poisonous, how long it takes to cook, etc.

- The gardener is concerned with the adult size of the plant, what type of soil and climate conditions it favors, how much fertilizer it needs, etc.

- The pharmacologist looks for medicinal effects in each plant.

Although there is overlap and dependency, each profession finds germane a different aspect of the flora. Each is abstracting the flora for its own purposes.

EXAMPLE: *To a top executive of the bank, the loan department is a module that makes money for the bank by accepting loan applications and issuing loans likely to be repaid. This abstract perspective—when turned into reality by the manager setting up the loan department—has to be made concrete by setting up detailed steps for the loan department to determine whether a loan is a good bet. Those details may actually change over time—based on experience—without affecting the abstract view taken by the executive.*

As this example suggests, abstraction and "management hierarchies" in organizations go hand in hand. Each higher layer in the management hierarchy takes an increasingly abstract view of the organization's architecture. When it comes to actually setting up the lower-level departments, there are a plethora of details handled internally.

EXAMPLE: *The manager of the bank's loan department is responsible for determining the detailed processes within that module for achieving the abstracted vision of that department held by top management. She may set up a multistep loan approval process, such as running a credit history on the loan applicant, appraising any collateral offered by the loan applicant, seeking the advice of an experienced underwriter, etc. Meantime, the higher management views the department in abstract terms like "quarterly profit and loss."*

Abstraction is effective because it enables issues of importance to a system as a whole to be considered without being obscured by distracting details. At lower levels of hierarchy, those details are dealt with, but in a smaller context constrained by the higher-level abstractions. An important issue is choosing the appropriate abstractions, using them to make the system simpler and easier to deal with, but not so simple as to be unrealistic. As Albert Einstein stated, "Everything should be made as simple as possible, but no simpler."

4.1.5 Encapsulation

An architecture focuses on the external behavior of the modules—as manifested by their interfaces—and how they interact. Implementers must take this interface and determine the internal design of the modules. An important architectural and implementation tool is *encapsulation*, which ensures internal details are invisible and inaccessible at the interface. This avoids other modules becoming dependent on internal details, making the system more difficult to change.

EXAMPLE: *In an abstract interface to the loan department, the customer is not responsible for invoking the steps of the loan approval process—that is entirely the business of the loan department. Encapsulation goes further and ensures these steps are invisible to the customer. For example, encapsulation ensures there are no other actions at the interface that provide visibility into the outcome of individual approval steps (such as the credit history report or the advice of the underwriter).*

Abstraction and encapsulation are complementary. Both seek separation of concerns (see Table 4.1 on page 116), the former by simplifying the external view and the latter by dogmatically enforcing abstractions by hiding internal details from the interface. Encapsulated details can be safely changed without affecting other modules.

EXAMPLE: *Which credit bureau the loan department consults to obtain a credit report on the loan applicant is encapsulated so that the bureau can be changed at any time without affecting the customer. Indeed, the entire credit bureau step is encapsulated so that it can be eliminated entirely if it proves ineffective.*

4.1.6 Modularity and Interfaces in Computing

For the remainder of the book, the principles of architecture design will be applied to computing (although they apply in other contexts as well). First, it is helpful to reflect briefly on the meaning and implications of architecture in computing.

Hardware/Software Dichotomy

The computer embodies many ideas, but the most powerful is programmability: Unlike earlier products, the functionality of a computer isn't determined at the time of manufacture, but is added later by software.

This makes the computer almost infinitely extensible. What can be accomplished with a computer is limited primarily by the programmer's imagination (and pragmatic constraints such as complexity and cost) rather than physical limitations.

Software Architecture

A software program running on a computer tells it what to do each step of the way. Although it isn't subject to the same physical limitations as the hardware, it is important to *impose* an architecture on software. The two most important reasons are to manage the inherent complexity (see Chapter 6) and to coordinate software provided by a number of competing and complementary firms (which is considered in this chapter). Software should be designed to be modular—decomposing it according to functionality—so that different firms or programming groups can implement different modules with minimum dependence among them. The principle of modularity as a "separation of concerns" is critically important in software.

Hardware and Software Interfaces

Interfaces are an integral part of the computing world for both hardware and software (see Section 4.1.3 on page 118). A hardware interface is a physical wire or fiber and connector and the precise definition of the electrical or optical signals it carries.

EXAMPLE: *In computers, the assorted jacks on the back (serial port, parallel port, monitor jack, power plug, etc.) are examples of interfaces. Each is associated with a set of physical (number of pins, geometry, etc.), electrical (voltage, etc.), and logical (order and meaning of bits) specifications.*

In software, an interface is the boundary between two software programs, or the boundary between two modules within the same software program. Its purpose is to allow the modules or programs to interact to accomplish some higher purpose, while encapsulating the inner workings, denying other modules access to them. The form of this interface is similar to interfaces found within organizations (see Section 4.1.3 on page 118). In particular, a software module interface consists of a set of actions, each action having a set of parameters passed to the module that customizes that action, and a set of returns from the module reflecting the results of that action. The action may change data within the modules as well as return values.

E X A M P L E :   *It might be useful within a larger software system to have a module that provides the same capabilities as a pocket calculator, such as adding, subtracting, multiplying, dividing, taking square roots, etc. Its interface could be similar to a pocket calculator, except there aren't physical keys and a physical display. The equivalent functions are invoked by other modules using actions like "add," "subtract," etc., with appropriate parameters consisting of the numbers to be added or subtracted.*

This calculator module can serve other programs needing numerical calculations. Significantly, the calculator interface reveals nothing about how the calculator performs these functions—these details are encapsulated, as they are in a real calculator.

4.2 Architecture of the Software Infrastructure

The architectural concepts, including decomposition, modularity, hierarchy, granularity, interface, abstraction, and encapsulation, aid the understanding and appreciation of the software infrastructure supporting networked applications. They are also applied to application design in Chapter 6. The more detailed functionality of the infrastructure is deferred to Chapter 7 and later chapters.

4.2.1 Goals of the Infrastructure

Well-principled architecture design is one goal of the infrastructure—in part to contain complexity—but there are others, such as

- Minimizing the cost and maximizing the performance (see Chapter 10).

- Minimizing the effort required to develop and maintain new applications, in part by including capabilities in the infrastructure required by a wide range of applications.

- Providing capabilities to support the operation of the system and contribute to its trustworthiness and reliability (see Chapter 8).

The layered architecture described next was not designed top-down by a single individual or organization. It is the result of the evolution of computing systems over many years, an evolution almost Darwinian in nature because it has involved many hundreds of hardware and software suppliers and tens or hundreds of thousands of individual contributors. Standardization plays an important role in coordinating these many players (see Section 4.3 on page 132). Many nontechnical considerations that help explain the technological trajectory are discussed in Chapter 5.

4.2.2 Layering

The form of modularity seen in the software infrastructure, at the top level of hierarchy, is *layering*, similar to the rings of an onion. The modules composing the infrastructure are layered, one "above" the other, where the terms "above" and "below" are interpreted logically, not physically. Each layer utilizes the capabilities of the layers below it and adds capabilities of its own to provide to the layers above it. Thus, layering is a way to achieve additional capability to adding infrastructure, making use of what already exists rather than building from scratch.

The software and hardware follow this modularity; in particular, the software is thought of as "riding on top of" the hardware, utilizing hardware capabilities to run programs, but abstracting the hardware's detailed characteristics from the application and user (this is the role of the *operating system* layer).

The *layering principle* sets out the constraints (see Figure 4.4):

- Each layer acts as a server to the layer above, providing actions whose implementations are encapsulated.

- Each layer is a client to the layer below, utilizing its available actions in the course of providing services to the layer above it.

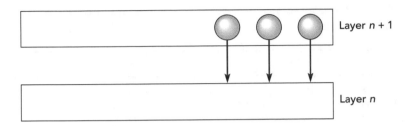

Layer *n* + 1

Layer *n*

Figure 4.4 The layering principle in software/hardware modularity.

- Each layer is permitted to interact with only layers immediately above and below. Thus, each layer serves to hide (encapsulate) the layers below it from the layers above it.

Functionally, the idea is to provide increasingly abstract and specialized services at each higher layer. Each layer is thus "simplifying, by hiding unnecessary detail" the layer below.

ANALOGY: *Consider a company that manufactures cyberwidgets. The architecture of the company defines four layers—supply, receiving, inventory, and assembly—and a building designed around these modules. The inventory layer is a module that is a server to the assembly layer and a client of the receiving layer, etc. The building has three floors, one for each of the receiving, inventory, and assembly modules. The supply layer encapsulates all the suppliers of parts assembled into cyberwidgets and is external to the building, but interacts through the trucks and drivers they send. The interaction among modules follows the layering principle in that the module corresponding to each floor (one layer) makes direct use of the capability of the floor below, but no others. The four layers are described in Table 4.2.*

The architecture of the building can support these layers by including means for each floor to make requests of the floor below (say, by an intercom system) and means to convey parts to the floor immediately above (such as conveyer belts) in response to requests.

This analogy has other features similar to the computer infrastructure. For example, specific functions analogous to "supply," "receiving," and "inventory" are required in networked computing

Table 4.2 A layered architecture for the manufacturer of cyberwidgets.

Layer	Functionality	Interaction with layer below
Assembly (third floor)	Assembles parts into finished cyberwidgets.	Requests specific parts as needed for assembly.
Inventory (second floor)	Stores parts awaiting assembly.	Indicates which parts are needed (in danger of starving assembly layer) or in excess supply (filling up allotted space). Requests and stores any parts that have arrived in receiving.
(Receiving (first floor)	Coordinates the supply of parts, receives parts, and pays suppliers.	Orders and receives parts, unloads, counts, and authorizes payment.
Supply (external)	Manufactures and conveys parts to be assembled into cyberwidgets.	There is no layer below.

(see Chapter 7). The coordination of supplier with assembly illustrates a problem in computing called *flow control*, described in Chapter 11.

The Layers in a Computing Infrastructure

Figure 4.5 illustrates the major infrastructure layers in a networked computing system. The functionality of each layer is summarized in Table 4.3.

How do the layers interact to get things done? Figure 4.6 shows two hosts participating in a networked application, each host executing a piece of that application and these pieces collaborating by communicating data through the network (as indicated by the arrow). The application does not access the network directly—this would violate the layering principle—but rather it involves the middleware and operating system layers. The middleware presents a standard interface to the application independent of the operating system and networking technology.

The middleware logically spans the two hosts (shown by dotted lines) because its goal is to hide the details of the operating system and network, including the distribution across hosts.

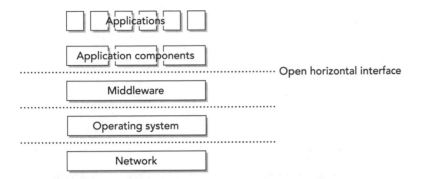

Figure 4.5 A simplified layered architecture for networked comput-ing software infrastructure.

Table 4.3 The major layers in a computer infrastructure.

Layer	Function	Analogy
Application (Chapter 6)	Provides specialized functionality directly needed by a user or organization (e.g., electronic commerce, information retrieval, or collaboration).	A firm is in a particular line of business (e.g., automobile manufacture) and defines various processes tailored to the operation of that business (e.g., assembly lines).
Application components (Chapter 6)	Specialized modules incorporated by many applications and purchased as a product from an outside company.	All automobile manufacturers buy components, such as tires and batteries, from common suppliers.
Middleware (Chapter 9)	Hides the heterogeneity and distribution of operating system and network from the application. Also provides capabilities useful to a wide range of applications.	Professional services, such as accounting, law, private investigation, etc., benefit all firms.
Operating system (Chapter 10)	Manages and hides the details of resources such as storage and printing. Also manages the details of interhost communications.	Resource management services, such as real estate, janitorial, and gardening, are useful to firms.
Network (Chapter 11)	Provides communication of data from one host to another.	To support interaction among its different locations, a firm uses telephone and overnight package delivery companies.

A Layered View of the Life and Social Sciences

At the risk of serious oversimplification, both the life and social sciences can be viewed in layers. The biological sciences draw upon understanding of physical phenomena from physics and chemistry and can be viewed as layered upon them. Physiology builds on biology to understand the overall organism, and medicine in turn builds on physiology. Of course, each "layer" adds substantial understanding to that supplied by lower "layers."

Similarly, the social sciences begin with an understanding of individuals in psychology and linguistics, and sociology adds understanding of the behavior of groups of individuals. Economics, political science, and law—which deal with the organization of commerce and society for higher purposes—are the "architects" of the social sciences.

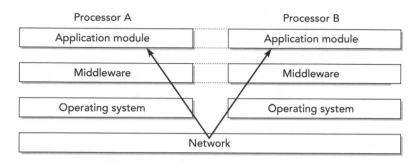

Figure 4.6 An example of application modules communicating through layers.

ANALOGY: *The mailroom in a large firm (analogous to middleware) provides workers with an abstracted letter and package delivery service. It relies on the post office and package delivery companies, or sometimes it may deliver a package directly inside the building. Those details are hidden (encapsulated) from mailroom clients.*

A top-down approach is followed in this book: Each layer is examined successively—starting with the application in Chapter 6—abstracting the layer below and appreciating what services it provides to the layer above. Much detail is ignored, focusing on issues important from an application perspective. This approach is quite similar to how computer systems are actually designed and implemented. Typically, in any given host, the layers are purchased from different companies, and it all works because of the layered modularity.

EXAMPLE: *Intel focuses on microprocessors, Compaq on desktop computers, Microsoft on operating systems, and Iona on middleware. Each is focused on one layer of the infrastructure, providing an interface promised to layers above.*

Data and Information in Layers

In Table 2.1 on page 18, data was described as "a collection of bits representing information." The infrastructure—both hardware and software—concentrates on storage and communication of data. On the other hand, what the application presents to the user is cer-

Table 4.4 How layers deal with data and information.

Structure and interpretation of data	Storage	Communication
The lowest layers deal with data in its most primitive form: a collection of bits. This portion of the infrastructure does not interpret those bits in any way.	The file system stores and retrieves bits without interpretation (see "File System" on page 91).	The network communicates packets and messages, both of which are presumed to contain bits without interpretation (see "The Network" on page 86).
	The operating system layer, which manages both storage and communication of data, usually assigns no interpretation to the data it manipulates on behalf of the application.	
The middle layers presume some structure for the data. Typically data is structured into numbers, character strings, and compositions of these basic types. In some cases, additional structure may be presumed.	A relational DBMS presumes that data is structured into tables (rows and columns of basic types) (see "Shared Data Tier: Database Management" on page 94).	The middleware layer communicates a structured composition of basic types (see Chapter 9).
The application assigns additional interpretation to the data.	Within the application, data is interpreted within the specific application context (for example, a number may be interpreted as a bank account balance).	

tainly information. The question then arises: Where and how is data turned into information? A rough answer is that this happens in the layers, where each layer adds structure and interpretation to the data it obtains from the layer below. As a rule, the infrastructure tries to make minimal assumptions about the structure of data, so that it can benefit a wide range of applications. However, moving into the middle layers, structure is added to the data so that more specific and useful facilities can be provided. The specific structure typically assigned to the data in different layers is described in Table 4.4.

The changing view of (often the very same) data as it moves through the infrastructure layers is at the heart of the separation of concerns that underlies the modularity of layering. Each layer avoids attaching any more structure and interpretation to the data it manipulates than is necessary to realize its functionality, thereby reducing its mutual dependence on other layers, including the application.

With this in mind, a definition can be assigned to the term "information" from the infrastructure and software perspective. If data is a collection of bits representing information, then information can be defined as structure and interpretation attached to data.

The Horizontal Layer Interface

Given the layered architecture, a key aspect of the infrastructure is the *horizontal layer interface*—illustrated by the dashed lines in Figure 4.5—which defines how each layer interacts with the layer below. Each layer interface is carefully documented, informing the layer above precisely how to invoke its services. One aspect of this interface is a presumed structure for data that passes between layers.

ANALOGY: *In the manufacturing example of Table 4.2 on page 126, the receiving floor provides a set of actions, such as "send next part that has arrived" and "obtain more parts with this number."*

These horizontal interfaces are said to be *open* when they are publicly available and not encumbered by intellectual property protections (see Chapter 5). Thus, any vendor is free to design, implement, and sell software that builds on an open interface without fear of violating legal protections, assuming the vendor possesses sufficient documentation to do so. Open interfaces not only enable different layers of the infrastructure to be designed (and manufactured, in the case of hardware) by complementary vendors but also support competition among vendors at each layer.

The Spanning Layer

The layered architecture just described is actually a simplification of reality. In practice—as a concession to competition in the industry—the infrastructure has some horizontal structure.

EXAMPLE: *In Figure 4.7, the layers are divided into modules at the granularity of an individual host. This heterogeneity arises not from the desire to have radically different functionality on different*

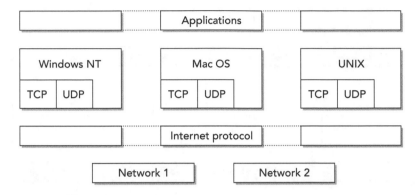

Figure 4.7 In reality, the architecture has structure in the horizontal as well as vertical direction.

hosts, but from the reality that different suppliers in the market-place are providing products similar in functionality but distinct as to details. The two layers shown in Figure 4.7 with this characteristic are the operating system (where there are several major OSs in the marketplace, including Windows 95/NT, MacOS, and UNIX—see Chapter 10) and the network (where there are a number of different technologies, such as Ethernet, wireless, asynchronous transfer mode, etc.—see Chapter 11).

Layers that are homogeneous in the horizontal direction, and can be assumed to be virtually ubiquitous on all computing platforms, have special significance because they divide the infrastructure into quasi-independent components that can be developed and advanced separately and can hide any heterogeneity below. Further, such layers provide a large existing market to vendors selling products at the layers both above and below and thus attract investment and competition. A layer with these characteristics is called a *spanning* layer [Cla97]. The following examples are illustrated in Figure 4.8.

E X A M P L E : *The internet protocol (IP) layer provides communication services to applications using a variety of network technologies (see Chapter 7). It is the foundation of the internet protocols and has reached such wide acceptance among consumers, universities, and many companies that it is virtually a spanning layer.*

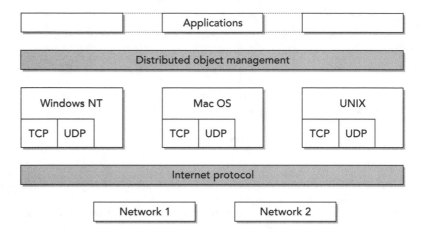

Figure 4.8 A spanning layer (shaded above) is uniform in the horizontal direction and almost ubiquitous.

The heterogeneity across different operating systems presents a problem to application developers. They must produce different versions for each operating system, creating a need for a spanning layer above the operating system. One candidate is distributed object management (DOM) (see Chapter 9).

How Layers Enable Business Applications

Evolving from departmental to enterprise and cross-enterprise applications (see Section 2.6 on page 52) creates difficult technical challenges. The legacy client/server departmental applications created an obstacle to data integration across an enterprise because they proliferated heterogeneous infrastructure and applications. Similar problems arise in social applications (see Section 2.3 on page 19), particularly those serving interest groups and the citizenry, where the groups are so large that users are not coordinated. Fortunately, these challenges can be addressed by the layers described in Table 4.3. The challenges and technologies addressing them are summarized in Table 4.5.

4.3 Standardization

The modular layered architecture and open horizontal interfaces provide a way to coordinate vendors of infrastructure and application software and encourage competition in the industry. However,

Table 4.5 Challenges to integration of data across an enterprise.

Problem (layer addressing this problem)	Nature of the problem	Solution
Communication of data (network)	Numerous networking technologies, such as Ethernet, token ring, asynchronous transfer mode, etc., use different ways of transferring data.	The internet—since IP is a spanning layer—allows data to be communicated across heterogeneous networks by subsuming and interconnecting them (see Chapter 11).
Representation of structured data (middleware)	Different computer systems represent standard data values (e.g., character strings and numbers) in terms of bits in different ways (see the sidebar "Any Information Can Be Represented by Bits" on page 10).	Transparently to an application, the representation of data can be automatically converted when communicated from one host to another (see Chapter 9).
Interpretation of data (middleware)	The application must consistently interpret data values. For example, a character string might represent a person's name rather than his address, or a number might represent a person's zip code rather than her telephone number.	The structure and interpretation of data can be described in mutually agreed-upon ways using metadata (see "Assistance from the Author or Publisher" on page 43) or through interface specifications (see Chapter 9).

they raise a daunting problem: At each horizontal interface, the products of different suppliers must be *interoperable*—they must work together correctly. To achieve this, there must be a single standard interface definition, so that each product at one layer is interoperable with all products at the layers above and below. The solution is to standardize the interface, through the process of standardization. A *standard* is a specification generally agreed upon, precisely and completely defined, and well documented, so that any supplier can implement it.

ANALOGY: *Standardization is common in many industries and professions. For example, standards are set for the legal profession by the Uniform Commercial Code and for the accounting profession by the Financial Accounting Standards Board.*

Standardization within Applications

Standardization applies not only to infrastructure but also to some applications, particularly those that cross enterprise boundaries (see Section 2.6.3 on page 64).

EXAMPLE: *EDI (see "Electronic Data Interchange" on page 67) was stimulated by a standard, ANSI X12 [Kee97]. X12 specifies the formats for the exchanges of many standard business messages, including the invoice (X12-810), tax information reporting (X12-826), purchase order (X12-850), notice of employment status (X12-540), mortgage appraisal request (X12-261), and many others. Without ANSI X12 (and an equivalent European standard, EDIFACT), EDI would be far less prevalent.*

The significance of standards like ANSI X12 is that many businesses can exchange messages without prior coordination or negotiation of formats. They can purchase rather than develop software to generate and interpret messages particular to specific business partners. Another example of application standardization is digital payments (see Chapter 8).

A standardized interface offers more value to users and organizations because it empowers them to mix and match products from different vendors complying with the standard. There are thus market pressures on suppliers to create and adopt standardized interfaces. The dynamics of standardization are influential in determining the direction of computing as well as the winners and losers among vendors. Some economic foundations for standardization are discussed in Chapter 5.

4.3.1 Reference Models and Interfaces

Recall that an architecture defines decomposition, functionality, and interaction. In order to standardize interfaces, the decomposition and functionality have to be determined, so these are the first issues in standardization. Together they constitute a *reference model*, which is an overall definition of modularity—including the location of standardized interfaces—and the decomposition of functionality.

ANALOGY: *The human heart and circulatory system, as illustrated in Figure 4.9, define a decomposition into lungs, heart, body, and veins and arteries that carry the blood between them. The simple connectivity is defined in the diagram. Interfaces might specify the constituents of the blood, the rate of heartbeats, the blood pressure, etc.*

The layered architecture of Figure 4.5 is a useful reference model. After agreement on a reference model, the interfaces among the modules can be standardized, including (in the case of software) a set of actions, parameters, and return values, which are called *formats*. In addition, there are often constraints or expectations related to the sequence of invocation of actions, which are called *protocols* (see Chapter 7). Once a reference model is established, the standardization process focuses on the detailed specification of interfaces, including formats and protocols. A goal is to leave room for vendors to differentiate their products based on the standards, for example, with proprietary extensions.

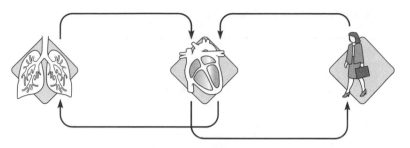

Figure 4.9 The circulatory system as a reference model.

4.3.2 Organization of the Standardization Process

Any formal standardization process requires a recognition of need by a standards body, industry organization, or government. A *standardization body* is an organization set up for the express purpose of promulgating standards (see the sidebar "International Organization for Standards (ISO)" for an example). The standards process also requires the commitment of monetary and human resources by a set of participating companies. A standards process may produce a single standard and dissolve, but more often there is an ongoing process of refinement and extension.

E X A M P L E : *The Internet requires complementary technologies and the coordination of a set of hardware suppliers (such as Cisco, 3Com, and Bay Networks), service providers (such as MCI and AT&T), and application suppliers (such as Netscape and Microsoft). These companies, together with university researchers, cooperate in a process of continuous refinement through the IETF (see the sidebar "Internet Engineering Task Force (IETF)").*

An increasingly popular approach in computing is a *technology web*, which is a set of companies coordinating complementary technologies without a formal process. (This isn't related to the Web information access application, except that the companies enhancing the Web are themselves a technology web.)

E X A M P L E : *The desktop personal computer is based on Intel microprocessors, the Microsoft operating system, various hardware suppliers, and various application software vendors—the Wintel*

International Organization for Standards (ISO)

ISO is an international, non-governmental federation of national standards bodies from over 100 countries, one from each country (the American National Standards Institute (ANSI) is from the United States). Its stated role is to "promote the development of standardization and related activities in the world with a view to facilitating the international exchange of goods and services." The technical work is carried out in a hierarchy of some 2,700 technical committees, subcommittees, and working groups with representatives from industry, research institutes, government authorities, consumer bodies, and international organizations. They come together as equal partners in the resolution of global standardization issues.

ISO standards are not always successful in the marketplace. For example, the Open Systems Interconnection (OSI) was an elaborate standard for networking protocols that has been supplanted by the internet protocols (see the sidebar "Internet Engineering Task Force (IETF)").

Table 4.6 Two types of standards.

Type	Description	Examples
De facto standard	A technology so commonplace that it is a standard in *reality*, even if not recognized by any formal body. It can be established in a couple ways: market power and voluntary cooperation. With *market power*, some product categories have winner-take-all effects resulting over time in a dominant solution (see Chapter 5). With *voluntary cooperation*, companies who recognize the need for interoperability voluntarily work together to recommend standards (see the sidebar "Object Management Group").	Market power: Windows operating system and the Hayes command set; voluntary cooperation: internet protocols (Chapter 7), Java (Chapter 9), and CORBA (Chapter 9).
De jure standard	A standard established by a formal process organized by government, an industry association, or standardization body. It may actually be mandated by law.	ISDN telephone interface; X.500 directory service; GSM digital cellular telephone.

technology web. Intel is particularly active in promulgating hardware interface standards through its Architecture Laboratory, and Microsoft is similarly active in software interface standards.

While the formal standards process is at times slow, technology webs support a rapid continual technology refinement. A technology web is typically limited to a small set of suppliers (often only one supplier for each of the complementary technologies), while most standards processes welcome all comers.

Two distinct types of standards—*de facto* and *de jure*—are described in Table 4.6. The computer industry moves so quickly that the de facto standard is increasingly popular.

4.3.3 Control and Enforcement of Standards

Issues with commercial, legal, and political implications surround the control and enforcement of standards. These issues heavily influence the competitive outcomes in the industry, and standards are increasingly a battleground for supremacy [Sha98].

As described in "The Horizontal Layer Interface" on page 130, many standards are *open* (publicly documented and unencumbered by intellectual property restrictions). For them, the primary "enforcement" is the marketplace, which favors products complying with the standard, in part because they are interoperable with complementary products.

A de facto standard may in principle be available for use by anyone, but there is a dominant proprietary *implementation* (an example is Adobe's Postscript). While a competitive vendor is permitted to build a standard-compliant product, the dominant vendor hopes the development cost would be prohibitive and market acceptance would be minimal.

EXAMPLE: *Competing implementations have occurred, contrary to the wishes of the dominant supplier, in the PC BIOS (code embedded deeply within the bowels of a PC implementation). Originally designed by IBM, it was successfully reverse engineered and implemented by Phoenix Technologies. Another example is the Intel Pentium microprocessor, which has been cloned by Advanced Micro Devices and others. They created a design independently by replicating the functionality and specifications and without using the original design.*

De jure standards are rare in the computer industry, but occur in communications, which is often subject to government regulation (see Chapter 12). The regulatory process may dictate a single standard but leave it up to industry to determine its details.

A standard may be publicly documented but incorporate patented ideas and require adopters to pay royalties. In this case, companies contributing technology to a standard are able to retain patent rights but are obligated by the standards organization to freely license the technology to all comers for a "reasonable and nondiscriminatory" royalty.

Further Reading

An extensive discussion of architecture design and the processes involved in creating them can be found in [BCK98]. A much more

Object Management Group

An important voluntary cooperative standardization effort is the Object Management Group (OMG) focused on object-oriented systems (see Chapter 6) and enterprise computing (see Section 2.6.2 on page 56). The OMG includes over 700 software companies who have found it in their best interest to join in promoting cross-platform standards, so that their products can participate together in enterprise applications. Strictly speaking, the OMG is not a standardization body, but rather simply makes recommendations as to the best technologies. Thus, it views its charter as the cooperative promulgation of de facto standards. The process followed by OMG is to identify areas that need standardization, request participating companies to contribute, evaluate those contributions by a technical committee, and make a final recommendation. Occasionally they ask members to merge their best ideas into a single proposal.

technical introduction to the design of distributed systems is [CDK94]. The business process reengineering described in [Dav93] is not dissimilar to the architecture design for software systems. Finally, strategies for using standardization as a competitive tool are discussed in [Sha98].

Industry and Government

5

Networked computing involves a large global infrastructure, computing and communications service providers, equipment and software suppliers, and millions of users (individuals and organizations). Its technologies must be considered in the context of a large, complex business and social system with many interacting economic, business, legal, and policy issues.

While networked computing has much in common with other industries, it also has special characteristics that distinguish it. Parts of this industry operate under economic constraints unusual for other industries, and government has an increasing role through intellectual property laws, regulation, and policies. For further elaboration of these issues and discussion of how suppliers and consumers can gain strategic advantage, see [Sha98].

5.1 Participants, Products, and Services

Networked computing is an industry with many different types of players, including suppliers of goods (equipment, software, information content) and services (communications and computing operations, application development). Any networked application builds on products and services provided by these myriad players and must find ways to coordinate them successfully.

5.1.1 Types of Suppliers

Individuals or organizations deploying networked computing applications can draw upon a variety of different suppliers, many pursuing quite distinct business models, as listed in Table 5.1.

5.1.2 Types of Consumers

There are several major categories of consumers of networked computing-related products and services:

- *User organizations:* Virtually all medium-to-large organizations, and many small ones, integrate networked applications into their operations. These applications range from highly customized to fairly generic, and they incorporate equipment and software products from a number of suppliers. The applications can be managed by internal information systems departments—which specialize in the development, integration, and operation of networked computing—or increasingly, all or some of these functions are outsourced to professional services firms.

- *Infrastructure service providers:* Network, computing, and middleware service providers purchase and deploy equipment and software, operate the systems, and provide customer service and billing.

- *On-line merchants:* These firms sell information content or other goods over the network. They are customers of network service providers and equipment and software suppliers.

- *On-line service providers:* These firms sell services over the network, such as information searching and retrieval, financial planning, stock trading, electronic banking, etc. The dividing line between merchants and service providers is not clean, as information content is typically embedded in services.

- *Cyberspace consumers:* The Internet—because it is available to so many individual users—has created this new category of consumers. These consumers desire communications (telephone service, email, etc.) and information access (the Web) and are customers of on-line merchants and service providers.

Table 5.1 Different types of suppliers for networked computing users.

Supplier	Description	Examples
Infrastructure equipment suppliers	Equipment includes computers, peripherals, and data and telecommunications switches. Increasingly, equipment suppliers specialize in each of these areas.	Computers: Compaq, Hewlett Packard, Dell; data network: Cisco, Bay Networks, 3Com; telecommunications: Lucent, Nortel, Siemens.
Infrastructure software suppliers	Infrastructure software includes operating system, database and Web servers, and middleware. Software is also embedded in network equipment.	Servers: Oracle, Netscape, Microsoft; operating systems: Microsoft, Apple, Sun; middleware: Iona, Microsoft; embedded software: Cisco, Lucent.
Infrastructure service providers	Network transport of data, audio, and video, including Internet service providers (ISPs) and telecommunications providers. Increasingly, operation of networks internal to organizations and internal computer operation are outsourced.	Networking: MCI, America Online; telecommunications: AT&T, Sprint, MCI; computing: EDS, Computer Science Corp.
Application service providers	Infrastructure service providers sometimes bundle applications.	Telephony (AT&T, MCI); information indexing and searching (America Online); payroll processing.
Content suppliers	Information content provided to consumers over the network.	Information services (America Online); entertainment video (TCI).
Application software producers	Application software products sold to users and organizations without the option of modification or customization (colloquially called shrink-wrapped software).	Personal productivity suites (Microsoft Office); network management (Bellcore).
Application framework producers	Partial applications—including *components* and *frameworks*—that speed application development (see Chapter 6), often with the aid of professional service firms.	Enterprise resource planning: SAP, Baan, PeopleSoft.
Professional services firms	Systems integrators—who design and deploy infrastructure and applications incorporating products from other suppliers—and custom application developers.	Systems integrators: Anderson Consulting, EDS; custom applications: Active Software.

5.1.3 Types of Information Goods

Information in different media (such as text, audio, images, video) is the primary good stored, retrieved, and manipulated in a networked application. When this information is bought or sold, it is called information *content*. An important distinction should be made between *static* and *volatile* content (see Section 2.4 on page 38). At its extreme, static content is created once and never changes, and at the opposite extreme, volatile content continually changes, expands, and becomes obsolete. Most content falls somewhere between these extremes.

EXAMPLE: *Real-time stock quotes (representing the last trading price) are highly volatile content, whereas historical stock quotes (representing prices in the past) are static. A digital encyclopedia is static but is updated annually and requires major revision every ten years or so. A movie is static; it is produced once and rarely modified thereafter.*

Much content has the characteristic that consumers don't want its entirety, but rather need to selectively narrow it to a relevant piece. Suppliers satisfying these consumers focus on *indexing* and *searching*, thus providing a *service* (searching for topical information) in addition to a *good* (the information itself). This can also be viewed as mass customization of an information good.

ANALOGY: *A high-end clothing store provides both goods (the clothes) and services (advising on color selection and performing alterations). Some clothing stores specialize in clothing customized to each customer.*

5.1.4 Types of Software Goods

Another good that is bought and sold is software—both application and infrastructure. There are two distinct approaches:

- The *software product*—sometimes called colloquially shrink-wrapped software—is developed with the hope that consumers will buy it (much like static content).

- The *custom-developed software application* is developed to a consumer's particular specifications and may have a single customer. The supplier and customer are the same if an information systems department develops and operates the application.

There are many intermediate cases. Custom-developed applications often incorporate products, because developing generic capabilities from scratch is much more expensive than buying them. Due to the escalating costs of software development, a new set of suppliers are focusing on reusable software components and frameworks intended as a foundation for new applications (see Chapter 6). For example, ERP vendors sell customizable turnkey solutions for standard business processes, and a customer hires a professional services firm to aid in the customization and integration into their environment (see "Enterprise Resource Planning" on page 60).

The software product and services are manifestations of push vs. pull (see Section 2.4.2 on page 47). In the product (push) model, the supplier defines and develops to a product specification and sells this off-the-shelf solution. In the services (pull) model, the customer provides a specification and commissions a supplier to develop an application to that specification.

Applications are not developed once and for all; once deployed, they move into a maintenance phase. Software products have a series of *releases*, each one fixing programming errors reported by customers and adding new capabilities and features or better performance. Custom-developed applications have similar maintenance needs.

Infrastructure software is normally sold as a product, as it is broadly deployed and not limited to a single organization. Customization of any sort is unusual; rather, the changing requirements of the collective consumers are incorporated into new releases. There are two categories:

- Infrastructure software *bundled with equipment* provides complementary functionality to the hardware (for example, the operating system supports the processor). It may be developed internally by the equipment supplier (Apple Computer or Cisco) or by a separate supplier (Microsoft Windows bundled with a personal computer). In either case, the software is sold bundled with the equipment and new releases may be sold separately.

- *Unbundled* infrastructure software is sold separately. For example, middleware (see Chapter 9) and databases (see Chapter 6) are by nature deployed across a heterogeneous mix of platforms, and thus bundling with one and only one platform makes no sense.

5.1.5 Equipment: The Component Model

The equipment supporting networked applications includes computers and peripherals (like the network interface) closely associated with users and infrastructure equipment such as server computers and network switches. Equipment suppliers have long used a component model, in which specialized component suppliers (such as manufacturers of microprocessor chips or memory chips) sell to many equipment manufacturers (see "Subsystems and Components" on page 80). (A similar component model is also gaining popularity in software—see Chapter 6.) The manufacturers differentiate themselves by assembling the components in different ways, adding their own specialized components, and gaining cost advantage with efficiencies in manufacturing or distribution.

5.2 Changes in Industry Structure

The structure of the computer and communications industries is changing rapidly. Major forces are the convergence of computing and communications in the context of networked computing, the changing application focus (moving from departmental to enterprise and cross-enterprise applications), and advances in the technologies themselves. The structure of the industry is also being changed by the trend away from vertical integration and the influence of venture capital.

5.2.1 From Stovepipe to Layering

The infrastructure hasn't always been layered (see Section 4.2.2 on page 124 and Figure 4.5 on page 127), especially in communications. From an economic perspective, the salient aspect of this architecture is its integration—within each layer—of functions required by all applications. In communications, this is called *integrated services*. The opposite architecture is the *stovepipe*, which dedicates a complete infrastructure to each separate application.

EXAMPLE: *In communications, the telephone network, cable television, and the Internet are each stovepipe networks dedicated to particular applications (telephony, video broadcast, and data). However, the Internet is moving toward an integrated services network that serves all applications (see Chapters 7 and 11). In computing, the stand-alone word processor and personal digital assistant are examples of stovepipe architectures.*

Both the stovepipe and integrated layer architectures are modular, allowing development, sales, and ownership of the infrastructure to be divided among firms, and each allows competition (competitive stovepipes or competitive layers). So why this trend toward layering? The economic forces behind this shift are summarized in Table 5.2. The layered architecture has disadvantages too: The burden is often on the customer to integrate the layers from different suppliers. Some users would prefer to purchase a turnkey solution.

EXAMPLE: *The difficulties users have integrating their personal computer with its various peripherals (modem, printer, etc.) partially offset the advantages of greater competition. Vendors have responded to this in different ways, including Microsoft's "plug-and-play" automatic configuration and Dell's customization and configuration (see the sidebar "Dell as a Subsystem Integrator"). Ease of use is also a major selling point for information appliances (see the sidebar "Information Appliances").*

5.2.2 Less Vertical Integration and More Diversification

Companies can become more or less vertically integrated and diversified, as defined in Table 5.3. These strategies are not mutually exclusive—one or both can be pursued. As a general statement, there appears to be a trend toward more diversification and

Dell as a Subsystem Integrator

Layering—and more generally, industry fragmentation—may require users to integrate complementary products to create a workable system. Particularly if there are numerous options available, this can make it difficult for the consumer to get everything working together.

While the success of Dell Computer has been attributed to its distribution model and customer service (see the sidebar "Dell Computer and Mass Customization" on page 68), it also performs a valuable subsystem integration function. The customer can interactively configure the desired peripherals, expansion cards, and software in the order, and Dell integrates these components and provides support.

System integration is a valuable service to the customer and a good opportunity for suppliers. Dell adds value only to the individual computer subsystem, but other firms (such as EDS and Anderson Consulting) perform similar system integration functions for the larger system.

Table 5.2 Forces driving the industry toward layering and away from stovepipe.

Force	Description	Example
Economies of scope	A common infrastructure supporting a variety of applications allows sharing of development, purchasing, administration, operations, and billing costs.	The Internet is cheaper to operate than separate email and Web networks.
Economies of scale	An infrastructure supporting a variety of applications is larger and thus may have lower unit costs.	The Internet has more users—and hence is larger—than a network that supports only email or only the Web.
Incremental costs	Each new application—leveraging an existing infrastructure—need not justify the cost of an entire new infrastructure.	Users add applications to a PC for the cost of software.
Larger market	Because the infrastructure is in place, application suppliers see a large existing market. This makes the spanning layer particularly important (see "The Spanning Layer" on page 130).	The Internet offers application developers a large number of users with Internet access.
Diversity of applications	A low incremental cost and larger market encourage greater application diversity, providing greater value to users.	More users subscribe to Internet access or purchase a personal computer because of the large number of applications.
Competition	The user can mix and match complementary technologies across layers. The greater competition may reduce prices and increase quality.	The user can choose from among many Internet providers and PC vendors without changing applications.
Multimedia	Applications can incorporate different media (text, graphics, audio, video) at will.	Remote conferencing (see Section 2.3.3 on page 27).
Single customer interface	In communications, the customer can deal with a single integrated services provider.	Today a user typically deals with separate telephone, television, and data providers.

less vertical integration in the computer and communications industries. Diversification is encouraged by the customer's desire for a
range of application solutions from a single supplier, while vertical

Table 5.3 Vertical integration and diversification.

Strategy	Description	Examples
Vertical integration	A company is vertically integrated when it makes (rather than buys) all the subsystems in its products. A company becomes more vertically integrated by acquiring suppliers that previously sold it components.	IBM makes everything from semiconductors to application software and provides professional services to install and operate applications. In acquiring Digital and Tandem, Compaq added a strong software and services business to become more vertically integrated. AT&T reduced vertical integration by divesting its equipment and computer subsidiaries. A system integrator (see the sidebar "Dell as a Subsystem Integrator" on page 145) is the least vertically integrated, as it purchases all its components.
Diversification	A diversified company provides products across different industry segments. It thereby achieves synergies, consistency of financial results, and provides customers with a "total solution."	By acquiring Tandem Computer, Compaq also diversified by adding reliable OLTP software and servers to its product line (see Section 2.6.1 on page 53). Telecommunications service providers are diversifying by accumulating telephone, cable television, wireless, and data networking assets.

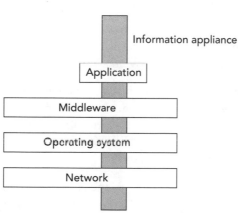

Figure 5.1 An information appliance captures a snapshot of an application and the layered infrastructure that supports it.

disintegration is driven by the improved competitiveness of more specialized firms (pursuing either integrated circuits, or equipment, or infrastructure, or applications). Both are driven by the forces

Information Appliances

The information appliance (IA) is a stovepipe architecture that packages a single (or small number of) applications within a small, inexpensive, relatively easy-to-use package. An example is a cellular telephone equipped with email and Web browsing. As shown in Figure 5.1, an information appliance captures a stovepipe snapshot from the layered infrastructure. In effect, an IA represents a return to the stovepipe architecture but still exploits layering with open interfaces. With the decreasing cost of electronics, some users may purchase a collection of information appliances rather than a single flexible (but more difficult to use) desktop computer.

There are also problems. One disadvantage is that IAs freeze functionality and standards at a point in time, forcing users to upgrade or replace them fairly frequently (making the manufacturers happy!). They also confront users with a proliferation of different user interfaces and, due to their limited display and keyboard power, may have difficult user interfaces (like the infamous "VCR programming problem").

behind the layered architecture. Companies that specialize in one layer are diversifying across a wide range of applications and services. But they are not vertically integrated in that they are supplying only part of the whole solution, and some other company is serving as the system integrator of the layers.

5.2.3 Venture Capital and Start-up Companies

Venture capital arguably plays a larger role in networked computing than any other industry—except perhaps biotechnology—and this is one powerful force behind vertical disintegration. Venture capitalists (VCs) fund new companies in the hope of hitting pay dirt with a few major successes that become public companies with high valuation. These investments are risky, and thus VCs diversify: Each VC funds multiple start-ups, and each start-up is typically funded by multiple VCs.

Why is this model so successful? There are a few basic observations:

- The barriers to entry, particularly in software, are lower than in many industries. Large capital investments are not needed from the VC, and the needed human capital is rewarded by equity.

- The trend from stovepipe toward layers with open interfaces allows small firms to fully participate with complementary products, without having to provide a total system solution.

- The technology and the industry move very rapidly, but size can be a disadvantage if slow decision making is the result. In addition, large companies with their installed bases find it more difficult to overcome supplier lock-in (see Section 5.3.2 on page 154).

- Start-ups have often proven financially lucrative to early employees as well as investors, and large companies cannot offer a comparable upside. Thus, start-ups sometimes have an advantage attracting the top talent necessary to bring a new idea to fruition.

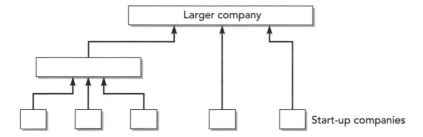

Figure 5.2 A process of absorption and consolidation creates new products in start-up companies and moves those products into diversified firms through consolidation and absorption.

Some start-ups succeed fabulously, others fail and go out of business, but a common process is the absorption of start-up companies into larger companies, as illustrated in Figure 5.2. It is increasingly common for new products to be developed by start-ups, often with collaborative marketing, sales, and distribution agreements with other firms. Moderately successful start-ups are often purchased by larger firms pursuing diversification, while wildly successful start-ups are taken public.

5.2.4 Computing/Communications Convergence

Convergence occurs when once-independent product categories or whole industries become—through the evolution of technology or the marketplace—either competitive or complementary. The evolution from centralized to networked computing (see Section 1.1 on page 2) has resulted in major convergence.

The overriding convergence between the telecommunications and computer industries, as a result of the networking of computers, illustrates both competitive and complementary forms of convergence. When users demand networked computing applications, they require both computers and communications, which become complementary.

EXAMPLE: *Computer equipment manufacturers believe the unavailability of high-speed Internet residential access is stifling their business opportunities. The obstacles are discussed in Chapter 12.*

At the same time, networked applications become competitive with traditional applications from the telecommunications industry, such as telephony, facsimile, and video conferencing.

E X A M P L E : *Internet telephony provides a two-way voice capability similar to the telephone network, but using the Internet (see Chapter 12).*

The computer/communications convergence is changing both industries irrevocably. The computer industry today encounters many more difficulties achieving interoperability—a stand-alone turnkey no longer offers much value—and thus is becoming heavily involved in standardization (see Section 4.3 on page 132). The telecommunications industry is being driven away from stovepipe solutions (see Section 5.2.1 on page 144). Together, these trends make the two industries more similar.

5.3 Obstacles to Change

While networked computing evolves quite fast, there are actually substantial obstacles to change in this industry. Surprisingly, without these obstacles the technologies might change even more quickly.

5.3.1 The Network Effect

When the value of a product or service to an individual consumer depends on the number of other consumers adopting it, this is called a *network effect* or *network externality*. The term "network" refers to the fact that the different instances of the product are logically connected (or possibly physically connected through a network). The term "externality" denotes the impact one consumer has on another without a compensating payment.

E X A M P L E : *You probably don't particularly care how many other consumers own the same automobile as you, as long as there is a sufficient critical mass of cars so that parts are available and mechanics know how to fix them. In the case of fashion, you may actively seek out clothing and colors not worn by too many other consumers.*

Clothing fashions often have *negative* externality if their loss of uniqueness causes them to have less value. Many networked computer products have a *positive* externality [Eco96]: The value increases substantially with the number of adopters.

EXAMPLE: *The telephone and the facsimile machine exhibit strong positive externality. The value of a telephone (or facsimile machine) depends on how many other people you can call (fax). To illustrate network effects without a physical network, a word processing program offers an individual user more value when there are many other users with whom he can share files. A computer programming language offers greater value when widely used because it is easier to find qualified programmers, complementary development tools, etc. An operating system offers greater value when widely adopted because it attracts a greater diversity of applications.*

Table 5.4 describes two types of network effects—direct and indirect. In terms of the impact of network effects on the marketplace, two concepts should be understood: critical mass and positive feedback. Early in the life cycle of a product or service with network effects—when there are few adopters—its value (as measured by consumer willingness to pay) may be lower than the supplier's costs, so that a supplier cannot make a profit. If the supplier overcomes this—say, by selling at a loss to get sufficient adopters—then eventually the willingness to pay will exceed the supplier's cost. This is called a *critical mass* of adopters.

After a product adoption exceeds critical mass, this increases its value to consumers further, thereby attracting new adopters, further increasing its value. This "success breeds success" phenomenon—called *positive feedback*—often results in dramatic and rapid market penetration. Positive feedback works in the reverse direction also: For a product losing adopters, there is increasing downside momentum because the value of the product is decreasing. Existing users derive less and less value—and become more likely to defect—while the product attracts few new adopters.

The result of critical mass and positive feedback can be a winner-take-all effect, in which a product category tips to a dominant supplier [Sha98].

Table 5.4 Two types of network effects in networked computing.

Type of network effect	Description	Examples
Direct	The value of a product or service depends on the number of other users available to participate.	Value of a packet network depends on the number of users connected to the network and available to participate in social applications.
	The value of a product or service depends on the number of complementary products with which data can be shared.	Value of a word processor depends on the number of compatible word processors with which files can be shared. Value of a Web browser depends on the number of compatible servers.
Indirect	The value of a product or service depends on the availability of software or content. A widely used product or service attracts more complementary software or content.	Large number of Web browsers attracts many information publishers. Large number of Microsoft Windows platforms attracts many application suppliers. Large number of music CD players attracts many available titles.

EXAMPLE: *The declining market share of the Apple Macintosh operating system and the rise in market share for Microsoft Windows illustrate positive feedback and a winner-take-all effect.*

Standardization and Network Effects

Strong network effects drive de facto standards (see Section 4.3.3 on page 136). A technical solution unencumbered by intellectual property restrictions that gains a modicum of success tends to be adopted by other suppliers wanting to offer greater value to *their* customers. The solution becomes more successful with time and eventually becomes dominant, establishing the de facto standard.

EXAMPLE: *A premier example of a de facto standard arising out of indirect network effects is the IBM personal computer. IBM did not successfully maintain intellectual property protection, and other suppliers exploited the critical mass and resulting application availability by producing compatible computers.*

A de facto standard can also be a product of academic research, particularly if an implementation of the technology is made widely and freely available and attracts complementary content or applications.

E X A M P L E : *The Internet technologies—originally developed by government-supported academic research projects—were widely available in the free Berkeley UNIX operating system. This attracted many complementary applications. By the time similar commercial networking became commonplace, the Internet had a large cadre of users (providing direct network effects) and a set of widely used applications (providing indirect network effects). The rest is history.*

Today product suppliers recognize the importance of network effects, and they commonly form consortia or use other means to define a dominant technology rather than waiting for the market to determine it. Their goal is to stimulate the market (and hence revenues and profits) more quickly and also to avoid stranded investments (which neither pay off nor can be recovered).

E X A M P L E : *The Automotive Network Exchange (ANX) electronic commerce initiative from U.S. automobile companies (see Section 2.6.3 on page 64) is based on standard internet technologies. Many companies are associated with the automotive industry and are candidates to join ANX. Cross-enterprise applications are subject to direct network effects, but these companies may form a critical mass, creating de facto standards. Clearly the founders of ANX have this in mind.*

The fundamental equation driving decision making in products with network effects is

Revenues = market share × size of market

It is possible for revenues to increase for one supplier, even as market share is ceded to other firms, as long as the total size of the market is increased sufficiently as a result of positive feedback.

E X A M P L E : *The digital versatile disk (DVD)—a format for storing digital data on an optical storage medium—resulted from industry cooperation because the manufacturers felt it necessary to define a*

The Success of the Web

The Web is a de facto standard that established a whole new industry and increasingly forms the basis for network applications (see the sidebar "World Wide Web" on page 37). The origins of its success are easy to see with hindsight. Information access has indirect network effects, and the availability of a browser encouraged a rush of complementary content. Of considerable importance was the ability of almost anyone to inexpensively publish content, creating a demand for browsers even before significant commercial activity. Netscape and Microsoft provided free browsers to create critical mass and stimulate demand for their complementary server products (for which they charged).

Arguably the greatest credit should go to the Internet itself, which by creating an open spanning layer (see "The Spanning Layer" on page 130) enabled new applications such as the Web to be globally deployed with a minimum investment for both developers and users (see Table 5.2 on page 146).

single standard before the product came to market. They were driven by content suppliers, who felt that incompatible products would confuse consumers and reduce the total market.

Both the OMG (see the sidebar "Object Management Group" on page 137) and the IETF (see the sidebar "Internet Engineering Task Force (IETF)" on page 136) are cooperative efforts to define de facto standards. In each case, companies cooperate to define a common solution in a marketplace where direct network effects would likely cause the market to tip to a dominant solution anyway.

This is not an entirely benign trend, as there is value in a winning solution from among competing choices arising from market forces—as opposed to vendor collaboration—as it may result in cost, performance, or features advantages.

5.3.2 Lock-In

A networked application comprises complementary, interoperable pieces such as application software, processors, operating systems, network, and peripherals). There are also *intangible* assets, such as time invested in learning the software, organizations set up to administer it, etc. Networked applications are more diverse than many other goods, such as automobiles. An automobile is a stovepipe "transportation application"—due to de facto standardization—and once you learn to drive one automobile, you can probably drive any other.

Multiple complementary tangible and intangible assets lead directly to *lock-in* [Far88], meaning a user or organization can't change one piece of the system in isolation, except by replacing it with a direct substitute. Alternatively, many complementary pieces have to be changed together. Lock-in is a barrier to selling new products, since a locked-in customer has to consider the tangible and intangible costs of making other changes as well. This is often so daunting and expensive that users keep what they have. Suppliers with a locked-in customer have an advantage over potential competitors.

Of course, lock-in isn't absolute; it comes in degrees. A user who simply wants to switch word processing applications will have an easier time than a user who wants to switch from a PC to a Macintosh. The degree of lock-in is quantified by the consumer's *switching costs*. Let's say a consumer is considering a new supplier for one piece of the computer system. The switching costs are the costs over and above the replacement of that one piece that the consumer must bear, typically including the cost of replacing complementary assets, including intangible assets such as trained workers.

Suppliers can take advantage of lock-in by successfully charging their customers higher prices than competitors for upgrades or complementary products (see the sidebar "The Value of Consumer Lock-In to a Supplier"). Thus, suppliers have a strong incentive to encourage lock-in of their own customers. An important impact of lock-in is the roadblocks to new technologies it engenders.

EXAMPLE: *Many large corporations, even today, store mission-critical information in database systems such as IMS, IDMS, and VSAM, even though these are considered inferior to modern relational databases (see "File System" on page 91).*

Lock-in is not entirely negative for the customer, who benefits from a long-term relationship with a single-source supplier. A locked-in customer—especially a major one—often has considerable influence over the evolution of products.

Supplier and Industry Lock-In

Suppliers in the computer industry can also suffer lock-in. Because each supplier is also creating a product that is only a piece of an overall system, it must pick and choose among complementary products.

EXAMPLE: *An application supplier has to choose a language and set of design tools, an operating system and computer platform, quite possibly a set of software components, a set of network protocols, etc. An equipment supplier has to choose among possible interfaces, integrated circuit components, etc.*

The Value of Consumer Lock-In to a Supplier

The supplier has an opportunity to sell upgrades, after-market products, etc., at higher-than-competitive prices to a locked-in customer. Of course, the supplier can't charge too much, or the consumer may switch anyway. Thus, the size of the premium prices and profit opportunities is directly related to the consumer's switching costs. The supplier must evaluate this carefully in setting prices.

A locked-in customer has a tangible monetary value to a supplier—something the supplier can take to the bank! Under certain conditions, the present value of future profits due to a consumer's lock-in can be shown to be equal to the consumer's switching cost [Sha98]. (The present value takes into account the time value of money by discounting profits in future years in accordance with prevailing interest rates.)

Microsoft vs. Everybody Else

The greatest battle in the software industry is between Microsoft, which gains increasing dominance of several product categories, and the other suppliers. It illustrates well the forces of network effects and lock-in.

One of Microsoft's primary allies is network effects. Obviously, Windows and Office maintain a strong position due to network effects, but the remaining competitive battle is for the corporate "back office." Microsoft is attempting to establish its NT operating system in competition with UNIX by exploiting the fragmentation of UNIX and resulting adverse network effects. The success of Microsoft's back-office server products will clearly depend on the success of NT, just as the Office application was established in part because of Windows. On the other hand, Microsoft concluded it couldn't overcome the momentum of the Internet and thus fully embraced Internet standards rather than going its own way.

The rest of the industry is using open standards as a way to battle Microsoft, pointing out to corporate customers the dangers of becoming locked-in to Microsoft. In the interest of open standards,

All these choices of complementary products have the potential for switching costs and lock-in. A supplier can also suffer lock-in to its own proprietary technologies. This comes in several forms, for example, the attraction of a lower incremental cost of upgrading a current product compared to creating a new one, or the need to continue supporting customers with legacy products.

EXAMPLE: *In the shift from centralized to decentralized computing, the suppliers of centralized computers (mainframe and minicomputers) were destabilized. Some never recovered. Even where they recognized the broad impact of the technological change, lock-in to existing products was difficult to overcome.*

5.3.3 Path-Dependent Effects

The cumulative effect of the obstacles to change that have been described—particularly lock-in and network effects—is that the industry as a whole has a considerable memory. Many standards have a lifetime greater than expected, given rapid technological advancement. Many of these legacy standards appear, in retrospect, to be almost accidental.

EXAMPLE: *The IBM PC platform, which became an industry de facto standard, illustrates industry lock-in. Consumers experience lock-in to this platform through their investments in software applications, add-on boards, etc. Intel and Microsoft experience lock-in through their accumulated investments in the microprocessor and operating system development. Indirect network effects cause the platform to have greater value to consumers because of large numbers of complementary products on the market (applications, add-on cards, experienced technicians, training courses and books, etc.). Even superior competing approaches have difficulty establishing themselves because they have to overcome all these advantages. Making improvements to the platform is difficult because of the coordination of complementary products.*

At any point in time, the marketplace does not necessarily allow the best or lowest-cost solution to dominate. Many seemingly minor or innocuous decisions by IBM in the original PC design remain today, even if better approaches would be available. This tendency of seemingly inconsequential decisions as a part of a standard (even de facto standard) to be irreversible and impact the marketplace much later is called *path dependency*. The ultimate consequence of "obstacles to change," the title of this section, is path dependency. Path dependency is a market failure that can prevent the best or most cost-effective solutions from achieving success.

they are doing some extraordinary teaming, such as OMG's CORBA and Sun's Java. If it were not for competition from Microsoft, it is not clear the rest of the industry would find teaming nearly so attractive.

5.4 Challenges for Suppliers

In networked computing, there are a variety of goods and services, such as infrastructure software and equipment, application software, system integration, custom application development, information content indexing and searching, and communications. Challenges that suppliers of these goods and services face—and the investments they make and the risks they assume—are quite distinct from those of many other industries. In particular, information as an economic good has some special technical and economic properties.

5.4.1 Properties of Information

Information can be captured in *discrete* or *digital* form, meaning it is represented by a set of symbols from a discrete alphabet. In computing, that alphabet is bits, and all information is represented by a collection of bits (see the sidebar "Any Information Can Be Represented by Bits" on page 10). A basic property of information represented this way is that exact replicas can be created, simply by making a copy of the data. In contrast to the manufacture of physical goods, this replication is very cheap.

The replication property leads to some unusual properties of information as an economic good, as in content that is created and sold. There are three distinct phases in the supply of content:

- *Creation:* Content has to be created or updated. This may require *authoring* (as in the case of a document, encyclopedia, music score, or a movie script), *producing* (as in a movie or music performance), or *collection* (as in the case of content that reports on some external phenomenon, such as the stock market).

- *Replication:* Once it has been created, one replica of the content is generated for each customer.

- *Distribution:* Content replicas have to reach the consumers. In networked computing, replicas can be inexpensively distributed over the network, or by physical transport of magnetic or optical storage media (as in a CD-ROM).

Although these steps parallel those for physical goods, there are some significant differences listed in Table 5.5. Supply economies of scale give substantial advantages to a high-volume supplier, which has significantly lower unit costs. While this is true in most manufacturing industries, it is more extreme for information content. The observation that creation costs are *sunk* and content is an *experience good* makes content creation quite risky. This can be overcome to some extent by building the *reputation* of the supplier (it turned out excellent content in the past) or through *recommendation* (see "Third-Party or Collective Recommendations" on page 44).

Table 5.5 Economic comparison of information and physical goods [Var95].

Property	Information content	Physical goods
Replication or manufacturing cost	Replication and distribution costs are small in comparison to creation cost.	Manufacturing and distribution costs are significant, even for relatively small production volumes.
Economies of scale	Unit costs decrease rapidly with sales volume because the major costs are one-time creation.	Economies of scale are limited by a significant manufacturing cost component.
Cost recovery	Creation costs are *sunk*; that is, cannot be recovered if there are no sales.	Some start-up costs (e.g., manufacturing capital equipment and real estate) can be recovered if there are no sales.
Value judgement	Content is an *experience good*, meaning the consumer must see it to judge its value.	A consumer can often judge the value without seeing the good (e.g., if it is consumable, such as motor oil).

The economic characteristics differ significantly for the suppliers of static and volatile content. Suppliers of static content deal with risk by diversification: They invest in a number of different content creations and recover most of their costs from their winners, leveraging the strong supply economies of scale that create high profits for these winners (see Table 5.3 on page 147). Suppliers of volatile content often avoid risk by selling information by *subscription*; that is, a consumer receives a continuous stream of updates for a fixed price (see "User Control: Subscriptions" on page 48). The investment in updating volatile content can be based on an accurate estimate of subscription revenues, and as a result, volatile content is a relatively low-risk business not as dependent on diversification.

EXAMPLE: *No book publisher would specialize in only books about mutual funds. On the other hand, Morningstar Mutual Funds successfully specializes in providing volatile information about mutual funds by subscription.*

5.4.2 How Software Differs from Information

From a supplier perspective, software is similar to information content, typically falling between the static and volatile extremes. The representation of software—like information—is data (in the case of software representing low-level processor instructions). Thus, replication is inexpensive, creation costs are significant, and there are strong supply economies of scale.

During development, software products have supply-side characteristics similar to static content: They are an experience good, and the costs of development (analogous to content creation) are sunk. Thus, software product development is risky, and suppliers respond by diversifying. On the other hand, the custom development of software—sold only once—benefits from no economies of scale. The high creation cost must be offset by the consumer's control over the features.

Creating custom or customized applications is relatively low risk, since development is undertaken on contract, with specified milestones, deliverables, and payment schedule. On the other hand, the supplier's profits are capped by the poor supply economies of scale. As a result, professional services organizations typically retain some ownership of custom applications, so that all or parts can be sold to others. Over time, they may develop a portfolio of customized products, resulting in a hybrid product services model (like the ERP applications—see "Enterprise Resource Planning" on page 60).

Software maintenance and upgrade costs are significant, whether the application is custom or a product. Charges for upgraded releases of the software—resembling the creation of volatile content—often represent a major source of supplier revenue, whether upgrades are sold by subscription or by new release.

5.4.3 Protecting Investments with Intellectual Property

As emphasized above, content and software both have a large cost of creation and low cost of replication. This is a double-edged sword. On the bright side, this leads to strong supply economies of scale and hence large rewards for successful products. On the dark side, it creates an opportunity for *piracy*—the unauthorized replication of content or software. Piracy is discouraged by granting *property rights* to the creator, a normal and necessary function of government. Since content and software don't have a physical manifestation, they are called *intellectual property*. The laws governing intellectual property (copyrights and patents) are discussed in Section 5.5.1 on page 165.

5.4.4 Selling Content and Software

Content and software suppliers face special pricing challenges, now discussed in the context of how they affect industry outcomes (see [Sha98] for a discussion of strategies). First, consider the nature of competitive markets. An idealized economic model is "perfect competition," in which there are many suppliers of a comparable product and no single supplier has control over the price. In such an idealized market, the price theoretically approaches the supplier's marginal cost (including incremental cost of production and a normal return on invested capital). Suppliers attempt to gain an edge by driving their costs lower than the competitor's.

EXAMPLE: *Perfect competition is a good model in agriculture, where a large number of producers can't easily distinguish their products and the price is dictated by the market.*

Strong supply economies of scale preclude such perfect competition in content and software. The incremental replication cost is practically zero, so that a supplier of a substitutable product that sells a higher volume is able to undercut a competitor's price, gain market share as a result, and eventually become dominant. Once one supplier achieves dominance, the basic assumptions of perfect competition are not valid.

EXAMPLE: *A few widely used and mature applications have a "standard" feature set (word processors, for example), making product differentiation difficult. Rather than perfect competition, a dominant product emerges and is difficult to displace because of its supply economies of scale. While it is relatively easy to develop a competing product, the dominant supplier has much lower unit costs. Lock-in and network effects also contribute to these winner-take-all effects.*

While all suppliers want to differentiate their products—to limit competition and improve profits—it is essential for content and software suppliers [Sha98]. Each must strive for sufficiently distinct features and performance to attract its own loyal customers.

Rejecting perfect competition, consider the opposite extreme of a dominant supplier. How should it price its product? Can it charge anything it pleases? Certainly not, as there are at least two pricing constraints. First, it must keep the price low enough to discourage competitive suppliers of a substitutable product. (In practice, the supplier has to worry about products that are similar, if not exact substitutes.) This is called *limit pricing*. Second, it can't charge more than consumers are willing to pay, which depends on the value the consumer places on the product. Pricing a product based on the consumer's value is called *value pricing* [Var95]. Value pricing is the dominant strategy for suppliers of content and software but requires an understanding of the customer's value proposition, discussed next.

Are Shrink-Wrapped Applications Poor Quality and Overfeatured?

Some users complain that software products have poor quality and excessive features, making them hard to use. If true, this is likely due in part to the industry tradition of fixed pricing. Keeping development groups employed requires steady revenue, which requires a steady stream of new products, an expanding customer base, or new releases sold to existing customers. There is thus pressure to frequently produce new releases with added features and a disincentive to improve quality if it lengthens the release cycle.

If software pricing were usage based, there would be greater incentive for high quality. Revenues would depend less on new features and releases and more on retaining users and getting them to use the application more. It would also better align pricing with value, benefiting suppliers. With the ubiquitous Internet, it is technically feasible to include usage monitoring and billing in software applications, but there might be customer resistance. Do you think it might become more common?

Value of Content

Because information is an experience good (see Table 5.5 on page 158), the supplier's reputation is important, since that is often the basis of choice. Where content is authored (as in works of literature), the consumer may attach more weight to the author than to the publisher. As a result, content suppliers choose authors carefully to protect their reputations.

For volatile content sold by subscription, the consumer is willing to enter a longer-term purchase agreement. *Timeliness* frequently affects value, and networked computing is an ideal medium, commanding higher prices than the same content distributed by slower means.

The value of content is reduced when there is too much of it, making it difficult for the consumer to find useful information. Content customized to the consumer's needs thus offers high value [Sha98] and is another strength of networked computing because it can make a dynamic and user-specific presentation of content. Similarly, a key to selling content is gaining the attention of the consumer in an increasingly information-rich environment.

It is often possible to get third parties to pay for content through advertising support, and this is an increasingly popular payment model on the Web. In spite of the fact that an advertiser derives little value from each consumer—after all, relatively few respond to the advertisement—the low replication costs make this a viable means of support. Advertising targeted to consumers most likely to respond offers greater value to the advertiser and is possible by observing the information accessed by the consumer to target advertising in this way. Thus, customized content can serve as the basis of customized advertising, increasing the advertiser's willingness to pay.

Characteristics like timeliness, customization, and low distribution cost suggest that the networked distribution of information offers greater consumer value than print media. Although not yet established in the marketplace, this means of distribution may become dominant in the future.

Value of Software

Software differs considerably from content in the value proposition to the consumer. A software application provides the user assistance in some task, including communication or collaboration with other users. From the user perspective, application software performs a *service*, replacing administrative assistance, travel, or alternative services.

EXAMPLE: *A word processor with voice dictation assists the user in creating a written document, providing functionality similar to a secretary taking dictation and transcribing the result. It is important for what it does; that is, its behavior. Similarly, a collaborative application replaces travel, another service.*

From an economic perspective, software is very much a hybrid between goods and services: The supplier cost structure is similar to information goods, while the value to the consumer is characteristic of services. In establishing the value to the customer—and hence the pricing—the factors listed in Table 5.6 should be considered. Information service providers that provide indexing and searching should take into account similar factors.

Some factors in Table 5.6 are intrinsic to the application itself—such as functionality, usability, and quality—while others can only be evaluated in the customer's context. To take full advantage of the latter, the supplier must *price discriminate*, charging different consumers different prices. In this respect, software products are quite distinct from custom-developed applications, for which there is a single customer and the price is determined by negotiation. Price discrimination is more difficult for products, but can be achieved by versioning and other means.

Versioning

A challenge in value pricing is that willingness to pay often varies widely among consumers, so it is difficult to establish a fixed price without significantly reducing revenues. The highest revenue often results from a high price, with a relatively small number of users benefiting from the application. This is unfortunate, given the low cost of replication. More users can benefit from the application,

Table 5.6 Factors affecting the value of a software application to the customer.

Factor	Description	Examples
Usage	How much the application is utilized.	Hours per day, number of simultaneous users, number of occasional users.
Functionality	Capabilities provided that users might otherwise have to do for themselves.	Voice rather than keyboard input for a word processor, user customization of menus.
Quality	Attributes that make the application better than other applications with similar functionality.	Time to perform a calculation, graphics with higher visual impact, less disk space required.
Usability	Ease of use and learning.	Speed of accomplishing task, lower training time or cost.
Impact	Tangible benefits of the application to the customer's organization or environment.	Cost reduction, increasing competitiveness, higher productivity, greater market share for their product or service.

while preserving supplier revenues, with *versioning* [Var97a]. In versioning a portfolio of similar products is offered, with individual versions differentiated by quality or features or performance. The consumers are induced to self-select, so consumers with high willingness to pay choose a higher-priced version.

EXAMPLE: *Airlines use versioning, offering different classes of service (coach, business, first) at different prices. Their pricing tries to induce travelers with a high willingness to pay to choose a higher class, without being too tempted by the lower (and cheaper) classes.*

Software is particularly easy to version. A full-featured and high-performance version—sold at a high price—can be modified to become lesser versions by selectively removing features or adding wait states and sold at a lower price. Notice that, contrary to the airline example, lower-priced versions of software or content actually incur *added* costs to the supplier [Var97a], even though they carry a lower price.

EXAMPLE: *Adobe sells a less-capable version of Photoshop—its image processing application—to makers of digital cameras, who bundle it with their cameras. IBM's and Dragon Systems' voice dictation applications come in versions distinguished by vocabulary size or specialization.*

Versions of information services are easily created by varying timeliness (adding delay) or customization.

EXAMPLE: *U.S. stock quotes are available free on the Web with a twenty-minute delay but are also sold by brokers with no delay. The U.S. Central Intelligence Agency consumes voluminous U.S. taxpayer dollars to scan and digest voluminous public information from around the world and condense it into targeted reports, suggesting that their customization provides high value to the government.*

Versioning may also become common in selling network services, such as Internet access. As discussed in Chapter 11, network services with different performance and quality characteristics (and associated pricing) will become available.

5.5 Government Roles

Thus far, the industry and its challenges have been emphasized. Governments also play a number of roles affecting networked computing, particularly since it is having an increasing impact on society (see Section 2.3.6 on page 35). The evolution of the industry thus depends on government policies, laws, and regulation, and that influence is growing.

5.5.1 Protecting Intellectual Property

In Section 5.4.3 on page 160, the importance of intellectual property to suppliers of networked computing was emphasized. The granting and protection of property rights are government roles. Governments grant limited-term exclusive property rights to inventors and creators to control exploitations of their works. Although creative work doesn't depend on such rights, the incentives to make such investments would be greatly reduced without them, given the high cost of creation and low cost of appropriation (see Section 5.4.1 on page 157).

The primary forms of protected intellectual property are technological innovations (protected by patents) and the original works of authorship (protected by copyright). Mere expenditures of time, money, and energy don't ensure protection by patent or copyright law. A copyrighted work must be original (have a modicum of creativity), and a patented invention must be novel, useful, and nonobvious to someone skilled in the art; and the inventor must apply for a patent and persuade a patent examiner that the specific claims defining the scope of the invention are sound.

Although not discussed further, there are also *trademarks* and *trade secrets*.

Benefits of Copyright

The copyright encourages the creation or authorship of original works of information content or software by granting to the author exclusive control—including the right to sell or license—over its replication. The intent of copyright law is to prevent others from appropriating, replicating, or displaying a work without the permission of the copyright holder. However, there are significant limitations on these rights. A significant one is a *fair use* defense against charges of infringement, which may include actions such as making a copy for students in a class. A copyright does *not* prevent others from *independently* creating or authoring similar works, even based on the same facts or ideas. However, an author does maintain control over a *derivative* work—one based on or derived from another work (for example, a movie based on a novel). A copyright is in force for a long time—typically fifty years beyond the author's lifetime.

The copyright law encourages the creation or authorship of works by providing protections that enhance their commercial value and also their orderly dissemination and use under the control of the copyright holder.

In the United States, an original work is eligible for copyright protection when reduced to tangible form—such as storing to a computer disk or printing on paper—which is called *fixation*. It is not necessary to attach a copyright notice (although a notice increases the legal rights, particularly in other countries, and is thus advisable). The digital representation of information and its dissemination over computer networks have raised sensitive new issues in copyright law. Some say major revisions of copyright law are needed, while others contend that current laws—interpreted in the new context—are adequate.

EXAMPLE: *In the United States, a National Information Infrastructure Task Force's Working Group on Intellectual Property Rights addressed this issue [Oke96]. Their conclusions, while comforting to those deriving income from works published on the Internet, have raised consternation from a broad cross section of interested groups, who fear that every substantial work on the Internet will carry license fees. For example, the Group recommended that a consumer purchasing a digital copyrighted work cannot sell that work to another—a right available to a magazine or book purchaser. The Group also failed to clarify the meaning of fair use in digital media and cautioned against redefining fair use before the technology matures.*

Uncertainty about copyright law has put a damper on the commercial networked distribution of information. However, a more serious and very legitimate concern is the difficulty in enforcing copyright laws in digital media (both networking and storage). Some content providers may have overreacted to this enforcement problem in ways that jeopardize consumer acceptance.

Copyrighting Software

Software can be copyrighted and usually is. The copyright enables the holder to exercise legal control over replicating the software, which she can exploit to license the software to the public. A *software license* lays out specific terms and conditions under which the software can be used or disseminated. There are some creative license provisions—such as *freeware* (software given away but for which copyright is retained) and *shareware* (software for which payment is voluntary)—made economically feasible by free replication and inexpensive distribution. Another licensing option is *copyleft*, which restricts the ability to make derivative works unless they are distributed free of charge. However, not all license provisions are

Intellectual Property as a Strategic Tool

Complex strategies revolve around intellectual property (IP) as a competitive tool. Patent rights allow the holder to decide whether to allow others to use an invention or not and under what terms. Companies not allowed to use an invention may be able to circumvent it by using different techniques, but that may increase their design costs or slow them down. If they do license it, they may be disadvantaged by license fees but may also invent improvements and patent those. A copyright is circumvented by independently achieving similar functionality, but does force a competitor to incur similar creation costs and slow its market entry.

EXAMPLE: *The first spreadsheet program was Visicalc. Since it was an immediate success, the functionality was soon copied by competitive programs, such as Lotus 1-2-3.*

The first IBM personal computer depended on the copyright of software included in read-only memory (called the BIOS) to prevent competitors from creating clones. The functionality of the BIOS was soon

necessarily enforceable, as there are limitations imposed by the copyright laws.

Infringement occurs when users or organization ignore or violate copyright holdings. Egregious infringement—such as setting up a factory to produce and sell large volumes of goods through licit and illicit channels—is called *piracy*. Piracy is a major problem in spite of copyright laws. Individual software companies and the industry as a whole devote considerable effort to uncovering infringement and piracy.

EXAMPLE: *The Software Publishers Association (SPA) is a trade association of software publishers in North America and Europe that works to eliminate software copyright infringement through various means. It conducts an education campaign to inform users and organizations about the copyright laws, their provisions, and their importance, and maintains hotlines for the reporting of abuses. It aggressively pursues suspected abuses through legal action. The SPA estimates that in 1996, 43 percent of the worldwide replicas of software applications were pirated.*

Benefits of Patents

A patent is a grant from the government of the right to make, use, or sell an invention for a fixed period of time after filing (twenty years in most countries). Exactly what is an invention? Informally, it is an idea that is both *novel* and practically *useful*. A patentable invention must have sufficient novelty over the "state of the art" to justify the grant of a monopoly and must not be obvious to one "skilled in the art." Like other forms of property, a patent can be used to prevent others from using the invention or can be licensed for compensation (called a *royalty*).

The patent encourages research and development by rewarding an inventor with exclusive limited-term rights, allowing him or her to exploit the invention for commercial gain or by deriving royalties. Less obvious is the public interest in seeing that inventions are publicly divulged—when the patent is issued or (in some countries) applied for—so that others can improve on them. Without patent protection, inventors might keep inventions secret, even as they are exploited in commercial products. The limited term of the patent gives the inventor a reasonable period of exclusivity and eventually removes exclusive property rights and puts the invention in the public domain for the benefit of all.

Software Patents

Patenting ideas embodied in software is controversial but has important ramifications for industry. Since software is an expression of an algorithm, it is subject to copyright law. Should it also be possible to protect the algorithms embodied in software by patents if they meet the "novel and useful" criteria? Traditionally, scientific principles and mathematical formulas were not eligible for patenting. Software was considered an expression of a mathematical formula and thus could not encompass patentable inventions. This led to a basic quandary: Much of the same functionality can be achieved in hardware or software, so why could hardware embody patentable inventions but not software? In the United States, courts have succumbed to the notion that software can embody patentable inventions. Officially, they are not called software patents, but rather "patents on methods or processes that can be embodied in computer programs," where the words "computer programs" could well be replaced by "digital hardware" without any distinction in the law.

5.5.2 Government Policies and Laws

Technology has tremendous power to do good but also has bad side effects. For example, automobiles transport people efficiently, but they also kill pedestrians. Society tries to accentuate the positive contributions while containing the negative, using public policies and laws as tools.

Networked computing has spawned some capabilities of concern to government policy makers. There is a natural polarization between those who would restrict technologies or their use and those concerned with preserving maximum individual freedom and unfettered innovation.

copied by Phoenix Technologies—and sold to competing suppliers—by carefully isolating the designers in a clean room without access to anything but the product specifications.

In both examples, firms relied on copyright, which other companies eventually circumvented. Patent rights are more fundamental, since they can prevent a competing product from exploiting the invention. Although some patents are fundamental and can't be readily circumvented, others are easy to circumvent but slow down a competitor. In intermediate cases, circumventing patents may force a competitor to increase the cost or reduce the functionality of its products.

Patents and Standardization

As discussed in Section 4.3 on page 132, competing firms increasingly participate in consortia or standardization efforts to define interface standards. This mechanism allows multiple suppliers to participate in designing and marketing complementary interoperable products in a system context. Patents are a major issue in such efforts. Many different arrangements are possible. A common approach is for all parties to agree—as a condition for participation—to license patents freely on "reasonable and equitable" terms. "Reasonable" means roughly to charge royalties sufficient to recover research and development expenses but not exclude competitors, and "equitable" means that differences in royalties charged different companies must be justified.

In a small consortium, patent rights are a key element of the negotiations, including the negotiations on exactly what is included in the standard.

EXAMPLE: *The DVD standard was agreed upon by two groups of companies. Each group had collaboratively created their own standard but decided that a single standard was necessary. They each brought*

Privacy

Personal privacy is threatened in many ways by networked computing. Bringing ordinary transactions on-line creates a wealth of information about personal habits and preferences. Further, by making databases available on-line, information about individuals—previously available from public sources—becomes easier to access.

In the United States, opposition to a national identity card has been based on privacy concerns. On the network, the equivalent is important to avoid fraud or mistaken identity across a network (see Chapter 8), since physical mechanisms for authentication (such as a person's face) are not available. Can a network "digital identity card" survive these forces of opposition?

Some strategies for providing greater value to consumers of information content—such as observing user behavior and tailoring content accordingly—also raise privacy concerns. For example, databases containing personal preferences and habits of individual citizens might be gathered and sold. However, there are big differences in approaches to these problems.

EXAMPLE: *The European Union has issued a directive that regulates what information can be collected on individuals and limits the uses of that information. The United States prefers to defer to industry self-regulation—with uncertain results thus far—except in the case of collection of information from children on-line. Differences in approach are problematic on the global Internet, leading to disputes among governments.*

Protecting Children

In the physical world, it is relatively simple to withhold certain products and services from children. For example, merchants can put questionable merchandise on a high shelf, or they can easily recognize an underage consumer and refuse a sale. These measures don't work on the network.

EXAMPLE: *In 1996 the U.S. Congress passed the Communications Decency Act, which banned "indecent" material from the Internet for the protection of children. There were several problems with this act, including the vagueness of the word "indecent" and the questionable jurisdiction of the United States over the Internet citizenry of other countries. The law was struck down by the U.S. courts as violating the freedom of speech provisions of the Constitution.*

This law—while not the solution—addressed a real problem. An alternative approach is for users or organizations to voluntarily add filtering software to their browsers.

EXAMPLE: *The World Wide Web Consortium has defined a Platform for Internet Content Selection (PICS) standard, in which a Web site can provide self-rating of its content or there can be third-party rating [Res97b]. Concerned individuals or organizations can install software that blocks sites with selected ratings.*

There are civil liberty concerns that PICS might be applied in a draconian fashion by some organizations, thus restricting constitutional protections of free speech. For example, protecting children from "indecent" material is not controversial, but should it be acceptable for a politically conservative private university to block student access to liberal causes (or vice versa)?

Law Enforcement and National Security

There is potential for problems when criminals or rogue nations utilize networked computing technologies for illegal ends. Criminal enterprises, like legal ones, can benefit from these technologies. Of particular concern [CST96a] is technology that ensures confidentiality—for example, encryption, discussed in Chapter 8—and compromises law enforcement tools such as court-ordered wiretaps. Forms of digital cash (see Chapter 8) could aid money laundering. Governments also want to prevent the availability of effective encryption technologies to other governments, which might foil electronic eavesdropping as a tool for furthering national security.

EXAMPLE: *The U.S. government has restricted the export of cryptographic technologies, products, and even related technical information by including them on the U.S. Munitions List maintained by the State Department. Computer and software companies in the United States assert that these controls hamper their export of advanced software products (and benefit overseas competitors*

patent rights to the negotiating table, and royalty arrangements were an integral part of the negotiations on the technologies incorporated.

without similar restrictions) and potentially stifle electronic commerce. Such government intervention may have hampered the security of public networks, making industrial espionage easier.

Public policy in these areas is in a fluid state, with eventual outcomes unclear.

Antitrust Law

Products in networked computing and software have economic characteristics that encourage winner-take-all outcomes, such as network effects and lock-in (see Section 5.3 on page 150). Companies increasingly cooperate in the setting of industry standards (see Section 4.3 on page 132). The acquisition of smaller companies is used as a faster alternative to internal development of complementary technologies (see Section 5.2.3 on page 148). All these observations attract the attention of government policy organs charged with preserving competition in the industry. For example, in the United States, antitrust laws penalize certain business practices that undermine competition. These include willful acquisition or maintenance of monopoly power, entering into agreements that unreasonably restrain trade (price fixing among competitors, for example), or tying the availability of one product in which a firm has market power to the customer's agreement to acquire a second product.

One easily applied tool of antitrust law is blocking mergers, when the market concentration that results is deemed to reduce competition. It is more difficult to separate already existing dominance due to winner-take-all economic forces from dominance due to predatory business practices. In networked computing, players that appear to be dominant at one point are sometimes undercut by later technological discontinuities.

E X A M P L E : *IBM was sued under the antitrust laws in the 1960s, as it was a dominant firm in both computers and applications at the time. However, the shift to decentralized and networked computing severely undercut its dominance.*

In view of the changeable nature of dominance, the apparatus has focused on preventing dominance in one product category from being used unfairly to further dominance in a complementary category.

EXAMPLE: *Microsoft's dominant position in desktop operating systems is viewed by many as a natural consequence of positive feedback in a network industry (see Section 5.3.1 on page 150). Although this dominance has not been directly challenged by antitrust officials, Microsoft has been accused of unfairly leveraging its operating system dominance to create a dominance in some applications.*

A policy dilemma is that product dominance has short-term benefits for the user, who sees better integration and ease of use. Over the longer term, however, it can deter new ideas and better implementations from entering the marketplace. Antitrust laws will likely have growing influence on the industry evolution, whether by outright enforcement or by indirect influence on business practices.

5.6 Open Issues

The changing nature of the industry and the societal discontinuity introduced by the Internet raise many unresolved issues.

5.6.1 How Is the Industry Organized?

As discussed in Chapter 4, the computer industry has shifted toward a more fragmented industrial organization in which different vendors contribute to a horizontally layered infrastructure and a diverse set of applications exploiting this infrastructure. This happened largely in the era of stand-alone computing, and networked computing is recasting the industry again. Network effects put a premium on interoperability across heterogeneous computing platforms, something much less an issue in an earlier era when each computer platform was in essence an independent commercial marketplace. The vision of the future, as discussed in Section 3.5, places unprecedented emphasis on interoperability. Standardization efforts like the IETF (see the sidebar "Internet Engineering Task Force (IETF)" on page 136) and OMG (see the sidebar "Object Management Group" on page 137)—each with wide industry participation—are concrete manifestations of this. The infrastructure for distributed applications can no longer be developed and deployed by individual companies or even small groups of companies; it has to be an industrywide effort.

In this respect, the computer industry is becoming more like the telecommunications industry, which has always recognized network effects and emphasized global standardization (see Section 5.2.4 on page 149). However, the telecommunications industry is also reorganizing (see Chapter 12). Major mergers are creating consolidated global telecommunications service providers offering a diversified portfolio of end-to-end services to multinational corporations. Telecommunications companies have traditionally offered turnkey applications, such as telephony and video conferencing, rather than commodity data transport services. This directly collides with the computer industry, where applications are sold independently of infrastructure.

The final outcome is not clear. What is the most effective industrial organization for the computer industry in the networked computing era and the telecommunications industry in an era of globalization, greater competition, and the growing importance of data services and computer applications? The organization of both industries will be much different, and the two industries may be more consolidated.

5.6.2 Sovereignty and the Global Internet

Political units are organized around geography, because historically interaction and socialization has been limited by geography. While the Internet is global in reach, governments and laws are territorial. When two users (or a supplier and a consumer) access the network in different jurisdictions, they are each operating under different laws. Increasingly, groups coalesce around interests or expertise without regard to geography (see Section 2.3.1 on page 19). Territorial laws and policies are increasingly ineffective in the face of this globalization. How, for example, do we enforce tax laws, restrictive policies on content, or prohibitions against encryption on a global network? The solution may be delegation of more government functions to international institutions, continuing a trend of the past century.

5.6.3 The Language of the Internet

Since the Internet is global, an important question is whether there will be a dominant language for collaboration and commerce on the Internet, or whether a diversity of languages will be preserved [Oud97]. There are strong network effects in language and positive feedback effects that tend to result in a dominant language. Many multinational companies and conferences choose English as the "official" language. On the other hand, native speakers of other languages would properly like to preserve their languages for Internet content and commerce. A technical solution would be automatic translation, but unfortunately, this technology is not yet sufficiently accurate.

5.6.4 Archiving Digital Information

Libraries have preserved the works of literature and many historical documents on paper media, but how will archiving of digital information occur [Kah97]? Fortunately, data can be replicated and hence preserved (see Section 5.4.1 on page 157). However, this begs the question of who does this archiving and who pays. Fortunately, publishing information on the network eases the logistical problem, as it can be systematically archived in a central repository.

However, archiving data is only part of the problem, since the meaning of the data—turning it into information—can only be extracted with the help of the application that created the data. This means that both data and associated applications must be archived—a technically feasible but daunting task. Does this mean that society must preserve instances of every computer platform and operating system in order to be able to run those archived applications?

5.6.5 A New Partnership

Many business and societal issues and problems emerge from networked applications, some of which have been discussed in this chapter. Doubtless there are many more. As with earlier technologies, the technology itself can mitigate many problems it creates. Further, there is an opportunity to coordinate new applications with changes in organizations, thus making more effective use of networked computing and minimizing adverse factors.

What is needed is a new partnership between technologists and other disciplines, such as law, economics, public policy, and business, to address problems and opportunities. Those responsible for policy or legislative initiatives need greater understanding of technology (I hope this book can help) and their side effects, and greater warning of potential problems and issues so they can be properly debated. Technologists must take a greater interest in the societal impacts of their work, which expand tremendously with the networking of computers. Technologists should draw attention to problems and feasible solutions and should work to mitigate undesirable side effects. Business and organizational experts should collaborate with technologists to define more effective means of melding applications with their societal and organizational context. Most of all, a new partnership will allow all the interrelated public, organizational, and technological issues to be properly and expeditiously addressed.

Further Reading

[Sha98] is a recent book that overlaps this chapter, focusing on the strategic implications for managers in the computing and communications industries, as well as customers of those industries. [OHE96a] contains much valuable information about specific products and vendors in client/server computing. A beginning text with a modern treatment of information economics is [Var87]. [Eco96] is a good introduction to network effects and [Dif97] is an excellent view into government policy implications for the industry.

Application Software

6

Applications were discussed in Chapter 2 from the perspective of the users and organizations that benefit from them. Applications don't just happen; they have to be conceptualized by someone who recognizes a need, needs must be analyzed to determine requirements, and software implementation has to be developed (see Section 3.4.2 on page 106). Most business applications are developed (or at least customized) for a rather specific need of an enterprise and its suppliers and customers. To ensure that the application meets those needs, works correctly, has adequate performance, and is sufficiently flexible and maintainable, it is important to follow a rigorous development process. It doesn't end there, either, as the maintenance and upgrade of the software is an ongoing process.

Application software can be acquired in a number of ways, which have their strengths and weaknesses from organizational, technical, and business perspectives. Like all of networked computing—but even more so—the business arrangements and associated technical approaches that surround the acquisition of application software are rapidly evolving. There is a trend toward outsourcing application development and reuse of software across different applications, and this is supported by new and evolving software development methodologies.

6.1 Some Overriding Issues

Application software development has to focus on much more than achieving the desired functionality. The development addresses other issues such as performance, flexibility, maintainability, etc. (see Section 3.4.2 on page 106). In addition, the various stakeholders have to be concerned with the costs, the risks, and the time to completion of the development process.

6.1.1 Software Complexity

A primary concern in application (as well infrastructure) design is complexity. The application may be decomposed into a large number of modules that interact in complicated ways, making it difficult for the designer to keep track of everything and understand and anticipate all possible behaviors. The characteristics of a good architecture discussed in Chapter 4 are important, in part as a way to contain this complexity.

There are many reasons why complexity is such an issue [Boo94]:

- The problem domain addressed by the application is often complex. The application is inherently no simpler than the problem.

- Today, software systems are designed top-down, from scratch. In much more complex domains—such as the organization of an economy—top-down design has proven ineffective. A self-organizing approach, such as the marketplace, has coped better with the complexity.

- Many other human activities are more constrained. For example, each economic agent operates under the constraints of laws and regulations, such as accounting standards, building codes, the uniform commercial code, etc. Although software suffers the curse of not being so constrained, a trend in modern software is to artificially impose more structure and standards.

- Human organizations are adaptable, because people are intelligent and adaptable. If some unexpected circumstance or problem arises, the people in the organization can react. In contrast, computers must be instructed in advance on how to deal with every eventuality. (In practice, a computer may just give up and turn the problem over to a human to deal with. This shouldn't happen often.)

- Most systems people deal with are continuous; they follow pre-dictable paths. Software is discrete, and in addition to having an astronomically large number of possible conditions, a program jumps among them in complicated ways. It is not feasible to exhaustively test all possible conditions, and unpredictable or undesirable behavior is inevitable.

- An application software development is a large team effort (of tens or even hundreds of thousands of programmers), with all the management problems that result. (The popular culture thinks of programming as a solitary and antisocial activity, but this is far from reality.) To be successful, the team must remain in close contact with the societal or business context for which the application is intended.

- A networked computing system integrates equipment and soft-ware from many different vendors (see Section 5.1 on page 139). Coordination, discipline, and a carefully conceived architecture design are necessary ingredients for success.

A primary technique for managing complexity is modularity (see Section 4.1.6 on page 121). Modularity occurs at different granulari-ties, starting with the separation of hardware from software, the separation of the hardware into hosts and network, and the separa-tion of software into application and infrastructure. Each of these large modules is hierarchically subdivided. This chapter deals with the modularity of the application software.

6.1.2 Acquiring an Application

Some distinct approaches to developing or otherwise acquiring application software are listed in Table 6.1. These are not mutually exclusive choices; rather, they can be combined in various ways.

EXAMPLE: *Most custom-developed business applications incorpo-rate a commercial DBMS (see "Shared Data Tier: Database Man-agement" on page 94) into a custom development, and ERP is an example of a commercial off-the-shelf (COTS) acquisition that is*

Table 6.1 Some distinct approaches to acquiring application software.

Approach	Description	Comments
Purchase	Buy an existing application, and configure it for local requirements.	Often termed *commercial off-the-shelf* (COTS), this is the minimum-cost approach, because development cost is split among multiple deployed applications. The organization and its processes must be molded to the application. Since other organizations have purchased the same application, there is little opportunity to gain competitive advantage.
Outsourced development	Hire another company to develop the application to specification.	With a fixed-cost contract, this carries low financial risk. However, the developers may not be as familiar with or concerned about detailed organizational requirements. There is opportunity to reengineer the process along with the application. Simply automating existing processes is rarely the best solution. The contractor's experience with similar applications improves the chances for success. The contractor can apply its experience to other contracts, reducing but not eliminating competitive advantage.
Internal development	Develop the software application in an internal information systems department.	This approach is most likely to result in an application closely matched to needs. However, this responsiveness may come at the expense of greater time to completion and development cost. The development organization is well positioned to maintain the application and manage future upgrades and extensions.

configurable and customizable (see "Enterprise Resource Planning" on page 60). Software components and frameworks provide a way to mix and match COTS and custom with a finer granularity (see Section 6.2.2 on page 198).

As intimated in Table 6.1, the appropriate path to acquiring application software is a crucial tactical and strategic decision, one that balances risks (failure, cost overruns, delays, failure to meet organizational needs), cost (development, maintenance, and upgrade), and the flexibility for future upgrades and extensions. The dimension most difficult to manage is the trade-off between meeting precise requirements on the one hand and cost and risk on the other. This reflects itself in two dimensions:

- *Internal vs. outsourced development vs. COTS:* Internal development is most likely to meet the precise requirements, but that benefit usually comes at a higher price (both monetary and risk). It is difficult for an internal development group to resist closely tracking expanding requirements, resulting in longer development cycles and more assumed risk. At the other extreme, major requirements compromises are likely with COTS. Outsourced development lies somewhere between—generally, requirements are flexible but have to be fixed at the start of the project (the developer will resist changes thereafter).

- *Fixed vs. time-and-materials pricing:* This consideration relates to the business arrangements between the acquirer and developer. In the fixed-price model, the acquirer contracts to pay a fixed price for a finished application that meets specific acceptance tests. In time-and-materials pricing, the acquirer pays an hourly rate for the developer's actual time spent. The fixed-price model has low risk to the acquirer, but does not readily accommodate requirements changes. Also, as discussed in Section 5.4 on page 157, the developer will strive to couple the negotiated price to the value of the application to the acquirer, rather than development costs. With time-and-materials pricing, the risk of cost overrun is transferred to the purchaser, but price is directly coupled to costs. This model better accommodates changing and expanding requirements but can increase time to completion and risk.

These conflicting goals result in a constant quest for the best mixture of COTS and custom-developed technology. Software components and frameworks appear promising as a way to better balance the conflicting goals (see Section 6.2.2 on page 198).

6.1.3 Development Methodology: Decomposition vs. Assembly

As illustrated in Figure 6.1 and defined in Table 6.2, there are two diametrically opposite methodologies for developing an application: decomposition and assembly. Normally these approaches are mixed.

ANALOGY: *Establishing the modularity of a software application is analogous to organizing a company. Making the company self-contained—developing all its departments from scratch—is decomposition. Outsourcing every function—development, marketing, manufacture, sales, etc.—and not hiring any internal employees is assembly. In practice, the two approaches are mixed. Manufacturing may be outsourced, but marketing will be performed internally.*

EXAMPLE: *A common methodology for business applications is to incorporate an off-the-shelf DBMS (see "File System" on page 91) and add custom-designed application logic. The application logic module is itself developed by either assembly or—more likely today—decomposition. This illustrates that if the modularity is hierarchical (see Section 4.1.2 on page 117), at each level of hierarchy the development of the next lower level can use either decomposition or assembly.*

Assembly and decomposition as development methodologies support the distinct business models discussed in Section 6.1.2 on page 179: Decomposition is custom development, whereas assembly uses COTS, with the added step of integration of the purchased components. Assembly in its purest form is not likely: If all the com-

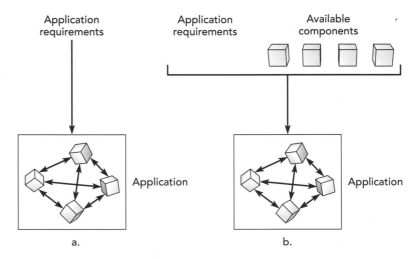

Figure 6.1 Two application development approaches: (a) decomposition and (b) assembly.

Table 6.2 Description of three methodologies for developing an application.

Approach	Description	Comments
Decomposition	Starting with application requirements, do an unconstrained decomposition into interacting modules. Custom implement and integrate those modules to realize the application.	This is the most common approach today, particularly when developed in one organization in its entirety. Decomposition is supported by the object-oriented programming methodology (see Section 6.2.1 on page 190).
Assembly	Find software components (subsystems available for purchase) that approximate application requirements. Assemble and integrate those components to realize the application.	The components are usually purchased from outside vendors and locally configured. Incorporating a commercial DBMS (see Section 6.3.1 on page 207) is an example of this. For application logic, this is supported by software components (see Section 6.2.2 on page 198).
Mixture	Usually an application is developed by assembling custom-designed modules with purchased components. The application and the custom modules are constrained by the component's functionality and interfaces.	For example, ERP applications provide a framework and components—with a high degree of configurability—but also allow custom modules to be added (see "Enterprise Resource Planning" on page 60). Often an experienced professional services firm is hired to design the business process and configure the ERP components.

ponents can be purchased to assemble an application, then it is likely a turnkey application can also be purchased. Thus, some custom development is usually associated with assembly, and in reality the possibilities span a continuum between decomposition and assembly. Assembly may be used only for an initial prototype, followed by internal development to refine either application functionality or performance.

Regardless of how the modularity is determined, the modules must be made interoperable in the *integration* phase. The typical methodology is to test and refine modules independently and then start grouping them to test interoperability. Where interoperability difficulties are discovered, modules may have to be modified, retested, and reintegrated.

Decomposition: Object-Oriented Programming

Decomposition is the most popular development methodology and is supported by *object-oriented programming* (OOP). In this case, the basic modules are called *objects*, which have well-defined interfaces that support abstraction and encapsulation (see Section 4.1 on page 113). OOP has three primary development phases:

- Architecture, which takes the form of decomposition of an application into its constituent objects. Typically this decomposition is hierarchical, with objects coming together to form modules, those modules coming together to form larger modules, etc. In this view, objects form the lowest level (finest granularity) of the hierarchy.

- Implementation of each object, with the goal of independence in implementation of the different objects (a separation of concerns).

- Integration of objects to make them interoperable, beginning with small groups and moving eventually to the application as a whole.

These phases overlap and together constitute only the development portion of the overall application life cycle (see Section 3.4.2 on page 106). OOP is described in more detail in Section 6.2.1 on page 190.

Assembly: Software Components

While OOP is currently popular, in computing there is always something new on the horizon. Today, one new trend is *component software*. Like objects, components form the basic modularity of the application, but the programming methodology is quite different. Components are presumed to predate the application and are purchased from a different company. The application is assembled from these existing components, often adding custom-implemented modules. This will be called *component-oriented programming* (COP) here (the terminology is nonstandard).

EXAMPLE: *In the future there will be available components representing typical business entities, such as the customer, account, invoice, purchase order, etc. A business application might then be assembled from these components, together with a DBMS. The development process will focus on configuring and integrating these components into a working application.*

In COP, the architecture phase takes the form "how can existing, available components be incorporated into the application." Ideally, development focuses on the integration of components, although it will typically be necessary to implement some customized subsystems.

Assembly offers considerably less freedom than decomposition. The application architecture is constrained by the desire to use existing components, and there are likely constraints on functionality and performance imposed by available components. For this reason, COP is viable only if there is a vibrant market in components, so that each development has available a reasonable diversity of components at a quality and price improved by competition [Szy98]. Today this market largely does not exist, except in the sense of some very large-grain components like the DBMS. However, the industry is working intensively on the underlying technology and standards that will enable a component marketplace (see the sidebar "Component Standards").

To summarize, in business terms the difference between OOP and COP is usually a make or buy decision. OOP focuses on decomposition into internally implemented and integrated modules, while COP focuses on assembly, configuration, and integration of purchased components. In practice, these approaches are mixed.

6.1.4 Software Reuse

Size and complexity of new applications are growing dramatically, and as a result, the costs of software developments and the length of the development cycle are often unacceptable. It is imperative that ways be found to contain the required effort and at the same time make applications more amenable to future change.

Component Standards

Today, three competing component de facto standards are emerging: CORBA from the Object Management Group, Java and JavaBeans from Sun, and DCOM from Microsoft. Each comes from a different perspective and strength: enterprise applications for OMG, the internet technologies for Sun, and the desktop applications from Microsoft [Szy98]. Each is working to expand its domain and hedging by providing bridges to the others.

The success of these competing standards will reflect secondary network effects, much like the operating system (see Section 5.3.1 on page 150). Each is working hard to achieve critical mass, where positive feedback kicks in. Application developers will prefer the standards with the largest repository of available components, and component vendors will prefer the environment with the largest market for applications. Positive feedback will create a tendency toward the winner-take-all effect. This is a classic standards war in its infancy.

ANALOGY: *The telephone industry faced a similar problem 50 to 70 years ago. Using the manual connection of phone calls by operators, every man, woman, and child on earth would have to become a telephone operator in a relatively few decades. Of course, what would happen in practice is a stifling of the growth of the service, which was avoided by direct dialing and the automation of call switching, eliminating the need for operators except in unusual situations.*

A key to reducing the cost and development time is *software reuse*. The objective is to avoid, as much as possible, the custom architecture and/or the implementation phases of application development, and instead adopt and modify an existing architecture and/or implementation. With successful reuse, the development focus shifts to assembly and integration (as is already the case with infrastructure equipment and software).

One significant opportunity is expanding the role of the software infrastructure, capturing much generic functionality required by all applications and making applications easier to develop. Aspects of this infrastructure most relevant to applications are discussed in later chapters.

Reuse is also achieved by software components, which are reused in many applications.

ANALOGY: *An electronic equipment manufacturer, in designing a new product, doesn't start from scratch. A number of electronic components and integrated circuits can be purchased. A major part of the hardware design is assembly of these components into the new product.*

Another dimension, not previously discussed, is *reusable architectures*. The idea here is to recognize that an application is rarely totally unique, so there may be an opportunity to share both an architecture and components.

The architecture is much more closely tied to the application and its requirements than are components. While there are some opportunities to reuse architectures, the reuse of components should be much more widespread.

EXAMPLE: *Many business applications share common elements, such as the customer, address, invoice, payment, etc. Components supporting these common entities can be used in many different applications. On the other hand, these components are combined in different ways in each application, say, supply-chain management and an internal accounting system. These applications demand distinct architectures.*

An example of a reusable architecture is a *software framework*. A framework is, roughly speaking, a reusable architecture for a particular application domain, bundled with objects or components that may already fit within that architecture.

EXAMPLE: *Enterprise resource planning (ERP) applications follow this model (see "Enterprise Resource Planning" on page 60). Each ERP application, such as supply-chain management, accounting, or human resource management, is a specific framework designed to support this business process, together with a set of objects or components that fit within that framework. Each framework and constituent components are configurable and can fit different business requirements. On the other hand, each tightly constrains the business process that it automates, as there are limits to configurability.*

Components and frameworks are complementary, since components fit into the framework and also constrain it. The term "constrain" is appropriate here, as the key to software reuse is to dampen the cherished freedom of programmers, causing them to conform to existing standards and designs. Choosing a framework limits the available components to those fitting in that framework.

6.1.5 Location of Data and Computation

Recall from Chapter 3 that the infrastructure supports four key capabilities on behalf of the application: communication across space, communication across time, computation and logic (together called processing), and the human-computer interface. The physical infrastructure has components that support these functions; namely, the hosts (computation and logic), storage managed by hosts (communication across time), the network interconnecting hosts (communication across space), and the human-computer interface (graphical displays, keyboards, pointing devices, microphones, TV cameras, speakers, etc.).

An application is decomposed into modules that are partitioned across a collection of hosts (presuming multiple hosts—see "Administration" on page 104). One question is how this partitioning is done.

EXAMPLE: *One such partitioning was discussed in Section 3.2.2 on page 92. In this approach, the partitioning is into* shared data, application logic, *and* presentation, *each of these managed by a different host. The shared data may be made available to multiple applications, or it may be specific to one application. For example, customer information may be needed by several applications, such as accounting (for invoicing and payments), sales (to manage contacts), and shipping (to ship products). Thus, this information may be kept in a data repository to be shared among different applications. On the other hand, information about unpaid invoices is needed in only one accounting application and may be kept on the same host as that application logic.*

Partitioning is important from several perspectives, such as ease of administration (Chapter 3) and performance (Chapter 10). In this chapter, the relationship between the data managed by the application and the application logic is the overriding consideration. This has a significant impact on the development methodology and the flexibility and extensibility of the resulting application.

There are two diametrically opposed models in wide usage: *tightly coupled* and *loosely coupled* processing and data. The difference is illustrated by the following analogy.

ANALOGY: *Consider an organization that is processing (using human workers, analogous to hosts) large volumes of paper records (analogous to data). The tightly coupled model divides the records into small pieces, each managed by a single worker, with those records stored in that worker's desk drawer. In the loosely coupled model, all the records are stored in a centralized vault in the basement, and each worker assigned work relative to a given record must retrieve it from the vault, process it, and immediately return the result to the vault. Tight or loose coupling refers to the proximity of workers and the records they access.*

The tightly coupled model is more expeditious and time efficient for the individual worker but raises significant coordination issues, for example, if two workers need to access the same record for different purposes. The loosely coupled model allows records to be better safeguarded. For example, the vault can be fire protected, the records can be logged as they leave or enter the vault, backup copies can be maintained (in case a record is accidently destroyed), etc. Also, the centralized vault makes coordination more straightforward: The keeper of the vault can check the same records out to two or more workers and keep track of who has them, who has made modifications, etc.

OOP utilizes the tightly coupled model, as it associates data and the processing of data together within an object. It is widely used for developing the presentation and application logic portions of the application. Storage and manipulation of large masses of data are the domain of the DBMS (see "File System" on page 91), following the loosely coupled model, where management of data is considered a separate function from its manipulation. These approaches are actually complementary and can be mixed. The application logic may use a tightly coupled model internally but also interact with a loosely coupled shared data repository (see Section 3.2.2 on page 92).

6.2 Tightly Coupled Data and Processing

Both the object and component programming methodologies tightly couple processing with data. As explained in Section 6.1.5 on page 187, this allows the structure of the data to be highly customized to meet application functionality or performance requirements, but it precludes easily sharing the data with other applications.

6.2.1 Object-Oriented Programming

Object-oriented programming emphasizes the decomposition of an application into modules called objects, which encapsulate both data and behavior that manipulates that data. Each object models some well-defined and self-contained functionality within the application, with the objective of separation of concerns among the different objects. Objects interact to achieve the higher-level functions of the application.

OOP is supported by object-oriented programming languages, representative examples being C++, Java, and Smalltalk. A *programming language* is a way to describe the operation of applications in a way the computer can understand and act upon. This book does not discuss programming and programming languages per se, but rather focuses on architecture.

What Is an Object?

Recall from Table 3.1 on page 78 that an architecture incorporates three aspects: decomposition, functionality, and interaction. OOP follows precisely this approach. The decomposition is into objects, the functionality of each object is defined by its interface, and the interaction results when one object exploits the functionality of another. Objects encompass all the principles of modularity described in Section 4.1.6 on page 121.

An important aspect of OOP is to align the decomposition of objects with the physical world that forms the application context. The architectural challenge is to define software objects within the application architecture that mirror real-world "objects" within the application context, making the transition from physical world to the software modeling or representation seamless.

Objects in the Physical World

As a way to understand the desired interfaces and interaction of software objects, it is useful to look first at objects in the physical world. Subsequently, software objects can be endowed with similar characteristics and capabilities.

Looking around, you probably see many "objects." In common usage, this means things that have a self-identity distinct from other objects and that individually serve some useful function, but also serve higher purposes by interacting among themselves.

E X A M P L E :   *A clock is an object that keeps track of time, but it is most useful if it interacts with a person, who observes that time. A purchase order is an object that expresses the desire to purchase a specific product or service from a vendor, but it is most useful when it interacts with that vendor, who then ships the product or provides the service. A bank account is an object that serves as a repository for money (but also reflects its time value), and it is most useful when it interacts with its owner to make deposits and withdrawals. In this pragmatic view, even a person (a customer or employee) can be considered an "object."*

From these examples, there are two distinct types of objects: those that have a physical manifestation but can be modeled (like a clock) and those that can be logical entities without a physical manifestation (like a purchase order or bank account). The latter can as easily be represented by data and processing. Physical objects can be modeled, but not represented, using data and processing (see the sidebar "Modeling and Representation").

Some objects can be customized or configured (like the clock, where the current time can be set), and other objects are immutable (like a brick), meaning they never change. Other objects are dynamic, meaning they do change with time. Usually the customization or change in an object can be captured by *attributes*, which are changeable properties owned by the object. The *behavior* of an object describes the manner in which its attributes change, particularly as time passes and as it interacts with other objects. Often, there is a direct coupling between this interaction and behavior.

E X A M P L E :   *A clock is an object that serves to tell the time. One of its attributes is the time it displays on its face, which reflects the passage of time. Another attribute is the energy remaining in its battery, which decreases with time and which determines how long it will continue to run before it stops. One of its behaviors is to change its display attribute. You can interact with the clock to set its time (change its display attribute to some desired value).*

Modeling and Representation

In a software application, there is a fundamental difference between modeling and representation. Real-world objects that are logical or informational in nature, such as an invoice, bank account, money, or a memorandum, can be directly represented by data within an application. This representation is equivalent to a physical representation, such as writing on paper. Real-world objects that only take a physical form, such as a motor or automobile, can be modeled by data and logic, but not represented. The model may be able to predict how the object behaves in the real world, but it will never replace it by performing the equivalent function.

Both modeling and representation have important roles. Modeling is often used for the control of physical objects.

E X A M P L E :   *In an automated highway system, the application may control various parameters, such as traffic light timing. For this purpose, the application may model the behavior of automobiles as they pass through the traffic lights.*

Table 6.3 Definition of some terms relating to object-oriented programming.

Term	Definition
Object	The smallest module in an object-oriented programming methodology. It may model or represent an object in the application environment.
Attribute	A numerical value or other data that summarizes some externally visible property of an object.
Method	An action available at an object interface for other objects to invoke (with parameters and return values).
Interface	The set of methods and attributes of an object, usually accompanied by documentation as to the functionality of the object and its methods.
Class	What is in common among a set of objects with the same interface and functionality. All objects with the same class share the same implementation and are called *instances* of the class.

In summary, an object (viewed in this abstract way) has two characteristics: its attributes and its behavior. It is these two characteristics that should be captured in a software object that represents or models an object from the physical world.

Software Objects

Software objects also have attributes and behavior, and they interact with other objects to realize some higher-order function. There is quite a bit of terminology surrounding objects that is summarized in Table 6.3. One useful feature of software objects is that they can model or represent objects in the environment of the application. This correspondence between environment and software makes applications more natural to design and implement.

EXAMPLE: *In commerce, customers and suppliers exchange goods for payment, where the payment can be a simple cash transaction or a more formal exchange of purchase order (authorization to ship goods and promise to pay), invoice (demand for payment), and payment. In electronic commerce (see Section 2.6.3 on page 64), except for physical goods, each of these objects from the physical world can be represented by software objects. There may be a*

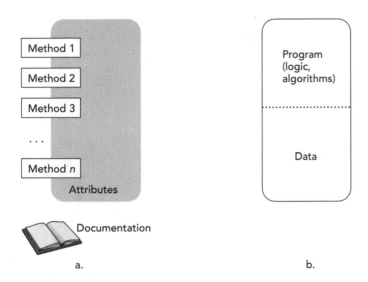

Figure 6.2 (a) External and (b) internal views of a software object.

> *software object representing the purchase order, another representing the invoice, and another representing the payment. In addition, within the electronic commerce application there are likely to be other objects representing the customer or supplier and also representing the goods being shipped.*
>
> *The attributes of these objects customize them to a specific purpose. For example, a purchase order has attributes such as a description of the goods being purchased, the agreed price, the name and address of the supplier (recipient of the purchase order) and the customer (originator of the purchase order), etc.*

The structure of a software object is shown in Figure 6.2, from an external perspective (a)—consisting of its interface and documentation—and an implementation perspective (b). An object has an interface (as described in Section 4.1 on page 113) that serves two purposes: It provides guidance to another interacting object, and it provides guidance to the implementer as to what attributes and methods have been promised.

What does the interface look like? Like the modules illustrated in Section 4.1 on page 113, an object offers a set of actions, each with parameters and return values, which are called *methods* or *operations*. (In this book, they are called methods.) In addition, objects may have attributes, which are numerical values or other data that are visible outside the object. Methods may be provided to examine or change the value of an attribute.

EXAMPLE: *An object representing a bank account will contain data representing attributes such as the account balance, the account number, and the customer owning the account. The actions include reading the account balance or making a deposit or withdrawal from the account.*

Internally, an object consists of data managed by the object (which includes the attributes and frequently other data as well) as well as program logic that operates on that data to implement the methods. Through encapsulation, the details of the implementation are hidden from other objects (see Section 4.1.5 on page 121).

One object interacts with another by invoking one of the methods at its interface, providing parameters and receiving return values. This is the same approach to interaction as described in Section 4.1.3 on page 118.

ANALOGY: *A pocket calculator provides an example of an object. It provides a set of actions such as add, subtract, multiply, divide, and clear. Each action is accompanied by a set of parameters, which are typically a pair of numbers to add, subtract, multiply, or divide. Each action has a return value, which is the result of the arithmetic operation and appears on the calculator's display.*

In OOP, every entity in an application is an object that interacts with other objects. This means that many things you might not think of as having "actions" must be cast into this form. The only way to interact with an object is through its methods, even for simple things like directly reading or modifying an attribute.

EXAMPLE: *A software object representing a driver's license would have attributes such as the name of the person, picture (which is a digitally represented image), address, date of birth, and a license number. The way these attributes are established in the first place, or changed, is through a set of methods that change attributes. For example:*

```
set_name: new_name -> status;
set_birth_date: new_birth_date -> status;
```

In these methods, the returned status *simply indicates whether the action was successful, or it describes some exceptional condition that may have occurred. The analogy to these methods for a license in the physical world would be to first erase the old attribute and then write in the replacement value for that attribute.*

A method may encapsulate much behind-the-scenes processing not visible at the interface. The set_birth_date *method, beyond changing the attribute, would doubtless do error checking. For example, it would check that the month is an integer between 1 and 12, and whether the date is reasonable (for example, a birth date more than 130 years ago or in the future might be rejected and that fact noted in the* status *return value). The method might also cross-check the license holder's birth date against government birth records to be sure it matches.*

Class: What Is in Common among Objects

In both the physical world and networked computing, there are frequently two or more objects (often *many* more) that share much in common.

E X A M P L E :   *A house typically has a clock in each room, where all the clocks have the same functionality but differ only in cosmetic ways. They may also differ as to the current value of their attributes, such as displayed time (if they are set differently) or energy stored in the battery.*

A typical bank will have a large number of savings or checking accounts with the same interface (methods and attributes) and same internal implementation, and differing only in the current value of their attributes. Each account has a different owner, a different balance, a different date of last deposit, etc.

A set of objects that share the same interface (methods, parameters, and return values), and have the same behavior, are said to have the same *class*. This class has a name, which is descriptive of the purpose and function of objects from this class.

EXAMPLE: *Class* `Bank_account` *describes a set of objects that represent bank accounts, one for each customer.*

When a number of objects have a common class, each of those objects is said to be an *instance* of the class.

EXAMPLE: *If a bank has customers Joe, Mary, and Sylvestor, each of whom has an account at the bank, then the application may have three objects that are instances of class* `Bank_account`. *One of them represents Joe's* `Bank_account`, *so, for example, its* `Customer_name` *attribute is "Joe."*

In practical terms, a class includes a description of an interface and a program implementing objects in that class. The class allows a single implementation to represent all objects that are instances of that class.

Visual Modeling of Application Architectures

OOP lends itself to visual representations of objects and the pattern of interaction among objects. Similarly, a diagram can show classes and relationships among those classes. A visual modeling language provides a standard way to do this, much as building architects represent architectural features in their blueprints. Visual modeling has two major advantages:

- Programmers can communicate ideas to one another, and document their designs, using these diagrams.

- Visual modeling tools can assist the designer in generating and manipulating these visual representations.

EXAMPLE: *The Unified Modeling Language (UML) is a standard modeling language [Har97]. A simple example of a UML diagram is shown in Figure 6.3. This diagram displays some classes, and the relationships among these classes are represented by arrows.*

Dealing with Legacy Systems

OOP methodologies have become popular over the past couple of decades, but applications created previously used different meth-

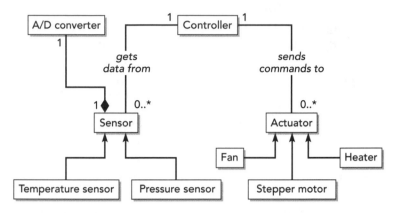

Figure 6.3 Example of a UML diagram applied to a building climate control system.

odologies. In enterprise computing, this represents a problem and a challenge, since there is a need to integrate different data and applications at the department level into applications automating business processes (see Section 2.6.2 on page 56). It is usually not cost effective, nor even advisable, to replace all these legacy applications. In an operational system, making radical changes is both expensive and risky.

If legacy applications need to be integrated with an application that utilizes OOP, it is possible to encapsulate them within objects in the new, integrated application (see Section 4.1.5 on page 121). Whatever interfaces were built into the legacy application can be recast as an object interface within the OOP application.

ANALOGY: *Rather than replace an old building, a cheaper and quicker approach is to renovate it. By adding a veneer of new paint, ceiling tiles, exterior siding, etc., the basic structural elements of the building can be preserved, while making the building appear to be new.*

However, the problem of partially replacing legacy applications, or integrating them with other applications, is usually much more difficult than this analogy suggests. Here is a better one.

ANALOGY: *In trying to renovate and cosmetically tune your house, you discover that (by basic architectural concept) it will never really meet your needs. A better approach would be to tear it down and start over. Unfortunately, there is the problem of where you live in the meantime.*

Especially business applications must be operational at all times—the business depends on it. Changing a portion of a legacy application, or integrating it with another, is an extraordinarily difficult challenge akin to rebuilding an ocean liner as it crosses the ocean.

Programming in OOP

Programming is the task of describing in detail what the computer is to do and what data to manipulate. An OOP language (such as C++ or Java) can express the notions of object, interface, class, etc., and describe the encapsulated implementation of object classes.

ANALOGY: *A program is analogous to a cooking recipe, with a set of actions in a specific order.*

There are two complementary aspects to any program, as listed in Table 6.4. One part (the algorithm) describes behavior, and the other (the data type) describes the data manipulated.

6.2.2 Software Components and Frameworks

Software reuse has the objective of reducing the cost and risk of developing new applications by either adopting the architecture of similar applications or modules used by other applications, or both (see Section 6.1.4 on page 185). While reuse was one of the original motivations for OOP, in practice it does not achieve much reuse. Software components and frameworks offer hope that much greater levels of reuse can be achieved (see "Subsystems and Components" on page 80). The basic idea is quite old (see the sidebar

Table 6.4 Two basic elements of a program.

Element	Description and purpose	Analogy
Algorithms	A specified sequence of steps designed to solve a problem (see Chapter 7). The algorithm determines the behavior of the program.	A recipe specifying the steps in preparing spaghetti—such as roll the dough, cut the noodles, boil the noodles, etc.—is an algorithm. These steps determine what the cook does and in what order.
Data types	A specification of the structure of any data manipulated by the algorithms (see "Data and Information in Layers" on page 128). Languages provide basic types of data, such as integers, characters, etc., and also ways to assemble these into more complicated types (such as a character string, which is an ordered set of characters).	The description of the ingredients manipulated in the recipe, such as the flour, the tomatoes, etc. The recipe also specifies more complicated ingredients, such as noodles, by indicating how they can be assembled (by combining flour and other ingredients in a particular way).

"Components, Frameworks, and the Industrial Revolution") but conceptually difficult to pull off in software because of its complexity. Some promises of component/framework technology include

- *Quality:* A component or framework used in many applications has been more thoroughly tested and has accumulated more operational experience.

- *Time to deployment or time to market:* Application development reverts to merely assembling components within a framework, possibly adding custom-designed components.

- *Low cost:* Components and frameworks benefit from being employed in multiple applications, thus amortizing their development cost.

- *Flexibility:* Components can be upgraded or replaced, or their assembly modified, to upgrade the application.

- *Competition:* In a market for components, different vendors will compete within each component category, increasing quality and reducing prices. The ability to mix and match components

Components, Frameworks, and the Industrial Revolution

The idea of components and frameworks for the physical world dates to the industrial revolution. Before that, products were handcrafted, meaning each instance of the product was individually fabricated by a craftsman. One innovation leading to the industrial revolution was standardized, interchangeable components.

EXAMPLE: *A particular automobile is a standard assembly of components (motor, steering wheel, axle, etc.) held together by a standard framework (steel frame and shell). To put out a new model, the designer may minimize effort by making a modification to an existing framework and adding new sheet metal. The manufacturer also uses many of the same components for different cars. Much of the new car's design is reused from the older design.*

Standardized components in a reusable framework led to

may reduce customer lock-in (see "Supplier and Industry Lock-In" on page 155).

What Is a Software Component?

Software components are reusable modules assembled to construct an application (see "Subsystems and Components" on page 80). Components (as well as frameworks) are usually developed, maintained, and supported by an outside vendor, as a separate business opportunity. Purchased as a product, they have to be accepted as is, although they may be highly configurable. The application developer may purchase or license components from a number of vendors and assemble them into an application together with custom-designed modules.

EXAMPLE: *An example of a component is an editor. Many desktop applications require editors of different types, for example, text editors, drawing editors, and organization chart editors. Even simple forms entry (as in a Web browser) requires an editor. Rather than developing custom editors for each application, it makes sense to develop editor components for each medium and assemble them into many applications.*

How does a component differ from an object [Szy98]? A primary difference is that since a component does not arise from decomposition of a specific individual application, it is harder to anticipate what other components it may have to interact with, including components from other vendors. This requires a considerably more disciplined approach to defining the ways components interact. Another challenge is that unlike an object, the purchaser of a component will not have access to any of its internal implementation, that being the proprietary intellectual property of a vendor. Encapsulation must be practiced much more dogmatically with components than with objects. Components should reduce the programming skill level required of application developers (component assemblers) while concentrating the skilled programming in the component vendors. Finally, OOP may or may not be used to develop a component, and if OOP is used, a component may be decomposed into multiple objects.

Components are not just a different way of programming; they represent a different industrial organization (see the sidebar "Components, Frameworks, and the Industrial Revolution"). Components move away from vertical integration, as applications are no longer developed monolithically but assembled from components provided by outside suppliers (see Section 5.2.2 on page 145). Earlier examples of this include the DBMS (see Section 6.3.1 on page 207) and the long-standing tradition of buying rather than making infrastructure software (principally the operating system).

Some detailed characteristics of components are listed in Table 6.5 together with analogies from the industrial or work world.

The standards and metadata have the greatest opportunities and challenges. Mixing and matching components from different vendors demands standardization. Metadata allows components to discover the useful services (methods, parameters, and return values) of other components, allowing them to adapt to one another. This capability makes it easier to envision different components interacting properly without that interaction being anticipated in their design.

Designing Components

In the component model, the programming task is split into two parts. The first is the implementation of the components themselves, and the second is the assembly of components into applications. These two tasks require different approaches. Component implementation uses a *system programming language* that allows the programmer to directly express algorithms and data structures, starting from the computer's basic capabilities. Most widely used system programming languages today are object-oriented. They allow the programmer to specify the interfaces and implementation of object classes, instantiate objects, prevent any actions violating encapsulation, etc. Programming in such languages requires considerable skill and patience.

Scripting and Visual Assembly

The assemblage of components should require less effort and less sophisticated programming skills than implementing objects or components. Approaches include visual and scripting assembly. An

remarkable increases in efficiency:

- The effort required to generate a new design is dramatically reduced.

- There is a natural decomposition into component and system manufacturers. Each is more specialized, separating their concerns and increasing their individual performance.

- Production of a large number of nominally identical components can be automated, increasing productivity and achieving higher economies of scale.

In computing equipment, integrated circuit components are also assembled in frameworks (printed circuit boards). Up until recently, software has been mostly handcrafted, but software components and frameworks will change that.

Table 6.5 Characteristics of software components [Kri98].

Characteristic	Description	Analogy
Modification	Components can be modified as they are incorporated into an application without access to the source program.	Parts bought from a vendor can be machined to change their characteristics prior to assembly.
Events	Components respond to action requests (through a method invocation) and also can issue notifications of changes in selected attributes. Other components can request to receive these notifications.	An assistant might be prepared to interrupt your meeting if an important call comes in. You indicate to your assistant what calls require notification.
Standards	Components adhere to predefined standards.	Interchangeable parts like screws and nuts can work together, even if they come from different vendors, but only if they adhere to standards of diameter, thread dimensions, etc.
Metadata	Components can describe themselves, so that other components can discover how to interoperate (these descriptions are metadata—see Table 2.8 on page 44).	Parts bought from a vendor are accompanied by paper documentation of their features.
Assembly	Two or more components can be assembled to form a larger-grain component. A component can be assembled from other components.	An engine is a component of a car but is itself an assemblage of components (pistons, gears, etc.).

environment for component assembly, as well as modification of components or implementation of new components, is called an *integrated development environment* (IDE).

EXAMPLE: *A number of software companies are marketing IDEs, for example, Microsoft's Visual Studio, IBM's VisualAge for Java, and Symantec's VisualCafe.*

In *visual assembly*, the components are displayed on the programmer's screen graphically, including displays of metadata, documentation, configuration, etc. The programmer assembles components by dragging and dropping visual icons representing them. A visual language for components is similar to UML for objects (see "Visual Modeling of Application Architectures" on page 196).

ANALOGY: *A building architect specifies the assemblage of components, such as bricks, sinks, windows, etc. The architect specifies their arrangement and interaction by a blueprint, which is analogous to a visual programming language. The design and detailed specification of the components is left to their individual manufacturer, in a process analogous to systems programming.*

Scripting assembly uses a textual scripting language specifically designed for gluing components together [Ous98]. The most popular scripting languages are Visual Basic on the desktop, and Tcl, Perl, and JavaScript in the server.

Frameworks

Assembling components still takes considerable work, because the developer must learn about available components, make choices, and do integration (including testing). There remains the need to create an architecture that meets application needs.

Frameworks allow an application to be developed with much less effort by providing an architecture as well as components. A framework can be thought of as a packaged application that can be both customized and extended.

ANALOGY: *Legos are a set of components that can be combined in different ways. They are not a framework, because the burden is on a child to decide what to build and how to combine the components to achieve that end. A Barbie doll is more like a framework. Barbie can be dressed up in different ways, but Barbie is still basically Barbie no matter how she is dressed. The ways in which Barbie's components are combined is predetermined, but there is some freedom to substitute components (like blouses, shoes, etc.) and mix and match.*

Frameworks generally allow modification or extension of components or of the framework itself, as well as the addition of custom components.

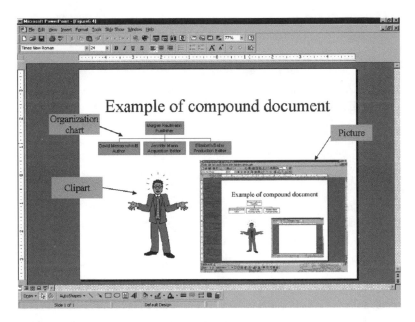

Figure 6.4 An example of a compound document.

Compound Document: Example of a Framework

The *compound document* is a successful framework allowing a number of components to share a common document window, including two competing standards—OpenDoc and Object Linking and Embedding (OLE).

Before the compound document, each window in the graphical user interface was managed by a single application, such as a spreadsheet, word processor, or drawing editor. Data could be cut and pasted from one window to another, but once pasted, it couldn't be modified. As a result, applications were driven toward more and more functionality, with duplication of some of that functionality among applications.

EXAMPLE: *In Figure 6.4, a presentation graphics editor, an organization chart, and clip art share a window. Also included is a cut-and-paste bitmap picture not managed by a component. Areas controlled by components may overlap, but the framework ensures that only one component (the foreground object) is presented to the screen.*

6.3 Loosely Coupled Data and Processing

Loosely coupling data and processing logically separates data from the application logic, treating data as a separate entity. The application logic can still be developed with the object and component methodologies, but the major part of the data is managed separately. A number of characteristics of data listed in Table 6.6 make this advantageous to an organization or individual owning the data.

Data that is tightly coupled to an application uses structures and formats defined by the application. Similarly, if data is to have an identity separate from an application, there must be a separately documented plan for structuring and organizing it. This is doubly necessary if the data is to be useful to more than one application.

ANALOGY: *A newspaper structures information by general topic (news, sports, classified advertisements), an airline sets its timetable by source and destination cities and time of day, and a dictionary organizes words by alphabetical order. Each of these structures helps the user or application find desired information.*

There are other, more pragmatic, disadvantages of tightly coupling processing and data:

- Many tasks relative to data are application independent, and capturing them in a database management system contributes to software reuse (see Section 6.1.4 on page 185).

- If an application crashes or fails, there may be irrevocable loss of tightly coupled data.

- Data comes and goes as the application executes, and there is no systematic way to archive that data for future use, except capabilities specifically built into the application.

- The data format is intimately tied to the application that created it. When the application is upgraded or replaced, information may be unrecoverable.

- Some flexibility in locating data on hosts is lost, with possible performance, cost, and scalability implications (see Section 6.1.5 on page 187).

Table 6.6 Characteristics of data that give it value independent of applications.

Characteristic	Description	Examples
Asset	Data underlies information and knowledge, increasingly important assets for many organizations (see Section 2.4 on page 38). Data's value is enhanced by decoupling it from specific applications.	Customer and employee information are core business assets. The goods traded in on-line sales are information.
Common source, shared resource	A given set of data originates from a single source, and yet this data (and the information and knowledge it represents) may be exploited by multiple applications. In the tightly coupled model, this data would have to be replicated within each application, which leads to coherency problems among those replicas.	Customer information can be incorporated into many business processes, for example, sales management and accounts receivable. Sales information can be used to forecast production, in supply-chain management, and in marketing strategy.
Interaction	The exchange of data with standard formats is a powerful mechanism for the opportunistic (and not necessarily anticipated) interaction among applications. The update of data by one application immediately becomes available to all applications sharing that data.	Information about customer purchases can later be used to target advertising. A knowledge base of problem reports in customer support can later be used in the development of the next version.
Decision tool	Data captures the condition of a business and is valuable as a tool for tactical and strategic decision making (see "Decision Support" on page 62).	Sales information can be used to divest products or stimulate related product development.
Archives	Data captures the history of a business, invaluable for discovering trends.	Data warehousing (see "Decision Support" on page 62).
Patterns	Data can be systematically searched, browsed, or mined to uncover unexpected patterns.	Data mining and OLAP (see "Decision Support" on page 62).

There is no single way of structuring data that suits all applications, so there needs to be more than one approach. Two premier data structuring models are widely used:

- *Relational model:* Data is organized into tables with rows and columns, in a model tailored to business applications (see "Shared Data Tier: Database Management" on page 94). Currently, this model is being extended to richer structures (see the sidebar "Extending Databases to Objects: ORDBMS and ODBMS").

- *Document model:* Data within documents is organized into hierarchical sections, paragraphs, tables, figures, etc.

6.3.1 Database Management

The database management system (DBMS) (see "Shared Data Tier: Database Management" on page 94) is a commercial product that manages large amounts of data on behalf of applications and is typically realized as a second-tier server on a centralized host (not infrequently a mainframe) that services a number of first-tier servers (with the application logic) (see Section 3.2.2 on page 92). In effect, the DBMS is a large-grain component that can be subsumed into or shared by applications.

EXAMPLE: *The DBMS is particularly relevant to business applications. Most organizations have a body of mission-critical data, including records of employees, customers, inventory, etc. This data must be shared among applications and must outlive applications that create it, so that they can be upgraded or replaced and still access the data.*

A DBMS bundles many capabilities related to the needs of mission-critical data and seeks to offer a range of services required by many applications:

- *Structured data model:* Databases offer structured ways of storing data that capture the relationships among data and enable standard queries to retrieve or modify it. This reduces the required functionality of the application. The database hides

Extending Databases to Objects: ORDBMS and ODBMS

The RDBMS and OOP have some dissidence:

- The RDBMS is able to store and manipulate only a small set of simple data, such as integers and character strings. There is need in today's applications for more complex data, such as images, audio, and video.

- The fact that there is no direct support for persistence in OOP creates complications, including the need to store mission-critical data in a DBMS. But the relational model does not directly support complex data possible in objects.

- The programmer must learn and use two programming languages: the OOP language and SQL.

Two new database product categories deal with these shortcomings: *object-relational DBMS* (ORDBMS) and *object DBMS* (ODBMS). The ORDBMS extends the RDBMS to include the ability to store and retrieve complex objects while retaining (and extending) SQL as the interface. The ODBMS abandons SQL and simply adds persistence

unnecessary implementation details such as the partitioning of data on hosts.

- *Persistence:* In the tightly coupled data processing model, when an application is no longer executing (because it crashed or was stopped), the data it is manipulating is lost. In contrast, persistent data outlives the application that created it. In most applications requiring database capabilities, it is a critical requirement that the data be long-lived (decades or longer), even in the face of system crashes or the upgrade of applications or the DBMS.

- *Scalability:* Since the needs of most organizations expand with time, a database improves its performance (such as the number of queries per unit time) as applications require. See Chapter for more discussion of scalability.

- *Transaction support:* The database multiplexes queries from many users or even applications into a single database and deals with many inherent problems and threats. The problems of shared access to common resources, and transaction support, are addressed in Chapter .

- *Access control:* A database allows control over who can access or modify data. This function, in a more general context, is discussed in Chapter .

Of these properties, persistence is the most fundamental and important. Mission-critical data must be reliably preserved for many years. Persistence is achieved in part by maintaining the data on nonvolatile storage (storage that is not lost in a power failure or a computer crash) and in part by managing it in the DBMS loosely coupled from the application logic.

The Relational Model for Structured Data

In the relational model (see "Shared Data Tier: Database Management" on page 94), data is stored in *tables* with rows and columns. This is one way to organize data in a DBMS.

EXAMPLE: *The table shown in Figure 6.5 illustrates information relevant to employees, specifically labeling the columns and rows. The columns, also known as* fields, *have identifying labels and represent*

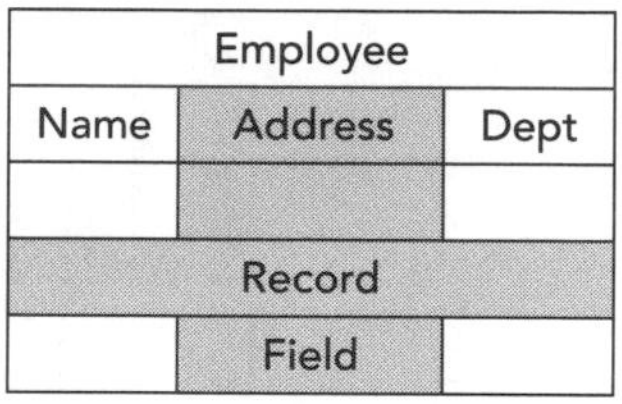

Figure 6.5 Example of a relational table storing employee data.

the employee's attributes. Each row, also known as a record, *represents an individual employee.*

The relational model is based on a solid mathematical foundation (set theory and predicate calculus) and forms the basis of a *relational DBMS* (RDBMS). The model also specifies a suite of *operations* on the data. Each operation accepts one or more tables, produces as an output another table, and in the process does some useful manipulation. Because the result of operations is a table, operators can be freely combined to form more complex operations. One operator produces a table, which is precisely what another operator expects. These operations are expressed in an internationally standardized *structured query language* (SQL).

EXAMPLE: *As shown in Figure 6.6, two simple SQL commands, PROJECT and SELECT, both produce a smaller table. The PROJECT operation removes fields, and the SELECT operation removes records, each based on criteria included in the arguments to the operation.*

Application Logic Interface: SQL

The application logic is typically programmed using the object or component model and must interact with the DBMS. As shown in Figure 6.7, application logic can store, access, and manipulate data in the DBMS using SQL. Typically, it operates one record at a time on a table that results from one or a series of SQL operators.

In addition to data in the DBMS, objects within the application logic will also encapsulate data. The application designer determines which data is stored in objects and which in the DBMS, including

directly to objects. There are merits and downsides to these approaches:

- The ORDBMS preserves existing applications and databases but allows them to be extended as desired into the world of complex data. Thus, the ORDBMS avoids many switching costs (see Section 5.3.2 on page 154) and offers a less radical migration path.

- The ODBMS is missing the structured query operators of the RDBMS. Also, the persistence is less useful in the long term because the persistent data is more difficult to reuse in future applications.

- The ODBMS eases the programming task, avoiding the extra step of deciding which data is persistent and consciously forming queries.

The ORDBMS vendors have significant switching costs in moving from RDBMS to the ORDBMS. Both vendors and customers have made huge investments in RDBMS technology, and this will be difficult for ODBMS vendors to displace.

The battles in this product category illustrate the immaturity of software technology. The RDBMS arose independently of and before the

(continued)

object model and is mis-
matched from it in some ways.
The marketplace will shake
out an eventual winner, but
before it does, there will likely
be some new technology on
the horizon.

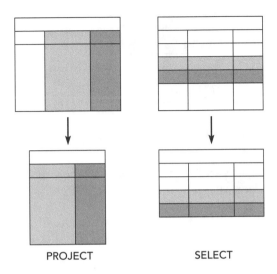

PROJECT   SELECT

Figure 6.6 Two examples of operations that perform data manipulation in SQL.

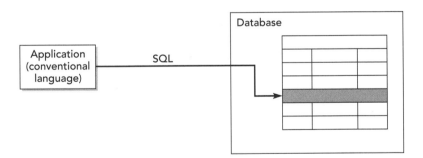

Figure 6.7 Application logic written in conventional programming languages manipulates relational tables by forming SQL queries.

duplication between the two. Factors to consider were listed earlier, such as persistence and data sharing.

Extending the DBMS

The relational DBMS predates the popularity of OOP, and thus the alignment of their data structuring models is not as close as it might be. As a result, some new categories of DBMS products are emerging (see the sidebar "Extending Databases to Objects: ORDBMS and ODBMS").

6.3.2 Document Management: XML

Documents (such as memoranda, proposals, and articles) are widely used in business and by individuals. Documents also encompass forms widely used in business, such as purchase orders and invoices (see the sidebar "Standardization within Applications" on page 134). They serve as the foundation of interaction, collaboration, and commerce, and document depositories form an important business or personal asset. The DBMS can manage documents, like other data. However, relational tables do not naturally represent the structure of documents. Today's DBMS can store documents in their entirety, but the *internal* structure of a document is not visible to the DBMS.

Another strong driver is the success and rapid propagation of the Web, which focuses on the presentation of information to users and is based on a document model. Unlike SQL and the DBMS, documents are especially appropriate for sharing data with other companies and consumers.

A *markup language* represents a hierarchical structure for a document—for example, sections, subsections, sub-subsections, sidebars, and images/figures—by attaching identifying *tags* to individual words, paragraphs, etc. Markup languages allow the document's structure to be exchanged among applications and also enable authoring tools that present specialized author interfaces from a common representation. ISO (see the sidebar "International Organization for Standards (ISO)" on page 135) has developed a standard called the Standard General Markup Language (SGML). SGML is considered too complicated for "everyday" uses, and thus the Web standards use a simplified subset of SGML, initially the Hypertext Markup Language (HTML). HTML has proven quite limiting because it focuses on the presentation of documents rather than their internal structure. W3C, the World Wide Web Consortium (which creates de facto standards for the Web) has defined a new markup language called XML (see the sidebar "eXtensible Markup Language (XML)") that stays within the confines of SGML.

eXtensible Markup Language (XML)

XML [Lau98] will govern document and data representation on the Web in the future. The term "extensible" refers to the language's ability to define new markup tags customized to particular purposes. XML focuses on expressing document *structure* rather than the presentation (formatting and display). As a result, a single document can be formatted and displayed in many different ways, depending on the needs of the user (as defined by the application).

XML also enhances information searches. (A simple example would be to search top-level section headings, or the document title, rather than all the text in the document.) The standard includes the Resource Description Framework (RDF), which allows the description of metadata about the document suitable for searching and similar purposes (see Table 2.8 on page 44).

A Document Object Model (DOM) defines standardized interfaces to documents thought of as objects. RDF and DOM allow documents to be treated as specialized components (see "What Is a Software Component?" on page 200), making documents active entities rather than static data. Clever application developers will build in many customized features using these standards.

EXAMPLE: *A number of specialized HTML editors (such as Adobe PageMill and Microsoft FrontPage) allow users to generate HTML documents without knowing the language. These editors present a standard "what you see is what you get" document editing interface. Standard word processors and page layout applications (such as Microsoft Word and Adobe Framemaker) offer the option of generating an HTML representation.*

XML opens up many possibilities for building business applications using the Web (see "The Web as the Presentation Tier" on page 103). If the *lingua franca* of communication between a business application and its presentation becomes XML, then XML supports an open interface between tiers like SQL, as shown in Figure 6.8. The application logic can generate the presentation in standard XML and access data using SQL. HTTP and CGI become standard protocols for supporting the multitier architectures (see Chapter 7).

Beyond just building applications, the XML-enhanced Web can be the basis for new businesses, as one Web site can seamlessly incorporate other Web sites. Businesses can be layered on top of one another much the same way the software infrastructure is layered (see Section 5.2.1 on page 144).

EXAMPLE: *Businesses might enter the Web-based "wholesale" sales of specialized goods, representing their catalog, pricing, etc., in XML. Various other businesses could then set up "retail superstores" that aggregate these wholesale goods in various ways, add a price markup, and sell directly to consumers. Because the wholesale goods are described in XML, the retailer can flexibly incorporate these descriptions into her own catalog, changing the presentation to conform to a uniform "look and feel." All this could happen dynamically and automatically as the consumer browses the catalog.*

XML or similar markup languages have tremendous potential for many applications requiring documents and for the exchange of information among applications. Direct support of XML can be expected in future database products, as well as document authoring applications.

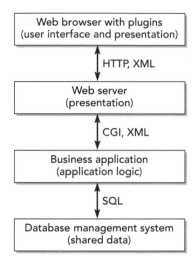

Figure 6.8 XML and SQL as the interface languages in multitier client/server applications.

Further Reading

The definitive references on software objects and components are [Boo94] and [Szy98]. Many business and nontechnical issues are also covered in [Szy98]. Both these books are long and detailed but well written, accessible, and highly recommended. Although both books discuss the application software development process, a more detailed treatise on application architecture and the application life cycle is [BCK98]. The management of software development projects is quite challenging and is briefly described in Chapter 3. This is the subject of many books, including [Pre96, You97, McC97].

Communications Support for Applications 7

In Chapter 6, application architecture and data structuring were discussed. Other than a brief mention of the locality between data and processing, the reality that both the data and processing are likely to be distributed across networked hosts and their associated storage was not explicitly addressed. The next issue is the communication services provided to distributed application modules, supported by the software and equipment infrastructure.

ANALOGY: *In the physical world, common communications mechanisms include the postal letter, the postal letter with return receipt, the registered letter (with guaranteed delivery), and the telephone call (which supports a conversation). Each of these services meets a distinct need when supporting geographically distributed activities, such as business processes.*

The overriding goal of the communication infrastructure is to hide—insofar as possible—the distributed nature of the application in order to simplify application development. Complete hiding isn't possible because the developer must choose the partitioning across hosts, making visible the distributed nature of the application, and performance and scalability will depend on this partitioning (see Chapter 10).

ANALOGY: *Suppose a widget is manufactured in two stages. Those stages could be located in the same building or in buildings in different countries. With the proper transportation infrastructure, the manufacturing process might be identical, but due to transportation delays the two-country approach would result in a longer time to complete the manufacture of each widget.*

When using object and component methodologies, the communications infrastructure must support the interactions among objects and components. If this interaction does not appear to depend on whether they are on the same host or on different hosts, the distributed nature of the application is hidden from the developer (except for important performance issues). This is an example of abstraction (see Section 4.1.4 on page 119), as the *implementation* of the communication must be different (one case requires communication over the network and the other doesn't), but these differences are hidden from the application developer. This abstraction can hide functional but not performance differences, as communication over the network will typically slow interactions.

7.1 Algorithms, Protocols, and Policies

The architecture decomposes an application into a set of interacting modules. The term "modules" should be interpreted broadly, including objects, components, a client host interacting with a server host, or two hosts achieving reliable data communication. Modules interacting correctly, achieving overall architectural goals, are said to be *interoperable*.

EXAMPLE: *The communication software and a modem connected to the computer are interoperable if the software successfully establishes a data connection and communicates data remotely using that modem.*

Interoperability is enabled by four elements—algorithms, protocols, formats, and policies—defined in Table 7.1. Protocols and policies govern the steps the modules follow to work together, algorithms work internally to the modules to realize the required behavior, and formats govern the interpretation of communications between the modules.

EXAMPLE: *Traffic laws, signs, and signals coordinate drivers. Some issues are addressed by policies (law), such as driving on a particu-*

Table 7.1 Four elements critical to achieving interoperability among interacting modules.

Element	Description	Example
Algorithm	A sequence of predefined steps designed to accomplish a specific task. A single computer program realizes an algorithm. Each module internally uses an algorithm that determines its contribution to a protocol, as well as other behavior.	A taxpayer follows a specified set of steps to fill out tax forms, such as "to determine the tax, if your adjusted gross income (AGI) is more than $20,000, take 10% of the AGI. If the AGI is less than $40,000, take $2,000 plus 15% of the difference of the AGI and $20,000."
Protocol	An algorithm performed cooperatively by two or more interacting modules, consisting of a sequence of communications from one module to another. The protocol coordinates the behavior of the modules to achieve interoperability.	A taxpayer and the government tax agency cooperatively follow a protocol. For example, the taxpayer fills out forms and mails them with a check, the agency returns a check if there is a refund, the agency sends notification of tax due, and the taxpayer returns that with a check.
Format	Each communication in a protocol includes information needed by the recipient module. The format defines the structure of the data in that communication.	The tax form and check sent by the taxpayer each have predefined formats.
Policy	A specific set of allowed and/or disallowed behaviors. The most fundamental policy is that interacting modules must follow the predefined protocol.	A taxpayer with income is required to file a tax return, and pay taxes due, by a certain date. The agency is required to treat all taxpayers equally.

lar side of the road. Other issues, such as the conflict between cars at an intersection, are handled by a combination of policy and protocol. A traffic light defines a protocol that specifies the sequence of lights (green, yellow, red), constraints on the lights in the two directions (green or yellow one direction, red the other), and driver behaviors (drivers can cross the intersection on green or yellow but not red). Each driver follows an algorithm to obey the protocol (for example, stop when light is red, go really fast when it is yellow). This protocol is buttressed by policies, including a law that drivers must stop for a red light.

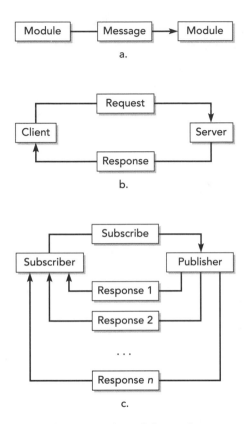

Figure 7.1 Three simple protocols widely used in computing: (a) send/receive, (b) request/response, and (c) publish/subscribe.

For every situation that arises, an algorithm or protocol must specify a well-defined action; it is not acceptable to just "give up." Because there are usually many different feasible scenarios, algorithms and protocols can be quite complicated. In fact, considerable design effort is devoted to dealing with the exceptional or unusual situations that seldom occur.

Protocols, formats, and policies are complementary, as they together govern the module interaction. To achieve interoperability, modules must know the details of all relevant protocols, formats, and policies and correctly implement them in internal algorithms.

Three simple but very common protocols are listed in Table 7.2 and illustrated in Figure 7.1. For these protocols, interoperability requires each message, request, response, and subscription to have

Table 7.2 Description of three simple but widely used protocols.

Protocol	Description	Application	Analogy
Send/ receive	One module sends a *message* to another, which receives it.	*Inform* or *direct* another module, for example, email.	Send a letter to a friend.
Request/ response	One module (called the *client*) sends a *request* to another module (called the *server*), and the server returns an immediate *response*.	Obtain *information* or a *service* from another module. This is the basis of client/server computing (see Section 3.2 on page 90).	Send an order form to a catalog retailer, expecting to receive goods by return post.
Publish/ subscribe	One module (called the *subscriber*) sends a *subscription* to another module (called the *publisher*), and the publisher sends back a sequence of responses.	Obtain information on an ongoing basis with a single request. This is the basis of information push (see Section 2.4.2 on page 47) and the basis of events (see "Designing Components" on page 201).	Send subscription order to a magazine, receive multiple issues.

a defined format understood by the recipient. Each protocol supports a different type of interaction. HTTP, the basis of the Web, uses a request/response protocol (see the sidebar "The Hypertext Transfer Protocol (HTTP)"). The publish/subscribe protocol is the most complex, as the number and timing of responses are determined by circumstances. It often requires a prior *discovery*, where the subscriber determines that there is an appropriate publisher to which to subscribe. There may also be an *unsubscribe* defined in the protocol to stop the flow of responses.

7.2 Abstract Communication Services

As in the physical world, no single communication service is suitable for all purposes. Some abstract communication services most useful to applications, and the role of the elements of interoperability in Table 7.1, will now be described. A *service* is a dynamic capability provided by the infrastructure for the use and benefit of the application. An *abstract* service is a view of the service that hides internal infrastructure implementing details (see Section 4.1.4 on page 119).

The Hypertext Transfer Protocol (HTTP)

HTTP is a request/response protocol that governs the interaction of a Web browser (the client) and a Web server (see the sidebar "World Wide Web" on page 37). The four basic steps are shown in Figure 7.2. The request is initiated by the user clicking on a hyperlink. The most common request is an HTML or XML document (see the sidebar "eXtensible Markup Language (XML)" on page 212), which is returned to the browser and displayed.

A *hyperlink* is a highlighted piece of text associated with a *uniform resource locator* (URL). The URL has three parts, representing the protocol (in this case HTTP), the name of the host desired, and the name of the desired document on that host.

E X A M P L E :   *A typical URL is http://www.eecs. berkeley.edu/~messer/ index.html, where http denotes the protocol, www.eecs.berkeley.edu is the name of the host, and ~messer/index.html is the name of the HTML document requested.*

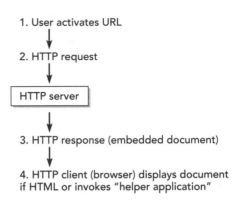

1. User activates URL

2. HTTP request

HTTP server

3. HTTP response (embedded document)

4. HTTP client (browser) displays document if HTML or invokes "helper application"

Figure 7.2 The HTTP protocol that forms the foundation of the Web.

These services are supported—behind the scenes—by protocols, policies, and formats.

Commonly available services are summarized in Table 7.3. An application is free to choose which service or services it utilizes. In the next section some concrete services provided by the internet protocols are described, where they generally map into the four categories of abstract services in Table 7.3.

7.2.1 Message Service

A message is a one-way communication of information from one module to another. Receiving a partial message is of no value to the recipient; so a message service will deliver the entire message or not deliver it at all.

E X A M P L E :   *An email application would use a message service. Whatever one user types is sent (as an atomic message) to the recipient. More generally, messages are commonly used in social applications (see "Communication Style" on page 23).*

Another characteristic of a message service is that one message does not share a context with another message—each message is self-contained and stands on its own. An application can create its own context for a group of messages, but the message service provides no assistance.

Table 7.3 Some useful abstract communication services.

Service	Description	Analogy
Message	A message with a pre-agreed format is sent to another module to inform or direct. The recipient is interrupted to receive it.	Judge Sylvia issues a subpoena to Bob, which is served on Bob in person.
Message with multiplexing and queueing	Like a message, except there can be multiple senders for a single recipient. The recipient is not interrupted to receive messages, but can retrieve them at will.	Alice, Harry, and June all send postcards to Bob. The postcards languish in Bob's mailbox until he retrieves them.
Message with reply	A message is coupled to an obligatory reply, also with an agreed format. The reply may return useful information or merely confirm an action or indicate a status.	Alice mails an order for tickets to a broker, who sends them back by return mail. Alice sends a letter with return receipt requested to Bob. The return receipt confirms the letter was received.
Conversation	A sequence of messages that possess a shared context. A conversation may be one-way (one module is always the sender and the other always the recipient) or two-way.	Alice telephones Bob. Each makes utterances in each direction, forming a conversation.
Broadcast	A one-way conversation in which there is a single sender and two or more (often a multiplicity) of recipients. Each recipient receives every message.	Television or radio broadcast to the public; a newspaper or magazine that sends out multiple issues.

EXAMPLE: *A pair of users may want to discuss a controversial topic by email, sending messages back and forth. The users create the shared context themselves, using phrases like "replying to your last idiotic statement." The message service is not aware of the context and treats each message independently.*

One consequence of the "no message context" is that a message service will not promise to deliver messages in the same order as sent. If the messages have no shared context, then they also have no order (in time) from the perspective of the message service. It is

Is a Message Delivered for Sure?

Sending a message is "open loop," like sending a letter. The sender does not receive an acknowledgment that the message was delivered. Can the sender be sure the message arrived?

The reliability of message delivery depends on the infrastructure investment. Messages can be delivered reliably when everything is running correctly. However, it requires more work to ensure that messages are not lost in computer crashes or hardware failures. There are elaborate middleware solutions to deal with such scenarios (see Chapter 9). A simpler solution is for the application to request a confirmation message from the recipient and consciously deal with lost messages.

A N A L O G Y : *Although your postal letters are delivered most of the time, you accept that they occasionally aren't. If it is critical to know, you purchase a special "return receipt requested" service or ask the recipient for confirmation.*

also possible that a message is never delivered (see the sidebar "Is a Message Delivered for Sure?").

A N A L O G Y : *If someone sends several of postcards back home over the course of a trip, the postal service will not necessarily deliver them in the order sent. The postal service is unaware of the common context of these postcards (the trip). It may even fail to deliver them all.*

Queueing and Multiplexing

Message services lend themselves to enhancements called multiplexing and queueing, which are attractive in some types of applications.

E X A M P L E : Message-oriented middleware *(MOM) is a class of infrastructure software that provides message services and includes multiplexing and queueing (see Chapter 9).*

Queueing, illustrated in Figure 7.3(a), deals with a situation in which a recipient may not be prepared to receive a message at all times (perhaps because it is busy doing something else). A message is sent to a queue (which is another module) associated with the recipient, rather than to the recipient directly. The message can reside in the queue as long as necessary, and the recipient retrieves messages waiting in the queue whenever it chooses. The service requires an intermediary queue and combines two protocols: send/receive (between sender and queue) and request/response (between recipient and queue). This illustrates how more complex protocols (or combinations of simple ones) can support useful communication services.

E X A M P L E : *The queueing of messages is used in deferred user-to-user applications such as email or voicemail (see Section 2.3.2 on page 22). The message service can queue an email message until the recipient reads it.*

A message service might provide *prioritization*, whereby some messages waiting for a recipient are presented ahead of others. The pri-

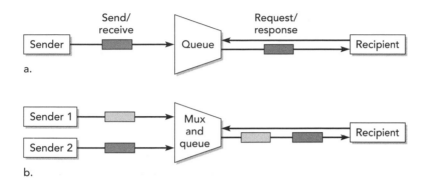

Figure 7.3 (a) Queueing allows sender and receiver to work independently, while (b) multiplexing allows two or more senders for the same recipient.

ority might be set by the sender or be related to the identity of the sender.

Multiplexing, illustrated in Figure 7.3(b), is a *combining* of messages for a given recipient from more than one sender. Messages are stored in a single multiplex/queue to be retrieved by the recipient when desired. Queueing can exist without multiplexing (although this is unusual), but multiplexing requires queueing, since it is possible for messages from two or more senders to arrive simultaneously, and one of them *must* be stored while the other is received.

ANALOGY: *Your mailbox is a queue for letters waiting for you to open and read them. It also multiplexes messages—mail from many senders arrives in your mailbox. The postal service provides a message service with multiplexing and queueing.*

EXAMPLE: *Figure 7.4 shows an example of a workflow application— the processing of purchase orders—that can utilize multiplexing and queueing. A number of workers may generate purchase requests that are multiplexed and queued for a single administrative assistant. A number of these assistants may forward these requests to a single purchasing department (again they are multiplexed and queued). If purchasing has a number of agents, they may all retrieve requests from the single queue as they free up time*

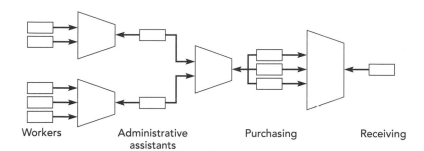

Figure 7.4 Example of multiplexing and queueing in a workflow application. The retrieval of a message from a queue is simplified to a single arrow.

to process them. The agents then forward the requests to the receiving department (where they are again multiplexed and queued) so that department is alerted to the future arrival of the purchased goods.

7.2.2 Message with Reply Service

Some applications need a *guaranteed* and *immediate* reply to a message. Typically this occurs when one module must sit idle awaiting information or a service from another. A *message with reply* service creates a shared context for the original and reply messages. There is an ordering—the reply message follows the original—and the reply is identified to the sender as a response to the message. The service would assume the sender is waiting for the reply, so the recipient should reply as soon as possible.

ANALOGY: *When a student is studying for an exam and has a question, she may send an email message to the teacher, who replies at his leisure. If he is too busy, he may not reply at all, as there is no obligation to do so. This is the message service. While the student is actually taking the exam, she will expect a reply to her question, and she will expect it as soon as possible. She will use a message with reply service.*

EXAMPLE: *User-directed information access applications like the Web would use a message with reply service (see "User-Directed Access" on page 40). When a user requests a piece of information, she is expecting the information to appear, and as soon as possible.*

A message service uses a send/receive protocol (or a more complicated variation in the case of multiplexing and queueing), whereas the message with reply service uses the request/response protocol.

Remote Method Invocation

A standard way for objects to interact is the method invocation (see "Software Objects" on page 192). Recall that an invocation takes the form

```
method: parameters -> return_values;
```

where the `method` specifies the action to be performed by the server object, `parameters` configure or specialize that action, and `return_values` return data to the client objects as a result of that action. As shown in Figure 7.5, it should be possible to make the method invocation work the same way, whether the client and server objects reside in the same or different hosts. In the latter case, it is called a *remote method invocation* (RMI). Because it is a form of communication between objects, RMI is another abstract communication service. In fact, since it involves a request from client to server object (`action`, `parameters`) and a response (`return_values`), it uses a request/response protocol.

Behind the scenes, the abstract RMI service requires substantial infrastructure. *Distributed object management* (DOM) and *distributed component platforms* (DCP) are two middleware technologies that provide an RMI service (described in Chapter 9). Because the form of object interaction is transparent to whether the objects are on the same or different hosts, DOM and DCP make building distributed applications much more like centralized applications. DOM and DCP also provide services that deal with special needs of such applications, such as the location and naming of objects (since the host needs to be identified as well as the object on that host) and security issues.

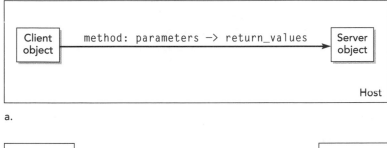

a.

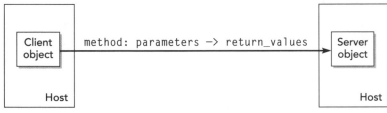

b.

Figure 7.5 Conceptually, an object method invocation can work the same way for two objects on the same host (a) or on different hosts (b).

7.2.3 Timing and Concurrency

While the message service may appear as just "a message with reply service that is missing the reply," this understates the difference. This is better understood by examining the timing of the underlying protocols, which describes what happens and when.

The timing can be appreciated from a protocol interaction diagram, illustrated in Figure 7.6 for RMI (which uses a request/response protocol). This diagram shows the evolution of time (from top to bottom), the specific steps in the protocol, and the time at which they occur. The horizontal arrows represent each individual communication, the direction of that communication, and the time it takes (because of delays in getting data through the network and other factors). The client object is blocked from the time it initiates the request until it receives the response. *Blocked* means the client object is inactive because it is awaiting its response, keeping it from doing any other work. Components of this blocked time include network and processing delays for the request, the time to invoke

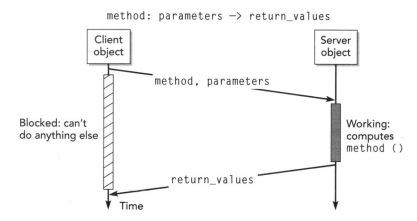

Figure 7.6 Protocol interaction diagram for a request/response protocol (stripes indicate that the object is blocked, waiting for a response; gray indicates that the object is processing a request).

the method and compute return values on those arguments in the server, and finally, the delay in the values returning to the client.

Blocking is not necessary, as seen in Figure 7.7. In the send/receive protocol, the sender is not blocked if it is not expecting a reply—it is free to go off and do other work. Since the sending and receiving objects are working on different tasks at the same time, they are said to be working *concurrently*. A request/response protocol—such as a message with reply or an RMI—does not allow the interacting objects to work concurrently during the course of their interaction. This distinction is important, because overall, more work may be completed when objects are working concurrently.

The addition of a message queue, also shown in Figure 7.7, gives the recipient more freedom to choose when it receives a message. Rather than receiving it immediately after it was sent, the recipient has the option to let it wait in the queue. Later, it can retrieve the object from the queue using a request/response protocol.

7.2.4 The Session

Sometimes an application desires to hold a conversation—a series of messages in both directions forming a single coupled interaction.

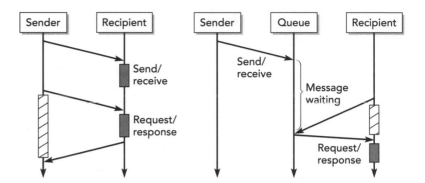

Figure 7.7 Protocol interaction diagram comparing timing of three protocols.

ANALOGY: *A conversation between Alice and Bob consists of a series of utterances, first from Alice to Bob, then a reply from Bob back to Alice, then from Alice to Bob, etc. Rarely does a conversation consist of only one utterance (which is amenable to a message) or only one utterance with one reply (which is amenable to the message with reply).*

All the messages within a conversation share a context: Each message has an interpretation that can be interpreted only in that context; that is, the interpretation of one message depends on the messages that preceded it. This implies that all messages must be delivered, and in the right order.

EXAMPLE: *An application that accesses a database repeatedly (see "Shared Data Tier: Database Management" on page 94) to store data and make queries benefits from a conversation. The queries (using SQL, if it is an RDBMS) are ordered; if one query changes the database, later queries should reflect those changes.*

Although an application can manage a conversation itself by building on the send or the request/response protocols, this is complicated since those protocols do not preserve an ordering of messages and may not even guarantee delivery of all messages.

A *session* communication service provides a conversation with a bidirectional sequence of messages, guaranteeing delivery of mes-

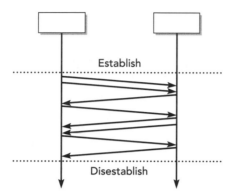

Figure 7.8 A session consists of establishment, a sequence of back-and-forth messages, and disestablishment.

sages in the same order as sent. Some details of a protocol supporting a session are pictured in Figure 7.8. A session has three phases: establishment ("let's agree to converse"), conversation, and disestablishment ("let's stop conversing"). During the conversation phase, it is typical for many more messages to flow in one direction than the other, and sometimes the conversation is unidirectional.

ANALOGY: *A session is analogous to a telephone call, which starts with the originating party dialing and the receiving party picking up the phone (establishment), and ends when both parties hang up their phones (disestablishment).*

Multimedia Transport

Multimedia applications incorporate combinations of audio, video, animation, images, graphics, data, and other media. Media such as audio, video, and animation can be transported over the network as long as they are represented digitally (see the sidebar "Any Information Can Be Represented by Bits" on page 10). Certainly people don't talk digitally, nor are the microphone or camera outputs digital. However, these media can be converted to digital by an audio or video coder, and converted back from digital by a decoder. Coders also *compress* the medium—which means they represent the medium with fewer bits—therefore consuming less storage and communication resources. Once the audio or video is digital—

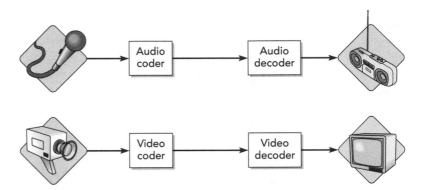

Figure 7.9 Immediate applications such as audio telephony or video conferencing require that the audio or video medium be transferred over the network in real time.

represented by data—it can be communicated over the network by forming it into a sequence of messages.

There are two distinct cases, depending on whether the application is immediate or deferred (see Section 2.3.2 on page 22):

• *Live audio or video:* In immediate applications such as remote conferencing (see Section 2.3.3 on page 27), the recipient is listening to the audio or viewing the video *as it is being created*, as illustrated in Figure 7.9. From the perspective of the communication service, this audio or video is called *streaming* (an analogy to water continually passing by in a stream).

• *Store-and-playback audio or video:* In deferred applications such as information access (see Section 2.4 on page 38), the audio or video is stored in a host and played back as the user watches it. An option, illustrated in Figure 7.10, is to temporarily store the audio or video in the user's client and play it back locally. If there is insufficient local storage in the client, or for other reasons, the audio or video may instead be played back by streaming from a remote host.

How is the audio or video partitioned into messages? Since the user probably perceives the entire audio or video presentation as

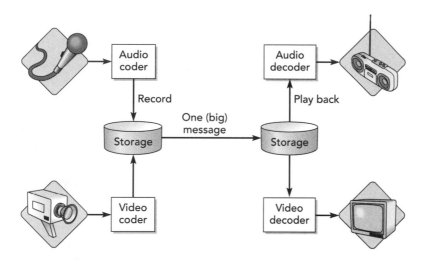

Figure 7.10 Deferred applications such as audio or video information access have the option of storing the medium on a local host before playback.

atomic, it is natural to think of it as a single message. In the store-and-playback case, this is an acceptable way to transfer the presentation to the client. Once the message is received, the presentation can be played back in its entirety. In the live case, however, the presentation must be divided into multiple messages.

EXAMPLE: *When Alice calls Bob, he answers, "Hello," and she replies, "Hi, this is Alice," and he replies "Hi Alice." The entire piece of the conversation from Bob to Alice including "hello" and "hi Alice" could not be transferred as a single message, since Alice would never have a chance to inject her "hi, this is Alice" in response to the "hello."*

The session—splitting the audio or video into a sequence of messages—is thus a natural communication service to support streaming audio or video. The coder divides the presentation into "natural" units, such as single utterances in the case of telephony, and sends each unit as a message. Since messages may be delayed by different amounts by the network, the relative timing of messages may have been modified at the receiver. To reconstruct the original timing (for example, the time between utterances), the service has to include synchronization information.

Multimedia applications frequently incorporate more than one medium, such as audio *and* video, or often multiple audio and video streams in a multiway conference. This generalizes the notion of session to multiple, logically connected streams. The service also has to support synchronization of these streams to make sure, for example, that video and its associated audio are time aligned.

7.2.5 The Broadcast

Thus far, the services described support point-to-point communication, as in the interaction of a pair of modules. Multipoint interactions involving three or more modules can be constructed by a composition of point-to-point interactions. Another mode occurring frequently enough to deserve its own service is the *broadcast*, in which identical information is sent to two or more recipients simultaneously.

EXAMPLE: *Remote learning with multiple students is an application of broadcast if it is cast as an immediate application (the students are viewing the presentation as it happens). Remote conferencing often involves multiple participants, and each participant may wish to hear (or see) all the other participants, which is done by using a broadcast from each participant to all the others (see Section 2.3.3 on page 27).*

The broadcast is a generalization of the session, but with multiple recipients. There are two ways to create multiple replicas of the messages originating from the sender:

- *Simulcast:* The sender creates the replicas and creates multiple sessions (one to each recipient).

- *Multicast:* The multiple replicas are created by the communication service rather than the sender. From the sender's perspective, multicast looks similar to a session.

Multicast is a service recently made available on the Internet (see Chapter 11).

7.3 Internet Communication Services

The most popular abstract communication services today are provided by the internet suite of networking technologies (see Section 3.3 on page 99). The internet provides specific variations on all the abstract communication services already discussed. There is nothing fundamental about the specific internet services; they are simply design choices.

Communication services, including the internet protocols, are layered (see Section 4.2.2 on page 124). This means that new and more specialized services can be deployed by adding a layer—leveraging an existing service on an existing network—rather than building it (service or network) from scratch. The internet services are layered as illustrated in Figure 7.11. Each layer provides a communication service at its interface but is called a protocol because it internally utilizes a protocol to realize that service (that protocol makes use of the service provided by the layer below). More than one service option can be defined at each layer, if needed to meet distinct application needs (see the sidebar "RMI Is Layered on Messages" on page 235 for an example of this).

EXAMPLE: *TCP and UDP are two "transport layer" services implemented using the IP service, which is the foundation of the Internet. Two more specialized services, RTP and IIOP, are implemented by adding a layer to UDP and TCP, respectively. An application is free to use any of these services (TCP, UDP, RTP, or IIOP) directly.*

These services are de facto standards from the IETF (see the sidebar "Internet Engineering Task Force (IETF)" on page 136), with the exception of IIOP, which is promulgated by the OMG (see the sidebar "Object Management Group" on page 137). Further detail on how these services are implemented is given in Chapter 11.

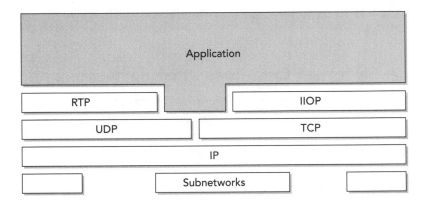

Figure 7.11 The internet suite of protocols, including those support-ing datagrams, sessions, and the RMI. These layers are implemented within the operating system and networking layers.

7.3.1 Internet Protocol (IP)

As a network of networks, the internet did not start from scratch, but rather built on existing networking technologies. Those tech-nologies (such as Ethernet, token ring, and Asynchronous Transfer Mode) are shown as the bottom layer, labeled "subnetworks." The *Internet Protocol* (IP), which forms the internetworking layer, can be viewed in two complementary ways. First, it is a protocol for inter-connecting subnetworks, with the result that end-to-end communi-cation services are possible in spite of the heterogeneity of the underlying layer. Second, IP is a spanning layer (see "The Spanning Layer" on page 130) that hides this heterogeneity through a stan-dard interface decoupled from specific networking technologies. IP is accessed by applications through an intermediary transport layer (UDP or TCP). Transport services customize the generic but limited service provided by IP to particular application needs.

7.3.2 User Datagram Protocol (UDP)

UDP is the most basic internet transport service. UDP provides a *datagram*, which is similar to a message, but with one important dif-ference: The number of bits in a datagram is limited. If an applica-tion wishes to send a message too long to be a UDP datagram, it must split up that message.

The service provided by UDP is quite similar to the postal service postcard analogy: Each UDP datagram is independent, and UDP does not recognize any shared context. UDP does not promise to deliver a datagram (although it obviously tries its best), and it does not promise to deliver datagrams sent to the same recipient in the sending order. UDP internally provides multiplexing and queueing similar to that described for messages in "Queueing and Multiplexing" on page 222. In order to receive datagrams, the recipient has to request them from the UDP layer.

7.3.3 Transmission Control Protocol (TCP)

TCP offers a type of session (called a TCP connection), although like UDP it does not directly support messages. Rather, TCP delivers a stream of bytes (eight-bit data) delivered reliably and in the same order they are sent. There is an establishment and a disestablishment phase to the protocol. There are two ways to communicate messages by TCP:

- *One message per connection:* To send a single message, a single TCP connection can be established and disestablished. The message is sent as a stream of bytes (with the constraint that the message must have an integral number of bytes). This high overhead approach (due to an establishment for every message) is most useful for sending long messages.

- *Application-defined message protocol:* Multiple messages can be sent per TCP connection if the application is willing to define its own protocol to do so. Fortunately this is simple, for example, by defining a special delimiter byte separating messages.

TCP doesn't offer multiplexing, although a recipient can open separate connections to multiple senders. It does provide queueing, as the recipient can ask for any data that has been received and is provided all the bytes that have arrived on that connection.

TCP, since it offers more facilities (including some discussed in Chapter 11), such as reliable and ordered delivery, is simpler to use than UDP. Why then would an application use UDP? The reason is

RMI Is Layered on Messages

An RMI consists of a request of the form (action, parameters) and a response in the form (return_values); each can be embedded in a message. The process of packing a list of data items (parameters and return values) in a message is called *marshalling*.

The request message must include a host and object identifier (so the invocation can be routed to the correct object). The message body must include a method identifier (so the right method can be invoked on that object) and the parameters. The response message includes the return_values, and the service binds the response with the request to the client object.

Marshalling is greatly complicated if the two objects are running on different platforms in different languages, since the representation of data is likely to be different. Therefore, a conversion is necessary somewhere in the infrastructure (see Chapter 9).

Internet Streaming Multimedia Protocols

The most basic protocol for multimedia streaming is the Real-Time Transport Protocol (RTP), which includes message sequence and timing information allowing a recipient to reconstruct the relative timing of messages. RTP normally utilizes UDP, because of its minimum delay, although there are other possibilities (such as TCP, with its reliability but higher delay). RTP also includes a definition of mixers and translators with the network that allow the coding to be changed or firewalls penetrated.

Associated with RTP is the Real-Time Streaming Protocol (RTSP) that allows applications to control sessions incorporating multiple RTP sessions; in essence, RTSP controls a remote multimedia server and is intentionally similar to HTTP, which controls a remote Web server (see the sidebar "The Hypertext Transfer Protocol (HTTP)" on page 220). Multipoint applications often use broadcast services, where recipients may enter and leave dynamically as time passes. The Session Description Protocol (SDP) provides a way for such "conferences" to be advertised and for hosts to enter and leave them. The

performance: Due to the overhead of establishing and disestablishing connections, sending individual short messages by UDP is much more efficient. Also, the reliable delivery of TCP is offset by greater delay because any data lost by IP has to be retransmitted.

7.3.4 Internet Inter-ORB Protocol (IIOP)

UDP and TCP allow communication in both directions to flow independently but do not directly support a message with reply service. The association of a message and its reply would have to be created by the application. Similarly, UDP and TCP don't directly support the remote method invocation (see "Remote Method Invocation" on page 225).

The OMG has defined a de facto standard called IIOP that provides RMI directly and transparently across the network. IIOP is a layer above TCP; it allows a series of RMIs to another host on a single TCP connection. See the sidebar "RMI Is Layered on Messages" to see how this layering is implemented.

7.3.5 Multimedia Sessions

As applications become more sophisticated, and especially as they incorporate streaming audio and video and similar media, there is an expanding need for protocols supporting complex combinations of real-time streaming media, such as audio and video, and also complex sessions incorporating simultaneous audio and video streams (see "Multimedia Transport" on page 229).

E X A M P L E : *A multipoint video conference may have a number of users participating, each originating video with its associated audio, which is broadcast to all the users.*

The IETF and W3C are standardizing protocols that support these complex multimedia sessions. (see the sidebar "Internet Streaming Multimedia Protocols").

Further Reading

[CST94] is a good introduction to the Internet, with an especially good discussion of some of the problems facing it in the future. [Pet96] and [Wal96] are excellent recent books on networks and their design philosophy, although both focus on low-level details omitted in this chapter. [Bak97] covers distributed object management and the remote method invocation.

Synchronized Multimedia Integration Language (SMIL) is a W3C standard that allows the composition of complex combinations of media from a multimedia server.

Trustworthiness: Reliability and Security

8

Networked computing is acceptable in mission-critical applications only if it is trustworthy. This means the application works correctly, almost all the time, and is secure against various external threats and natural disasters. As the applications of networked computing expand to encompass critical infrastructure, business applications, and electronic commerce, trustworthiness becomes a crucial issue for business and the larger society. The impact of failures or inappropriate penetration could be widespread and damaging.

8.1 Facets of Trustworthiness

Several major facets of trustworthiness are listed in Table 8.1. Any trustworthy application must combine these elements. What must be done right to have hope for a trustworthy system? The answer is many things, including important human and management elements. Further, a computer system is only as trustworthy as its weakest link. These elements must not only be combined carefully, but they also interact.

8.1.1 Program and System Correctness

A major source of unreliability is flawed computer programs. Software applications and the infrastructure that support them are very large, complex, and can experience an astronomically large number of possible conditions (see Section 6.1.1 on page 178). Although any application is subjected to extensive testing, including alpha- and beta-site testing with actual users (see Section 3.4.2 on page

Table 8.1 Important aspects of networked computing system trustworthiness.

Factor	Description	Analogy
Intrinsic reliability	The application operates correctly, all the time, even in the face of inevitable equipment and facility failures and natural disasters. This assumes no deliberate internal or external threats or vandalism.	A bank's financial systems should be designed and managed such that, in the course of normal operations, customers are served well and no financial errors are made. This includes contingency plans for major disasters such as floods and earthquakes.
Security	The system continues to operate reliably and protects its confidential information in the face of aberrant or malicious behavior on the part of unauthorized parties.	The bank designs its facilities and operations to prevent criminal behavior such as robberies, sabotage, and theft of confidential information.
Human elements	Trustworthiness is dependent on competent and honest operators, who faithfully follow established policies and procedures and make good decisions. A crucial component of security is operational vigilance for unusual or suspicious activity.	No matter how well the bank's systems are designed, they are vulnerable to problems caused by incompetent or dishonest workers. The bank posts guards at branches and crucial facilities to report suspicious activity and deter lawbreakers.

106), it is simply not possible to thoroughly test all possible conditions. Thus, latent program errors (colloquially called software bugs) are inevitable.

ANALOGY: *The transportation system works well most of the time, but occasionally there are accidents.*

These bugs are observed, and corrected as they are observed, as part of maintenance and new releases. Serious flaws may be manifested at the time of installation, in which case it may be necessary to "roll back" to a previous release. Serious bugs can cause the application or computer system to *crash*, meaning an unrecoverable error necessitates a restart from scratch.

EXAMPLE: *The Nasdaq stock exchange upgraded the software on both its primary and backup computers (for compatibility) in July 1994. This caused their systems to crash, and the exchange was forced to halt trading for two hours while the previous release was restored [OST97].*

Bugs in their most benign (but most difficult to detect) form don't cause crashes but "merely" incorrect results.

EXAMPLE: *The Pentium processor was found to encounter errors in its floating point arithmetic, caused by a bug in its microcode (software embedded within the chip). Although it rarely occurred, when the bug was detected, Intel was forced to supply replacements to many customers.*

Human Element

Every application has to be configured during installation for its local conditions, and during its operations innumerable decisions are made by its operators. Even the best laid plans of its designers are dependent on vigilance and competent decisions during installation and operation.

EXAMPLE: *A telephone switching center in New York City inadvertently went on battery backup (during a power system overload compounded by a backup generator failure) in September 1991. The designers had included alarm bells and warning lights to warn of this condition, but they were ignored by operators for six hours until the batteries discharged. Because the center was crucial to local air traffic control, 400 flights were canceled and tens of thousands of passengers were inconvenienced [OST97].*

Emergent Behavior

A large application is decomposed into individual modules whose behaviors are individually well understood. However, when many modules interact in complex ways (see Section 6.1.1 on page 178), surprising and unanticipated behaviors (called *emergent behaviors*) are sometimes observed. Emergent behavior is not an error per se; rather, it is a natural phenomenon that can be beneficial but is most often undesirable or even destructive.

Diversity, Reliability, and Security

A diversity of technologies and vendors may increase the likelihood of either downtime or security holes, in part because the operators have less familiarity with each individual technology. On the other hand, in the absence of such diversity, problems that do occur can be more severe.

ANALOGY: *Genetically diverse animal populations are more resistant to disease. If all animals in a population were genetically identical, they could readily succumb to the same disease.*

When an application incorporates multiple identical copies of the same program, very minor errors can spawn serious problems because of subtle interactions among the multiple copies. In this regard, software components (see "What Is a Software Component?" on page 200) are a double-edged sword. On the one hand, widely used components are more thoroughly tested and thus have fewer bugs. On the other hand, since they are distributed more broadly, they might interact in surprisingly destructive ways.

EXAMPLE: *A small flaw in a software upgrade in a telephone switch in New*

ANALOGY: *A system as complex as the worldwide economy exhibits emergent behavior, such as business cycles and recessions, that cannot be well anticipated or explained in terms of the behavior of individual economic actors. On the other hand, by studying the behavior of the system in the large (in macroeconomics), insights—if not complete understanding—can be gained.*

Emergent behavior can cause crashes, but more benign forms cause deterioration in performance or functionality. Prevention of emergent behavior, or even of recurrence, is difficult. The widespread replication of the same technology seems to increase the likelihood of emergent behavior (see the sidebar "Diversity, Reliability, and Security").

Availability

Availability refers to the fraction of the time an application is running when it is needed. Availability is reduced by *downtime*, which is a period of unavailability because of scheduled maintenance (including installation of software upgrades, or fixing of bugs or configuration errors or problems), hardware failures, recovery from crashes, power failures, etc. Availability is usually expressed as the percentage of time the system is available. The relationship of downtime and availability is shown in Table 8.2.

There is a trade-off between the economic impact of downtime in comparison to the cost of high availability. In many essential systems, such as an air traffic control system or telephone network, the social and economic cost of downtime is so great that extraordinary measures (and costs) are undertaken to ensure high availability (1 hour per 20 years is achieved in telephone switching systems). In many other applications, lower availability may be tolerated in the interest of lower cost. For example, 99 percent availability might be acceptable in a typical business application, if the downtime came in many short periods rather than one long failure per week, or if it could be scheduled at less critical times (2 a.m. Sunday morning, for example) [Ber97].

Downtime is not the only impact of application crashes or aberrant behavior. There may be permanent loss of data, which has its own

Table 8.2 Relationship of downtime to availability [Ber97].

Downtime	Availability
1 hour per day	95.8%
1 hour per week	99.41%
1 hour per month	99.86%
1 hour per year	99.9886%
1 hour per 20 years	99.99942%

economic or social cost. The issues are thus how often downtime occurs, what is the restoration time, and how much if any data is lost.

High availability requirements can increase the costs of development, equipment, and worker training or salaries (hiring more skilled operators). Development costs are increased by greater attention to recovering gracefully from unusual conditions and more time and attention paid to program correctness and testing. Avoiding downtime even during inevitable failures of hardware and communication links requires *fault tolerance*, in which a failed piece of equipment is automatically replaced by a redundant replacement. Some useful technical tools for increasing availability are listed in Table 8.3.

These features are complementary. For example, if one processor fails, switching to a redundant processor will prevent loss of data if there is a replica, or if the data is persistent. Data replication has many uses besides fault tolerance (see the sidebar "Uses of Data Replication").

8.1.2 Security: Countering External Threats

Intrinsic reliability addresses unintended or natural problems. Security addresses hostile threats from workers or citizens with nefarious purposes, such as vandalism (corrupting data or disrupting operations) or theft of data or services. The greatest external threats arise

York City in January 1990 cascaded throughout the country, causing over 50 percent of the telephone traffic to be blocked in the AT&T nationwide network for over seven hours [OST97]. The same upgraded software had been replicated across the country, and the replicated flaw interacted, causing each switch to crash the switches with which it interacted.

Similarly, if a security flaw is exploited in a particular technology, the damage is potentially more severe if that technology is widely deployed.

Uses of Data Replication

There are a number of motivations for data replication besides aiding in fault tolerance. Replication can improve performance by keeping a replica of data closer to where it is needed. In networked computing, usually "closer" means "on this side of a communication link bottleneck," which leads to the idea of *caching* described in Chapter 12.

ANALOGY: *If you are living in a two-story house and don't appreciate the time and effort to run up and down the stairs, you might purchase two copies of a book you are reading and keep one copy on each floor. That way, a copy will be close at hand at all times.*

Similar issues arise when users collaborate on common information, as in collaborative authoring (see the sidebar "Collaborative Authoring" on page 28). The data must be replicated, one copy for each user. Replication of data where the copies are all being modified simultaneously means that changes to any one copy must be reflected as soon as possible to the other copies. A similar issue is document *version control*. When multiple users are making changes to a document, there is a need to recover older versions of the document if not all users agree with the changes.

Table 8.3 Techniques for fault tolerance and graceful crash recovery.

Feature	Description	Analogy
Equipment redundancy	Provide backup equipment (hosts, network switches, communication links, etc.). Upon failure of the primary equipment, switch to the redundant backup.	Keep a spare car in the garage. If you have car trouble, get a ride home to use your spare car.
Data replication	Keep replicated copies of data. Upon loss of data, restore from the replica (losing changes in the interim).	Leave a spare copy of your income tax returns with a friend. In case a fire destroys either copy, use the spare.
Data persistence	A property of data that outlives the program that created it (see Section 6.3.1 on page 207). Upon a crash, data can be recovered when the program is restarted.	Take written notes at a meeting. In case you can't remember what happened, fall back on the notes.

when hosts are connected to a network, especially the global Internet, since this allows virtually anybody to attempt access. Various means have been developed to counter these threats, although not yet with complete effectiveness.

ANALOGY: *Once access to bank branches is given to the general public, both customers and bank robbers can enter. Countermeasures such as glass partitions, surveillance cameras, and alarms can deter criminals but also create a less friendly and functional environment for the customer.*

This analogy illustrates two downsides to security. First, it is expensive—like high availability, high security increases design costs, capital investments, and operational costs. Second, security is invasive—there is a trade-off between helping legitimate users accomplish their purposes easily and preventing vandalism or theft.

Good security requires an understanding of both the inherent vulnerabilities of the application and the nature of potential threats. Unfortunately, such comprehensive understanding is infeasible, so vigilance and continual learning of new threats are necessary

[OST97]. Security is an ongoing process, including new measures to counter newly identified threats [CST98].

EXAMPLE: *CERT is a clearinghouse located at Carnegie Mellon University that "studies Internet security vulnerabilities, provides incident response services to sites that have been the victims of attack, publishes a variety of security alerts, researches security and survivability in wide-area-networked computing, and develops information to help you improve security at your site."*

Two aspects of security are easy to overlook, so they should be emphasized up front:

- An individual security measure is rarely effective in isolation. Security is by nature a *system* composed of many complementary measures, and they are only effective in concert.

- People are as important to security as technology. Although people external to an organization or administrative domain are a security threat, employees or other insiders are a much greater threat, as they have greater opportunity for mischief. Conversely, worker training, competence, and vigilance (fortunately more the norm than dishonesty and maliciousness) are the most important ingredients of effective security.

Analogy: The Postal System

It is useful to consider briefly an analogy to the postal system, which encounters in the physical world many of the same security objectives and issues as networked computers. Some features of postal system security are illustrated in Figure 8.1, focusing specifically on sending a document through the mail.

Assume that Alice wants to send a message (using a postal letter) to Bob. To begin, Alice writes her message on paper using permanent ink, making it difficult to modify surreptitiously. This provides assurance to Bob that the message was not modified in transit by some third party, say Eve. (The fictitious names Alice, Bob, and Eve are commonly used by computer security people to keep straight the parties to a security protocol.) Formally, the paper and permanent ink provide evidence of the *integrity* of the message. Also, to assure

Availability, Security, and the Market

High availability computer systems were pioneered by Tandem Computer in the 1970s, and since then other vendors have entered the market. These systems are used in applications such as OLTP (see Section 2.6.1 on page 53), where downtime is expensive.

The market is arguably less effective in fostering security. Threats are diffuse and difficult to characterize, and the cost benefits of security are difficult to quantify. Much core technology (the UNIX operating system and the internet technologies) were developed in a benign environment of trusted users (the university research community) and thus were originally lax on security.

The most effective market mechanism for promulgating good security is to make sure the risks (and costs) of security breakdowns are borne by those in a position to deploy the security necessary to counter those risks.

EXAMPLE: *In the United Kingdom, by law, the risk of theft of money from automatic teller machines (ATMs) is borne by the consumer, whereas in the United States it is borne by the bank. As a result, banks in the United States have deployed much stronger ATM security measures.*

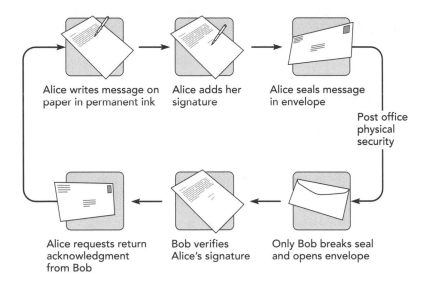

Figure 8.1 How the postal system provides some security features in a message from Alice to Bob.

Bob that Alice was the source of the message (and not Eve pretending to be Alice), Alice may affix a signature that Bob can check against a copy of her signature that he keeps in his files. The signature provides *authentication*—a provable identification of Alice. Alice may also not want Eve to read the message, which she would like to keep confidential (between her and Bob). For this purpose, Alice seals her message in an envelope to keep away prying eyes. During transit, the postal system maintains physical security, allowing access only to postal workers, who are presumed honest and trustworthy. Once it arrives, Bob can unseal the envelope to read the message and examine the signature to authenticate Alice. He may notify Alice (using a return letter) of successful delivery. Later, Bob may find it necessary to prove in court that Alice sent him the message (for example, if it is a legal contract). For this purpose he would produce the message and argue that since it was written in permanent ink on paper—and thus difficult to modify without detection—and contained Alice's signature, Alice must have sent it. The inability of Alice to later deny she sent the message is called *nonrepudiation*.

It is important to note that some of these security measures would falter if they had not been combined. For example, Alice might be able to repudiate the message if she had not been authenticated (by her signature) or if she could claim the message was altered in transit (the message didn't have integrity).

Even with all these measures, the postal system has inherent vulnerabilities. Bob's mailbox—in order to be accessible to a postal worker—is also accessible to any passerby (such as Eve), who can steal a letter or insert a fake letter. The envelope also allows Eve to determine that Alice sent Bob a message (by her return address), even if she can't examine the contents. To counter some of these threats, the government has established *legal sanctions*—including laws against the theft of mail from, or insertion of unauthorized mail into, a mailbox. If Bob is especially worried about these threats, he could rent a post office box, which restricts access to his mail (by giving him an exclusive key) and thus maintains physical security all the way from Alice to him.

Threats to Networked Computing

Many of the security measures in the physical world must be transferred to networked computers. Messages crossing the network, whether they originate with a user (such as an email message) or with an application (such as module-to-module interaction) are data (a collection of bits). This is a security challenge, because the infrastructure, in order to manipulate and process those bits (for example, replicate them—see Section 5.4.1 on page 157), must inherently be able to observe and modify them. Without additional measures, there would be no way to prevent a message from being examined or modified in transit, or to detect that this happened.

Similar observations apply to the other security elements identified in the postal system analogy. Each message must include identification of sender and recipient, also represented by bits, which can easily be observed or modified. In an internet, for example, it is possible to pretend to be a different host by faking the sender identification information (this is called *spoofing*).

Computer Viruses

Between executions, programs are stored in a special *executable* file in the computer storage (such as magnetic disk). During these dormant times, programs are vulnerable to infection by a virus. A virus attaches itself to an executable (called a host) in a way that causes its own execution each time the host is invoked. The virus can then replicate itself by attaching its own replica to other executable files, and at the same time, it can consume resources or destroy data.

ANALOGY: *In biology, a virus is an infectious agent that can multiply by replication only in living cells of animals, plants, or bacteria. Viruses can consume resources or act destructively. Similarly, computer viruses infect computer systems and can multiply by self-replication.*

Viruses must be taken seriously whenever an executable is moved from one host to another, using a floppy disk or transferring over the network. Fortunately, there are excellent utilities for detecting and eradicating viruses.

ANALOGY: *It is easy to put a deceptive return address on a postal envelope. You are wise not to trust the return address as a form of authentication, but to look for a more secure authentication of the sender (such as a signature) inside the envelope.*

Networked computers are susceptible to more subtle threats as well. One threat, particularly in a network environment, is the *computer virus*. This is a piece of executable program that can "infect" computer files, self-replicate, and cause damage (see the sidebar "Computer Viruses").

Like criminals that might break into a post office, hosts are susceptible to *intrusion* by unauthorized access through the network. Ways are needed to prevent these intrusions by admitting authorized users and preventing access to others. Frequently it is desired to provide *conditional* access to some applications but not others.

EXAMPLE: *A Web server is often intended to be accessed by anybody on the Internet. At the same time, there may be other applications or stored information on the same host that should have restricted access.*

Even if access is denied to any but authorized users, others might gain entry by spoofing the identity of an authorized user. To counter this attack, there have to be user authentication measures analogous to the signature in the postal system. Similarly, if legal contracts are "signed" over the network, or orders for goods placed, a forgetful or unscrupulous user might later repudiate the transaction unless there are security measures to prevent this.

A malicious attacker may mount a *denial of service attack*, injecting vast amounts of artificial work or communications causing a host or network to become overloaded and degrading the performance for legitimate users.

ANALOGY: *Your teenage child might retaliate for the punishment of being banished to his room by tying up the phone.*

EXAMPLE: *In 1988, a student at Cornell University unleashed a worm on the Internet that resulted in a denial of service to a large num-*

ber of UNIX hosts. A worm is similar to a virus (see the sidebar "Computer Viruses" on page 248), except it replicates by exploiting operating system vulnerabilities to get itself installed and executed on another computer.

8.2 Computer and Network Security Measures

How can the myriad external threats to networked computer systems be countered? This is the role of security measures. Networked computing security includes a number of building blocks analogous to those in the postal system, which are listed in Table 8.4. Fortunately, these capabilities are sophisticated and capable of achieving a much higher level of security than in the postal system analogy. However, to be effective, they have to be *used*, which unfortunately can be invasive (in cost or convenience) to legitimate users. Among other things, these security measures create serious administrative or operational issues.

The most important point is that the capabilities in Table 8.4 work in concert and must be deployed in a coherent *system* backed by well-trained and vigilant operators, a coherent set of established security policies, and criminal laws and penalties. Again, the overall security is only as good as the weakest link.

8.2.1 Encryption Ensures Confidentiality

The confidentiality of data stored or communicated across the network is achieved by *encryption*. Suppose Alice wants to send a confidential message to Bob while preventing an eavesdropper, Eve, from reading the message. The idea is for Alice to *lock* (encrypt) a message so that it can only be *unlocked* (decrypted) by Bob, who has the unlocking *key*. Eve is unsuccessful in unlocking the message to view it because she does not possess Bob's unlocking key.

A N A L O G Y :   *In the physical world, a lockbox can be used to provide confidentiality. The lockbox requires an unlocking key to open. To be analogous to encryption, a special lockbox that requires two keys—a locking key to lock and an unlocking key to open—must*

Table 8.4 Pillars of a computer security system.

Capability	Description	Analogy
Authentication	Messages received over the network may be received from anyone and anywhere. Authentication enables a recipient to verify the identity of a sender.	On paper documents, a signature is appended. The recipient of a telephone call may be able to identify the caller by recognizing her voice.
Message integrity	A message is a collection of bits and may easily be modified as it crosses the network. Message integrity ensures that the message has not been modified since created by the sender.	Paper documents created in permanent ink are difficult to modify without detection. Although additions are possible, they are difficult to achieve without detection.
Confidentiality	A message passing the network might be read by an eavesdropper. Confidentiality ensures that a message can only be read by the intended recipient.	The sender of a letter encloses it in an envelope to keep away prying eyes. A postcard, on the other hand, does not provide confidentiality.
Nonrepudiation	A sender might later claim never to have sent a message. Nonrepudiation enables a recipient to prove (in court if necessary) that the sender did send the message.	A recipient of a document (purchase order or contract, for example) will require a signature on it so he can later prove the identity of the sender. Additional assurance is provided by signing two copies of the document, one kept by the sender and one sent to the recipient.
Access control	A host connected to the Internet will be vulnerable to theft or vandalism by unauthorized parties. Access control restricts access to hosts, or particular applications, to authorized and authenticated users.	Postal patrons are allowed into the public area of the post office, but only postal employees can enter secure areas where mail is sorted. Employees are authenticated by a picture badge.

be assumed. First, Alice locks a message in the lockbox to protect it from being read by Eve. Second, Bob unlocks the lockbox to obtain the contents—the message from Alice.

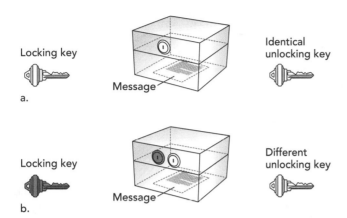

Figure 8.2 Two types of lockboxes, which are analogous to a symmetric and asymmetric encryption system.

Encryption comes in two distinct flavors: symmetric and asymmetric. These are analogous to two distinct types of lockboxes, depending on the relationship of the locking and unlocking key, as illustrated in Figure 8.2.

- *Symmetric locking and unlocking keys:* The lockbox requires identical keys to lock and unlock the lockbox. There are two replicas of this key—one held by Alice and one by Bob.

- *Asymmetric lock and key:* The lockbox has two different keys, a locking key to lock the lockbox (possessed by Alice) and an *unlocking* key (possessed by Bob) that unlocks the box. Alice's key cannot unlock the box—it can only lock it. Only Bob's key can unlock the lockbox to recover the message once it has been locked.

The symmetric lock and key is conceptually simpler, but there are advantages to the asymmetric lock and key, as will be seen shortly.

As shown in Figure 8.3, in networked computing a message is data (a string of bits) and the locking or unlocking key must also be data. The analogy to the lockbox is an *encryption algorithm*—a mathematical algorithm that takes as input the message and the key and generates as its output the encrypted message (also data, another

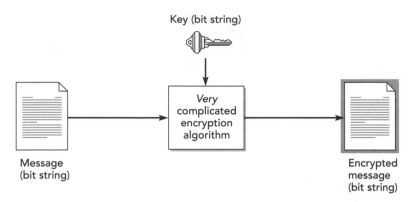

Figure 8.3 The encryption algorithm hides a message from anybody without a complementary decryption key.

string of bits) (see the sidebar "Any Information Can Be Represented by Bits" on page 10). This encryption algorithm is designed so that the original message can be recovered from the encrypted message by a *decryption algorithm*, which requires the unlocking key. Together, the encryption algorithm applied by the sender, followed by a decryption algorithm applied by the recipient, constitutes a *confidentiality protocol* (see Section 7.1 on page 216).

Strictly speaking, recovering the message from the encrypted message is not impossible. For example, Eve could try unlocking the message by systematically trying all possible unlocking keys. Rather, it must be assumed that this type of attack is *computationally impractical*. This means it is not possible—using a computer that Eve can afford—within a period of time that makes the resulting message useful to her.

The time it would take to try all keys depends on the *key length* (number of bits in the key) and the speed of available computers. The key length can be made sufficiently long to foil this attack for any desired period, for a particular computer technology.

E X A M P L E :   *For a 128-bit key, there are $2^{128} = 3 \times 10^{38}$ different keys. If a computer could try 100 million keys per second (a rough time for today's fastest desktop computers), this attack would take 3×10^{30} seconds, or 10^{21} centuries.*

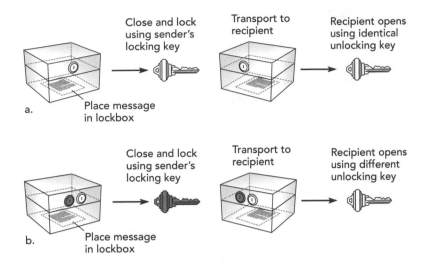

Figure 8.4 Using a lockbox to preserve confidentiality: (a) symmetric and (b) asymmetric.

Symmetric vs. Asymmetric Encryption

The lockbox analogy illustrates confidentiality for the two cases in Figure 8.4. The requirements for confidentiality are different in the two cases:

- *Symmetric encryption:* The locking and unlocking keys are identical. Eve must not possess a replica of this key.

- *Asymmetric encryption:* The locking and unlocking keys are different. Eve must not possess a replica of the *unlocking* key, but it doesn't matter if she possesses a replica of the locking key, because that would not allow her to unlock the message.

The last statement is important, but to be valid, an additional important assumption is necessary: It must be computationally impractical for Eve, possessing a replica of the locking key, to turn that into a replica of the unlocking key. Fortunately, there are asymmetric encryption algorithms with this property.

In the asymmetric case, it is permissible to distribute replicas of the locking key publicly. Bob, who wishes to receive confidential messages from many people (including Alice), can give a replica of the locking key to anyone he expects might want to send him a confidential message. Bob need not worry that Eve will then possess a replica of the locking key, since it will not help her unlock a message sent by Alice (or anyone else). The locking key can be made available to anyone to send Bob confidential messages (for example, it can be included in directories or published on Bob's Web home page). For this reason, the asymmetric locking key is called a *public key*, and the asymmetric unlocking key is called a *secret key* (since only Bob can possess it).

For the symmetric case, the single key must be a *secret* key, not divulged to anybody other than the sender and recipient. This makes the symmetric approach logistically troublesome to Bob, since he must somehow get a replica of this secret locking key to Alice. Obviously, he can't just send the unlocking key to Alice over the network, lest Eve capture it in transit. Further, he must trust Alice not to give it to anyone else or use it herself to read confidential messages to Bob from others.

E X A M P L E :   *If Bob is a merchant selling goods over the network, literally anybody is a potential consumer who might buy Bob's goods, including Alice. If Alice wants to use her credit card to make a purchase, she would like to avoid its interception by Eve, who might use it improperly to make her own purchases. The asymmetric encryption protocol is preferred, since Bob can simply publish his public key, and Alice can use it to encrypt her credit card number. Eve, who does not possess Bob's secret key, cannot view the credit card number.*

To summarize, the two approaches are illustrated in Figure 8.5. In subsequent figures, an encrypted message is denoted by a shaded box as in Figure 8.5.

E X A M P L E :   *The most widely used de jure symmetric encryption standard is the data encryption standard (DES), formally called DEA-1 by ISO (see the sidebar "International Organization for Standards (ISO)" on page 135). A widely used de facto asymmetric encryption standard is RSA, named after its inventors Rivest, Shamir, and Adleman.*

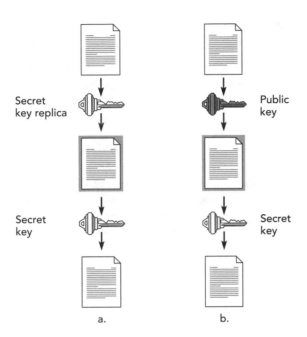

Figure 8.5 (a) Symmetric and (b) asymmetric encryption confidentiality protocols.

An important characteristic of the asymmetric encryption protocol is that the roles of the two keys can be reversed: Alice can encrypt a message using her secret key, and Bob can decrypt the result using Alice's public key, and the original message is recovered. This reversed protocol does not provide confidentiality, since anybody with Alice's public key can recover Alice's message. However, it will be useful later for authentication and message integrity.

This description might lead you to conclude that only asymmetric encryption is useful. Unfortunately, asymmetric encryption and decryption require roughly one thousand times more computational effort than symmetric encryption and decryption. Thus, symmetric encryption is superior for "bulk encryption" of large amounts of data and is widely used for this purpose. In practice, the two approaches are often combined (see Section 8.2.4 on page 262).

8.2.2 Authentication

Bob has to worry that he may be dealing with an impostor who *claims* to be Alice. Compared to the personal interaction of the physical world, impersonation is easy over the network.

EXAMPLE: *When Alice visits an Unlimited store in the local mall, there are a number of clues that this is a legitimate business—such as the store, the sign out front, etc. Over the network, Alice should be skeptical of a seller claiming to be Unlimited, since an unscrupulous person (such as Eve) could more easily set up a Web site claiming to be Unlimited and collect money from Alice without delivering goods. In their store, Unlimited authenticates Alice by requesting a picture identification or credit card. Over the network, Eve might more easily impersonate Alice, and Alice might then have to pay for goods actually ordered and received by Eve.*

Authentication allows Bob to verify that the person claiming to be Alice is in fact Alice. In practice, both Bob and Alice should authenticate one another. Examining how authentication is done in the physical world gives some clues as to how it can be done in networked computing:

- Bob could compare a person's face with Alice's picture shown in her picture identification card and, if it matches, authenticate her as Alice. This authentication depends on Alice's physical characteristics.

- If a person can produce Alice's credit card—and the issuer of the credit card confirms that Alice has not reported it stolen—Bob might authenticate that person as Alice. This authentication depends on the person presenting something only Alice should possess.

In both these cases, authentication depends on a trusted third party, called an *authority*—either the issuer of Alice's picture identification or the issuer of her credit card. In fact, it is impossible to authenticate Alice without the aid of an authority. Depending on someone to authenticate themselves is inherently suspect.

Biometrics

The two physical-world authentication techniques have analogs in networked computing. The first, based on a person's physical characteristics, is called *biometrics*.

EXAMPLE: *If Bob wants to authenticate Alice, and has obtained some unique physical characteristics of Alice from a trusted third party (her picture, fingerprint, or the pattern of the iris of her eye, for example), then Bob can verify that physical characteristic.*

Biometrics requires a trusted way to gather the biometrics data on the person being authenticated. This is most widely used to authenticate a person entering a physical facility such as a bank vault, computer center, or ATM, where the data is gathered under the complete control of the authenticator.

Shared Secret

Asking the person claiming to be Alice to produce something that only Alice should possess, as confirmed by an authority, is the most practical authentication over a network. In the physical world, that "something" is a physical object such as a picture identification or a credit card. Over the network, that something can't be a physical object and thus must be a *secret*. A secret is data—a string of bits— or something equivalent, such as a password, which only one person knows. A *password* is a nonsensical string of characters (letters, punctuation marks, numbers) that the person has chosen at random and committed to memory. Authentication proceeds by challenging a person claiming to be Alice to produce Alice's secret. There are at least several subtleties in doing this securely:

- It is a bad idea for Alice to give her secret to Bob for purposes of authentication, since Bob could later use it to impersonate Alice.

- It is doubly bad for Alice to send her secret to Bob over the network, as Eve could intercept it and later use it to impersonate Alice (and Bob would have it as well).

- There must be an authority that Bob trusts to verify Alice's secret.

There are thus three valued properties of an authentication scheme based on a secret:

- Bob should not be required to know Alice's secret in order to authenticate her.

- Alice should be able to prove she has a secret without revealing it.

- Bob should be able to verify the secret with an authority he trusts.

The first property can be achieved using asymmetric encryption keys. The idea is for Bob to acquire Alice's *public* key and then verify that the person claiming to be Alice possesses Alice's corresponding *secret* key. This is secure if Alice's public key is confirmed by an authority that Bob trusts. The second property can be simultaneously achieved using a *challenge/response protocol*.

EXAMPLE: *In a commonly used protocol, Bob generates a random integer k, encrypts it using Alice's public key, and sends the result to Alice with the challenge to respond with k + 1 encrypted by Alice's secret key. In order to meet that challenge, Alice has to decrypt the message to obtain k, add unity, and encrypt the result using her secret key. Both require Alice to have her secret key. Bob, knowing Alice's public key, can decrypt the response from Alice to confirm that the result is, in fact, k + 1. This protocol depends on the reversal of the role of the public and private keys in the asymmetric encryption protocol. Notice that it does not require Alice to reveal her secret key, or Bob to possess it.*

The third property is a bit more difficult. Bob must somehow verify Alice's public key with an authority he trusts. The way this works is similar to the driver's license authentication in the physical world. Alice presents Bob with a credential called a *digital certificate* (analogous to a driver's license) that was issued to her by a trusted authority (analogous to the motor vehicle bureau). The digital certificate provides Bob with Alice's public key in a way that he can trust.

Digital Certificates and Certificate Authorities

Bob must confirm Alice's public key with a trusted authority in order to authenticate Alice. A side benefit is that once Bob has Alice's

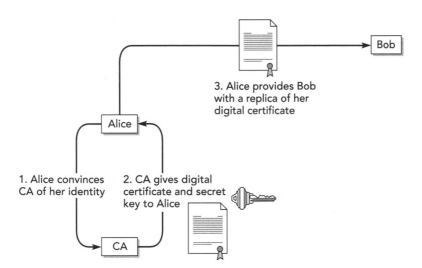

Figure 8.6 Alice uses a digital certificate to provide an authenticated public key to Bob.

Certificates and a National Identity Card

U.S. citizens have always resisted a national identity card because of privacy concerns. In the physical world, it has been possible to get along without one. However, authentication on the network for general purposes such as electronic commerce requires the equivalent in networked computing—the digital certificate. Are citizens finally ready to accept this?

public key, he can also use it to send Alice confidential messages—and be assured that Alice and only Alice can read them—as well as authenticate her. The trusted authority is called a *certificate authority* (CA), and what the CA provides in order to verify Alice's public key is called a digital certificate.

ANALOGY: *A digital certificate is analogous to a driver's license that Alice might use to prove her identity to a merchant. Alice establishes her identity with the driver's license bureau, which is analogous to the CA. The bureau issues a driver's license, analogous to the digital certificate.*

The CA is a company or government agency that specializes in issuing digital certificates. The protocol that Alice uses to obtain one and later use it is shown in Figure 8.6. (The driver's license bureau of the physical world could be substituted for the CA without any difference in the protocol.) The three steps are as follows:

1. Alice proves her identity to the CA (for example, the CA might require Alice to appear in person and present her birth certificate, social security card, and driver's license). The CA then

generates a new unique matched pair of asymmetrical encryption keys on behalf of Alice. The CA gives the secret key to Alice (which she must *keep* secret) along with a digital certificate that contains both her identity and her matching public key.

2. To establish her identity, and also her public key, with Bob (or to anyone else), Alice supplies the digital certificate provided her by the CA.

3. Presuming that Bob trusts the CA, he can use the public key from the certificate not only to authenticate any person claiming to be Alice (by the challenge/response protocol, establishing that the person has Alice's secret key) but also to send confidential messages to Alice.

EXAMPLE: *The most prominent CA is VeriSign, a company that specializes in security and makes money by issuing certificates. Like all CAs, VeriSign maintains strict internal security practices. For example, revealing Alice's secret key to a third party would be an egregious act.*

In security, there is often a catch. What is to prevent someone from making his or her own digital certificate and claiming it comes from the CA? For example, why can't Eve manufacture a digital certificate that attaches her public key to Alice's identity? Alternatively, why can't Eve modify Alice's digital certificate to substitute her public key for Alice's? If Eve can do either, she can fool Bob. These problems can be circumvented by using message integrity.

8.2.3 Message Integrity and Nonrepudiation

Recall that the *integrity* of a message sent by Alice is the assurance that the message was not modified in transit to Bob (analogous to a paper document written in permanent ink), and *nonrepudiation* allows Bob to prove that Alice created the message (analogous to a signed document). Integrity is necessary for nonrepudiation, since without it Alice can always repudiate the message by claiming it was modified after she created it.

Integrity and nonrepudiation can be achieved by using the asymmetric encryption protocol in reverse—encryption with the private key followed by decryption by the public key. Alice can encrypt her message to Bob with her secret key, and Bob can decrypt it using Alice's public key. While this does *not* provide confidentiality, Bob *can* be sure the message was not modified after Alice encrypted it. Why? Anybody can decrypt Alice's message and modify it, but they lack Alice's secret key, which would be needed to re-encrypt it.

This asymmetrical encryption reversal can also prevent Alice from repudiating the message. If Bob keeps a copy of the encrypted message and also a copy of Alice's digital certificate, he can prove in court that encrypting the message required the secret key corresponding to Alice's public key (as verified by the CA)—which could only be done by Alice—and that the message was not later modified by him or anyone else. Alice's only defense would be that her secret key was accidently revealed to someone else before the message was sent, but her case is weak if she did not report this to an authority.

For computational efficiency, a slightly different approach is used to achieve integrity and nonrepudiation, called a *digital signature*. It uses essentially the same idea, so details are omitted.

The security of the digital certificate (see "Digital Certificates and Certificate Authorities" on page 258) also depends on integrity and nonrepudiation. When the CA issues Alice's digital certificate, it attaches its own digital signature. Integrity of the certificate ensures that the certificate was not modified and that it originated with the CA.

ANALOGY: *If the CA is analogous to the driver's license bureau and the CA-issued digital certificate is analogous to a driver's license, its digital signature is analogous to the seal authenticating the license and the plastic encasing of the driver's license that prevents it from being modified.*

The last detail is that Bob requires the CA's public key to check its signature on Alice's digital certificate. This is usually addressed by building it into software.

EXAMPLE: *Web browser software includes the public keys of a set of*
CAs (and the user can add more). This allows the browser to check
the authenticity and integrity of any certificate issued by one of
those CAs. The browser can obtain authenticated public keys of
Web servers from certificates supplied by those servers and use
these public keys to check the integrity of messages, send confi-
dential messages to the server, etc.

Although all these protocols sound complicated, they are normally
embedded in the software applications, so the user need not deal
with them directly. The purpose of this discussion has been to
understand what security protocols can accomplish and what
assumptions are necessary to assume they are trustworthy.

8.2.4 Combining Techniques

Several security capabilities and techniques have been described. In
practice, if Alice and Bob interact over the network, they desire a
combination of confidentiality, authentication, integrity, and nonrepudiation. The techniques can be combined in different ways to
achieve this, as illustrated by the following examples. Assume that
Alice and Bob each possess her or his own secret key and a digital
certificate issued by a CA.

EXAMPLE: *Suppose Alice wants to communicate a message confi-*
dentially to Bob, and Bob insists on authenticating Alice and verify-
ing the message integrity. Alice can encrypt the message twice, first
using her secret key (to assure integrity and also authenticate her-
self to Bob) and then encrypting the result using Bob's public key.
She also sends him a copy of her certificate. Bob can obtain Alice's
public key from the certificate and her original message by decrypt-
ing the message with his own secret key (ensuring confidentiality)
followed by Alice's public key (authentication and integrity).

Suppose Alice wants to send a lot of messages to Bob confiden-
tially but is concerned about the computational cost of asymmetri-
cal encryption. (For example, she might want to actually talk to Bob
confidentially for a while, and her computer or Bob's might not be
able to keep up.) What she can do is create a random key for a
symmetrical encryption protocol. This key, called a session key, will

be used only once. She can communicate this session key confidentially to Bob using asymmetrical encryption and Bob's public key, which she obtains from his digital certificate. Subsequently, she encrypts the messages using symmetrical encryption with the session key, and Bob and only Bob is able to decrypt it.

This last example illustrates a benefit of a session (see Section 7.2.4 on page 227). It creates a shared context for a sequence of messages, allowing a one-time session key to be communicated to Bob only once and used on many messages.

The possibilities are numerous, but these examples illustrate some important combinations. These techniques are widely used to provide secure communication over the network.

E X A M P L E : *Netscape Communications defined an open de facto standard called Secure Socket Layer (SSL) that adds authentication, confidentiality, and integrity to sessions using the internet's TCP (see Section 7.3.3 on page 235). This protocol is widely used, particularly for secure connections between a Web server (such as retail, brokerage, and banking sites) and the browser. SSL's operation is indicated by a "key icon" in the lower-left corner of a Netscape Navigator window.*

8.2.5 Security Policies

Usually security features are built into software applications and don't disturb the user. However, they can be invasive as, for example, when a user must obtain a digital certificate to participate in a secure application. As a result, strong security techniques are sometimes not used, in spite of the resulting vulnerabilities. To avoid problems that might result, a critical element of security is a set of *security policies* established by an organization as part of a comprehensive plan for achieving a desired trade-off between security and ease of use (see Section 7.1 on page 216). Policies establish, for example, when confidentiality and authentication are required or not required. Policies are enforced primarily by system administrators, who configure hosts and applications in accordance with those policies.

Legal Sanctions

No matter how many security measures are taken, it is possible for an intruder to gain access by surreptitious or fraudulent means. An extreme example would be breaking and entering a physically restricted facility, but there are other ways, such as a confidence game or blackmail. In these cases, the intruder may have broken federal or local laws and can be apprehended and prosecuted.

EXAMPLE: *A particularly notorious individual who gained surreptitious access to many systems is Kevin Mitnick [Haf95], who was convicted of a felony.*

Laws and legal sanctions are the ultimate protector of computer systems.

Access Control

One essential security measure is *access control*, which determines and limits user access to individual applications, to individual hosts, or to entire intranets (see Section 3.3 on page 99). An important security policy concerns access rules based on "need to know" and "need to use" criteria. Access control requires several elements:

- A secure access database describing access authorizations for each user.

- Authentication protocols to authenticate each user requesting authorized access.

- Some way to prevent access to unauthorized users.

This third element is provided by the firewall (see Section 3.3.1 on page 99).

Firewalls

A tool for access control is the *firewall*—equipment imposed on a network link that connects a protected enclave (the intranet) from the global Internet. The firewall is configured to restrict communication passing through, and it offers a focal point for enforcing policies on access to the intranet. Further, a firewall often restricts communication protocols and applications.

ANALOGY: *Countries typically have checkpoints at their border crossings where laws relative to contraband, immigration and emigration, etc., are enforced.*

If hosts were intrinsically completely secure, they could be directly connected to the global Internet, but in practice hosts and their applications have security loopholes. The greatest loophole is the users with legitimate access to the host, who are often not as trained in or conscious of security issues as would be desirable. If an intruder gains access to a legitimate user account, for all practical purposes that host is compromised. Thus, it is better if intruders cannot reach the host at all. Unfortunately, it isn't as simple as a blanket denial of access to all outsiders, because an organization typically wants unrestricted access to some applications, such as

Web servers targeted at the general public. Thus, access control (using firewalls) may be necessary.

ANALOGY: *A country usually restricts its borders but also allows other countries to operate embassies and consulates within its borders. Those other countries may be permitted free passage and unrestricted access to their own embassies.*

An intranet offers no protection against threats *within* the trusted enclave. Most organizations also have internal compartmentalization, restricting access using firewalls *within* an intranet. Firewalls are discussed further in Chapter 11.

8.3 Electronic Payments

Electronic commerce has challenging security requirements because it involves the transfer of money, with the threat of large economic losses (see Section 2.6.3 on page 64). In addition, acceptance by the general public depends on its confidence in the intrinsic security against various threats, such as theft of money and credit card numbers, being stuck with charges made by others, etc. It is wise for a merchant and a customer to authenticate one another—so that the customer is not duped by an unscrupulous merchant, and the merchant is assured of payment—and the merchant obviously also demands nonrepudiation of a customer's order. All these can be achieved using security capabilities already discussed.

A security issue unique to electronic commerce is electronic payments. The ramifications of a security lapse in electronic payments are severe—the possibility of widespread forgery or theft. A customer may be concerned about privacy and thus desire confidentiality in his or her purchases. This requires, among other things, that purchase information not be made known to anybody but the merchant and that the customer's financial information remain with the financial institution. These issues place challenging requirements on an electronic payment system.

In the physical world, payments are made by cash, credit cards, debit cards, and personal checks. Credit and debit cards can be used on-line, presuming appropriate authentication and confidentiality. Electronic funds transfer from one bank account to another can also be used, which works like a check. There are, however, reasons to consider innovative alternatives:

- It may be possible to improve user convenience.

- Added security measures can reduce the vulnerability of all parties to fraud.

- A credit card payment, having a substantial transaction cost, is not economic for small purchases. Particularly in the sale of online information, there is a desire for small payments, (like fractions of a cent, often called *micropayments*). Thus, payments with small transaction costs are desirable.

- Many consumers are concerned about privacy and don't relish any ability of merchants or financial institutions to track these purchases.

There are two basic approaches to payments, whether electronic or not:

- *Account authorizations* linked to purchases (such as credit and debit cards), in which payment is transferred from financial institution to merchant, drawing upon the customer's account (a debit) or as a loan to the customer (a credit).

- *Tokens of value* carried by the consumer, such as cash, stamps, and increasingly in the future, something called a *prepaid smartcard* or *digital cash.* These tokens of value have intrinsic monetary value (either directly, like a coin, or indirectly backed by a financial institution or the government, like a bill) and can be exchanged for goods and services. They can be stored in a card (similar to a credit card) or on the disk drive of a desktop computer. Payment is direct from consumer to merchant by transferring the appropriate token(s) without an intermediary.

EXAMPLE: *A postage stamp is a token of value that can be exchanged for a single specialized postal service. It is affixed to the item being mailed.*

8.3.1 On-Line Credit Card Systems

Credit cards, today common for payments by telephone or over the network, work well for relatively large payments. They also have problems:

- Consumers are concerned about the theft of credit card numbers. This theft can occur by eavesdropping (which is countered by confidentiality, such as the Secure Socket Layer used by many electronic commerce Web sites) or by merchant employee theft.

- Consumers are concerned about privacy. Each merchant can track the purchases of a given consumer (because the same credit card number is used each time), and the financial institution can track all purchases made on a given credit card.

These concerns are addressed by an electronic credit/debit payment system called SET.

Secure Electronic Transaction (SET)

SET is a standard for on-line credit/debit card transactions established by Visa and Mastercard. In a conventional credit card transaction, the consumer deals with the merchant, and the merchant deals with the financial institution. The consumer provides credit card information to the merchant, who both authorizes the charge before fulfilling the consumer's order and submits it to the institution for payment. A key shortcoming addressed by SET is the availability of the credit card information to the merchant, which enables the tracking of purchases and increases the possibility of theft of credit card numbers.

SET logically partitions the transaction into the order and the payment authorization. The *order* for goods and services—and fulfillment of that order—is conducted between the consumer and the merchant. The *authorization for payment* is conducted between the consumer and the financial institution, which credits that payment to the merchant. This partitioning ensures that the merchant has no visibility of credit card or financial information, and the financial institution has no visibility of the order. The protocol has all the previously discussed security features, including authentication of all parties and confidentiality.

Questions about Digital Cash

New tokens of value, such as digital cash, raise a number of questions.

One obvious one is who will back the value. Is it backed by the financial institution, as in a demand deposit withdrawal, or is it backed by the Federal Reserve Bank, as in paper money, or is it backed by somebody else? What happens if a token is lost or stolen? Can the value be restored, or is it irrevocably lost? Can the thief spend it, and if so can the thief be traced? Another issue is whether digital cash is subject to regulation and if so by whom and for what societal purpose. For example, value tokens add to a nation's money supply, the size of which is tracked and controlled by a central bank to preserve monetary value. What is the impact of the global reach of the Internet and electronic commerce? Who pays for the underlying infrastructure and operation of a digital cash system, and how do they recover those costs? Is it the government recovering costs through taxation (or selling the cash they manufacture), or financial institutions through fees? Does digital cash replicate the anonymity of coins and bills, such that purchases cannot be traced?

SET includes two more subtle features. First, the authorization actually passes through the merchant, so that the consumer has the appearance of dealing only with the merchant. This authorization is encrypted, and the merchant does not have the secret key necessary to view it. Of course, the merchant does obtain confirmation from the financial institution that it will receive payment before order fulfillment. Second, the order and authorization are linked so that the customer cannot later repudiate the purchase, for example, by claiming that the payment was for other goods never delivered. This uses a variation on the digital signature, called a *dual signature*, which allows both merchant and financial institution to verify (and prove) the linking.

Digital Cash

Another on-line payment mechanism is *digital cash*, which is a token of value in networked computing—analogous to bills and coins in the physical world—that can be directly exchanged for goods or services. There are many nontechnical issues raised by any new token of value (see the sidebar "Questions about Digital Cash"). There are also interesting technical issues.

Like everything in networked computing, a token of value in a digital cash system must be represented by data; that is, a string of bits. Presumably, this data includes the monetary value, as well as possibly other things. This raises some troubling questions.

First, how can somebody accepting digital cash be convinced of its monetary value? The answer is it must have an issuer (such as a central or financial institution) that stands behind it. The issuer must not be able to repudiate it, and the merchant must verify its integrity. A consumer will obtain digital cash by taking an account withdrawal in digital cash. (Financial institutions love this idea, because to them it is an interest-free loan!) The digital cash carries a digital signature of the issuer, assuring its integrity (it cannot be modified by anybody else without detection) and also precluding the issuer from repudiating its value.

Since digital cash is data, unlike coins and bills it is easy to replicate. What, then, is to prevent the consumer from spending it more than once?

E X A M P L E : *Unless countermeasures are taken in the digital cash protocol, it would be easy to withdraw $1 from the bank, make 999,999 copies of it, and then make a $1,000,000 purchase. Naturally, the bank must ensure this cannot happen.*

This problem is circumvented by including a unique *identifier* in each token. The identifier is a big number, just like the serial number on a physical bill. A replica can be detected by comparing identifiers. The question is, where and when is the identifier checked? The issuer can detect multiple spending by refusing to deposit a token, when a token with the same identifier was previously deposited. To enable this double-spending detection, a token can be spent only once, and then it must be returned to its issuer for credit to a bank account (or a new issuance of digital cash). Digital cash is thus different from physical cash in that a merchant accepting payment by digital cash cannot spend that token again—it must be deposited in the issuing institution.

Another issue raised by the unique token identifier is the possibility of tracing of financial transactions, with privacy implications for the consumer. This issue is addressed by *anonymous* digital cash (see the sidebar "Privacy and Anonymous Digital Cash"). It preserves the spending anonymity of physical cash; namely, when a merchant receives physical cash for payment or a financial institution receives physical cash for deposit, there is no record of who spent the cash or what they bought.

If an institution can match identifiers of tokens it issues against the identifiers of tokens it accepts for credit, it has a complete trace of how the cash is spent, in light of the single-spending attribute. Fortunately, while the identifier must be unique to prevent multiple spending, it need not be known by the institution when the token is *issued*. The key idea behind anonymous digital cash is to hide the identifier from the financial institution at the time of issuance. While this requires enormous ingenuity, it has been shown to be possible.

8.4 Open Issues

Trustworthiness is arguably one of the least mature areas of technology and one that raises contentious policy issues.

Privacy and Anonymous Digital Cash

There is a tension between the desire of consumers for privacy in their purchases on the one hand, and a societal interest in preventing tax avoidance and money laundering on the other. The latter encourages audit trails for monetary transactions. Already, with the level of credit and debit card purchases, a great deal of information is becoming available about the spending patterns and lifestyles of many consumers. If in an electronic commerce system all purchases are logged and traced, the private lives of individuals would be an open book to financial institutions. For example, if every purchase of gasoline, payment of toll on a highway, and minor purchases of snacks and drinks were logged, it would be possible to effectively track the location of individuals almost as effectively as by surveillance.

David Chaum is the most eloquent and persistent advocate of privacy in electronic transactions and has developed protocols for anonymous digital cash. To quote him [Cha91]:

> We are fast approaching a moment of crucial and perhaps irreversible decision, not

(continued)

merely between two kinds of technological systems, but between two kinds of society. Current developments in applying technology are rendering hollow both the remaining safeguards on privacy and the right to access and correct personal data. If these developments continue, their enormous surveillance potential will leave individuals' lives vulnerable to an unprecedented concentration of scrutiny and authority.

8.4.1 How Do We Deal with Increasing Vulnerability?

Networked computing integrated into vital societal functions carries vulnerabilities. Even technological security, such as that discussed here, cannot by itself be completely effective. Physical security, employee integrity, operational vigilance, and many intangibles are involved. Further, all possible threats cannot be anticipated, so the update and addition of security measures throughout the life cycle of an application is inevitable.

Most unsettling is the observation that network breakdowns or break-ins can be massive, with much wider impact than physical breakdowns or break-ins. Further, the magnitude of the risks is difficult to quantify, and as a result the insurance industry has not been active in offering means for spreading these risks as it has in other human activities.

How will these problems be addressed? One clear need is additional research, seeking more effective security systems and greater robustness and reliability. Another need is for a much more vigorous response on the part of government and law enforcement, especially in developing more effective means for deterrence, detection of illegal or harmful activities, and investigative techniques.

8.4.2 National Security and Law Enforcement Needs

Government policy and laws applying to cryptographic technology must make some difficult trade-offs, and this is an area of strong disagreement between governments and industry [CST96a].

On the one hand, strong encryption technology—the basis of all the security tools discussed—is extremely important to networked applications such as electronic commerce. A credible threat to any country is economic espionage, which can be countered by maintaining confidentiality in commercial network traffic. The government has a law enforcement obligation to counter domestic and foreign threats to commerce and industry, and thus should encourage encryption technology. On the other hand, the government relies upon electronic eavesdropping to address legitimate national security threats and court-ordered wiretaps in criminal law enforcement and prosecution. These require a government to decrypt intercepted messages, which motivates it to keep "strong" encryption away from criminals, terrorist organizations, and foreign governments. (Here, "strength" is generally related to the number of bits in the encryption keys.)

One strategy employed by the U.S. government has been to legalize any and all encryption within the country but to disallow the export of strong encryption technology. Industry complains that this not only makes U.S. software less competitive globally but also stimulates viable overseas competitors. A U.S. government response has been to propose "key escrow" schemes that allow a back door for "authorized" access to encrypted information by forcing keys to be deposited with an escrow organization under legal obligation to disclose them in national security and criminal cases. Industry has found these proposals unsatisfactory, arguing in part that individuals and businesses should be afforded the strongest protections available in the technology. Also, these proposals are difficult to implement globally, across multiple jurisdictions. These policy issues are far from settled and will doubtless be debated for some time.

8.4.3 Individual Privacy

The degree to which individual privacy will be maintained in electronic commerce remains an open issue. Commercial enterprises have incentives to track the purchasing habits of their customers in a legitimate attempt to improve their business strategies, but consumers worry that this information can be misused. Similarly, an increasing number of information access applications on the Web are supported by advertising, and the more information available about users, the higher the advertising rates. This tension between the interests of sellers and information providers on the one hand and consumers and users on the other has an uncertain outcome.

EXAMPLE: *The Open Profiling Standard and TRUSTe are industry ini-*
tiatives to make visible to the consumer where the self-provided
information is used and to lend some control over personal infor-
mation. An objective is to reassure consumers, so that privacy con-
cerns don't become a major impediment to consumer acceptance.

8.4.4 Theft and Piracy of Software and Information

A concern on the part of sellers of information and software is the
ease of replication and unauthorized dissemination over the network. Security measures such as encryption provide sellers some
tools to enforce license provisions. However, there are limitations,
since information must be decrypted in order to be read or viewed,
opening opportunities for copying if not outright piracy. Like other
security measures, they are also inevitably invasive to the consumer.
Some strategic issues for sellers are discussed in [Sha98].

Further Reading

An excellent overview of the various compromises to trustworthiness is [CST98], and the implications for essential societal infrastructure are summarized in [OST97]. [Ber97] gives a good practical
picture of computer system reliability. [Sch96] is an excellent com-
pendium of security protocols. Cryptography policy is considered in
great detail in [CST96a].

Middleware

Middleware is a software infrastructure layer (see Section 4.2.2 on page 124) that falls between the application and the operating system (discussed in Chapter 10). Layering allows additional capabilities to be added to an existing infrastructure (the layers below), and middleware is a good illustration. While the lower infrastructure layers (operating system and network) have existed for some time and have a fairly established (albeit evolving and expanding) set of capabilities, middleware is a diverse and changing software product category. Further, just as there are different network protocol layers for different purposes (see Section 7.3 on page 233), there are different middleware solutions serving different categories of applications. Layers added to the infrastructure become increasingly specialized.

ANALOGY: *Companies providing new services built on an existing infrastructure are analogous to middleware. Examples include FedEx's overnight package delivery (built on an existing airport and highway infrastructure) and the Schwab OneSource mutual fund marketplace (which consolidates the offerings of many mutual funds on a single statement). Note that these examples serve quite different and specialized purposes—a characteristic of middleware.*

Middleware can serve many purposes, either singly or in combination, including

- *Abstraction and complexity management:* Middleware can isolate an application from heterogeneous operating systems and networking protocols. For example, middleware might allow an application to be transparently ported to different operating systems—or even run across hosts with different operating systems—without imposing onerous application development effort. In this role, middleware potentially becomes a spanning layer (see "The Spanning Layer" on page 130).

- *Location independence:* Middleware can partially hide the application partitioning across hosts, making it appear to the application developer as if the application were running on a single host. This simplifies application development and makes that partitioning more configurable, for example, allowing the number of participating hosts to be automatically adjusted according to performance requirements (see Chapter 10).

- *Software reuse:* Middleware can incorporate generic functions useful to many applications—especially in a networked environment—reducing application development cost and time (see Section 6.1.4 on page 185).

- *Software portability:* Middleware can provide a uniform execution environment, so that one application program can run on different platforms with minimal reprogramming.

- *Mobile code:* In a form of dynamic portability, program execution can be moved from one host to another. This can have several advantages related to performance and interoperability.

- *Interoperability:* Middleware can simplify interoperability (see Section 7.1 on page 216) by predefining formats and protocols for common tasks.

- *Scalability:* Middleware can support scalability by automating load balancing or parallelism (see Chapter 10).

Middleware is becoming much more important as an enabler for enterprise and cross-enterprise applications (see Section 2.6 on page 52). The reason is that many such applications must integrate legacy departmental or enterprise applications, which run on heterogeneous platforms and languages. Middleware is one approach to mitigating these incompatibilities by performing automatic conversions within the infrastructure. Middleware is also viewed as an enabler of more flexible applications that can adjust to changing needs, another important requirement for the future (see Section 1.1.3 on page 6).

There is no single widely accepted middleware solution, especially not one providing all the capabilities listed. Also, there is no precise boundary between capabilities provided by middleware (adding an infrastructure layer above existing operating systems) and distributed operating systems (enhancing the operating system layer to manage two or more hosts). Different approaches are vying for dominance, and maturation may or may not bring widely accepted solutions. However, when applications span administrative and organizational boundaries, middleware provides a way to address the heterogeneity of the resulting computing environment. Thus the emergence of social and electronic commerce applications is stimulating some ambitious de facto middleware standardization efforts that may lead to greater uniformity.

This chapter doesn't attempt to catalog and discuss all flavors of middleware, but rather focuses on some important capabilities of value to applications and illustrates them with specific middleware products and product categories. A broad definition of middleware is assumed; that is, some capabilities discussed here might be considered by some vendors as part of distributed operating systems rather than middleware.

9.1 Message-Oriented Middleware as an Aid to Workflow

As discussed in Section 7.2.1 on page 220, some applications require a message communication service with multiplexing and queueing (see "Queueing and Multiplexing" on page 222), Such applications typically include repetitive tasks with irregular arrivals and completion times. Many such applications—those in the workflow category—are deferred (see Section 2.3.2 on page 22) and support multiple users, like the purchase order example in Figure 7.4 on page 224. Networking protocols provide limited support for queueing, so this has led to *message-oriented middleware* (MOM), which provides higher-level messaging and queueing services.

9.2 Transaction Processing

While not explicitly addressed in Chapter 6, an application may be distributed over multiple hosts. For example, if the application is composed from objects or decomposed from components, those objects or components may actually be partitioned across different hosts and interact through remote method invocations or messages. This reality introduces complications. For example, one host may crash, resulting in the loss of only a portion of the application (see Section 8.1.1 on page 239). How does the application recover gracefully from such a catastrophe?

Another complication is that applications must commonly coordinate a set of distinct *resources*, whether on common or different hosts.

EXAMPLE: *A travel reservation system manages airline seats, hotel rooms, and rental cars. A bank's financial system manages accounts and transfers of money among them.*

Often these resources may reside on different hosts and even within different administrative domains. As seen shortly, the coordination of the multiple resources also introduces coordination issues.

Transaction processing greatly simplifies application development by consistently handling many problems that arise within the middleware infrastructure, removing that burden from the application developer [Ber97].

9.2.1 Example of the Challenges: Travel Reservations

A travel reservations application illustrates the challenges addressed by transaction processing.

EXAMPLE: *Planning a trip requires coordinated reservations for hotels, airplanes, rental cars, etc. The managed resources are airplane seats, rental cars, hotel rooms, etc. For consistency, the rental car and hotel reservation must coincide with arrival of the airplane, on each of multiple legs of the trip. If consistent reservations*

*are not available (for example, there is no airplane seat that day),
then the hotel and rental car reservations should not be made.*

How is a situation like this handled? One approach would be to
make sure an airline reservation is made before a rental car and
hotel reservation. However, there may be no rental cars available—
or perhaps no hotel rooms—on the day of arrival. So, there is no
feasible order for reserving resources that guarantees consistency.

Another approach would be to take two passes: Confirm availability
of all resources (without reserving them), and then return to lock
them in. This approach is undercut if there are other reservations
being made at the same time. (If two sets of reservations overlap in
time, they are said to be *concurrent*—see Chapter 10.)

EXAMPLE: *If the travel reservation application confirmed the availability of consistent airline seat, rental car, and hotel availability,
when it returned to lock them in, it might find the airline seat was
the last available and in the meantime was given to another
customer.*

Other things can go wrong. For example, the crash of a participating host or application might leave the reservations partially
incomplete.

EXAMPLE: *The travel reservation application might think it had
locked in a reservation for an airline seat, but not be informed that
an airline's host crashed and lost the reservation before the database update was completed. At the airport, the customer would
discover the problem.*

It would be quite complicated to deal with all these cases in the
application, made worse by the participation of distinct administrative domains (the airline, rental car company, and hotel company).

Similar issues arise in a number of networked applications. Later,
two more—distributed databases and electronic commerce—are
discussed. Transaction processing deals with these issues in a
generic way, simplifying application development and contributing
to software reuse.

9.2.2 What Is a Transaction?

In everyday language, a transaction is a series of related reciprocal actions or communications between two people (such as a bank teller and customer). Users also participate in transactions with information systems (such as a customer using an automatic teller machine). One of the earliest commercial applications of computing, on-line transaction processing (OLTP) systems (see Section 2.6.1 on page 53), manages large numbers of these transactions.

More recently, the term *transaction* has been formalized in computing to have a specific meaning: It is a group of related resource management actions that are *atomic*; that is, they are all completed successfully (called a *commit*), or the resources are left as if none of the actions had ever happened (called an *abort*).

EXAMPLE: *In the travel reservation system, if all the consistent reservations that make up a complete itinerary are grouped together as a transaction, then by definition, consistent reservations in the itinerary were successful, or else no reservations were made.*

The application logic can group together a set of resource actions as a transaction and not have to worry about all the complicated issues arising when some actions are successful and others aren't. The application logic must still deal with the possibility of an abort, but that is simpler: Abort is the same as if the transaction hadn't been attempted.

EXAMPLE: *In the travel reservation application, either a consistent set of reservations was successfully made, or none of the reservations were made (as if they had not been attempted). There are no intermediate cases to worry about.*

Internal to the transaction processing middleware, there are many possibilities to deal with. Of course, it would be even easier to declare that a transaction always completes successfully. Unfortunately, this isn't realistic: There are a number of unavoidable problems that can cause an abort, such as a system crash or a request for a resource that simply isn't available.

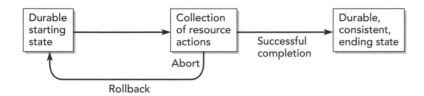

Figure 9.1 A transaction consists of a sequence of resource-manipulation tasks logically coupled to one another, which either succeed or fail as a unit.

A transaction is illustrated in Figure 9.1. It starts and ends in a consistent, durable state. The *state* of a resource manager is a set of conditions (for example, the reservations for a traveler in the travel reservation system). A state is *consistent* when resources are not at odds with one another (for example, the day of arrival and hotel reservation are consistent) and it is *durable* if it outlives the transaction that created it. By definition, the intermediate inconsistent, transient states—corresponding to only a portion of a transaction's resource actions—are not durable. If something goes awry in the midst of a transaction (such as the unavailability of a resource or the crash of a resource manager), it is *aborted*. In that case, there is a *rollback* to the initial durable state. The hoped-for outcome is that all the consistent resource actions in the transaction are successful, so the transaction is declared successful, and the resource managers are left in the second consistent, durable state.

9.2.3 Transaction Processing Architecture

The *transaction processing monitor* is a middleware product that coordinates a set of *resource managers* involved in the transaction and serves as coordinator of the application and these resource managers. To benefit from transaction processing, the application must conform to a predefined architecture (shown in Figure 9.2) and a set of policies and protocols:

- *Architecture:* The application logic and distinct resource managers being coordinated must be distinct and visible to the middleware transaction manager. Typical resource managers are database servers and MOM queues (see Section 9.1 on page

The ACID Properties of Transactions

The acronym ACID is often used to describe four important properties of transactions:

- *Atomicity:* A transaction either all completes or all fails, there is no such thing as a partial completion.

- *Consistency:* A transaction must leave the system in a consistent state at the end of the transaction, or it must abort, returning all resources to their initial state.

- *Isolation:* Concurrent transactions are allowed, but they don't interfere with one another (this is discussed in Chapter 10).

- *Durability* (or persistence): A transaction leaves the resources in a permanent state after it commits—a state that outlives the transaction.

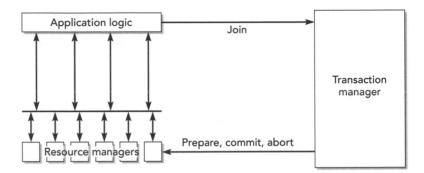

Figure 9.2 Architecture of the application, transaction manager, and resource managers.

275). Commercial products in these areas conform to the policies and protocols necessary to participate in transactions.

- *Policies:* Each transaction initiated by the application must be registered with the transaction manager. Each resource manager must be prepared to roll back all actions related to a given transaction and also participate in the appropriate protocols.

- *Protocols:* When the application logic declares the transaction complete (the last resource action), the resource managers participate in a voting protocol with the transaction manager. The transaction manager informs the application logic as to successful completion (a commit) or abort of the transaction.

When the application logic registers a transaction (a *join*), it is provided a unique transaction identifier (ID) that it uses to identify each resource action. Each resource manager has to be prepared to roll back to the initial durable state in case of an abort; to be prepared for that, the resource manager must keep track of all resource actions and be prepared to reverse them. When the application declares the transaction complete, the transaction manager conducts its voting protocol. If all resource managers agree that the transaction was completed successfully, they are told to wrap up the transaction (a commit). If one or more of them doesn't agree (or fails to respond), then the transaction is aborted, and each resource manager is directed to roll back.

Some complications arising when two or more transactions are concurrent within the same resource manager (concurrent transactions) are discussed in Chapter 10.

Application Examples

Transaction processing benefits applications requiring coordination of resources across hosts and for which reliability and availability are important (see Section 8.1 on page 239). In pragmatic terms, such applications generally incorporate multiple databases and message queues, often across administrative domains (see the sidebar "Open Transaction Processing Standards").

A simple application of transaction processing is an automatic teller machine network [Ber97]. The implementation of such a network would define transactions like Deposit, Withdrawal, and Request-Balance. Each such transaction involves at minimum a database in the bank owning the ATM and a database in the bank with the customer's account. Defining these operations as transactions ensures the consistency of these databases, so both banks have a consistent and durable view of the results of the transaction, and money is not destroyed or created.

Another application is a brokerage house customer stock-trading system, which may have to access roughly ten different stock exchanges [Ber97], where a typical transaction is ExecuteTrade. Obviously, it is important that databases in the brokerage (crediting or debiting a customer account) and at the stock exchange end in a consistent and durable state after each trade.

An important application of transaction processing is electronic commerce [Tyg96]. A typical transaction would be a Purchase, which includes an order, a payment authorization, a fulfillment of the order (delivery of goods from merchant to customer), and a payment (from financial institution to merchant) (see Section 8.3 on page 265). The transaction involves resources in both the merchant and a couple of financial institutions. A number of problems arise if a Purchase is not atomic—for example, the customer pays for merchandise but doesn't receive it, or a merchant ships the merchandise but never receives payment.

Open Transaction Processing Standards

TP protocol standards are important for two reasons. Consistent with the open systems philosophy, they increase competition by allowing customers to mix and match elements (databases, MOM) from different vendors. In addition, in applications such as electronic commerce, it is increasingly common to run transactions across company and administrative boundaries, where detailed coordination is not practical.

OSI TP is a de jure standard established by ISO (see the sidebar "International Organization for Standards (ISO)" on page 135). Like many ISO computing standards, it is not widely implemented, largely because it came along slowly. OMG (see the sidebar "Object Management Group" on page 137) is defining a de facto standard Object Transaction Service (OTS) as part of its CORBA standards (see Section 9.4 on page 287). Many database and MOM vendors plan to implement OTS.

9.3 Mobile Code and Mobile Agents

With *mobile code* (MC), as illustrated in Figure 9.3, a program is sent to a target host (as a message) and then executed there. A *mobile agent* (MA) is similar, except that data is sent along with the code. The idea with both MC and MA is that computation can be dynamically moved where it is most advantageous. The program code does not need to be preinstalled on the host where it is to run, because it is dynamically moved there as needed.

ANALOGY: *Sending an appliance repairman out to a residence with a set of tools to repair a refrigerator—as opposed to bringing the refrigerator to the repair shop—is analogous to MC. Sending an insurance agent out to a residence with loads of information on insurance policies—as opposed to asking the customer to come to the insurance office—is analogous to an MA.*

Although the MC and MA ideas are simple, the advantages are subtle, and implementation faces numerous challenges.

9.3.1 Interactivity and Scalability

Some advantages of MC and MA are illustrated in Figure 9.4. One advantage is that MC and MA can dynamically move processing cycles from one host to another. There are two important performance implications. First, if the presentation (or a portion of it) is moved to a client, the user will experience faster response, because each user interaction will not experience the delay of messages sent over the network (see Chapter 11). For example, animations executed in a server but presented in a client are generally not feasible. However, the MC message will typically be large, resulting in a noticeable delay to get it to the client.

ANALOGY: *Although the insurance agent wastes time traveling to reach a customer's residence, once there she can hold a give-and-take conversation with that customer much better than she could by the exchange of postal letters.*

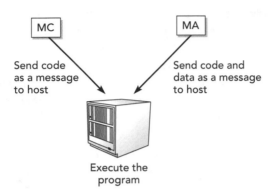

Figure 9.3 Mobile code (MC) and mobile agent (MA) allow a program execution to be moved from one host to another.

Mobile Code, Agents, and Objects

MC and MA are invariably used in the context of objects or components (see Section 6.2 on page 189). The object or component offers a convenient unit of code to transport to another host, where it can interact with other objects or components already residing there.

Considering the object approach, in technical terms MC is a class or assembly of classes—which are instantiated and executed in the target host—and an MA is an object or assembly of objects. A class includes its implementation (a program in some appropriate language), which is transported to the target host in a message. An object includes both the class and the data stored in the object, all of which can be enclosed in a single message (see Section 7.2.1 on page 220).

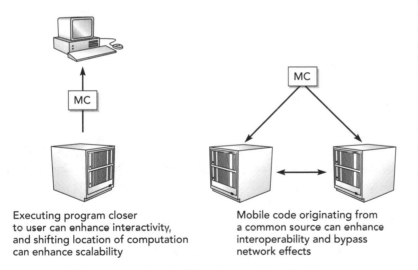

Figure 9.4 The advantages of mobile code include interactivity, scalability, and interoperability.

E X A M P L E: *Java (an MC system discussed shortly) has been successfully used in the Web. The MC (called a Java applet) is retrieved from a Web server and executed in the browser.*

Mobile Code and Network Effects

As discussed in Section 5.3.1 on page 150, new direct applications are difficult to establish due to direct network effects. Early adopters derive very little benefit and have low willingness to pay. By aiding interoperability, mobile code can bypass this problem [Mes96a], since one user's license can permit her to opportunistically provide another user with compatible MC.

ANALOGY: *In the genesis of the facsimile machine, imagine that fax was implemented in software. Even if another user had no fax, if you could send a fax machine (as MC) followed by a fax, there would be no network effect. Even the first adopter would derive full benefit.*

Applications with strong network effects are the most compelling for MC, including direct-immediate applications with the peer-to-peer architecture (see Section 3.1.3 on page 81).

If the licensing and pricing of mobile code (see "Copyrighting Software" on page 167) is done like phone calls, the originator pays the license fee (and it is free to the responder). Alternatively, usage-based fees could be

Another advantage is that MC allows computation to be moved dynamically to whatever host is appropriate, based not only on interactivity considerations but also on available resources. This is particularly valuable in moving computation from a server to a client, because clients automatically scale in proportion to the number of users (see Chapter 10 for a discussion of performance).

ANALOGY: *A company running short of workers, instead of hiring more, might train its customers to perform more functions. For example, a copy shop might ask customers to three-hole punch the pages. As the number of customers increases, the total capability expands accordingly.*

9.3.2 Interoperability

As shown in Figure 9.4, one powerful benefit of mobile code is *interoperability*. In a distributed environment, installing interoperable pieces of a distributed application on the hosts—and keeping them updated with compatible upgrades—is a daunting administrative problem. At minimum, the application need must be anticipated so the software can be installed. Mobile code can bypass these issues: If the distributed pieces are sent from a single source using MC, then interoperability is easier, and the need does not have to be anticipated. This is particularly advantageous interorganizationally, where coordination is more challenging. MC also bypasses network effects (see the sidebar "Mobile Code and Network Effects").

ANALOGY: *Suppose the repair of a piece of complex equipment requires a close collaboration between customer and factory. The manufacturer—rather than taking the time to train a customer's employee to work on the equipment while collaborating with its factory technicians—sends one of its own expert repair technicians to the customer's premises for that purpose.*

EXAMPLE: *MC is part of the proposal for the network computer (see the sidebar "An Ultrathin Client: The Network Computer (NC)" on page 98). A major argument in favor of the NC is the reduction in administrative costs by avoiding the configuration of individual clients.*

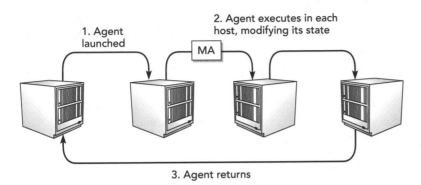

Figure 9.5 Information access using a mobile agent.

paid by both originator and responder (see the sidebar "Are Shrink-Wrapped Applications Poor Quality and Overfeatured?" on page 162).

9.3.3 Mobile Agents

MAs provide an intriguing way to implement information access applications, as illustrated in Figure 9.5 (see Section 2.4 on page 38). The conventional approach has been to move data to join the computation, resulting in the shuttling of data about the network. An alternative is to leave the data in place and move the computation using MAs.

ANALOGY: *You might send an assistant (mobile assistant) to visit all the libraries in town seeking particular information, rather than browsing the on-line catalog and having a book sent to your office. The mobile assistant can browse the stacks, looking inside books and possibly finding something not evident from the catalog entry. The assistant can accumulate and bring back information in his briefcase.*

An MA (rather than MC) is needed because the agent can "sweep up" information and bring it along. In addition, the agent can adaptively choose its itinerary based on what it finds.

9.3.4 Mobile Code and Agent Middleware

Mobile code and agents require *mobile code middleware* support. This middleware addresses one key issue—software portability—and other issues, such as security. Executable code is not easily portable from one host to another, as there are differences in computer

Java and Information Appliances

Information appliances provide a vertical application in a stand-alone and easy-to-use package (see the sidebar "Information Appliances" on page 147). Java is ideal because it allows information appliances to be upgraded over the network. This addresses two of their limitations: They don't have a magnetic or optical storage device for loading new applications, and their embedded applications become obsolete over time.

instruction sets and operating systems. A lot of the advantage is lost in a network environment if MC can execute on only one specific platform (such as UNIX, Windows, or MacOS). The mobile code middleware provides a platform-independent abstract machine to the mobile code, so that it can execute anywhere. In addition, it is dangerous to execute code from an untrusted source, and MC middleware can enforce security policies that restrict sources of MC or the action available to the MC.

Java Mobile Code

An example of MC middleware is Java from Sun Microsystems [Arn96, Fla96]. Java is several things. First and foremost, it is a "pure" object-oriented language, one that unlike C++ requires programs to be composed exclusively of objects. Java also defines an entire *mobile code system*, including a *virtual machine* and a set of *libraries*. MC and MA are generally based on objects and components, and Java is an example of this (see the sidebar "Mobile Code, Agents, and Objects" on page 283).

The Java *Virtual Machine* (VM) defines the instruction set of a virtual microprocessor and then *emulates* this virtual microprocessor on a real microprocessor. The primitive instructions for the VM are written in *bytecode*, composed of instructions for the VM. A Java compiler translates the Java source code into bytecode that can then be executed on any platform with a VM. This model of execution is called "write once, run anywhere" (see the sidebar "Java as a De Facto Standard").

Unfortunately, portability requires much more than platform-independent program execution. Programs require access to network, machine (memory, storage, etc.), and user interface (display, keyboard, mouse, etc.) resources. Thus, a mobile code system must provide similar resources, but in a platform-independent way. To this end, Java provides a set of libraries, with well-documented interfaces for a suite of standard actions (such as accessing files, creating graphical objects, connecting to the network, etc.). These libraries must be maintained on each platform. A mobile code system must also provide security measures (see the sidebar "Java and Security").

9.4 Distributed Object Management

Two objects (or components) can interact even if they reside on different hosts, for example, by using a remote method invocation (RMI—see "Remote Method Invocation" on page 225). Interacting objects on different hosts are called *distributed objects*. Exploiting this capability, applications can be decomposed into distributed objects (or assembled from distributed components), which are partitioned across multiple hosts. Distributed objects introduce practical difficulties. For example, how can RMI be made to work even if the hosts have different operating systems, or the objects are implemented using different languages? How can an object on one host identify objects on another host, or maintain a reference to such objects? It doesn't make sense for every application developer to address these and similar issues independently. Rather, distributed objects require *distributed object management* (DOM) middleware. To the application developer, the major benefit of DOM is that it makes a distributed application appear more like a centralized application, as the interaction among objects is similar whether objects are distributed or reside on the same host.

ANALOGY: *Two companies will have difficulty collaborating on a project if one uses English and the other Spanish. A service to facilitate this collaboration is an automatic translation from English to Spanish and Spanish to English that is transparent to the employees involved.*

As illustrated in Figure 9.6, without DOM (at the top), application software has to be ported to different platforms and has to provide its own object-interaction communications (using, say, TCP/IP—see Section 7.3 on page 233). With DOM, the application programmer uses RMI for object interaction, and interoperability is achieved regardless of platform and language.

EXAMPLE: *Two pieces of an application, one written in the Java language on a Windows NT platform, and the other written in C++ running on a UNIX platform, would be interoperable (could invoke one another's methods).*

Java as a De Facto Standard

Although Java began as an elegant solution to the technical problem of software portability, it soon became a weapon in industry battles, creating winners and losers. Because programs written in Java can in principle run under any operating system, Java potentially turns the operating system into a commodity (a good differentiated by price and quality, but not functionality or features). Sun advanced Java using industry alliances—in part to undercut the dominance of Microsoft Windows—following a multiprong strategy:

- Gain broad industry support by licensing under attractive terms. Encourage others to add enhancements and complementary technologies.

- Avoid the de facto standard from splitting into incompatible versions by a licensing provision that affords Sun control over what is included in a single "pure Java" (in effect creating a de jure standard based on copyright protections).

- Try to establish the Java environment as its own operating system with

(continued)

thin-client products that run only Java (see Section 3.2.3 on page 96).

Java has strong network externalities (see Section 5.3.1 on page 150) and is only useful (beyond a programming language) if widely adopted. Thus, Java is an interesting case study in establishing a de facto standard.

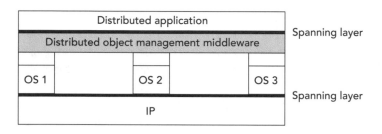

Figure 9.6 DOM middleware adds a spanning layer isolating the application from its distribution and heterogeneous operating systems and languages.

This also allows more flexibility in partitioning an application across hosts without affecting its architecture or functionality (contributing to scalability—see Chapter 10). Two de facto standards are competing for dominance (see the sidebar "Competing Distributed Object Visions: DCOM and CORBA"). The most compelling need for DOM is in enterprise and interenterprise applications (see Section 2.6 on page 52), since these encounter the greatest platform and language heterogeneity. Such applications should be easier to develop and manage because of DOM, which has the potential to provide an infrastructure similar to the Internet but richer and with higher levels of abstraction.

The proponents of DOM have ambitious goals, subsuming capabilities discussed earlier in this chapter (messaging services, transaction processing, and mobile code). There is hope for realization of this vision—it has the support of the largest software companies and a viable standardization process—although it has proceeded so quickly that many important capabilities (such as transaction processing) seem to be afterthoughts.

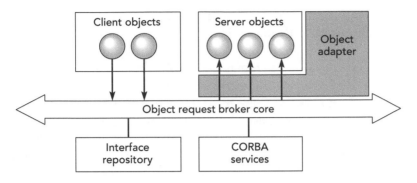

Figure 9.7 The architecture of CORBA.

9.4.1 One DOM Standard: CORBA

Some challenges to integration of data across an enterprise (or cross-enterprise) were listed in Table 4.5 on page 133: *communication*, *representation*, and *interpretation* of data. The DOM addresses these problems, and the architecture of one DOM platform—CORBA from OMG, shown in Figure 9.7—illustrates how [OPR96, Sie96, Ran95, Bak97]. Also see the sidebar "The OMG Process" for a discussion of how CORBA standards are developed.

Communication and Representation of Data in CORBA

The first issue is how data is communicated between two objects (the protocol) and how it is represented (the formats) (see Section 7.1 on page 216). The heterogeneity of object languages and platforms is finessed by communication through an intermediary—the *object request broker* (ORB)—rather than directly. The ORB arranges whatever translations are necessary to allow a client object to perform an RMI on the server object (see the sidebar "RMI Is Layered on Messages" on page 235). Internal to the ORB is a communication protocol and a universal format for marshalling of method parameters and return values. The flavor of this protocol built on the internet TCP/IP is IIOP (see Section 7.3.4 on page 236).

A N A L O G Y :   *The ORB is analogous to an English-to-Spanish translation service that is invoked automatically whenever two companies collaborate.*

Java and Security

MC is a security threat (see Section 8.1.2 on page 243) because—like a computer virus (see the sidebar "Computer Viruses" on page 248)—it is an executable program originating from a potentially unknown source. Fortunately, MC is *knowingly* executed (unlike viruses, which propagate surreptitiously), and thus it is easier to enforce security policies.

MC security is addressed by appropriate policies (enforced by the VM) that establish a trade-off between safety and functionality. The unit of security in the Java system is the VM, and the policies govern the allowable access of VM to various resources at the granularity of objects (typically different for objects with a local or remote origin). An object's ability to read and write local files or its access to the network may be restricted. A VM is like a firewall between MC and the remainder of the environment (see "Firewalls" on page 264).

The Java system is complicated enough that loopholes for determined adversaries are inevitable. Security policies tend to be invasive, precluding desired functionality. An effective security measure for the future may be authenticating the origin and integrity of MC using a digital

(continued)

signature (see Section 8.2 on page 249). Less restrictive security policies might be imposed on MC if it is authenticated as originating at a reputable source (such as a major software company) and if it has integrity.

A remote client object can invoke a method on a local server object as intermediated by the ORB. Also included is an *object adapter*, which manages local objects, such as invoking them when their methods are called and routing each RMI to the appropriate object. Aside from communication protocols and formats, another issue is how a client object specifies the location of a server object and how it knows that object exists in the first place. Dealing with the first issue (and deferring the second), each object in the DOM is assigned an *object reference* when it is created. This reference is unique and stays with the object even if it moves to a different host or is temporarily stored on disk. Thus, a server object can use that reference as long as it likes. This *location transparency* is especially important for mobile objects.

Interpretation of Data in CORBA

The common interpretation of data among objects implemented by different programmers in different languages is an issue. How does one object know the names, parameters, and return values of another object? CORBA provides two forms of assistance: an *interface definition language* (IDL) and an *interface repository* (IR).

ANALOGY: *An IDL and IR are analogous to a memorandum that describes to the employees of two companies the precise ways in which they will collaborate. This memorandum is not a part of the collaboration itself, but rather documents in advance how it will take place.*

IDL is a language defined for the express and limited purpose of describing the interface (but not the implementation) of an object's class. The implementation is presumed to be in a system programming language (such as Java or C++). The steps in implementing a class would be

- Describe and document the class interface using IDL.

- Automatically translate the IDL description into a template in the implementation language (called a language *binding*).

- Use that template as a starting point for implementing the object class.

IDL also serves as documentation for the class interface that can be published. (One can imagine a whole library of interface specifications and many pleasant evenings spent poring over them.) More interestingly, IDL serves as the basis of *discovery* of the interface, so that a client can interoperate with an object without knowing its interface in advance. A given ORB publishes IDL descriptions of the classes it harbors in a database called the *interface repository* (IR).

ANALOGY: *The graphical user interface (GUI) is an analogous capability for an application's presentation. Before the GUI, "command line" interfaces forced users to memorize application directives in advance. The GUI features a self-describing menu interface, where available commands are displayed and chosen by the user without consulting manuals.*

9.4.2 Services Offered by DOM

A DOM also captures as *object services* common facilities needed by many applications, contributing to software reuse (see Section 6.1.4 on page 185). Representative CORBA services include

- *Life cycle and relationship services:* (No, this isn't a dating service, but that would be a reasonable analogy.) Life cycle services specify standard interfaces for operations common to all object systems, such as `create`, `destroy`, `move`, and `copy`. Relationship services provide standardized ways of composing objects into larger modules.

- *Naming and trader services:* The object reference allows interaction with an object once it is known, but ways of finding objects are needed. The naming service maps the name of an object into a reference. (Name servers are common on networks and are discussed further in Chapter 11.) The trader service allows objects to be found by function rather than name or reference. The trader service is also being standardized by ISO (see the sidebar "International Organization for Standards (ISO)" on page 135).

- *Security services:* These specify the standard security capabilities of authentication, access control, and confidentiality (see Section 8.2 on page 249).

Competing Distributed Object Visions: DCOM and CORBA

Two de facto distributed object management standards are engaged in a classic standards war. In terms of strategies and models for industrial organization, they are dramatically different. DCOM is promulgated by Microsoft, which controls the dominant Windows platform. CORBA is developed by OMG (see the sidebar "Object Management Group" on page 137), an industry consortium with more than 700 participating companies.

DCOM, not being designed by committee, is today more real but doesn't benefit from the give and take and infusion of ideas from a multiplicity of companies. CORBA is more ambitious in its goals, including platform independence and its aspirations to subsume other middleware functions such as transaction processing and mobile code.

The healthy competition between two standards will result in shorter time to market. On the other hand, network effects are strong (see Section 5.3.1 on page 150), and two standards may confuse the marketplace and slow adoption.

The OMG Process

The process used by OMG (see the sidebar "Object Management Group" on page 137) has similarities to the IETF (see the sidebar "Internet Engineering Task Force (IETF)" on page 136). Officially the OMG doesn't call itself a standardization body, but rather a consortium of companies cooperating to define a DOM architecture and interfaces within that architecture. The stated goal is designing "a common architectural framework for object-oriented applications based on widely available interface specifications." The hope is that the open interfaces will be implemented by multiple vendors.

Once the OMG decides a given interface is needed, it issues a request for proposals and guides the refinement of proposals submitted through comment and consensus, sometimes by suggesting that companies work together to integrate their best ideas. Unlike the IETF, proposals need not be accompanied by a working implementation, but companies with successful proposals must agree to market a commercial implementation within one year.

- *Transaction services:* These provide standard interfaces to transaction processing (see Section 9.2 on page 276).

9.4.3 Interoperability among ORBs: IIOP

Each organization will select, install, and administer its own ORB, implying that a given distributed application might span ORBs from different vendors, or separately administered ORBs from the same vendor. This requires interoperability among ORBs (see the sidebar "Portability vs. Interoperability"). CORBA has defined a General Inter-ORB Protocol (GIOP) that defines the payload of messages among ORBs. GIOP can be implemented on top of any reliable transport protocol (see Chapter 11), but the most common are the standard internet protocols (GIOP over internet is called IIOP—see Section 7.3.4 on page 236).

9.5 Open Issue: Are Middleware Service Providers Needed?

Telecommunications has always featured a service provider that planned, deployed, and operated telecommunications facilities as a public infrastructure (see Chapter 12). Although companies have traditionally provisioned their own computing and internal networking, it is increasingly common to outsource networking and occasionally computing facilities. The question arises, will the rising importance of middleware expand the role of service provider? Today, the Internet provides at least one service—domain name services, discussed in Chapter 11—not traditionally provided by telecommunications networks. An expanded suite of services could include many things, such as MOM and DOM, encryption key distribution and escrow, directory services, payment mechanisms, etc.

A public infrastructure supporting mobile or nomadic computer users suggests more strongly the need for supporting middleware services, if users are to be afforded comparable services regardless of location (see "Nomadic and Mobile Access" on page 102). Advocates of ultrathin clients like the network computer (NC) also advocate a major role for a service provider in which the user provides only a platform for application execution, but all storage is maintained centrally (see Section 3.2.3 on page 96). Another manifestation of this trend is free services like electronic mail provided on Web sites with advertiser support.

Which part of the distributed computing environment is a public infrastructure, and which part should be provided by users for their own needs? Who will design, construct, and operate the public infrastructure needed for distributed applications, and how will it be paid for?

Further Reading

[OHE96a] is an excellent general reference on middleware technologies, including those discussed in this chapter. [OHE96b] gives a more complete description of distributed object management in particular. [Ber97] is a good general reference on transaction processing and computer system reliability in general, while [Gra93] is the most authoritative and extensive reference on the subject. [Fla96] is a recommended reference on Java, especially for those with prior programming experience. Although there is not yet an ideal reference on CORBA, [Bak97] can be recommended (note that it emphasizes one vendor's products).

Portability vs. Interoperability

Portability and interoperability are distinct but complementary goals. The objective with *portability* is to avoid lock-in (see Section 5.3.2 on page 154) by building application elements that are easily moved from one platform to another. Java provides portability for a single language but does not promise interoperability with application elements written in a different language.

Interoperability bypasses network effects (see Section 5.3.1 on page 150) by allowing application elements to work together even though they were developed on different platforms in different languages. CORBA offers interoperability (an object in one ORB can be a client of an object in another ORB) but does not promise portability: Generally an application developed on a vendor's CORBA-compliant ORB can't easily be moved to a different ORB. ORB vendors have no strong desire for portability because lock-in benefits them.

Java and CORBA (or ActiveX and DCOM) are complementary, since customers may like to avoid both lock-in and network effects. In the future, DOM middleware will support both portability and interoperability.

Performance and Quality

10

In most networked applications, there are performance and quality objectives which, if violated, adversely impact the utility. These objectives strongly depend on the specific application context. Not meeting them may reduce the quality of the user experience, or cause annoyance, or worst of all, cost money.

EXAMPLE: *After clicking on a Web hyperlink, time spent waiting for display of the linked page is wasted. Displaying poor-quality (muddy or distorted) video in a video conference will reduce the quality of the experience. Delaying execution of a stock trade may cost a customer money.*

Identifying performance and quality objectives is an important part of application needs assessment (see Section 3.4.2 on page 106). These objectives then have direct impact on the architecture and design of the application—especially the mapping of application functionality onto multiple hosts. The network and communication links also affect performance and quality, as discussed in Chapters 11 and 12.

10.1 Performance and Quality Metrics

In the operation of a networked application, *performance* refers to quantitative measures such as the aggregate number of users accommodated and the speed of response to each user. *Quality* refers to qualitative measures of the user experience, such as the fidelity of audio or video reproduction. Important quality metrics include program correctness and reliability (see Chapter 8). Performance can be objectively measured, while quality benefits from subjective assessment, asking users to rate their experience.

ANALOGY: *Analogous questions could be asked about a work group completing some repetitive task (such as processing license applications). How many applications is the group processing per week? How often do they make mistakes? How satisfied are the applicants with the experience?*

It is usually not meaningful to address the performance or quality of a monolithic application as a whole, as there are many aspects and perspectives. It should be modularized and dealt with hierarchically, like other aspects of computing.

10.1.1 Performance

While performance can be quantitatively measured, requirements must be related to user or organizational needs. Like availability and security (see Chapter 8), there is a trade-off between performance and cost, so it is important to understand what performance is sufficient.

ANALOGY: *What are the performance characteristics of a rope? When used to tow a vehicle, the right metric is the force it can exert without breaking. If used to rappel down a mountain, an important metric is length. It is inefficient to use a really long rope to tow a vehicle, or the strongest rope to rappel down a mountain.*

The first step is to divide the application into individual tasks. A *task* is a small, manageable collection of actions that are not usefully subdivided. (A task is similar to a transaction—but without the formal requirements—see Section 9.2.2 on page 278.)

EXAMPLE: *In Web browsing, one task is clicking on a hyperlink and retrieving a new page. The task is complete when the page is displayed, and in the meantime the user is idle. In a stock trading system, a task is one trade, including order and fulfillment.*

ANALOGY: *A complete application is analogous to the work group in social applications (see Section 2.3.1 on page 19). Like the work group, it has the goal of completing some well-defined project. The application task then becomes analogous to the task group in the social application. Looked at in this way, achieving high performance in the networked application faces similar challenges to achieving high productivity and output from a work group.*

For some tasks, an important performance parameter is *completion time*. For repetitive tasks, the number of tasks completed per unit time (called the *throughput*) may hold the greatest interest. Not infrequently, both are important.

EXAMPLE: *For a Web browser, the individual user is concerned about individual task (information request and response) completion time. The task throughput for one user is dominated by the time he spends reading the retrieved material and hence is not relevant to application design. However, the Web server supports a large number of users making requests, and the number of users served is directly related to task throughput.*

For a stock trading system, the throughput must exceed the largest expected daily volume of trades divided by the trading hours, or else some customers won't be served on busy days. The execution time for a market order is important (lest the stock price change), but the fulfillment time is not (since the customer is not waiting, and it has no impact on price).

ANALOGY: *For a bridge authority, a single task would be one car passing over the bridge. The driver of that car is primarily concerned about completion time, but the bridge authority is primarily concerned about the throughput (which directly relates to its toll revenue).*

For repetitive tasks, are completion time and throughput related? Naively, one might assume that reducing the completion time and increasing the throughput go hand in hand. This is *not* the case, as illustrated in Figure 10.1. Shown are two cases:

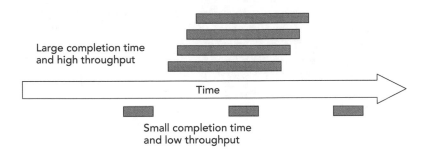

Figure 10.1 Relationship of task completion time and throughput for repetitive tasks.

- In the first case, the execution of tasks overlaps in time (said to be *concurrent*), for example, if multiple hosts are working cooperatively on the tasks. The completion time for each task is long, and yet the throughput is high.

- In the second case, the tasks are not concurrent; each task is completed before the next task begins. Because of a large idle period between the end of one task and the beginning of the next, the throughput is low, and yet the completion time is short.

EXAMPLE: *In the Web browser, the user waits for a new page to be displayed before clicking on a hyperlink on that page, so these tasks are inherently not concurrent. The user probably stops to examine and read each page, leaving a substantial gap between tasks. Even if task completion time is short, task throughput is dominated by user behavior.*

The stock trading system could have a set of hosts performing trades concurrently. Each new order would be routed to an idle host, decoupling throughput from completion time.

10.1.2 Quality

Important quality metrics relate to the subjective quality of audio, images, and video media. Any audible or visible elements not present in the original source (such as noise or distortion) are called *artifacts*. ("Artifact" simply means man-made or artificial. In this context, artifacts are artificially introduced by the computer system or network.)

EXAMPLE: *Distortion causes an audio signal to sound unnatural, while noise is a "hissing" component most evident when the audio is silent. For images and video, artifacts take the form of visual effects such as unnatural mosaic patterns, fuzziness caused by lowered resolution, etc. Artifacts are introduced by compression algorithms designed to reduce the bitrate necessary for representing the source (see Chapter 12) and by impairments introduced within networks (see Chapter 11).*

Another common detrimental artifact in direct-immediate applications (such as telephony or video conferencing—see Section 2.3.2 on page 22) is *delay*. Any delay between the original source and reproduced signal in excess of approximately 0.25 to 0.5 seconds makes a two-way conversation difficult. The speed-of-light propagation delay is substantial in a global network (see Chapter 12), so this is a particular problem over long distances. In deferred applications (such as audio or video-on-demand or broadcast), delay is less critical.

10.1.3 Factors in Performance and Quality

The factors listed in Table 10.1 contribute strongly to performance and quality. While technology and equipment both improve in cost and performance characteristics over time, for an application developer the goal is achieving adequate performance in *today's* technology and equipment. The application architecture is thus the primary consideration. In Table 10.1, as in the remainder of the chapter, the restaurant analogy of Table 3.2 on page 93 is used frequently.

10.2 The Role of Concurrency

Recall that two tasks are concurrent when they overlap in time. There are two important motivations for concurrency listed in Table 10.2. In many applications, concurrency is unavoidable due to functional requirements.

Table 10.1 Some important determinants of performance and quality.

Factor	Description	Analogy
Application architecture	Architecture determines the partitioning of the application onto multiple hosts. It also addresses the relative location of data and processing (see Section 6.1.5 on page 187).	A restaurant can organize its kitchen and table service in various ways. For example, gourmet and fast-food restaurants are organized quite differently.
Technology	Electronics, magnetic and optical storage, and fiber optics are rapidly advancing. Application performance benefits directly from these technology advances.	Agriculture and food preparation technologies reduce the cost of food over time, thereby reducing the cost of restaurant meals.
Equipment	Computing systems and networks make use of technology to provide processing, storage, and communication services to applications.	Kitchen equipment such as microwave ovens and conveyer belts substitute for labor, improve speed, and reduce costs.

Table 10.2 Two motivations for concurrency in networked applications.

Motivation	Description	Analogy
Intrinsic functional requirements	The application requirements may require concurrent tasks, such as multiple users working independently.	In a restaurant, multiple customers are ordering and eating their meals at one time.
Performance objectives	A single host or communication link may not be fast enough to meet task completion time or throughput requirements.	A fast-food restaurant may find that one cook cannot serve up meals fast enough, so more cooks are hired. A single waiter may not be able to serve all customers, so more waiters are hired.

EXAMPLE: *Many applications support multiple users simultaneously. A stock trading system has many brokers or customers entering and executing orders. If each such order and execution is considered a task, then they must be concurrent.*

In other applications, concurrency is dictated by performance objectives. If one host can't provide needed throughput, it can be increased by assigning those tasks to multiple hosts.

EXAMPLE: *In an email forwarding and routing application, the entry, sending, and delivery of one email message is a task, and the primary performance objective is throughput. As the number of users and messages increases, eventually one host can't accommodate them. Throughput can be increased by adding a second host, assigning half the messages to it. The tasks on the two hosts are then concurrent.*

Often the two motivations in Table 10.2 go together: A large number of users performing tasks simultaneously requires concurrency for both functional and performance reasons.

10.2.1 Concurrency with Multiple Hosts

If task throughput must be increased, adding hosts to work on tasks concurrently may help. A couple of simple approaches (for two hosts) are shown in Figure 10.2. As tasks are initiated, they can be routed to different hosts, or alternatively, they can all be routed to a single host, but that host can delegate those tasks it is unable to accommodate.

ANALOGY: *A restaurant maître d´ can assign waiters to different tables, or can assign all tables to one headwaiter, who in turn delegates them to other waiters as necessary.*

EXAMPLE: *It is common for a Web server to route requests from different users to multiple hosts. For example, an on-line stock brokerage might have dozens of hosts handling trading. Each new user who initiates a trading session is routed to the host that currently has the lightest load.*

Often life isn't this simple. One obstacle is dependency among tasks, so delegation to different hosts creates communication overhead that limits throughput. Another is the location of data needed by tasks, which may also create communications overhead (see Section 6.1.5 on page 187).

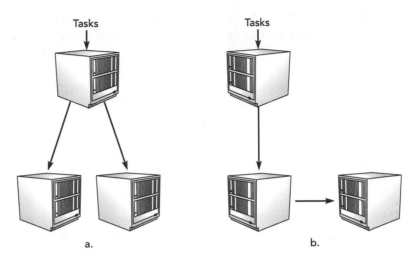

Figure 10.2 Task throughput can be increased by (a) routing or (b) delegation of tasks to multiple hosts.

10.2.2 Concurrency in a Single Host

Concurrency in a *single* host is necessary if concurrency is an intrinsic requirement and a single host offers adequate performance. Tasks can be concurrent in the same host using *time-slicing*, as illustrated in Figure 10.3 (for the special case of two concurrent tasks). The idea is simple: The host alternates execution back and forth between tasks (each switch is called a *context switch*), working on the first for a while and then the second for a while, returning to the first. Although the two tasks are never executing simultaneously, they are concurrent because their execution overlaps in time.

ANALOGY: *A single waiter can serve multiple tables in the restaurant by dividing her time among the tables. First she fills the water glasses at one table, then switches to bringing a meal to another table, then switches to bringing the check to a third table. Considering the start-to-finish service to one customer as a task, she is performing concurrent tasks by context switching.*

Multitasking—concurrent tasks in a single host—is an important feature of modern operating systems. Because computers are very fast, multitasking is not evident to a user, who perceives that a host

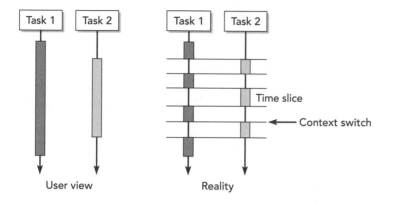

Figure 10.3 Time-slicing allows concurrent tasks in the same host.

can run different applications concurrently without apparent impact of one on the other.

EXAMPLE: *Multitasking allows a personal computer to overlap the printing of a document with some activity supporting the user, such as editing a document. The user may not be aware that there is a concurrent printing task, because the computer is fast enough to keep up with both the user's requests and the printer needs, while dividing its attention between the two.*

One important motivation for multitasking is *fairness*. On a single host, the alternative to multitasking would be to execute tasks sequentially, one after the other. This may be "unfair" if one task has a very long completion time, shutting out other tasks. The impact of concurrency on fairness is illustrated in Figure 10.4. The individual time to completion of each task is inevitably greater (since the computer is switching among them). Nevertheless, a short task may complete sooner—because it is allowed to start sooner—if the tasks are concurrent. Exactly the same idea applies to communications (see the sidebar "Why Networks Use Packets").

EXAMPLE: *Without multitasking, a user would have to wait for a document to completely print before doing anything else. This could be a long time. The user would prefer to "edge in" other tasks, even at the expense of increasing printing time.*

Different Forms of Multitasking

There are two forms of multitasking: *cooperative* and *preemptive*. In cooperative multitasking, tasks must periodically and temporarily give up control voluntarily. In preemptive multitasking, tasks need not worry about this, as context switching is invisible to tasks. The operating system invisibly preempts every task whenever it wishes to pass control to another, and later restores the first task without it realizing that it was interrupted.

Why Networks Use Packets

Multitasking has a precise analogy to the communication of messages. Like a task, a message isn't useful until received in its entirety. Consider sending two messages across a communication link, as illustrated in Figure 10.5. Each message consumes the link for a period of time proportional to the number of bits in the message. A very long message, given exclusive access to the link, may delay the arrival of many other shorter messages.

> **E X A M P L E :** *If a message payload includes a very large executable file, it may be many megabytes in length. On a slow link, this might take many minutes to transmit.*

To address fairness, messages can be communicated concurrently by fragmenting each message into *packets*. As shown in Figure 10.5, two messages arriving simultaneously must contend for the same link, and if the communication of the long message is completed before the shorter starts, the shorter message's arrival is delayed. Packetization allows them to be communicated concurrently, by interleaving packets. Because messages are fragmented into packets, a network such as the Internet is called a *packet network* (see "Switching" on page 87).

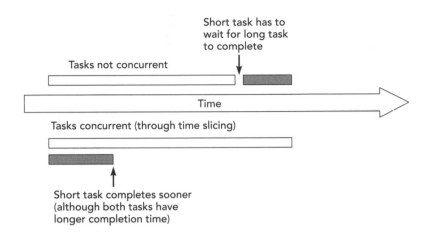

Figure 10.4 Multitasking in the same host contributes to fairness.

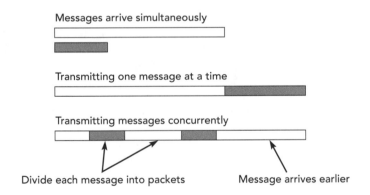

Figure 10.5 When messages are fragmented into packets, contending messages can be communicated concurrently by interleaving of packets.

10.2.3 Resource Conflicts and Transactions

Although concurrency is important for meeting requirements or improving performance, it introduces many subtle complications into application development. One of the most important is the *resource conflict*, which is an incorrect result due to an adverse interaction between two concurrent tasks manipulating the same resource. The prevention of conflicts is an important role of transaction processing (see Section 9.2 on page 276). Transaction processing prevents these conflicts, which is the transaction *isolation* property (see the sidebar "The ACID Properties of Transactions" on page 279).

EXAMPLE: *Suppose George is withdrawing $100 from a joint bank account at one ATM, and concurrently his wife Linda is depositing $100 into the account at another ATM. After completion of both transactions, the bank account should be unchanged. However, consider what might happen with the common account information manipulated by both transactions:*

- *George's transaction reads the account balance.*
- *Linda's transaction reads the account balance.*
- *George's transaction subtracts $100 and replaces the balance.*
- *Mary's transaction adds $100 and replaces the balance.*

The end result is that the balance ends up $100 too large, making the bank unhappy. It could easily work the other way, with the balance $100 smaller, making George and Linda unhappy. In either case, the result is incorrect, and money has been created or destroyed.

ANALOGY: *In the restaurant, when a customer orders a glass of milk, the waiter goes to the refrigerator, removes the bottle of milk, pours a glass, and replaces the bottle. Suppose two waiters do this concurrently. What could happen is the second waiter goes to the refrigerator while the first waiter is pouring and concludes incorrectly the restaurant has no milk.*

The goal might be to prevent concurrent transactions from *interacting* at all, but this is impossible.

EXAMPLE: *If one transaction reserves the last seat on a flight, there is no seat available to give to another, concurrent, transaction. The first transaction has affected the second. The best hope is to avoid a conflict, such as neither transaction getting the seat or both getting the same seat.*

In transaction processing, conflicts (but not interactions) are avoided by guaranteeing *serial equivalence*, illustrated in Figure 10.6. The result of two concurrent transactions is precisely the same as if the transactions were sequential, that is, one followed the

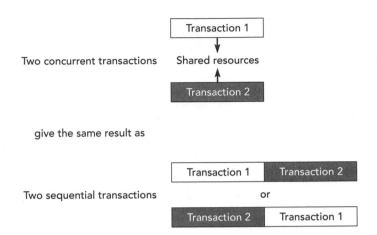

Figure 10.6 A transaction provides serial equivalence to concurrent transactions.

other. Serial equivalence says nothing about the *order* of the transaction equivalence—it could be the first followed by the second, or the second followed by the first—but merely that the result will be equivalent to one or the other of these cases.

E X A M P L E :   *If two concurrent transactions attempt to book the same last-remaining airline seat, serial equivalence dictates that one will obtain the seat and the other won't. It doesn't indicate which customer will be lucky.*

Serial equivalence is implemented using *resource locking*. One transaction applies a lock to resources during periods of possible conflicts, preventing another transaction from conflicting.

A N A L O G Y :   *One waiter might lock the refrigerator while pouring a glass of milk, so that a second waiter will not be able to check for milk availability until after the milk bottle is returned.*

10.3 Scalability

An important performance consideration in application architecture design is scalability. An application is *scalable* if its performance metrics can improve, as necessary and essentially without limit, by adding equipment (more hosts, more network connections, etc.) and without the need for replacement of existing equipment. Further, equipment cost hopefully increases at most linearly with performance metrics, so that the cost per unit of performance is constant or declines. Most (but not all) networked applications require scalability to accommodate a growing user base.

EXAMPLE: *An application supporting the purchase or sale of stocks should be able to accommodate increasing sales volume, essentially without limit. An application supporting requests for location of packages in a package delivery service should be able to accommodate more requests as the customer base increases.*

There are two keys to scalability. First, processing needs to be partitioned across multiple hosts in such a way that more hosts can be added as necessary. Second, close attention has to be paid to the coupling of data and processing (see Section 6.1.5 on page 187) and communication costs.

A number of other characteristics have to be right. The most important are

- All the hosts have to be kept busy. "Busyness" is measured by a performance metric called *utilization*, which is the fraction of time the host is doing useful work (a utilization of 1.0 means the host is busy all the time). To the extent the utilization is below 1.0, application performance metrics for n hosts cannot approach n times a single host.

- Communication among hosts must be kept in check. There is overhead in this communication, and the application partitioning must consider the performance implications.

- Operational data *originates* from a single source but is typically *used* by multiple applications, implying one-to-many communications. Similarly, in decision support, data originates from many operational sources but must be aggregated in one place, implying many-to-one communications. The storage and communication requirements for such data must be taken into account.

A number of typical problems arise that can adversely affect scalability.

Scalability in Production

Networked application scalability has a close analogy to the production of goods and services [Var87]. A production process has inputs (raw materials, labor, capital goods, etc.), called the *factors of production*, and outputs a quantity of finished goods. When that output quantity increases as fast or faster than the factors of production, the production has *constant* or *increasing returns to scale*. This desirable property (analogous to scalability) implies a constant or decreasing cost of factors of production per unit output, that is, economies of scale. The factors of production are analogous to hosts, networking equipment, wide area network services, software licenses, etc., and the production is analogous to the number of users served, or transactions per unit time, or other performance metrics.

10.3.1 Blocking

One common way to delegate work from one host to another is the remote method invocation (see "Remote Method Invocation" on page 225). This service invokes some action on the server, but the client is blocked while waiting for the reply, which reduces its utilization and defers continuing the remainder of the task. On the other hand, a message service (not demanding an immediate reply) allows the client to continue working immediately after delegating work to a server.

EXAMPLE: *The workflow (purchase order processing) application of Figure 7.4 on page 224 illustrates the delegation of work to other hosts (and in this case workers too) using a message service. Each host (and worker), after delegating the next stage of one repetitive task, can immediately move on to the next task.*

Two objects interacting remotely will incur greater overhead than if they were local. One manifestation is a greater delay in interaction across the network (this is discussed in Chapter 12). The application partitioning should take this into account by minimizing communication overhead and mitigating its impact.

10.3.2 Duplicated Work

Scalability requires a partitioning of tasks onto hosts, but this is rarely straightforward because of dependencies among tasks. One possible problem is creating more work *in aggregate* because of the partitioning, typically because a given operation must be artificially repeated *n* times (or at least more than once) just because there are *n* parallel work units.

ANALOGY: *Suppose the government birth certificate bureau finds that a single clerk can't handle the load, and so hires n clerks. However, an inept manager splits the birth certificate records randomly among the clerks, so each client must talk to multiple clerks to find his records, and there is a large duplication of effort. A competent manager divides the birth records alphabetically, so a client goes directly to the right clerk.*

10.3.3 Faulty Load Balancing

If scalability is to be achieved, each host must be well utilized, which requires *load balancing*.

ANALOGY: *A fast-food restaurant will increase the number of order takers with the expected customer load, but all order takers must be kept busy. Fortunately, the arriving customers—who join the shortest line—perform load balancing.*

As this last example suggests, queueing is effective for load balancing if arriving tasks can observe the tasks waiting in queues and join the shortest one (this is a valuable function provided by MOM—see Section 9.1 on page 275). In general, delegating work to the currently least-utilized host is effective but may be upset by dependency among tasks.

ANALOGY: *In the fast-food restaurant, each order placed must also be picked up. If there is a single pickup worker, as the number of order takers is increased, there will develop a long line at pickup. This load balancing problem can be overcome by assigning each worker to both order taking and pickup.*

10.3.4 Congestion

In many applications, the workload varies irregularly or randomly with time.

EXAMPLE: *In the purchase order processing workflow application of Figure 7.4 on page 224, the number of purchase orders generated will vary day by day. In a stock trading system, the number of trades will vary minute by minute, driven in part by current market conditions (such as balance of buy and sell orders).*

An unfortunate consequence of these fluctuations is *congestion*, which is a temporary overutilization of resources due to temporarily high arrivals.

ANALOGY: *Highway congestion results from too many cars trying to use the highway (a finite resource). It results in increased delays for cars reaching their destinations.*

Congestion results from too many tasks contending for a host's computational resources, or from too many messages contending for a network's communication resources. It impacts performance directly by delaying task initiation, or increasing task completion time, or in the case of communications, delaying the time of a message arrival.

Congestion impacts scalability since, as the load grows, some resource becomes congested, and that congestion inhibits performance. Possible points of congestion should be anticipated and ways incorporated to increase those resources as load increases. Congestion of one resource can limit performance, even if other resources are not congested.

ANALOGY: *The fast-food restaurant experiences variations in customer arrivals and adjusts the number of order takers, cooks, etc., accordingly. However, fixed resources such as tables and chairs do not vary, and they limit the number of customers served.*

Congestion in Processing

Both the arrival rate of tasks and their completion time can be irregular. This is illustrated in Figure 10.7. The important point is that both the number of tasks arriving and the task completion times fluctuate and contribute to fluctuations in host utilization. Resources such as hosts must be sized to meet anticipated *peak* demand.

EXAMPLE: *The rate of orders in a stock market trading system is irregular, depending on the actions of numerous individual investors and affected by market conditions. The completion time of an order is also irregular, depending on how easily a buyer or seller is found. Electronic mail messages arrive irregularly, although there are some patterns—for example, more arrive during the day than at night, etc. Similarly, the time spent reading each email message is irregular.*

Congestion on Communication Links

Sharing a host between tasks is synonymous with sharing a communication link among messages (which are fragmented into pack-

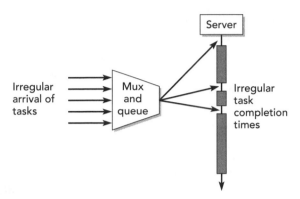

Figure 10.7 Multiplexing and queueing of tasks for a server.

ets—see "Why Networks Use Packets" on page 304). Like a host, a communication link has a finite peak capacity, and the portion of that capacity consumed by messages depends on both arrival rate and length (synonymous with task throughput and completion time). Thus, congestion issues also arise in communication links.

Mitigating congestion is a function of the network (see "The Network" on page 86). It utilizes tools synonymous to those previously discussed for hosts:

- The network associates queues with each communication link. Packets can temporarily arrive faster than they are accommodated on the link, with the excess packets queued. Later, when packets are arriving more slowly, the queue can be emptied.

- Like multiple hosts, the network can provide multiple links for packets to travel, even between the same source and destination. Like load balancing in hosts, the network tries to balance the packet load on the alternative links.

- The network provides congestion information to the hosts that allows them to mitigate that congestion (analogous to highway traffic reports on the radio).

Congestion in networks is discussed further in Chapter 11.

Congestion in Storage

Getting data from where it originates or is modified leads to communications congestion. Particularly in decision-support applications—where data from many operational systems is aggregated—congestion can also occur in storage systems.

EXAMPLE: *Data warehouses have so much data pouring in that the accumulated data can be outrageously large (many terabytes and even petabytes). Such large amounts of data cannot be accommodated by disk storage and thus must rely on so-called tertiary storage devices (such as magnetic tape). Tertiary storage suffers much greater access time than disk, and thus applications that rely on tertiary storage suffer from scalability problems.*

10.3.5 The Role of Application Architecture in Scalability

Scalability is an important consideration in the design of the application architecture (see Section 3.4.2 on page 106). Of course, scalability may not matter in some applications if the performance requirements are modest in relation to current technology and it is certain they will not grow. Such situations are, however, rare. Usually an application is designed with the expectation of success, the demands may increase, and it is difficult to predict where performance requirements will saturate.

Fortunately, there is much that can be done to aid scalability. As the modularity of the application is determined, the architect should be aware of the obstacles to scalability that have been discussed. The following steps are helpful:

- The application should be modularized so that as the workload grows, it can be split into more and more submodules that can be assigned to different hosts.

- Care should be taken to minimize communications requirements among submodules and also dependencies among tasks delegated to submodules. This depends heavily on what performance metrics are important.

- Duplication of effort across hosts should be avoided.

- Scheduling of tasks should be effective in balancing computational and communications requirements, avoiding "hot spots."

- In the face of irregularities in computational and communications requirements, the utilization of both hosts and communication links should be adjusted to limit congestion.

Addressing all these issues is difficult enough in architecture design, but it is far more difficult to modify the architecture of an already operational application.

Designing High-Performance Systems

The following are typical steps in designing a high-performance and scalable application architecture:

1. Break the application down into small, atomic tasks, where each task will be assigned to one host (to avoid communication overhead).

2. Characterize the resource requirements of each task. For example, how much processor execution time and memory and storage space does it consume? This step is best left to an expert with detailed knowledge of the internal workings of computer systems.

3. Analyze the communication patterns among tasks and, in particular, the communication burden on the network created by assigning tasks to different hosts.

4. Understand the scheduling constraints on tasks. What tasks are dependent on the prior completion of others? This determines how much parallelism is possible: If one task must be completed before another, there is completion-time advantage to assigning them to different hosts.

5. In light of these constraints, tentatively assign tasks to different hosts in a way that attempts to achieve the maximum parallelism and minimizes communication requirements. Establish prioritizing in each host: What tasks should be completed most urgently because results are needed by another task?

6. Analyze the proposed host assignment in terms of hot spots— points of congestion in either processing or communication—

Today's Operating Systems

Three widely used operating systems for servers and desktop computers are UNIX, MacOS, and Windows.

UNIX is relatively easily ported to different hardware platforms, so incompatible variations are provided by several vendors. A freeware version called Linux has become popular for desktop computers.

MacOS and Windows are each tied to a particular microprocessor. MacOS has lost significant market share, in part because Apple Computer pursued a proprietary hardware/OS strategy, and in part because it has lost its technological edge (for example, it has cooperative but not preemptive multitasking—see the sidebar "Different Forms of Multitasking" on page 303).

Windows is the dominant desktop operating system, and Microsoft is also making it a vibrant competitor to UNIX with a modern version called Windows NT.

as well as underutilized resources. What bottlenecks will ultimately limit overall application performance? Remember that performance is evaluated in terms of application requirements, such as response time to users. Attempt to modify task assignments—or add communication or processing resources—to eliminate these bottlenecks, thus improving overall performance.

Throughout all these steps, the scalability of the design should be evaluated. Specifically, how can processing and communication resources be added to improve performance as needed? This may lead to additional design modifications.

A similar design methodology can be used in designing the social organization portion of a business process (see "Business Process Reengineering" on page 58). In that case, hosts are replaced by workers, but many similar considerations apply. The best outcome will be achieved by considering the tasks assumed by workers and by networked computing together, as they often have mutual dependencies that affect the overall performance and efficiency of the business process.

10.3.6 Mobile Code and Scalability

Mobile code (see Section 9.3 on page 282) can aid scalability, since it allows computation to dynamically move among hosts, even where the necessary software code does not previously reside. This provides added possibilities for locating computation where there is low utilization, or reducing communication overhead, or both. For example, in client/server applications the server becomes congested as the number of users (and clients) grows. The number of clients expands directly with users, so scalability is enhanced if load can be shifted there.

EXAMPLE: *Web browsers can directly support the user interface (text, graphics, dialog boxes, etc.) but generally not anything specific to an application (presentation or application logic—see Section 3.2.2 on page 92). There are problems if these elements must execute exclusively on the server. First, any interaction between user and application suffers from message latencies, slowing response time. Second, presentation services are limited to those directly supported by the browser. Third—and this is the scalability argument—the server becomes congested as the number of users increases. Mobile code can avoid all these problems by dynamically moving presentation and application logic specific to the application to the client. This was an early application of Java (see "Java Mobile Code" on page 286).*

A N A L O G Y :   *If your restaurant has exhausted its space, you can still expand by entering the catering business, preparing food in your customers' kitchens.*

Another example arises in data-intensive applications. It is not practical to move massive databases around to different hosts, so there are only two other possibilities: Access the data over the network (which is the point of the three-tier client/server architecture—see Section 3.2.2 on page 92), or move application logic to the host where the data resides. The latter trades lower communication overhead for additional load on that host.

A N A L O G Y :   *A worker needing repeated access to a body of records can be physically co-located with the records, rather than using company mail to make requests for and receive those records.*

The most compelling application of mobile code is in applications that span administrative domains. From the perspective of scalability, flexibility in locating computation is desired, but it may be administratively difficult or impossible to ensure that needed software is installed. In principle, mobile code allows computation to be located anywhere.

10.4 Operating Systems

The operating system is the portion of the software infrastructure primarily responsible for supporting concurrency, such as managing and scheduling tasks in multitasking, and packetization and scheduling of messages in communications (see Section 4.2.2 on page 124, where the location of the operating system in the architecture of the infrastructure is described).

Operating Systems and Winner-Take-All Effects

Several factors discussed in Chapter 5 contribute to winner-take-all and path-dependent effects for operating systems:

- *Indirect network externalities:* A dominant operating system attracts a large base of application developers, offering users a large suite of applications. It is easier to share files and run direct applications for users with the same operating system.

- *Path-dependent effects:* New entrants must match the expanding accumulated investment to provide competitive features and maturity. As with all software, large supplier economies of scale reduce the unit costs for an operating system with high market share.

- *Lock-in:* Users accumulate application software for a particular operating system and gain familiarity with its operation and administration, increasing switching costs.

Over time, it is inevitable that one operating system gains dominance, like the "natural monopoly" tendencies that

(continued)

have long dominated tele-communications policy (see Chapter 12).

EXAMPLE: *In 1998, Windows has a 90 per-cent market share for new desktop computers. In 1998, the U.S. govern-ment filed an antitrust suit against Microsoft, not on the basis of the Windows near-monopoly (which is legal), but alleging illegal business practices by tying other applica-tions and services to Windows to extend that monopoly.*

Middleware layers (see Chap-ter 9) and the thin-client model (see Section 3.2.3 on page 96) may reduce the visi-bility of the operating system over time. This would give an opening to other operating systems.

When a single program is written and compiled, it executes as a *process*, which provides an executing environment that hides (abstracts) many details of the physical host and its peripherals. The operating system supports multiple concurrent processes through multitasking (see the "Different Forms of Multitasking" on page 303), which allows concurrent programs on the same host through time-slicing (see Section 10.2.2 on page 302). The process hides from each program the existence of other concurrent programs (unless it wishes to interact with them). With preemptive multitask-ing, a program is not aware that it is being suspended to do a con-text switch to another program.

EXAMPLE: *You doubtless have experience starting two or more applications on a personal computer, such as an email application and a word processor. Each application is a program executing as a separate process.*

This last example illustrates one motivation—running multiple applications—for having multitasking and processes. Another is the need for concurrent tasks on one host within a single application (see Section 10.2.2 on page 302), typically because of an intrinsic application requirement (such as supporting multiple users). A third motivation is mitigating the blocking that programs experience while they wait for an external request (see Section 10.3.1 on page 308). Structuring an application as concurrent processes allows a host to continue doing useful work even when one process is blocked waiting for an external request to be satisfied.

EXAMPLE: *A task needing information from a remote host may need to wait for a time before receiving a response. Meantime, other tasks can continue their work, increasing host utilization.*

Further Reading

[Sil97] and [Tan97] are excellent references on operating systems, with much more detail than given here. [Hwa98] discusses scalabil-ity, primarily from a hardware perspective.

Networks

11

The network allows hosts to communicate in support of a networked application. The communication services provided to the application were discussed in Chapter 7, with additional communication facilities provided by the middleware layer (such as distributed object management) discussed in Chapter 9. This is about all that is necessary to know—from a functional viewpoint—except for one important issue: How do hosts find and address one another? In addition, traffic within the network strongly influences application performance and quality metrics (see Chapter 10) because it impacts the reliability and delay of messages sent from one host to another.

The global Internet was an important development as the first packet network that connected not only organizations of all sizes, but also individual citizens (see the sidebar "Origins of the Internet"). This enables, for the first time, the widespread deployment of electronic commerce and social applications (see Chapter 2). For this reason, the Internet is used as a concrete example to illustrate many general concepts.

11.1 Functions of a Network

The fundamental role of the network—carrying messages from one host to another using switches connected by communication links—was described in "The Network" on page 86. The internet technologies, manifested most visibly by the public Internet, are most popular today, in part because they allow existing LAN networks to be

Origins of the Internet

The local area network (LAN), specifically Ethernet, allowed interconnection of hosts within a building. Its biggest application was allowing users to log in and access files in different hosts, send email to one another, etc. It demonstrated the value of interconnecting hosts and allowed development of an early suite of networked applications.

In the early 1970s, the U.S. Defense Advanced Projects Research Agency (DARPA) funded research into wide area computer networking. Since LANs already existed, this project interconnected existing LANs, rather than designing from scratch a new end-to-end network. It resulted in the *internet protocols* (see Section 3.3 on page 99), which have been extended and refined in the IETF (see the sidebar "Internet Engineering Task Force (IETF)" on page 136).

Wide area networking was also studied by ISO (see the sidebar "International Organization for Standards (ISO)" on page 135), resulting in the Open Systems Interconnection (OSI) standards. The differences in process are striking. OSI defined an elaborate and complete protocol suite *before* implementation, whereas the internet protocols arose from university

incorporated into a WAN by internetworking (see Section 3.3 on page 99). The abstract message services supported by the network—message, message with reply, session, and broadcast—were outlined in Chapter 7, together with concrete internet examples. As mentioned in the sidebar "Why Networks Use Packets" on page 304, for reasons of fairness (one large message can't delay others inordinately), messages are fragmented into smaller packets for network transport.

The network performs a number of important functions besides empowering hosts to find and address one another. It allocates limited communication resources to different applications and users, and ultimately it controls quality metrics of interest to the application.

11.1.1 Sharing: Statistical Multiplexing

The essence of the network topology of Figure 3.6 on page 89 is that backbone communication links are shared among hosts, users, and applications. This sharing is the essence of the favorable economics behind a public network.

ANALOGY: *Although it is an overused (and sometimes misleading) analogy, the network shares some characteristics with the public highway system. The highways connect everybody's parking lot or garage (except for the small problem of the oceans) and are shared by all citizens. A better analogy—and the one used here—is the railroad system. Like the Internet, in the United States the railroad system is privately owned, but ownership and use is shared by a number of companies, and the system transports a variety of goods for the benefit of every segment of the economy.*

Any specific communication link may forward packets from a number of hosts to a number of other hosts, depending on the network topology. Sharing reduces the number of communication links and thus serves to reduce the unit communication costs. It also implies packet queueing and multiplexing at each link (see "Queueing and Multiplexing" on page 222), since packets arrive from a number of different hosts. Queueing allows packets arriving from different

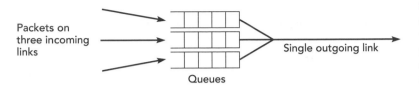

Packets on three incoming links → Queues → Single outgoing link

Figure 11.1 A switch stores incoming packets in queues and sends them to outgoing links one after the other (special case of three input links and one output link shown).

sources at the same time (this is called packet *contention*) to be accommodated by delaying all but one of them.

The queueing and multiplexing function within a network switch is illustrated in Figure 11.1. Packets are stored in queues as they arrive, and the switch chooses one packet at a time to be transmitted on the link, thus performing multiplexing.

ANALOGY: *Queueing and multiplexing occur when a single railroad track is shared among different trains. Trains coming from different origins are multiplexed at a station or switching yard. While two or more trains may arrive simultaneously, all but one will wait.*

The dynamic sharing of a communication link in the network is called *statistical multiplexing*. Specifically, the capacity of a given link—called the *bitrate*, or sometimes the *bandwidth*—is constant and is measured in bits per second (bps). On the other hand, the packets multiplexed on the link vary in their demands on the link, depending on what the application and users are currently doing. The demand on the link is best characterized by the average bitrate required to support the aggregate packets from all sources, which is the product of the average packet size (in bits) and the average rate of arrival (in packets per second).

EXAMPLE: *A typical voiceband data modem connecting a personal computer supports a bitrate of 33,300 bps, while a switched Ethernet LAN may have a capacity of 10 million bps. If the average packet size is 8,000 bits, the modem can accommodate at most 33,000/8,000 = 4.125 packets per second, whereas the Ethernet can accommodate up to 1,250 packets per second.*

research projects that developed, prototyped, and tested them incrementally. The internet used a process of continuous improvement by researchers, rather than top-down design.

The most telling difference was the availability of prototype internet implementations in freeware distributions of Berkeley UNIX. A number of applications were developed and refined in parallel with protocol refinement. The applications impacted the protocols, and vice versa, in an empirical environment. By the time OSI implementation started, the Internet was already soundly established, along with a suite of compelling applications. Because of network externalities and lock-in (see Section 5.3 on page 150), OSI lost, illustrating the power of early to market and positive feedback with winner-take-all effects.

In practice, both the packet size and the rate of packet arrival are irregular—as is their aggregate bitrate demand—so that at some times the packets may be arriving too fast (or may be too big), and at other times they can easily be accommodated by the link. In the former case, packets accumulate in the queues, and in the latter case, the queues are gradually emptied. As long as the aggregate bitrate demand is less than the link capacity, statistical multiplexing works well.

Network Congestion

Packets arriving too fast (or that are too big) result in an increasing number of packets waiting in queues. This is a manifestation of congestion (see Section 10.3.4 on page 309), which increases the time required for each packet to traverse the network from one host to another, because the packet is spending time in queues waiting to be transmitted.

From an application perspective, the performance parameter of interest—called the *message latency*—is the time that elapses between the generation of a message in one host to the receipt of that complete message in another host. (Latency is the time the message is latent, or "hidden" and unavailable to the application.) A message has to be fragmented into packets, and those packets have to be reassembled into the original message at the destination. One component of the message latency is the congestion-induced time that packets sit in queues awaiting transmission on communication links (see Chapter 12 for discussion of other contributors to latency). Thus, the direct impact of network congestion on the application is increased message latency.

EXAMPLE: *A remote method invocation (RMI) is constructed from two messages, the first from client to server marshalling the parameters, and the second from server to client marshalling the return values (see the sidebar "RMI Is Layered on Messages" on page 235). The client is blocked until the return, and this blocking time includes two message latencies. Thus, network congestion forces the client object to wait before resuming its work.*

The storage capacity of queues in the packet switch is finite, so severe congestion can result in a packet arriving at a switch to find the queue full. The packet must then be discarded. Thus, it cannot be guaranteed that packets actually arrive at their destination during periods of congestion, unless additional measures are taken in the network protocols (see Section 11.2 on page 330).

11.1.2 Packet Forwarding and Routing

The network must find a route from source to destination host—consistent with the network topology—for each packet. To support this function, each packet looks like the following:

Header	Payload

The two elements of the packet are as follows:

- A *packet header* includes information meaningful to the network, such as the source and destination of the packet, the size of the payload, etc.

- The *packet payload* includes data to be delivered to the destination. For example, it might include the message (or fragment of a message) that should be delivered to the application.

The network has no interest in the content of the payload, other than its size. Thus, to the network, the payload is merely data, whereas the application interprets it (so that it becomes information—see "Data and Information in Layers" on page 128). The routing of packets makes use of information in the header identifying the intended destination of the packet.

A N A L O G Y: *A packet is analogous to a single railroad train. The train includes an engine with driver, which maneuvers the train through the railroad system and is analogous to the packet header. The passengers and freight are analogous to a packet payload.*

Another—in some ways better—analogy to the packet header is the postal envelope (see "Analogy: The Postal System" on page 245). The envelope, like the header, includes sender and recipient identification and address. The recipient discards the envelope to access the enclosed letter.

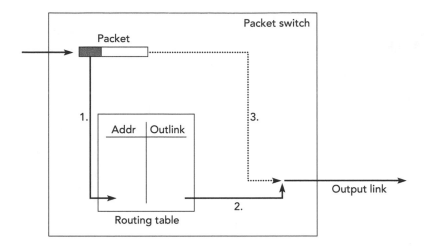

Figure 11.2 The forwarding of a packet requires the three steps shown. Routing updates the routing table based on the network topology.

EXAMPLE: *The header used by the basic Internet Protocol (IP) includes an IP address, which uniquely identifies the destination host. In the latest version of IP (Version 6), the IP address is 128 bits, which is capable of identifying $2^{128} = 3 \times 10^{38}$ hosts (older versions of IP use only a 32-bit address). This very large number—even considering inefficiencies, it represents about 1,500 addresses per square foot of the earth's surface—anticipates a future in which many devices will have Internet access (see Section 1.2 on page 7).*

As shown in Figure 11.2, each switch maintains a *routing table* consulted by the switch to determine the appropriate output link for each packet (from among all those connected to the switch). For each packet, the switch follows these steps:

1. While the packet is queued (as in Figure 11.1), the destination address (or more likely some portion of the address) in the packet is noted. That address is used as an index into the routing table.

2. The appropriate output link is read from the table, and meanwhile the packet is queued until there is an opportunity to transmit the packet.

3. When the chosen output link is available (no other packet is being forwarded), the packet is transmitted on the chosen link.

This entire process is called packet *forwarding*. The entries in the routing table must be chosen carefully so that forwarding gets the packet closer to its destination, depending on the network topology. The updating of routing tables is called *routing*, and packet switches that implement this function are called *routers*. Each router periodically exchanges network topology information with nearby routers, which over time propagates through the entire network. Multicast requires a more complicated routing (see the sidebar "Simulcast and Multicast").

11.1.3 Name Services

For purposes of packet forwarding, a destination address is included in each packet header (128 bits in the latest IP). Users would find it unpleasant to deal with these addresses directly. To make it easier for users, hosts are also assigned *names*, which are mnemonic and more easily remembered by people. A source must include the destination address—a host name will not suffice—so the host name has to be converted to an address within the infrastructure. This is the function of a *name service*.

A N A L O G Y :   *Telephone numbers are currently ten to thirteen digits. While users do successfully deal with telephone numbers, IP addresses would be much larger—the equivalent of thirty-five digits—and would be very difficult for users to remember.*

E X A M P L E :   *A typical name is* `info.sims.berkeley.edu`*," and a typical form of an IP address (older 32-bit variety) is* `128.55.156.273`*" (expressed in octal rather than binary). In the Internet, the name service is the domain name system (DNS). For example, when the user invokes a hyperlink in a Web document, the URL (see the sidebar "The Hypertext Transfer Protocol (HTTP)" on page 220) includes the host name where the page can be found. The application then obtains the IP address of the host from the DNS before initiating the HTTP protocol. The DNS is like the telephone white pages: Knowing the name of a person or company, the white pages provides their telephone number (their telephone network address).*

Simulcast and Multicast

In a broadcast communication service, replicas of the source messages are communicated to multiple recipients. As discussed in Section 7.2.5 on page 232, this is useful for applications such as multiparty video conferencing and remote learning and can be accomplished by simulcast or multicast, as shown in Figure 11.3. *Simulcast* requires that the source send replicas independently to each destination, but it has two problems:

- Simulcast is not scalable (see Section 10.3 on page 306). In some applications, the number of destinations may be *very* large. As the number of recipients increases, both the processing requirement and network access link bitrate increase, so eventually both resources are exhausted.

- Simulcast is inefficient. For example, on the network access link, the same data is sent repeatedly—once for each destination—when once would suffice.

In the Internet, these problems are mitigated by *IP multicast*, which replicates the data *within* the network for all recipients. To the source, multicast looks essentially the same as unicast, and the network makes replicas as "close" (in terms of network

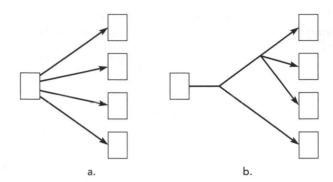

a.   b.

Figure 11.3 (a) Simulcast and (b) multicast allow communication of the same information to multiple hosts.

Structure of Names and Addresses

For reasons of network scalability, both names and addresses are hierarchical (see Section 4.1.2 on page 117). Addresses, which indicate where the host is connected to the network topology, reflect the "network of networks" structure. The Internet topology has a two-level hierarchy, where the two levels are "network" and "internetwork." An IP address has this hierarchical structure of the form (Network, Host), where Network is a unique identifier for a given network, and Host is a unique identifier for a host topologically connected to that network.

ANALOGY: *Telephone numbers have a similar hierarchy, with a country code, city code, and local number uniquely identifying a telephone.*

Host names also have a hierarchical structure, where the levels of hierarchy are delimited by a "dot" notation, representing the administrative partitioning of the network.

EXAMPLE: *In "info.sims.berkeley.edu," "edu" indicates that this host is administered by an educational institution, "berkeley" indicates that this educational institution is Berkeley, "sims" designates the school within Berkeley, and "info" distinguishes this host from others within that school. Except for "edu," these represent administrative boundaries.*

There is no particular relationship between administrative and top-ological structure; a given organization may be geographically distributed.

E X A M P L E : *The IBM Corporation has many offices in cities around the world. All IBM host names include "*ibm.com*" (often with a country mnemonic added) in spite of the fact that these hosts connect topologically in many different geographical locations.*

11.1.4 Flow Control

Anytime one entity (a producer) sends a stream of messages to another (a consumer), as illustrated in Figure 11.4, there is the question of whether the consumer can keep up with the producer. For example, the producer might be running on a faster computer, or the processing required to generate messages may be much less than the processing required to consume them. *Flow control* is a protocol that the producer and consumer use to prevent the producer from generating data faster than the consumer can accept it.

A N A L O G Y : *A restaurant ensures it can serve all customers that arrive by requiring a reservation. The customers and restaurant participate in a reservation (flow control) protocol.*

A typical flow control protocol requires acknowledgment of messages by the consumer, and a policy that the producer must limit the number of unacknowledged messages sent.

E X A M P L E : *Flow control might be executed on a per-packet basis. The producer could keep track of past packets sent and receive acknowledgment from the consumer that those packets have been accepted. If the producer ensures there are no more than n unacknowledged packets (by refusing to send more), an intermediate*

topology) to the recipient as possible to conserve network resources. Each recipient must subscribe to the source.

A N A L O G Y : *IP multicast is like a radio network. The programs at the source are not broadcast directly to the listeners, but rather to a limited set of radio stations. Each listener tunes into the broadcast (analogous to subscribing) without knowledge of the source.*

While efficient and scalable, multicast places special burdens on routers. They must be prepared to replicate—not simply forward—packets within the network and also accept subscriptions. Routing is more complicated, since subscriptions must flow from recipient back toward the source.

Figure 11.4 With a producer/consumer communication, flow control is required to prevent overflow of intermediate queues.

The Value of a Name

Internet domain names have serious political and commercial implications. Commercially, companies want to protect their trademarks and not allow others to use those trademarks in domain names. This also has value to consumers, who can often guess a domain name. There are often geopolitical implications as well. Except in the United States, domain names end in a mnemonic for the country. If countries split or unite, should their domain names change accordingly?

In light of this, it is surprising that domain names can be obtained for a very small administrative fee with minimal restriction. Some enterprising folk have speculated on names that might be of value to large companies in the future. So the question arises, should domain names be subject to trademark laws? If a company owns the trademark for "xyz," should that trademark also apply to domain name "xyz.com"? What should be the process for assigning names? Generally, courts in the United States have invalidated domain names that may cause consumer confusion with registered trademarks.

queue with a capacity of n packets cannot overflow. This is roughly how TCP implements flow control (see Section 7.3.3 on page 235). UDP, on the other hand, does not provide flow control, so this burden is shifted to the application (see Section 7.3.2 on page 234). A message with reply protocol (such as RMI) has implicit flow control, since the reply from the recipient provides an implicit acknowledgment that it is ready to receive another message.

11.1.5 Congestion Control

Network congestion tends to be unstable; that is, some congestion causes more congestion. To understand this, it is important to distinguish traffic *offered* to a network (the aggregate packets that sending hosts *wish* to communicate) and traffic *carried* by the network (the aggregate packets actually delivered to the destination hosts). The carried traffic cannot exceed network capacity; that is, the utilization of each link in the network cannot exceed 1.0. However, the offered traffic *can* exceed the network capacity. If it does, queues within the network must accumulate the excess offered traffic, and eventually become full, causing packet loss. The instability results from senders attempting to get lost packets through by resending them, resulting in an artificial increase in offered traffic and making the congestion more severe.

E X A M P L E :   *Protocols that provide reliable delivery of packets, such as TCP, achieve reliability by retransmitting lost packets. For these protocols, every lost packet will result in at least one retransmission, which increases the offered traffic. This increase in offered traffic will cause a higher percentage of packet losses, making the problem progressively worse.*

A qualitative curve illustrating offered versus carried traffic is shown in Figure 11.5. The network "capacity" is the hypothetical carried traffic if every link in the network were running at full utilization and there were no retransmissions. Unfortunately, as the offered traffic increases, the carried traffic peaks out at less than full network capacity (reflecting packet loss and retransmission), and further increases in offered traffic cause the carried traffic to actually decrease because of increased retransmissions.

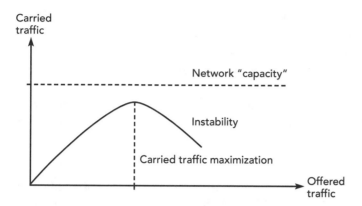

Figure 11.5 Networks often display unstable behavior, and the goal of congestion control is to limit the offered traffic to the point where the carried traffic is maximum.

Clearly, somehow restricting offered traffic to a level that maximizes carried traffic is to the user's collective social benefit. *Congestion control* is a protocol and associated policies engaged in by the network and its sources to attempt to maximize the carried traffic. It works by artificially limiting the offered traffic, keeping it within the stable region. Each user participating in congestion control is restricting his or her personal behavior in the interest of this social benefit.

A N A L O G Y :   *Metering lights at the entrance to a major highway is a form of congestion control. By limiting offered traffic, carried traffic (drivers actually reaching their destinations) is increased. Some drivers languish at the metering light to help speed other drivers to their destination.*

Flow control and congestion control are different. Flow control is a protocol implemented between a single source and a single destination with the goal of keeping the destination from being inundated by too many messages. Congestion control is a protocol the *aggregate* sources of traffic and the network participate in, with the goal of keeping the network operating in the region of greatest carried traffic. Flow control is required regardless of the traffic conditions in the network.

Types of Congestion Control

Congestion control must resolve the social issue of how the burden of restricting offered traffic is distributed among users and applications. Representative alternatives are asking each source to generate the same fraction of their desired traffic, placing a maximum offered traffic restriction on all sources, or somehow allocating more offered traffic to "compelling" uses. Choosing the right approach is a contentious issue.

From a social perspective, there are at least three generic options listed in Table 11.1. All three approaches encourage users and applications to shift their demand from periods of congestion to less busy periods—the incentives approach through pricing and the others through restrictions to offered traffic.

Both the voluntary and incentive approaches have the significant advantage that sources presumably know something about the "importance" of their traffic, and they can voluntarily allocate the limited network resources during periods of congestion to the most compelling purposes. Mandated policies are inflexible in this regard. However, voluntary approaches are easily circumvented by "bad" citizens, who are rewarded for doing so. Pricing incentives preserve user flexibility without creating bad citizens, since users generating more offered traffic during periods of congestion assume a disproportionate share of costs.

How is congestion control realized? From a technical perspective, there are two basic approaches listed in Table 11.2. Unlike the network, each source cannot see the global picture. Thus, a source-initiated algorithm must be designed in such a way that the sources collectively reduce the offered traffic appropriately, without global knowledge. Similarly, pricing incentives have to be designed to encourage the desired collective behavior.

EXAMPLE: *The Internet TCP incorporates congestion control, which was introduced after the Internet experienced considerable congestion instabilities. Each TCP source estimates congestion by noting the incidence of lost packets and voluntarily reduces offered traffic.*

Table 11.1 Alternative approaches to congestion control.

Approach	Description	Examples
Voluntary policies	Sources voluntarily adhere to policies restricting offered traffic, acting for the collective good. "Bad" citizens ignoring these policies are rewarded by receiving a larger share of the carried traffic, and they create congestion, impacting others.	Protocol implementations adhering to the widely used Internet TCP de facto standard (see Section 7.3.3 on page 235) include congestion control. Hosts can avoid TCP congestion control by using another transport protocol, such as UDP (see Section 7.3.2 on page 234).
Mandatory policies	Policies are mandated for the allocation of offered traffic.	Metering lights at highway and bridge entrances are mandated, with legal sanctions for violation.
Pricing incentives	Pricing for network services is adjusted to influence offered traffic. Sources shifting offered traffic to less congested times are rewarded by lower prices, and revenue is generated to upgrade overloaded facilities.	Telephone companies use time-of-day pricing, generally increasing prices during periods of peak demand. Supply and demand are matched for most goods and services through pricing mechanisms.

Table 11.2 Two technical approaches to implementing congestion control.

Approach	Description	Analogy
Source initiated	Sources detect network congestion, or are informed by the network (either directly or through pricing adjustments), and limit the offered traffic. This has the advantage that sources can offer the most compelling traffic or time-shift less compelling traffic.	Customers finding long lines at ATMs and teller windows may voluntarily leave, returning later. Alternatively, the bank may charge lower fees for customers served during light periods, rewarding those customers who choose them.
Network policing	The network enforces limits on the traffic it will accept from each source. The network may engage in flow control with each source, or it may silently drop excess traffic.	Highway metering lights are an involuntary flow control. A restaurant only accepting customers with reservations may stop answering the phone when they become fully booked.

Congestion and Network Externalities

Recall that an externality is an impact of one user on another without a compensating payment. Congestion is thus a network externality but one very different from the type discussed in Chapter 5. There, one added user *increases* its value to other users, because there is one more user to participate in applications. Congestion has the opposite character: One more user *reduces* the value of the network to other users because of the increased congestion he causes. Adding a user to a network is thus a classical double-edged sword.

Network policing can take the form of *admission control*, in which session establishment requests are refused if the session would adversely impact existing sessions (see Section 7.2.4 on page 227). Another form of policing discards selected packets. This is indiscriminate—important messages could be discarded as easily as unimportant—but this can be redressed by asking the sources to attach a *priority* to each offered packet, and the network can discard traffic in order of priority (starting with the lowest).

When offered traffic is mandated, the usual goal is some measure of *fairness*. Another difficult question is the interpretation of fairness: Is it fair to equalize offered traffic for different sources or give each source a fraction of its desired offered traffic? In practice, attempts at fairness inevitably impose a much greater burden on some sources than others.

EXAMPLE: *Different applications have different inherent traffic requirements. Thus, mandating equal offered traffic will, for example, be quite restrictive to some and not to others.*

Except for pricing incentives, these approaches do not allow sources complete freedom to choose the traffic they offer at times of congestion. A primary advantage of pricing incentives is that users or applications with compelling needs are able to satisfy those needs (with a price penalty). The primary objection to pricing is the cost of the infrastructure (see the sidebar "Cost of a Congestion Control Infrastructure").

11.2 Quality of Service (QoS)

Networked applications are concerned with performance parameters such as task throughput, task time to completion, or interactive delay (see Chapter 10). The impact of inevitable network impairments (such as packet latency and loss) therefore depends on the application.

EXAMPLE: *Applications using distributed objects interacting through RMI will experience greater blocking time—and hence increased task completion time or reduced task throughput—when the packet (and hence message) latency increases (see "Remote*

Method Invocation" on page 225). Streaming audio and video will experience greater end-to-end delay as the packet latency increases (see Section 11.2.2 on page 332). Packet loss may have even more serious consequences.

To the extent the application incorporates interhost communication over the network, its performance parameters are impacted by network *impairments*, including

- *Packet and message latency:* Packet latency is caused by the speed-of-light propagation delay, transmission time, queueing delay, and processing time in the software infrastructure (the first two are discussed in Chapter 12). Message latency is caused by the latency and loss of packets composing the message.

- *Packet and message loss:* Once a message is fragmented into packets, loss of one or more of those packets causes loss of the message. In practice, if loss is unacceptable, a protocol such as TCP is used to guarantee packet delivery using retransmission. In this case, packet loss results in increased message latency (but not loss).

- *Packet corruption:* Communication links can cause bit errors (changing a "0" to a "1" or vice versa). This is especially a problem on wireless communication media. If a packet must be delivered with integrity, then a bit error in a packet is equivalent to a packet loss (see Section 8.2.3 on page 260).

In summary, the application is concerned with *message* latency, loss, and corruption (or their impact on higher-level communication services such as the RMI), and in a packet network these concerns are translated into *packet* latency, loss, and corruption. These latter characteristics are called *network quality-of-service* (QoS) parameters.

11.2.1 The Internet Transport Protocols and QoS

The internet UDP, TCP, and RTP protocols (see Section 7.3 on page 233) are called *transport protocols*, while IP is a *network protocol*. The purpose of the transport protocol is to condition or customize the network protocol to the needs of the application. One of those conditionings is in QoS.

Cost of a Congestion Control Infrastructure

Today's internet protocols emphasize simplicity and low cost, and this is reflected in congestion control. Whether more sophisticated approaches are needed, desirable, or affordable is controversial. Those opposed mention the cost of a pricing infrastructure, including the required metering of source usage and the billing of users. Relating congestion in a particular part of the network back to the sources causing that congestion—and notifying them of a price increase—is also not a simple technical problem.

On the other hand, today's internet protocols—like the standby service on airlines—transfer the risk of congestion to every user. This risk reduces the value of the network service and thus probably also users' willingness to pay. Thus, the appropriate question is not the absolute cost of a congestion control infrastructure, but rather that cost in relation to the resulting revenue possibilities and benefit to users.

IP provides a *best-effort datagram* service. Datagram refers to the fact that packets each stand on their own; they do not share a context (like a session). The term "best effort" describes the QoS; that is, IP makes no guarantee that a given datagram is delivered, nor does it guarantee its latency if it is delivered. It simply makes its best effort to deliver the datagram and deliver it as early as possible. The philosophy behind IP is to keep it simple and make it a "lowest-common-denominator" communication service that can be enhanced by the transport protocol.

UDP does not add much to IP, except some additional addressing to specify the destination process (in addition to destination host, as in the case of IP) (see Section 10.4 on page 315). UDP also promises not to deliver corrupt packets.

Many applications demand *reliable* delivery of messages, meaning they are actually guaranteed to be delivered and to be uncorrupted. This feature is offered by TCP—in the context of a session—by retransmitting packets that are lost or corrupted. The destination acknowledges each received uncorrupted packet (by sending an acknowledgment packet in the reverse direction), and the source retransmits packets for which it receives no acknowledgment. TCP also incorporates flow control and congestion control.

Why not *always* stipulate reliable delivery for all transport protocols? The reason is that a penalty is paid in latency for reliable delivery, because retransmissions consume extra time. Some applications prefer some unreliability in exchange for lower latency. One example is direct-immediate applications using audio or video media, as discussed next.

11.2.2 Integrated Services

The Internet originated as a data network, but recently its capabilities have begun to overlap the telephone network, providing audio and video incorporated into immediate interactive and collaborative applications (see Section 2.3 on page 19). In short, the Internet has become an *integrated services* network, defined as one providing the full range of services needed by applications (data, audio, video, and others).

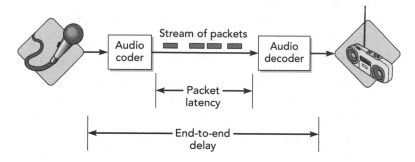

Figure 11.6 Network packet latency is one source of end-to-end delay in a streaming multimedia service.

An integrated services network must satisfy a wide range of application needs generally satisfied by a range of transport protocols.

EXAMPLE: *The RTP transport protocol is one response to the particular needs of streaming multimedia services (see the sidebar "Internet Streaming Multimedia Protocols" on page 236).*

An issue particular to direct-immediate applications is delay. As illustrated in Figure 11.6 for an audio service, subjective quality is adversely affected by end-to-end delay (from the microphone at the source to the speaker at the destination), particularly in a direct-immediate application such as audio conferencing. The audio medium is streamed over the network as a sequence of packets, and one component of end-to-end delay is packet latency. In this case, the added latency of reliable delivery is problematic, and more likely a datagram service would be used.

Expanding the capabilities of the Internet—making it an integrated services network that provides good performance and quality for all services—is an ongoing issue (see the sidebar "The Evolution of the Internet").

11.2.3 Pricing Network Services

The pricing of network services is a concern to users and organizations but crucial to the economic viability of service providers. Users collectively finance and utilize a shared network—and the actions of

The Evolution of the Internet

The Internet did not start out trying to be all things to all users. For many years it was designed, prototyped, and operated with a limited best effort service model and used for a more narrowly defined set of applications. Improvements have been added incrementally as problems arose, such as scalability and congestion. Recently, driven by integrated services (including audio, video, and multicast), the Internet has been retrofitted to meet those needs. It is a testament to the flexibility of the original design that this is possible. On the other hand, the question arises when it might be better (from the perspective of cost, performance, or whatever) to design a completely new network around the expanded requirements (called a *greenfield* approach).

The Internet is an interesting test of the relative merits of a process of incremental improvement and expansion versus a greenfield approach. Certainly when compared to the networks that preceded it, the Internet is *itself* a premier example of greenfield thinking. On the other hand, for networks, the obstacles of network externalities strongly favor a process of continuous

each user affect others—making pricing a complex issue. As in any social context, the concern is how to finance, deploy, and operate the network to maximize the *collective* benefit to the users, and how to divide costs among those accruing those benefits.

The challenges are similar to the pricing of software (see Section 5.4.4 on page 160). Like software, networks benefit from large economies of scale: In the absence of congestion, new users can be accepted at a very low marginal cost. This is troublesome in a competitive market, because prices are driven toward marginal costs, which are much lower than average costs. Pricing therefore cannot be based strictly on costs, but must take into account the value to the customer. Sophisticated pricing strategies—similar to value pricing and versioning in software—are needed to make network services a viable business.

Before setting prices, the first question is the costs:

- *Fixed costs:* Each user requires an access link to the network and also permanently shares in the use of an access switch with a modest number of other users. Relatively fixed costs also include customer support, billing, marketing, etc.

- *Usage-related costs:* It is more difficult to allocate the cost of the backbone network, since it is not dedicated to a single user. The backbone facilities (switches and communication links) must be sized in anticipation of the aggregate traffic, and frequent and heavy users have a greater impact on these costs than light users. Thus, the backbone costs attributable to a given user are reasonably approximated by the traffic generated by that user, measured by total number of bits (number of packets times size of packets) or a similar measure.

- *QoS-related costs:* When users request QoS guarantees, such as reliable or delay-bounded delivery of packets, there are costs associated with resources reserved for one user and not shared with other users.

- *Congestion costs:* In a packet network, congestion results primarily in increased latencies, which can be considered a "cost" to the collective users, not in monetary terms, but in terms of productivity or aggravation or other indirect measures. Each user offering traffic during congestion is increasing the latencies experienced by other users and thus creating a "cost" to them.

Each of these costs can potentially be reflected in the pricing, and each has a strong argument in its favor:

- A fixed price for Internet access based on the fixed costs is non-controversial. No other user will be willing to offset fixed costs directly attributable to another user.

- A component of price based on usage is more controversial. It can be the basis of value pricing—using usage as a basis of price differentiation—since heavy users may have a higher willingness to pay.

- QoS predictability offers direct value to the user but would be futile in the absence of associated pricing mechanisms because rational users would always choose the highest quality option. QoS could also form the basis of versioning (see "Versioning" on page 163) as a strategy for deriving more revenues from users with a greater willingness to pay.

- Congestion pricing creates a source of revenue for a congested network that can be used to expand capacity. As a form of congestion control by providing incentives, it gives users freedom of action without creating bad citizens (see Section 11.1.5 on page 326).

At present Internet pricing is simple (see the sidebar "Today's Internet Pricing"). In the future, the Internet likely needs more sophisticated pricing strategies, particularly as it provides an increasing number of service models with QoS differentiation (see Section 11.2.2 on page 332). The strongest counterargument is the cost of the infrastructure supporting pricing (see the sidebar "Cost of a Congestion Control Infrastructure" on page 331).

improvement, allowing new features to be systematically propagated to existing users (see Section 5.3.1 on page 150).

11.3 Network Security

By its very nature, a public network is a security risk, as it opens up access to each connected host to everybody (see Chapter 8). Fortunately, measures can be taken to mitigate these security risks.

11.3.1 Secure and Insecure Authentication

Protecting a host requires access control and associated authentication of users. Unfortunately, some simple authentication
approaches commonly used are insecure. A common approach is to
ask a user to supply a password, which is checked against a stored
replica. Alternatively, the IP address of a host is sometimes used to
authenticate it. An intruder who gains physical access to a network
(or surreptitiously installs a program in a host connected to a network) can monitor network traffic. This *sniffing attack* can uncover
valuable information, such as the IP address of hosts or user passwords. It is possible for an attacker to masquerade as a different
host by *spoofing* an IP address, making it appear that packets are
originating from another host. Authentication based on a shared
secret or certificate is much more secure (see Section 8.2.2 on page
256).

11.3.2 Security Flaws in Public Servers

Many Internet hosts must offer publicly available servers, for example, to send and receive email and provide Web services. Not infrequently, these servers have security flaws. Once external access to
these servers is allowed, attackers can exploit them. Web servers
are especially vulnerable given the capability to extend them—
using a *common gateway interchange* (CGI)—allowing the HTTP
server to invoke an arbitrary program or script. Sometimes ordinary
users add CGI extensions, and they frequently have security flaws.

11.3.3 Firewalls and Packet Filtering

As described in Chapter 8, firewalls create a *trusted enclave* that is
partially isolated from the global Internet (less draconian than physically isolating the enclave). Several common configurations for firewalls [Gar96] are shown in Figure 11.7. The elements of these
configurations include the following:

- The firewall acts as a *packet filter*, examining all IP packets and
  passing only those meeting specific criteria, such as destination,
  or running specific transport protocols (such as TCP), or supporting specific applications.

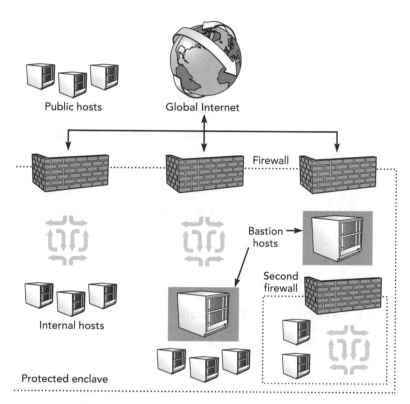

Figure 11.7 Typical firewall configurations.

- *Bastion hosts* are special hosts *within* the enclave. If there are bastion hosts, the firewall only allows IP packets to pass to and from the bastion hosts (other packets are blocked).

- *Public hosts* are special hosts *outside* the enclave. This is where, for example, a public HTTP server might run.

Bastion hosts provide external services, such as email, and can execute *proxies* for the benefit of applications running on nonbastion hosts. (A proxy is a program that acts on behalf of another.)

Finally, in the double-firewall architecture, a second firewall interior to the bastion hosts provides an additional layer of protection. For example, an intruder gaining access to the bastion host can't penetrate to hosts within the interior enclave. This architecture is

Firewalls Limit Innovation

Key to the success of the Internet has been keeping the network simple and allowing additional capabilities (new transport protocols or applications) to be added. It has traditionally been possible for a single programmer to make an innovation and distribute it widely in very short order.

Sadly, this capability is lost where firewalls are added. Since firewalls specifically limit protocols and applications, new innovations are available to users within a trusted enclave only when the firewall is upgraded. Since firewalls generally incorporate only standardized protocols and applications, the practical impact of this is to greatly increase the importance of standardization activities like those of the IETF (see the sidebar "Internet Engineering Task Force (IETF)" on page 136). Strong security is invasive to users and organizations in many ways.

especially common with extranets (see Section 3.3 on page 99), where the bastions provide extranet functions and the interior firewall provides additional protection for sensitive internal activity.

Firewalls are also used to compartmentalize an organization. For example, access policies may reasonably prohibit the engineering department from accessing human resources servers, and firewalls can enforce such policies. Recall, however, that firewalls are effective only as part of a security *system*, which should include confidentiality, authentication, and operational vigilance.

11.3.4 Where to Use Encryption and Authentication

The encryption techniques described in Chapter 8 assure confidentiality, but the question arises, "Where do you use encryption?" Chapter 8 incorporated encryption into applications (such as SET, PGP, and SHTTP). This is the most secure approach, but it places additional burdens on application developers and is relatively invasive to users (who must deal with passwords, secrets, etc.). Armed with an understanding of the network, there are other possibilities that trade a bit lower security for less intrusiveness. They differ as to the protocol layer where authentication and encryption are implemented and also in position in the network topology:

- *Firewall-to-firewall:* An organization frequently has two or more geographically separated locations, each with a protected enclave. Confidential internal communication among locations can be achieved using leased dedicated facilities (a *private* network). A *virtual private network*—a private network embedded within the public Internet—is less expensive. This can be achieved using encrypted semipermanent IP connectivity among firewalls, which do the encryption and decryption and authenticate one another to avoid spoofing attacks.

- *Host-to-host:* Authentication of hosts and encryption of IP packet payloads can be performed at the IP layer. The IETF is standardizing these capabilities (called *IPsec*).

- *Process-to-process:* Secure sockets layer (SSL) was originally proposed by Netscape Corporation to provide authentication and confidentiality in Web browser-to-server connections, but it is available for any application.

- *Link-by-link:* The previous approaches encrypt only (IP or TCP) packet *payloads*. When IP packet headers aren't encrypted (because network routers must examine them to do packet forwarding), an attacker can do *traffic analysis*; that is, see who is communicating with whom and the amount of traffic. This privacy concern can be redressed by encryption and decryption on communication links between packet switches (including packet headers). Link encryption is particularly attractive on wireless communication links (which are relatively easy to monitor).

These possibilities are not exhaustive, but serve to illustrate a range of possibilities.

11.4 Open Issues

Because Internet service and the selling of content over the Internet are new businesses, there are many unresolved issues.

11.4.1 The Future of the Internet

The Internet is a research infrastructure that "grew up" to find itself a commercial phenomenon. As a research infrastructure, some capabilities required to make it a viable commercial network were naturally not addressed, and as a result it misses some arguably important capabilities. Foremost among these is the lack of QoS configurability and the lack of an infrastructure to support any but fixed pricing. An unanswered question is whether these capabilities are really needed and, if so, how they will be deployed.

11.4.2 Making Money on the Internet

The Internet is a new communications medium, and like all new media, its most compelling uses need shaking out. It is particularly unclear how money is best made on the Internet. Earlier anecdotal evidence suggests that most predictions will be wrong. For example, television in its early days was said to be the death of both radio and movies. What actually happened was the movies became stronger than ever, and radio metamorphosed into a resource for mobile citizens.

Currently, Internet information suppliers are finding it difficult to charge for usage and are using advertiser support (like radio and television). However, an enabling infrastructure for micropayments is missing, and purchasing by credit card is cumbersome (who wants to bother typing in long numbers—over and over—for each merchant?). Will a payment model emerge?

Further Reading

A superior general textbook on network protocols is [Pet96], and [Wal96] is a more advanced book that has a chapter on network pricing. A more complete discussion of pricing issues is given in [Mac95a,b,c]. [McK97a, McK97b] are good general introductions to social issues in network design. A well-written general reference on network security is [Gar96], and one specifically addressing Web server security is [Gar97]. An encyclopedic reference on security on the Internet is [Atk96].

Communications

The communications industry provides various communications and network services. Its impact on networked computing is manifested in two principal ways. First, the availability of networking services—especially nomadic and broadband access—depends on the evolution of the communications industry, which is the primary network service provider. Second, digital communications—the technology underlying the communication links connecting hosts and packet switches—directly impacts network performance and thus application performance.

12.1 Communications Service Providers

The computer industry emphasizes direct sales of equipment and software to end-users (individuals and organizations). Systems integrators develop and deploy new applications, and more recently there is a growing emphasis on outsourcing of operations as well (see Section 5.1 on page 139). In contrast, communications has always emphasized a *service provider* that constructs and deploys facilities and leases communications services to end-users and organizations. Thus, the industry has a vertical structure consisting of three levels: equipment and software suppliers, network service providers, and end-users (individuals and organizations). There are several reasons service providers play a more prominent role in communications than computing:

- Communications networks require *public rights of way* for communications facilities that are buried in trenches along highways or railroad tracks, or strung from telephone poles. Given the associated regulatory and logistical problems, end-user organizations are generally precluded from constructing their own communication links between facilities.

- Direct network externalities favor a public network—rather than a proliferation of private networks serving subsets of customers—because such a network can provide greater value to users (see Section 5.3.1 on page 150).

- Sharing facilities among many users is economical, both because of statistical multiplexing (see Section 11.1.1 on page 318) and economies of scale.

An exception to the service provider model is the local area network (LAN), traditionally installed and operated by an internal networking support organization. (This is also changing, with many companies choosing to outsource their internal network operations.)

There are an expanding number of communications service providers:

- *Telephone operating companies* have been a government-sanctioned and regulated monopoly for most of the past century. Their business model has emphasized turnkey applications (such as telephony or video conferencing), although they also lease communication facilities. Foreign attachments (such as voice-band data modems or facsimile machines) providing nonvoice services over a voiceband channel have been permitted for a couple of decades. The most common Internet access link for residences exploits a foreign attachment—the voiceband data modem. These firms also operate the Internet backbone.

- *Cable television* (CATV) *service providers* emphasize video broadcast and video-on-demand applications to residences over coaxial cable facilities paralleling the twisted-wire-pair facilities of the telephone companies. (The twisted pair consists of two wires twisted about one another, and the coaxial cable consists of an inner wire encased in a cylindrical sheath. The latter has considerably greater capacity, as needed for multiple channels of broadcast-quality video.) CATV companies have a local franchise and are subject to regulation. While CATV is available to a high percentage of residences in the United States, it is not as common in most other countries.

- *Wireless service providers* offer primarily radio-based telephony (the mobile phone or cellular phone), although there are a few wireless Internet providers. There are independent companies as well as major telephone operating company divisions or subsidiaries. Most wireless services require a government license for the radio spectrum they use, although there is a trend toward unlicensed radio spectrum with associated "etiquette" policies (relaxed rules that restrict interference with other users).

- *Internet service providers* (ISPs) offer Internet access to consumers and businesses. These companies lease high-speed access to the Internet backbone and lease a number of lower-speed connections to consumers and companies, aggregating their traffic into the backbone. Increasingly telephone operating and CATV companies have entered this business.

The core competency of these service providers is customer service and operations, not technology. They rely on equipment and software suppliers (much like end-users depend on computer manufacturers).

Today this industry is experiencing chaotic change brought on by the rising importance of data services (including the Internet and networked computing), deregulation and greater competition, and industry globalization. There are numerous divestitures, mergers, and start-ups. Amid all this chaos, a few general trends can be discerned:

- In consonance with the globalization of industry and rise of the multinational corporation, most competitive communications providers can provide businesses with turnkey end-to-end communications services on a global basis. Thus, the industry is reorganizing around a smaller number of service providers, each operating on a global scale.

- The rising importance of data in relation to voice—as a revenue generator and as a fraction of the overall traffic—is shifting the technology from data retrofitted onto voice networks to integrated networks that can handle multimedia applications.

- The greater mobility of users, together with low-cost portable computers and information appliances, is shifting the emphasis from users in fixed locations to providing users with networked and application services seamlessly from any location, even while in motion.

Among these trends, most germane to this book is the rise of data networking and the Internet, which have captured the attention of communications companies. The Internet is a destabilizing force, in many ways analogous to the impact decentralized computing had on the companies emphasizing centralized computing (see Section 1.1 on page 2). The computing industry moved from stovepipe applications (supported by vertically integrated companies) toward layering (supported by a fragmented industry—see Section 5.2.1 on page 144). Likewise, traditional communications companies—emphasizing vertical integration and turnkey applications (such as telephony and video conferencing)—are retrenching to provide digital communications and integrated services networks, with applications coming from elsewhere.

12.1.1 Communications Regulation

Another striking difference between communications and computing is the role of government. In many countries, the communications infrastructure is government owned—like the postal service and the highways. Where communications providers are privately owned, as in the United States, they have been government regulated. Some reasons for this include

- Communication facilities based on wire and fiber communications media often require a public right of way—a street or highway—which in turn requires a franchise from the government.

- Like the highways and postal system, communications has been viewed as a *natural monopoly*; that is, society could not afford duplicate communications infrastructures. The companies thus operated as government-sanctioned monopolies, relying on regulation to keep prices and profits in check.

- There is a societal interest in achieving *universal service*—keeping prices of basic communications service very low so that almost everyone can afford it. This has resulted in a system of cross-subsidies (long distance subsidizing local service, and businesses subsidizing residential). Since such subsidies are antithetical to free markets and competition, this also suggests the need for a regulated monopoly.

- Communications is a crucial infrastructure for national defense and for dealing with natural disasters, and thus it may be too important to entrust to the vagaries of free market competition. Facilities hardening and strict availability objectives, unjustifiable in a competitive industry, have been mandated by regulation.

Many industry observers argue that due to technology advances, communications is no longer a natural monopoly. For example, communications services to residences can now be offered by several wireless technologies, satellite, cable television, and telephony facilities. Wireless is particularly propitious to competition, since facility costs are more incremental than in wired approaches. Since universal service is a reality in developed countries, cross-subsidies may no longer be needed.

In addition, there is today much greater faith in the free market and the benefits of competition in increasing efficiency, reducing prices, and speeding the adoption of new technologies. If universal service remains an objective, economic theory prefers a targeted user subsidy (like "food stamps") since it does not interfere with the market.

The first deregulation step in the United States was the separation of long distance and local service providers (called *local-exchange carriers* (LECs)), with a phase-out of cross-subsidies from long distance to local service. More recently, LECs have been encouraged to accept local-access competition, with the right to compete in long distance promised in return. Further, LECs have been allowed to enter the cable television and other businesses outside their service territory. Recent laws have mandated that carriers freely connect their network to other networks. While this is clearly in the customer's interest—due to the benefits of network effects—the purpose of the law is to prevent interconnection restrictions from being used as a competitive strategy.

Meantime, the Internet has flowered without regulation. Indeed, this may account in part for its dramatic success and growth. As Internet public policy issues have arisen, it appears increasingly likely that some activities on the Internet will be regulated (see Section 5.5.2 on page 169).

12.2 Current Developments in Data Communications

Communications has experienced rapid changes in technology and industry structure. Networked computing is impacted by several issues relating to the communications industry, and as a result, computer companies have become increasingly active in trying to influence it.

12.2.1 Broadband Network Access for Residences

While the commercially available Internet access is adequate for businesses, many residential users crave higher bitrates than they are able to get. The primary vehicle is voiceband data modems, offering bitrates up to 34.4 kilobits per second (kbps). Less widely used is ISDN at 128 kbps. *Broadband* access—speeds approximating the 10 megabits per second (Mbps) of Ethernet LANs in the office—is an elusive target. Some computer equipment vendors believe this may stifle their future business opportunities, since demand for more computing power is increasingly tied to networked applications (see Section 5.2.4 on page 149). This may also stifle opportunities for businesses selling large-volume information (especially in audio and video media) over the network, and some social applications needing high bitrates, such as remote conferencing (see Section 2.3.3 on page 27). Some technical implications of bitrate bottlenecks are discussed in Section 12.3 on page 352.

Broadband Internet access has proven a daunting technical, economic, and regulatory challenge. There are two basic approaches:

- Utilize an existing medium—the telephone twisted pair or CATV coaxial cable—and achieve broadband by adding sophisticated digital communication electronics.

- Install new facilities, leveraging advanced fiber optics or wireless media.

The installation of residential access fiber optics is economically difficult to justify. The fiber and its electronics are not the problem—it is the cost of digging trenches or stringing wires. This is accentuated by two adverse economic factors:

- Achieving a reasonable unit cost depends on economies of scale; thus, incremental installations responsive to actual service orders are uneconomic. A substantial sunk investment in facilities to serve an entire neighborhood at once is necessary.

- One expects only a small fraction of residences (called the *penetration*) to initially subscribe to broadband access. They must bear the facilities cost for everybody. If there are competitive access offerings, each will achieve an even lower penetration.

Putting these together, the service provider sees a high risk that its investment will not pay off and cannot be recovered (this is called a *stranded* investment). Similar reasoning led the government to conclude decades ago that communications was a natural monopoly, and a high penetration (universal service) required government intervention. It may be that broadband access remains today a natural monopoly.

Fortunately, several technologies bypass these barriers: fixed wireless networking, satellite, and retrofitting of existing communications media (twisted pair and coax). *Fixed wireless networking* uses wireless radio technology to provide service to fixed locations. The investments are more incremental; that is, a wireless transceiver need only be installed at residences actually subscribing. Satellite direct-broadcast services (such as DirecTV) are already delivering broadband to residences for television (although they do not provide a link in the reverse direction).

Internet Roaming

Some ISPs provide worldwide access with a local telephone call by constructing dedicated access points or contracting with locals to construct and operate them. Another expeditious approach—modeled after roaming in cellular telephony—uses bilateral arrangements among ISPs so that each provides access to the other's customers. A third approach is to create a third-party settlement process. A third party forms an association of ISPs that collectively agree to provide service to one another's customers. A roaming customer invokes a settlement (payment from one ISP to another) by way of the association, and the customer is billed through their home ISP. This works very similarly to credit card settlements (in that case the association is Visa or Mastercard) or floral delivery services.

E X A M P L E : *iPass is a third-party settlement company. ISPs joining iPass allow their subscribers to roam worldwide, accessing the Internet with a local phone call to another ISP that is an iPass member.*

The obstacles to such an arrangement are mainly technical: A single software and protocol implementation has

The options for using the existing telephone and cable television media include

- The twisted wire pair already installed for the telephone can carry much higher bitrates on the access link than voiceband data modems (which in contrast transmit data through the entire telephone network). The relevant technology is the *digital subscriber loop* (DSL). Bitrates of tens of Mbps are possible for short distances, and Mbps for longer distances.

- The CATV coax can accommodate high bitrates by displacing television channels (roughly 30 Mbps per TV channel). Unlike the telephone twisted pair, CATV broadcasts to a large number of homes over the same coax, so this link is multiplexed (see Section 11.1.1 on page 318).

Both options bypass a primary disadvantage of the voiceband data modem; namely, the need to suspend access while making telephone calls. Ideally, Internet access should be continuously available.

Hybrid approaches—combining existing communication media with new facilities in ways that exploit the best characteristics of both—are also promising. Examples include *fiber-to-the-curb* and *hybrid fiber/coax*, both of which exploit modern fiber-optic technologies in the shared portion of the access network (which is economically more feasible) and use existing media for per-residence access.

Many broadband access options are *asymmetric*—providing a higher bitrate toward the residence—which is appropriate for publication applications such as the Web (URLs are small in comparison to the HTML pages, images, video, etc.). However, direct applications have symmetric bitrate needs, and opportunities such as mobile code (see Section 9.3 on page 282) may reverse the asymmetry (see Section 2.3.2 on page 22).

12.2.2 Nomadic and Untethered Internet Access

Many users want unfettered Internet access while traveling, that is, nomadic or mobile access (see "Nomadic and Mobile Access" on page 102). Today the dominant nomadic access uses voiceband data modems and the telephone. Alternatives are arising, including

to work with all ISPs. What is needed is *IP dialtone*, where no special configuration is needed to call any number of ISPs.

Figure 12.1 The Nokia 9000 is a combination cellular phone and computer terminal in a small package. *Source:* **The Nokia 9000i Communicator—a GSM 1900 digital wireless phone with the ability to fax, send and receive emails, or access the Internet.**

- *Roaming:* Internet access works worldwide using local telephone numbers. The most promising of these approaches uses third-party settlement, so that each service provider doesn't have to construct worldwide facilities (see the sidebar "Internet Roaming").

- *Wireless nomadic and mobile access:* Digital cellular telephony systems are being retrofitted to provide data services, and new wireless networks (both satellite and terrestrial) are being constructed for this purpose (see the sidebar "Wireless Access Protocol (WAP)" on page 350).

- *Broadband nomadic access: This* might be achieved using DSL technology, with a service analogous to the public telephone.

EXAMPLE: *Many nomadic users will use an information appliance rather than complete computer to access the Internet (see the sidebar "Information Appliances" on page 147). An example of a wireless information appliance is the Nokia 9000, pictured in Figure 12.1. In addition to standard personal digital assistant functions*

Wireless Access Protocol (WAP)

Economies of scale in terminal production and user nomad-ism are motivations to stan-dardize on common protocols and "air interfaces" for wire-less data services. WAP is an industry consortium pursuing de facto standards. WAP is currently focused on making the mobile terminal (includ-ing cellular telephone) a thin client based on Web technol-ogy (see "The Web as the Pre-sentation Tier" on page 103). The architecture of WAP—typical of similar efforts to define wireless interfaces—is shown in Figure 12.2. WAP defines a Wireless Markup Language (WML) that exploits the extensibility of XML (see Section 6.3.2 on page 211) to define a markup language specific to wireless terminals with limited display capabili-ties. XML or HTML can be converted to WML by a *filter*. To reduce the processing requirements of the portable information appliance, WAP defines a *proxy* for the wire-less device. The proxy per-forms many functions on behalf of the portable device and also converts media such as images and video to a form appropriate for the wireless channel. WAP also uses Web technology to define better user interfaces for standard telephony features (such as call forwarding).

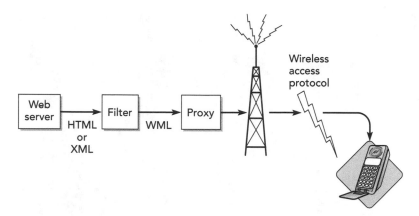

Figure 12.2 The WAP architecture for wireless Internet services to untethered information appliances.

(calendar, address list, etc.), it includes a cellular telephone, facsim-ile, and Internet applications (messaging, email).

12.2.3 IP Telephony

Just as telephony and audio conferencing can be incorporated into networked applications (see Section 2.3.3 on page 27), the stan-dard telephone service—using either standard phones or com-puter terminals—can be accommodated over the Internet. This is called *IP telephony* or *Voice over IP* (VoIP). As illustrated in Figure 12.3, there are three cases of VoIP to consider:

1. Special Internet phones (that speak IP directly) can realize a telephony service using a session (see "Multimedia Transport" on page 229). Alternatively, one or both of these phones could be replaced by a desktop computer or information appliance (similar to the Nokia 9000 shown in Figure 12.1).

2. A special conversion device called an *IP telephony gateway* can connect the public telephone network (PTN) to the Internet. It converts between formats and protocols used in the public telephone network and those of the Internet, allowing a plain old telephone (POT) to make a call to an IP telephone—that call being completed over the concatenated telephone net-work and Internet.

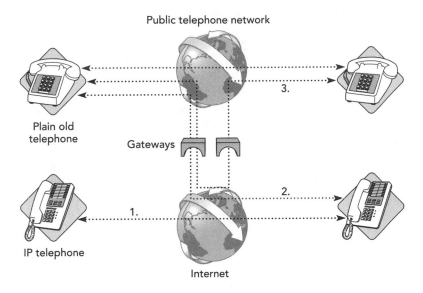

Public telephone network

Plain old
telephone

Gateways

IP telephone

Internet

Figure 12.3 IP telephony allows telephone calls over the Internet from either standard phones or special internet phones.

3. A telephone call can be made between two POTs over the Internet using *two* gateways. This concatenates the PTN at the two endpoints with the Internet in the middle.

IP telephony phones and gateways must be interoperable. Thus, the success of IP telephony hinges on standardization, given the resulting direct network externality.

E X A M P L E : *The standard for VoIP with the greatest momentum is the International Communications Union (ITU) H.323. It is built on RTP (see the sidebar "Internet Streaming Multimedia Protocols" on page 236) and uses bitrates from 56 kbps down to 5.3 kbps. RTP uses UDP for low delay, and H.323 can suffer up to 15 percent packet loss with good voice quality.*

Today IP telephony is used by corporations wishing to save on internal long distance costs. The most effective approach is to integrate IP telephony into a company's PBXs, so that the switch can automatically choose the best option, IP or PTN. Telephone companies are also likely to offer IP telephony to POTs customers using gateways.

12.2.4 Integrated IP Networks

Digital communication links have traditionally been shared between the Internet, PTN, and other communications networks. Since the data traffic has been a fraction of the PTN voice traffic, this retrofitting of data on a predominantly voice network makes sense. However, data traffic is growing much faster than voice, and by 2001 to 2003 should be bigger. In not too many years—as voice becomes a fraction of the total traffic—it makes more sense to carry voice on the data network. Thus, stand-alone IP data networks also providing multimedia services (including voice telephony) are likely. This should make Internet access even more common—expanding opportunities for consumer electronic commerce—and also higher speed, improving its performance for remote conferencing and other social applications.

EXAMPLE: *In a 1998 milestone, a new company—Level 3 Communications—planned on investing more than $8 billion in an international fiber-optic backbone and local IP-based network. This is the first network constructed exclusively for IP.*

12.3 Impact of a Communication Link

Communication links connect packet switches and carry large amounts of data (as a sequence of packets—see Chapter 11). From the perspective of the network, and ultimately the application, the primary impact of a communication link is the latency and corruption of packets. When added to the communication protocol (see Chapter 7), these impairments—latency and packet loss—result in added message latency and reduced application performance (see Chapter 10).

Communication links accept a continuous stream of bits at a constant bitrate. Each bit traverses the link at the speed of light (or a large fraction thereof, depending on the medium). The bit reaches the other end with a delay (called the *propagation delay*) equal to the distance traveled divided by that speed. This leads to the counterintuitive observation that the bitrate is unrelated to the rate the bit traverses the link, but rather is determined by the space each bit takes up on that link.

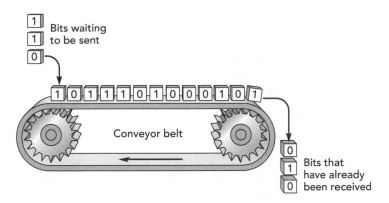

Figure 12.4 Conveyor belt analogy to a communication link.

A N A L O G Y :   *A mechanical analogy to a communication link is a con-*
veyor belt, as shown in Figure 12.4. The conveyor belt moves at a
constant speed. Two piles of wooden blocks—one with blocks hav-
ing a "0" embossed on the side and the other containing blocks
embossed with a "1"—are used to communicate bits. Blocks
(drawn from the appropriate pile) are placed on the belt at a con-
stant rate (the bitrate). At the destination, the bit embossed on
each arriving block is noted to recover the original bit stream.

Since the conveyor belt moves at a constant speed, the bitrate is
completely determined by the size of the blocks, that is, the space
each one takes up on the belt. The time it takes a single bit to
travel the entire belt is the propagation delay, determined by the
speed of the belt and proportional to the distance.

An optical fiber communication link works this same way, except
that the "blocks" in this analogy are replaced by optical pulses. A
communication link thus has two key parameters: the bitrate B and
the propagation delay τ. The product of these two parameters—the
bitrate-delay product $B\tau$—is another important parameter (equal to
the number of bits in transit at any given time). The bitrates that can
be achieved by modern fiber-optic technologies are quite impres-
sive (see the sidebar "Fiber Optics and Optical Networking").
Bitrates are expressed in kilobits per second (kbps), megabits per
second (Mbps), gigabits per second (Gbps), and terabits per second (Tbps). While voiceband data modems can achieve tens of

Fiber Optics and Optical Networking

The premier communications media for new installations are fiber optics and wireless radio. There is also considerable interest in retrofitting legacy facilities for broadband Internet access (see Section 12.2.1 on page 346). Like electronics and storage, advances in fiber optics over the past couple of decades are remarkable. The capacity of a single fiber is, for all practical purposes, unlimited, but limitations of the associated electronics are bypassed by *wavelength division multiplexing* (WDM). Independent bit streams are carried by different wavelengths (colors of light) over the same fiber, thus vastly increasing its total capacity.

The total bitrate of a fiber often exceeds the needs of one packet switch. The fiber can be shared over multiple bit streams not only by WDM but also by *synchronous optical networking* (SONET), in which the bits from different bit streams are interleaved. All bitrates carried by SONET are multiples of a basic rate, 51.84 Mbps. In SONET terminology, a bitrate of $n \times 51.84$ Mbps is called an OC-n. The highest SONET rate that has been standardized in 1998 is OC-192 (9953.28 Mbps), and commercially available systems that carry 32 OC-48 bit

kbps, fiber optics is today into the tens of Gbps range, with Tbps commercial systems on the way in a few years.

For users at fixed locations and with the luxury of fiber-optic access, bitrates are seldom a limitation on application performance. For others—such as users in residences and nomadic users—bitrates remain a severe limitation.

12.3.1 Impact on Message Latency

Hosts send messages to one another using a communication link, and they care about the message latency—the time elapsing between when a message is sent and when it is received in its entirety (see Section 7.2.3 on page 226). There are a number of contributors to message latency, including processing time in the host software infrastructure and queueing delay in packet switches. The contributor of interest here is the communication link, with two components:

- *Transmission time* is how long it takes to transmit the message on the link (analogous to the time it takes to put all the blocks composing the message on the conveyor belt).

- *Propagation time* is the time it takes the message to traverse the link at some fraction of the speed of light (analogous to the time it takes one block to traverse the conveyor belt).

Since the transmission time depends on the size of the message, but the propagation time doesn't, their relative importance depends on message size. The crossover is when the message size equals the bitrate-delay product, where the two contributors are equal. Thus, there are two distinct cases:

- *Bitrate-limited:* For large messages (much greater than the bitrate-delay product), the dominant contributor to message latency is transmission time. Increases in bitrates will substantially reduce message latency.

- *Delay-limited:* For short messages (much smaller than the bitrate-delay product), the dominant contributor to message latency is propagation delay. Further increases in bitrates will have limited impact on message latency.

ANALOGY: *For the conveyor belt, in the bitrate-limited case, the blocks are large, and only a fraction of the blocks composing a message are in transit at any time. In the delay-limited case, the blocks are small enough that all blocks composing the message occupy only a portion of the belt.*

EXAMPLE: *On fiber optics, bitrates of 2.5 Gbps are routinely available in 1998. The propagation delay across the United States is roughly 30 milliseconds, for a bitrate-delay product of 75 Mb. Thus, messages shorter than 75 Mb—which is quite large—are already delay-limited.*

There are two important points. First, there are ways of mitigating message latency (discussed in Section 12.3.2), but they depend on whether the communication links are bitrate- or delay-limited. Second, as fiber-optic (and wireless) technologies advance, available bitrates increase, but propagation delay remains constant. Thus, over time communication links become delay-limited. This observation has profound implications for networked computing, because as all technology performance parameters advance (electronics, storage, and communications), the speed of light increasingly looms as the ultimate performance limitation.

Consider the worst-case propagation delay—halfway around the globe—which is about 0.15 seconds. For social applications this delay is modest, but for hosts trying to cooperate on a computation it is huge.

EXAMPLE: *Over the next decade or so, the processor instruction rates will approach 10^{10} instructions per second. If such a computer were blocked waiting for a response with a round-trip propagation delay of 0.3 seconds, it would miss 3 billion instructions.*

The speed of light is an increasingly serious limitation even *within* a computer or a single integrated circuit. For applications distributed over wide geographic areas, it is particularly important for the future.

12.3.2 Mitigating Communications Bottlenecks

For some users, bitrate is a serious performance limitation, especially those using voiceband data models or wireless access. Over

streams for an aggregate capacity of 79.626 Gbps are available. In the laboratory, bitrates greater than 2 Tbps over a single fiber have been demonstrated [Ram98]. This capacity is so great as to be almost inconceivable.

EXAMPLE: *The telephone network uses a bitrate of 64 kbps to represent speech. At this rate, a 2-Tbps fiber could carry over 31 million simultaneous telephone conversations.*

Up until recently, networking used optical communication links in conjunction with electronic multiplexing and switching. The next step is networks—called *optical networks* [Ram98]—that perform more multiplexing and switching functions in the optical domain, bypassing the speed limitations of electronics.

time, more advanced technologies will relax this situation, although application demands have a way of keeping up with technology advances. Regardless, wide area wireless access will doubtless be a bottleneck, as will propagation delay. Fortunately, there are widely used measures to mitigate these problems, as discussed in this section.

Data Caching

Suppose a client is repeatedly accessing data from a remote server, and there is an unacceptably high message latency. *Data caching* can help. Each time the client accesses data, it is stored in local memory or storage (called a *data cache*). If the client accesses the data more than once, it can be accessed locally (without a message latency) all but the first time.

EXAMPLE: *Web browsers typically cache recently accessed pages. Not infrequently, the user will request the same page again.*

A variation on this approach is as follows: The server not only returns the particular data requested by the client but also tries to *anticipate* future requests and send additional data along as part of the response. This *predictive caching* algorithm can eliminate message latencies completely for those requests that can be predicted.

EXAMPLE: *In a Web browser, when the user requests a certain page, it is likely that her next request will be a hyperlinked page. (The other possibilities are a URL typed in by the user or accessed from a stored bookmark.) Thus, a predictive caching algorithm might return not only the page requested but also all hyperlinked pages. That way, if the user clicks any hyperlink on that page, the result will be available in a local cache.*

ANALOGY: *You search for information first in reference books on your desk, then in your office at work, then in your local library, and as a last resort from remote libraries. Each of these is a cache attempting to supply the information needed most often. A decision to purchase a reference book is predictive caching.*

Predictive caching is effective on delay-limited communication links—where the expanded message will not increase the message latency appreciably—but not on bitrate-limited links. Thus, it will become increasingly important in the future.

Data Compression

When message latency is bitrate-limited—as is often the case today for users accessing the network by a voiceband modem or wireless link—a helpful technique is *data compression*, which reduces the number of bits required to represent the data (and thus the message size and latency). Compression removes *redundancy* from the data, which occurs when not all bit patterns occur with the same relative frequency. The trick is to ensure that the most frequent bit patterns are represented by fewer bits, and the least frequent by more bits.

Lossless data compression allows the exact recovery of the original data. This type of compression is the best available for most data. On the other hand, data representing media to be displayed to users—audio, images, graphics, facsimile, video, and animation—does not have to be reproduced precisely and can suffer *lossy* compression. In this case, while the possibility of recovering the original is forgone, a "reasonable rendition" can be represented by discarding information not subjectively important to the human aural or visual system. In contrast to lossless compression, which typically reduces the number of bits by a factor of two or three, lossy compression can typically reduce the required bits by 100 with reasonable quality (see the sidebar "JPEG and MPEG").

Mobile Code

Mobile code is another response to unacceptable message latency (see Section 9.3 on page 282), since it can move computation closer to the data it processes (see Section 6.1.5 on page 187). Alternatively, moving computation to a client improves interactivity by executing application logic locally rather than on the server. Mobile code suffers the initial delay required to transport the mobile code (which is often quite large but will become less serious as communication technology achieves higher bitrates).

Caching and Copyright Law

A policy issue arising in caching is the fair use of copyrighted material (see "Benefits of Copyright" on page 166). While viewing the information is fair use—why else would the information be made available on the network—making a permanent copy and distributing it to others would be a copyright violation. Caching is an intermediate case without nefarious intentions but possibly a copyright violation. This is another difficult legal question arising in the digital age.

EXAMPLE: *The current copyright law in the United States seems to make caching legal, as it says a work is protected by copyright only when it is "fixed in a tangible medium of expression, when its embodiment… is sufficiently permanent or stable to permit it to be perceived, reproduced, or otherwise communicated for a period of more than transitory duration." However, there is currently discussion of not permitting the "transitory fixing" of copyrighted material, which would seem to rule out caching, except with explicit permission.*

JPEG and MPEG

The Joint Picture Experts Group (JPEG) and Motion Picture Experts Group (MPEG) are both standardization efforts under the auspices of ISO (see the sidebar "International Organization for Standards (ISO)" on page 135). JPEG is the most commonly used compression algorithm for images and MPEG for video. MPEG is not only used in networked computing but also has become the standard video encoding for digital television in the United States. Both standards can be configured to different compression ratios, of course affecting the quality. MPEG includes many system features as well as compression.

MPEG is an excellent illustration of standardization as a collaborative design process. No single company would possess the range of expertise necessary to set the requirements for or design MPEG. The MPEG standardization committee designed many new algorithms rather than simply specifying existing algorithms.

12.4 Open Issues

The communications industry is undergoing massive consolidation and change, bringing numerous contentious issues.

12.4.1 Is Communications Regulation Needed?

A major question for the future is the appropriate balance between regulation and free markets. This will strongly influence the availability of broadband services to residences and hence the ability of consumers to fully participate in the networked computing revolution. It will impact the availability of an infrastructure for opportunistic nomadic connection to the global network—the networked computer equivalent of the pay telephone. Who is going to develop, capitalize, and deploy both these infrastructures?

12.4.2 Regulation of the Internet

IP telephony raises thorny policy issues. Much of its attraction derives from the lack of regulation of IP networks. But how does a fully competitive market (IP telephony) compete against a regulated one (PTN)? Should similar regulation be extended to all telephony, regardless of the medium? That would "level the playing field" but would also subject one Internet application to regulation, and not the others.

Further Reading

A general textbook on digital communication is [Lee94]. [Per85] gives a good background on fiber-optic technology, and [Ram98] is a comprehensive textbook on optical networks. [Abe97] gives a thorough treatment of broadband access, including technical, business, and economic aspects. [CST97a] gives a good background of the history, applications, and technology of wireless communications, and [Rap96] and [Pah95] give excellent coverage of the technology of wireless communications.

Glossary

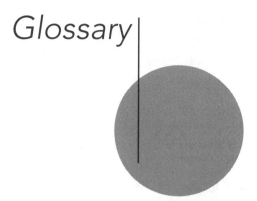

abstraction   Making a subsystem or service more transparent and flexible by hiding irrelevant detail.

access control   In computer security, a limitation on which users or hosts can access a particular resource or application.

action   At an interface, a behavior that is promised by a subsystem, configured by parameters and having return values.

address   A data token representing the topological access point for a host on the network. The address is used to forward a packet and is often obtained from a name server.

administration   The ownership and operation of a computing infrastructure and associated application.

algorithm   A specified sequence of steps designed to accomplish a specific task.

application   Computer software that performs useful functions on behalf of a user or organization, involving the storage, processing, and communication of information.

application logic   The portion of the application program—distinct from the presentation and the shared data—that constitutes the assumptions and operations that define what the application does.

architecture   A decomposition of a system, including a definition of the functionality of each sub-system and its interaction with other subsystems

assembly   In software development, creating a system from components. The opposite of decomposition.

asymmetric encryption   An encryption protocol in which two complementary keys are required, one for encryption and the other for decryption. For confidentiality, the encryption key can be made public, but the decryption key must be kept secret. Sometimes called public key encryption.

atomic   Cannot be split into constituent parts and retain its usefulness.

attribute   For a software object or component, data representing an observable and changeable property.

authentication   In security, obtaining assurance of the identity of a user (or other entity, such as a host). It requires an authority.

authority   In security, some entity that is trusted and can provide assistance.

autonomous publisher   A publisher that chooses what information is supplied to a user, or when it is provided, or both. The opposite of interactive information access.

availability   A metric describing the fraction of time an application is running reliably.

awareness application   An application that autonomously informs the user of newly available information.

batch processing   A style of noninteractive computing in which a task is completed in its entirety before the results are made available.

biometrics   In security, authentication based on some physical characteristics of the user. The alternative is authentication based on a secret.

bit   Short for "binary digit," an atomic piece of data assuming the value "0" or "1." It is the basis of computer-mediated information.

bitrate   The rate at which bits are sent on a communication link. Sometimes called bandwidth.

blocked   A condition of one object that has invoked a method of another object and is awaiting a response (including return values) before it can resume.

broadcast   A publication-immediate style of social application in which identical information is communicated to a group of users. It is an immediate version of mass publication.

browse   Interactive access, looking for relevant or useful or interesting information.

business application   An application serving business purposes, including commerce.

business logistics   In electronic commerce, a cross-enterprise application that coordinates material flows, finished goods, services, and workers.

business process   A collection of related activities including everything from acquiring resources to delivering a product or services to customers. It spans multiple departments and possibly also enterprises.

business process reengineering   A systematic design of a business process, including networked computing, workers, and interfaces between them.

cache   A place for temporary storage of data.

centralized computing   A computing model in which a relatively few mainframes run batch programs.

challenge/response   In security, a protocol for authentication in which one entity challenges another entity to prove that it possesses a secret—usually without revealing it.

citizenry   A large group of users without a specific purpose or goal.

class   In object-oriented programming, what is in common among a set of objects with identical functionality and implementation, but with different attributes and encapsulated data.

client   An entity that performs its function by making one or more requests of others. It initiates requests and does not have to be available at all times. In this book, the term is applied to a host that provides a user interface and application presentation and also to an object that invokes the method of another object.

client/server   A networked computing system architecture in which hosts are specialized into clients and servers.

collaboration style   Describes social applications allowing users in a group to coordinate their activities or shared resources.

collaborative authoring   A direct style (immediate or deferred) of social application that supports a work group authoring a document.

common off-the-shelf (COTS)   A product (equipment or software) purchased and integrated into an application, rather than designed and built.

communication link   A channel that communicates a string of bits from one geographic location to another (usually in both directions).

communication style   Describes social applications allowing users in a group to share information.

complexity   In software development, attributes such as a large number of modules interacting in complicated ways, requiring many designers.

component   A subsystem that is purchased as is from an outside company.

component-oriented programming (COP)   In software implementation, a programming methodology based on assembly and integration of software components. COP requires a component supply industry, programming tools, and also standardization of component interfaces.

composition   Bringing together existing subsystems, as the first step to assemble a system.

compression   An algorithm that reduces the number of bits required to represent information by exploiting either human visual or audio system properties, or the different frequency of occurrence of bit patterns.

computer   Equipment that executes programs, allowing them to store, manipulate, and communicate information under software control.

concurrent   Describes two or more tasks that are overlapped in time.

confidentiality   A property of communicated or stored data that is unintelligible to someone monitoring it. Typically achieved by encryption.

congestion   Temporary overuse or oversubscription of a resource when the total demands on it fluctuate with time.

congestion control   In networking, the avoidance of congestion by artificially reducing total source traffic.

congestion pricing   For a network service (or other shared resource, such as server capacity), a component of price based on the aggregate usage.

consumer electronic commerce   Electronic commerce involving the citizenry (and possibly enterprises).

convergence   Applied to industries, when two industries become, for the first time, strongly complementary or competitive.

copyright   Government-sanctioned property rights for original content or software. It does not prevent anyone from independently creating a similar work—even based on the same facts or ideas.

critical mass   For a product or service with network effects, when the number of adopters increases to the point that the value of the product or service exceeds the supplier or service provider cost.

cyberspace   Within a wide area network, such as the Internet, the public place where the citizenry access information and interact without regard to geographic distance.

data   A collection of bits representing information.

data mining   An application that processes massive amounts of data using statistical tools looking for unexpected and useful patterns pointing to commercial opportunity.

data warehouse   A very large nonoperational database aiding decision support and acquired by consolidating and archiving information from multiple operational databases.

database   A file containing data with a predetermined structure. The relational database is the most common.

database management system (DBMS)   A large-grain component that manages the storage, processing, and retrieval of information from one or more databases. Other functions include data integrity and security. It is typically assembled into an application.

decentralized computing   A computing model in which inexpensive personal computers are dedicated to single users but are not yet networked.

decision support   An aspect of a business application supplying information to management about operational issues.

decomposition   The partitioning of a system into cooperating subsystems that interact to realize some higher purpose.

deferred style   Describes social applications in which users can participate at different times.

departmental application   A business application primarily serving one functional department, such as accounting, human resources, or manufacturing.

deployment   Everything required to turn a completed and tested application into an operational application, including installation and testing of infrastructure, installation of software, training of workers, and import of legacy data.

desktop computer   A personal computer or workstation accessed by a single user and used for running personal productivity applications and for the presentation of networked applications.

digital cash   Data representing monetary value—functionally similar to cash in a wallet—that can be used to make payments over the network.

digital certificate   In security, a message with integrity and nonrepudiation, provided by an authority, that provides a user's identity and public key for asymmetrical encryption. Others can use it to authenticate and communicate confidentially with the user.

digital library   A large, well-organized, and well-indexed repository of information.

digital signature   In security, data added to a message that assures its integrity and authenticates its source. It is the foundation of nonrepudiation.

direct style   Describes social applications in which users communicate directly with other users with known identity.

discussion forum   A publication style of social application that supports discussion and brainstorming of an interest group. The newsgroup and listserver are deferred versions, and the chatroom is an immediate version.

distributed object management   Middleware that allows objects to interact using remote method invocations across different hosts, as well as other functions.

distributed system   A system that incorporates two or more hosts communicating with one another. A distributed application is synonymous with networked application.

diversification   The business strategy of a company that accumulates a portfolio of different products across industry segments.

document   A form of structured data, typically containing text, images, video, and audio, that is self-contained and suited to capturing or presenting information and knowledge to users.

domain name   A name associated with a particular host that is easy for users to remember.

electronic commerce   Conducting business among enterprises (also called a cross-enterprise application) or between enterprises and the citizenry.

electronic data interchange (EDI)   An early electronic commerce application that allowed businesses to electronically exchange information on industry-specific forms.

electronic money management   In electronic commerce, reducing transaction costs by making and receiving payments electronically.

embedded computing   A computing model with networked computers built into everyday products, giving them added features and sophistication.

encapsulation   Subsystem implementation details that are hidden and inaccessible. Encapsulation seeks to enforce abstractions and enable implementation details to be changed without affecting interoperability with other subsystems.

encryption   An algorithm transforming data and an encryption key to make it unintelligible to anyone without a decryption key. The original data can be recovered by a decryption algorithm and decryption key.

enterprise   A unit of economic organization and activity, such as a company or a university.

enterprise applications   A business application primarily supporting a business process, as opposed to a departmental mission.

enterprise resource planning (ERP)   A packaged application serving a business process fairly standardized across companies, but configurable and extendable to meet the needs of individual enterprises.

equipment   A component included in the infrastructure that typically incorporates integrated hardware and software. Examples are a computer or switch.

event   An action or occurrence that happens externally and beyond the control of an observer, who may request notification.

extensible markup language (XML)   A markup language expected to replace HTML in representing documents on the Web. Unlike HTML, it stresses document structure rather than formatting.

extranet   An extension of an intranet across the public Internet using security tools to ensure confidentiality and authentication.

fat client   A partitioning of an application that includes much functionality in a client host.

fiber optics   A communications medium using pulses of light guided through a cylindrical glass strand.

file   Data named and stored as a unit for the benefit of some application.

file system   A service of an operating system that stores and manages files stored hierarchically in folders or directories.

firewall   Equipment imposed on communication links into and out of an intranet and enforcing security policies, thereby creating a protected enclave.

flow control   In networking, artificially limiting the rate at which a source generates data to match the rate a recipient consumes it.

format   The way a document is displayed to the user. Alternatively, a specification of the structure and interpretation of data contained in a message.

framework   A reusable architecture for a software application, often accommodating modification and extension.

granularity   A property of an architecture that defines the number of subsystems and the range of functionality of each. Granularity can range from coarse-grain (few large subsystems) to fine-grain (many small subsystems).

groupware   A collection of social applications that support the activities of work groups.

hardware   The electronics and physical embodiment—as distinct from software—comprising equipment.

hierarchy   A decomposition in which subsystems are themselves decomposed into subsystems, enabling a system to be viewed at different granularities.

host   Computer connected to the Internet or other network.

hyperlink   An association between information and the address of another document containing related information. In the Web, a hyperlink is indicated by a special formatting, the user can access the associated page by clicking with a mouse.

hypertext markup language (HTML)   The first markup language representing documents on the Web, focused on formatting and display rather than structure.

immediate style   Describes social applications in which users must participate at the same time.

implementation   The concrete realization of functionality embodied in a hardware and/or software design.

index   A list of topics or terms, with associated hyperlinks or references to information pertaining to those topics or terms.

information   Applied to people, patterns or meaning in data that affect their perspective, understanding, or behavior. In the infrastructure, structure and interpretation attached to data, usually added in an infrastructure layer or application.

information appliance   A stovepipe system providing some packaged application. Often it is small, portable, and battery operated.

information management   The organized storage and manipulation of large repositories of information.

information systems   A department within an enterprise with primary responsibility for acquiring, deploying, and operating an infrastructure and application.

infrastructure   Equipment and software deployed for the benefit of all applications.

instance   In object-oriented programming, an object belonging to a particular class is an instance of that class.

integrated   In an infrastructure layer or network, the property of being able to accommodate all media required to support a variety of applications.

integration   In software development, making modules or components interoperate once they have been individually implemented and tested.

integrity   In security, assurance that a message or file hasn't been modified since it was created by an authenticated entity.

intellectual property   Information or ideas with commercial value for which the government has granted exclusive property rights, including copyright, patent, trademark, and trade secret.

interactive   A style of application in which the user has frequent opportunities to direct or inform. The opposite of batch processing.

interest group   A group of users sharing a common interest in a subject, hobby, profession, or goal.

interface   The external view presented by a subsystem, carefully designed and well documented. It defines how other subsystems can interact with it and also informs the implementer of promises to other subsystems.

internet   A network consisting of interconnected subnetworks (in practice, a wide area network interconnecting local area networks). Also refers to a set of de facto standards for both networking protocols and applications. The (uppercase) Internet is a global public internet.

Internet Protocol (IP)   The lowest-layer protocol in the internet that allows subnetworks to be networked. IP is often synonymous with internet, as in "IP telephony."

interoperable   Describes two subsystems or modules that successfully interact to achieve some higher purpose.

interpretation   Attaching significance to structured data in some application context.

intranet   A private network constructed for the exclusive use of an enterprise using the internet architecture, standards, equipment, and applications.

key   In security, data required to encrypt or decrypt.

knowledge   In computing, a large amount of information well organized and indexed, making it useful to users.

latency   For a message, the time elapsed from creation to reception in its entirety. The most important performance metric of the network, the term can also be applied to packets.

layering   In the infrastructure architecture, decomposition as modules layered on top of one another. Each layer makes use of the services of the layer below, adds capability that specializes its function, and provides services to the layer above. Each layer provides integrated support for many different applications.

legacy application   An application developed some time ago—using obsolete technology—that remains operational.

license   A granting of a right to make, use, or sell products incorporating intellectual property, often in exchange for a fee or royalty.

limit pricing   For a product or service with large supply economies of scale, a price low enough to discourage competitive products or services, taking into account a competitor's high creation cost.

link   See communication link.

load balancing   Where concurrent tasks are assigned to different hosts, the utilization of each host is about equal.

local area network (LAN)   A network connecting hosts within a building or campus.

lock-in   For a supplier or consumer, the obstacle to adopting new products or services arising from the tangible and intangible costs of switching.

mainframe computer   A physically large, high-performance, and expensive computer, used by large organizations to run mission-critical applications requiring reliability and security and managing large amounts of data.

markup language   A specialized language for representing the structure and formatting of documents—especially valuable in making documents portable.

mass customization   The tailoring of a product or service to each customer, usually dependent in part on a business process application.

mass publication   A publication-deferred style of social application in which identical information is communicated to a group of users. An immediate version is broadcast.

medium or media   In digital information, a reference to a particular type of information—such as a document, numbers, audio, or video. In communications, the physical channel— such as wire pair, coaxial cable, fiber optics, or radio.

message   An atomic unit of information sent from one user to another, or from one module to another, to inform or direct. There is one sender, but there may be more than one (or even an indeterminate set of) recipients. Also, an abstract communication service that allows one module to send a message to another.

message with reply   An abstract communication service in which one module sends a message to another and receives a shared-context immediate reply.

message-oriented middleware   A middleware category that supports sophisticated messaging services with multiplexing and queueing.

metadata   A description of the content of a body of data, most often conveying information that is not easily extracted from the data itself (such as human judgement).

method   For an object, an action the object is prepared to perform, customized by parameters and with return values.

middleware   A software infrastructure layer that falls between two other layers and translates or hides them from one another. Typically, middleware falls between the application and operating system. Distinct middleware solutions support different application categories.

mobile agent   Mobile code that transports data with it. Sometimes used for searching through multiple information repositories.

mobile code   A program that can be opportunistically transported to a host for execution—not requiring program code to be previously stored in that host.

mobile computing   A computing model in which networked computers can be taken anywhere—including moving vehicles—without losing networking connectivity.

modeling   Using a system of mathematical postulates, data, and inferences to imitate or emulate a physical entity and predict its behavior. Unlike representation, modeling cannot substitute for that physical entity.

modularity   A system decomposition into subsystems (called modules) that have desirable properties, such as separation of concerns, interoperability, and reusability.

multicast   In networking, an implementation of broadcast in which the network internally replicates data and forwards it to separate recipients. An alternative to simulcast.

multimedia   The combination of information from different media (text, images, video, audio, etc.) within the same document, social application, or infrastructure.

multiplexing   A service that allows a recipient to receive messages from multiple senders. Necessarily combined with queueing, since two messages may arrive simultaneously.

multitasking   A feature of modern operating systems that supports concurrent tasks in a single host through time-slicing.

name service   A network service that provides a host address associated with a host domain name.

navigate   Follow a prescribed route to find useful information.

network   Collection of equipment that allows one computer to communicate with another, incorporating switches and communication links.

network computer (NC)   An ultrathin client host. Often it does not host application programs, but provides only the user interface.

network effect or externality   Applied to products and services, when their value to the consumer depends on the number of other consumers who have adopted the same product or service. The value may increase (as in a social application) or decrease (as in congestion).

networked application   A computer application that is distributed across two or more hosts.

networked computer   Any computer connected to a network (same as a host).

networked computing   A computing model in which hosts—including mainframes, servers, and desktop computers—are connected to a network and execute networked applications.

nonrepudiation   In security, the ability to prove that a message has integrity and was created by an authenticated user.

notification   Autonomously informing a user about external events.

object   In software, the smallest unit of modularity in a program, consisting of an interface and an implementation.

object database (ODBMS)   A database that adds persistence to objects, avoiding the use of SQL and supporting complex data structures.

object-oriented programming (OOP)   A programming methodology based on decomposition into interacting objects. OOP is supported by OOP languages such as C++ and Java and various development tools.

object-relational database (ORDBMS)   A relational database with extensions allowing it to manage complex data types and objects, but continuing to use SQL.

on-line analytical processing (OLAP)   An application providing multidimensional views into a relational database—usually for decision support.

on-line transaction processing (OLTP)   A departmental application supporting service agents gathering and disseminating information.

operating system   A layer of software infrastructure that performs a number of functions, including management of storage and communications and support for task concurrency within a single host.

packet   A unit of data transported across a packet network, including a header (with address information) and payload (message or fragment of a message transported on behalf of the application).

packet forwarding   In packet switching, the choice of an output link based on a packet header and a routing table.

packet header   In packet networks, the portion of a packet not needed by the application but added for packet forwarding and protocol implementation.

packet payload   In packet networks, the application data portion of a packet.

packet routing   In packet switching, the updating of routing tables, with the goal of forwarded packets reaching their destination while traversing the fewest links or encountering the least congestion.

patent   Government-sanctioned property rights for an invention (idea that is useful and novel).

peer   An entity that deals with other peers symmetrically, as equals. As distinct from client/server, where a client acts and the server responds.

performance   Quantitative measures of operation, such as speed of processing repetitive tasks or the completion time of a single task.

persistence   Applied to data, a property that outlives the application that created it. Often, mission-critical enterprise data has to persist for decades, and persistence is an important capability of databases.

personal computer   A desktop computer suitable for less computationally intensive tasks.

policy   A specification of permitted and prohibited behaviors. An important tool for both interoperability and security.

portability   The ability of software to run on platforms from different vendors.

positive feedback   For a product or service with network effects, when the number of adopters exceeds critical mass, the market is self-sustaining and increases rapidly.

predictive caching   An algorithm that attempts to predict what information will be needed so it can be sent in advance to a cache located near the recipient.

presentation   The portion of the application concerned with presenting information to and obtaining directions from the user through the user interface.

privacy   Freedom from unnecessary intrusion into one's activities, habits, communications, or financial affairs.

process   An abstract machine supporting a single executing program within the operating system. Multitasking allows multiple concurrent processes.

processing   Manipulation of data by a computer under control of a software program.

processor   An engine that executes a single computer program. A computer or host incorporates one or more processors.

propagation delay   The delay on a communication link due to the finite speed of light.

protocol   An algorithm performed by two or more interacting modules, including communication among them.

publication style   A style of application in which users communicate indirectly with other users—often not known to them—by making information available in a form and place where it can be accessed by others.

publish/subscribe   A protocol used for one module to obtain a series of updates from another, consisting of a subscription from the first module and a series of responses from the second.

pull   Applied to either information access or social applications, a style in which the user initiates an interaction or access. Examples include searching, browsing, and navigation.

push   Applied to either information access or social applications, a style in which a source or publisher autonomously initiates an interaction with the user. Examples include autonomous publication, messaging, and notification.

quality   Qualitative measures of merit, such as program correctness, reliability, and subjective measures of audio or video fidelity.

quality of service (QoS)   Control and reproducibility of performance and quality parameters. May be applied to networks or servers.

queueing   A service that stores messages temporarily until the recipient is willing or able to access them.

recommendation sharing   A publication-deferred social application that collects advice or judgement from many users to guide other users.

recommender system   An application that provides recommendation sharing.

redundant   In system reliability, nonoperational equipment that can take over immediately on a failure.

relational database   A database in which the data is kept in a row-columns tabular structure.

reliability   A property of an infrastructure or application that operates correctly almost all the time.

remote conferencing   A direct-immediate style of social application that attempts to re-create a face-to-face meeting over geographic distance.

remote learning   Remote conferencing and collaboration applied to education.

remote method invocation (RMI)   An abstract communication service allowing an object on one host to invoke the method of an object on another host and immediately receive the return values.

replicate   Make an exact copy of an original work, equivalent to the original in every respect. This is possible for digital information, by simply copying the data representing it.

representation   Taking the place of some entity, from which that entity can be recovered. For example, data can represent speech (in the sense that intelligible, accurate, and natural speech can be recovered from it), or a document, or other forms of information.

request/response   A simple protocol used for one module to obtain information or service from another, in which a request is sent by the first module followed by a response from the second.

reuse   Infrastructure, subsystems, and components that can be assembled and integrated into multiple applications.

scalable   An architecture with the property that performance metrics can be improved as necessary, by adding equipment. In addition, it usually means the cost increases no faster than performance metrics.

scheduling   Establishing in advance when something will happen. Social applications support the scheduling of task groups, and operating systems schedule processing tasks.

secure electronic transaction (SET)   In electronic commerce, a standard for on-line credit card payments to merchants, with many features to ensure privacy, confidentiality, and security.

security   Protection against hostile or greedy threats.

send/receive   A simple protocol used for one module to inform or direct another, in which a message is sent by the first module and received by the second.

server   An entity that does not initiate an interaction, but satisfies requests from other entities. It must be available at all times. The term is applied to a host existing primarily to satisfy requests from clients, and to an object whose method is invoked.

service provider   A company providing services—such as networking or applications—to other companies by operating an infrastructure it owns or leases.

session   An abstract communication service that allows one module to send another a shared-context sequence of messages guaranteed to be delivered in the same order as sent. Often a session is bidirectional and requires an establishment and disestablishment.

simulcast   In networking, an implementation of broadcast in which the source replicates data and sends it to separate recipients. An alternative is multicast.

social application   An application serving a group of users.

software component   A software module that can be purchased and integrated with other components or subsystems to assemble an application.

software program   Embodies a series of specific instructions to the computer, determining its functionality.

spanning layer   A special infrastructure layer that hides any heterogeneity in the layers below it and is also ubiquitous.

standard   A specification of an architecture (reference model and interfaces) that is generally agreed upon, precisely defined, and well documented.

standardization body   An organization dedicated to defining and promulgating standards, usually with the assistance of many companies.

statistical multiplexing   Sharing a communication link among packets from different sources and destinations, resulting in more efficient use.

storage   That portion of the equipment infrastructure devoted to keeping data from the time it is created until it is used.

stovepipe   An architecture and associated business model in which separate infrastructures are built for different services or applications. The opposite of layering.

structure   Applied to data, a pattern and organization that is specified and adhered to. Examples include data structures and databases.

structured query language (SQL)   A standardized and widely used language for applications to manage data in a relational and object-relational database.

subscription   A request from a user to receive autonomously published information, usually narrowing down the request to a specific topic or subject (called an information channel).

subsystem   A portion of a system that realizes some defined self-contained purpose and is itself a system.

supply-chain management   An enterprise resource planning application that monitors and coordinates the flow of materials, goods, services, and payments between suppliers and customers.

switch   Within a network, equipment that routes packets from one communication link to another in accordance with its destination address.

symmetric encryption   An encryption protocol in which the same key is used for encryption and decryption. For confidentiality, the key must be kept secret. Sometimes called private key encryption.

system   Something with a defined higher-order purpose that is not atomic, but is created by decomposition of subsystems.

system integration   The phase of system implementation in which subsystems are made to interoperate.

task   For either a user group or a computer application, some atomic behavior with a short-term goal.

task group   A group of users completing a short-term task, interacting simultaneously and typically with their undivided attention.

telephony   An audio conferencing service, equivalent to the familiar service provided by the public telephone network (PTN).

terminal   In the era of time-shared computing, equipment that provides the user interface, offering only textual display and keyboard input.

testing   Trying out a system in a realistic operational context to gauge whether it works correctly and reliably.

thin client   A partitioning of an application that places little or no application functionality in a client host.

three-tier client/server   A client/server architecture in which there are two specialized types of server, one providing application logic and the other managing shared data.

time-sharing   A computing model in which terminals allow a group of users to run different applications or share applications on a centralized computer.

transaction   A set of resource management actions that are atomic, consistent, isolated from other transactions, and durable. Transaction processing is middleware that supports transactions and thereby simplifies application development.

transport protocol   A layer immediately above the network protocol (such as IP) that specializes it to application needs. In the internet, two widely used examples are UDP and TCP.

trustworthiness   Term applied to a system or application when it works correctly, almost all the time, and is secure against internal and external threats.

two-tier client/server   A client/server architecture with only one kind of server, as distinct from three-tier.

ubiquitous computing   A computing model in which networked computers are unobtrusively sprinkled throughout the physical environment.

usage pricing   For a software application or network service, a component of price based on monitoring of how much the product or service is used.

user   A person who benefits from a networked computing application.

user interface   The interface between a desktop computer and a single user, incorporating information output (graphics, audio, video) and input (keyboard, pointing device, microphone, camera). The portion of the application managing the user interface is the presentation.

utilization   For host processing or link, the fraction of the available capacity actually utilized.

value pricing   Base the price of a product or service on the consumer's willingness to pay rather than costs.

versioning   For a product or service, supplying similar flavors that differ as to functionality, features, quality, or performance.

vertical integration   A business strategy in which a company chooses to make rather than buy all subsystems for its products.

virus   In security, a program that attaches itself to a host program (or other executable file) and surreptitiously runs—replicating itself by attaching to other programs and possibly causing harm—whenever the host program runs.

voice over IP (VoIP)   Provision of a standard telephony service using an internet in whole or in combination with the public telephone network.

Web   A publication (deferred or immediate) social application—typically used for mass publication—in which a Web client is used to browse or navigate through information provided by a Web server. The information is provided in pages, which typically contain hyperlinks to other pages.

wide area network (WAN)   A network that interconnects local area networks over a wide geographic area. The Internet is a WAN.

wireless   In communications, links not requiring wire, coaxial, or fiber media.

work group   A group of users collaborating to complete a longer-term project (such as a design, proposal, etc.).

workstation   An especially powerful (in terms of processing speed) desktop computer, often used for computationally intensive tasks.

World Wide Web (WWW)   Same as Web.

References

[Abe97]   G. Abe. *Residential Broadband*. New York: Macmillan, 1997.

[Abr92]   N. Abramson. *Multiple Access Communications: Foundations for Emerging Technologies*. Los Alamitos, Calif: IEEE Press, 1992.

[Arn96]   K. Arnold and J. Gosling. *The Java Programming Language*. Reading, Mass.: Addison-Wesley, 1996.

[Atk96]   D. Atkins et al. *Internet Security: Professional Reference*. Indianapolis: New Riders Publishing, 1996.

[Bak97]   S. Baker. *CORBA Distributed Objects Using Orbix*. Essex, UK: Addison-Wesley Longman, 1997.

[BCK98]   L. Bass, P. Clements, and R. Kazman. *Software Architecture in Practice*. Reading, Mass.: Addison-Wesley, 1998.

[Ben98]   W. Bennis and P. Ward Biederman. "None of Us Is as Smart as All of Us." *IEEE Computer*, March 1998.

[Ber97]   P. Bernstein and E. Newcomer. *Principles of Transaction Processing*. San Francisco: Morgan Kaufmann, 1997.

[Bie97]   A. Biermann. *Great Ideas in Computer Science: A Gentle Introduction*, 2d ed. Cambridge, Mass.: MIT Press, 1997.

[Bir96]   K. Birman and R. van Renesse. "Software for Reliable Networks." *Scientific American*, May 1996.

[Bol96]   W. Bolton. *Mechatronics: Electronic Control Systems in Mechanical Engineering*, 2d ed. Reading, Mass.: Addison-Wesley Longman, 1999.

[Boo94]   G. Booch. *Object-Oriented Analysis and Design with Applications*, 2d ed. Redwood City, Calif., Benjamin Cummings, 1994.

[Cai97]   F. Cairncross. *The Death of Distance: How the Communications Revolution Will Change Our Lives.* Boston: Harvard Business School Press, 1997.

[Cat97]   R. Cattell and D. Barry, eds. *The Object Database Standard: ODMG 2.0.* San Francisco: Morgan Kaufmann, 1977.

[CDK94]   G. Coulouris, J. Dollimore, and T. Kindberg. *Distributed Systems: Concept and Design.* Harlow, UK: Addison-Wesley, 1994.

[Cha91]   D. Chaum. "Numbers Can Be a Better Form of Cash than Paper," pages 151–156 in *Smart Card 2000,* ed. D. Chaum. Amsterdam: North Holland, 1991.

[Cla97]   D. Clark. "Interoperation, Open Interfaces, and Protocol Architecture," in *White Papers from the Unpredictable Certainty,* Computer Science and Telecommunications Board, National Research Council. Washington, D.C.: National Academic Press, 1997.

[CST94]   Computer Science and Telecommunications Board, National Research Council. *Realizing the Information Future: The Internet and Beyond.* Washington D.C.: National Academies Press, 1994.

[CST95]   Computer Science and Telecommunications Board, National Research Council. *Evolving the High-Performance Computing and Communications Initiative to Support the Nation's Infrastructure.* Washington, D.C.: National Academies Press, 1995.

[CST96a]   Computer Science and Telecommunications Board, National Research Council. *Cryptography's Role in Securing the Information Society.* Washington, D.C.: National Academies Press, 1996.

[CST96b]   Computer Science and Telecommunications Board, National Research Council. *The Unpredictable Certainty: Information Infrastructure through 2000.* Washington, D.C.: National Academies Press, 1996.

[CST97a]   Computer Science and Telecommunications Board, National Research Council. *The Evolution of Untethered Communications.* D.J. Goodman, Chair. Washington, D.C., National Academies Press, 1997.

[CST97b]   Computer Science and Telecommunications Board, National Research Council. *White Papers from the Unpredictable Certainty: Information Infrastructure through 2000.* Washington, D.C., National Academies Press, 1997.

[CST98]   Computer Science and Telecommunications Board, National Research Council. *Trust in Cyberspace.* S. D. Crocker and F. B. Schneider, Chairs. Washington, D.C.: National Academies Press, 1998.

[Dav93]   T. Davenport. *Process Innovation: Reengineering Worth through Information Technology.* Boston: Harvard Business School Press, 1993.

[Dif97]   W. Diffie and S. Landau. *Privacy on the Line, the Politics of Wiretapping and Encryption.* Cambridge, Mass.: MIT Press, 1997.

[Eco96]   N. Economides. "The Economics of Networks." *International Journal of Industrial Organization* 14(6):673–699 (October 1996).

[Fan97]   C. Fancher. "Smart Cards." *Scientific American*, August 1996.

[Far88]   J. Farrell and C. Shapiro. "Dynamic Competition with Switching Costs." *Rand Journal of Economics* 19(1):123–137 (Spring 1988).

[Fla96]   D. Flanagan. *Java in a Nutshell.* Sebastopol, Calif.: O'Reilly, 1996.

[Gam95]   E. Gamma, R. Helm, R. Johnson, and J. Vlissides. *Design Patterns: Elements of Reusable Object-Oriented Software.* Reading, Mass.: Addison-Wesley, 1995.

[Gar89]   B. Garson. *The Electronic Sweatshop: How Computers Are Transforming the Office of the Future into the Factory of the Past.* New York: Penguin Books, 1989.

[Gar96]   S. Garfinkel and G. Spafford. *Practical Unix and Internet Security.* Sebastopol, Calif: O'Reilly, 1996.

[Gar97]   S. Garfinkel and G. Spafford. *Web Security & Commerce.* Sebastopol, Calif.: O'Reilly, 1997.

[Gil97]   P. Gilster. *Digital Literacy.* New York: Wiley, 1997.

[Gra93]   J. Gray and A. Reuter. *Transaction Processing: Concepts and Techniques.* San Francisco: Morgan Kaufmann, 1993.

[Gre96]   R. Grenier and G. Metes. *Going Virtual: Moving Your Organization into the 21st Century.* Upper Saddle River, N.J.: Prentice Hall, 1996.

[Gut95]   M. Guttman and J. Matthews. *The Object Technology Revolution.* New York: Wiley, 1995.

[Haf95]   K. Hafner and J. Markoff. *Cyberpunk: Outlaws and Hackers on the Computer Frontier.* New York: Touchstone Books, 1995.

[Har97]   P. Harmon and M. Watson. *Understanding UML: The Developer's Guide.* San Francisco: Morgan Kaufmann, 1998.

[Haw96]   G. E. Hawisher and C. L. Selfe, eds. *Literacy, Technology, and Society: Confronting the Issues.* Upper Saddle River, N.J.: Prentice Hall, 1996.

[How85]   D. Howe, ed. "The Free On-Line Dictionary of Computing." *http://wombat.doc.ic.ac.uk/*

[Hwa98]   K. Hwang and Z. Xu. *Scalable Parallel Computing: Technology, Architecture, Programming.* New York: WCB/McGraw-Hill, 1998.

[Ing98]   D. E. Ingber. "The Architecture of Life." *Scientific American*, January 1998.

[Jon97]   K. Jones. "Auto Net To Pave E-Commerce Way." *Inter@active Week*, September 15, 1997.

[Kah97]   B. Kahle. "Preserving the Internet." *Scientific American*, March 1997.

[Kat92]   M. Katz and C. Shapiro. "Product Introduction with Network Externalities." *Journal of Industrial Economics* 40(1):55–83, (March 1992).

[Kee97]   P. Keen and C. Ballance. *On-Line Profits: A Manager's Guide to Electronic Commerce*. Boston: Harvard Business School Press, 1997.

[Kep97]   J. Kephart, G. Sorkin, D. Chess, and S. White. "Fighting Computer Viruses." *Scientific American*, November 1997.

[KFN93]   C. Kaner, J. Falk, and H. Nguyen. *Testing Computer Software*. Scottsdale, AZ: The Coriolis Group, 1993.

[Kri98]   D. Krieger and R. Adler. "The Emergence of Distributed Component Platforms." *IEEE Computer,* March 1998.

[Lau98}   S. St. Laurent. *Xml: A Primer.* Foster City, Calif.: IDG Books, 1998.

[Lee94]   E. Lee and D. Messerschmitt. *Digital Communication*, 2d ed. Boston: Kluwer Academic Press, 1994.

[Les97a]   M. Lesk. "Going Digital." *Scientific American*, March 1997.

[Les97b]   M. Lesk, *Practical Digital Libraries: Books, Bytes, and Bucks*. San Francisco: Morgan Kaufmann, 1997.

[Lyn97]   C. Lynch. "Searching the Internet." *Scientific American*, March 1997.

[Mac95a]   J. MacKie-Mason and H. Varian. "Pricing the Internet," in *Public Access to the Internet,* B. Kahin and J. Keller, eds. Cambridge, Mass.: MIT Press, 1995.

[Mac95b]   J. MacKie-Mason and H. Varian. "Pricing Congestible Network Resources." *IEEE Journal on Selected Areas in Communications* 13(7) (September 1995).

[Mac95c]   J. MacKie-Mason and H. Varian. "Some FAQs about Usage-Based Pricing." *Computer Networks & ISDN Systems*, December 1995.

[McC95]   S. McCanne and V. Jacobson. "vic: A Flexible Framework for Packet Video." *Proceedings of the Third International Conference on Multimedia '95*, pages 511–522.

[McC97]   S. McConnell. *Software Project Survival Guide*. Redmond, Wash.: Microsoft Press, 1997.

[McK97a]   L. McKnight and J. Bailey. "Internet Economics: When Constituencies Collide in Cyberspace." *IEEE Internet Computing*, December 1997.

[McK97b]   L. McKnight and J. Bailey, *Internet Economics*. Cambridge, Mass.: MIT Press, 1997.

[Mes96a]   D. Messerschmitt, "The Convergence of Telecommunications and Computing: What Are the Implications Today?" *IEEE Proceedings*, August 1996.

[Mes96b]   D. Messerschmitt, "Convergence of Telecommunications with Computing." *Technology in Society* 18(3).

[Mit96]   W. Mitchell. *City of Bits: Space, Place, and the Infobahn*. Cambridge, Mass.: MIT Press, 1996.

[Mok97]   P. Mokhtarian, "Now That Travel Can Be Virtual, Will Congestion Virtually Disappear?" *Scientific American*, October 1997.

[Neg96]   N. Negroponte and M. Asher, eds. *Being Digital*. New York: Vintage Books, 1996.

[Neu95]   P. Neumann. *Computer Related Risks*. Reading, Mass.: Addison-Wesley, 1995.

[Oak96]   R. Oakman. *The Computer Triangle: Hardware, Software, People*. New York: Wiley, 1996.

[OHE96a]   R. Orfali, D. Harkey, and J. Edwards. *The Essential Client/Server Survival Guide*, 2d ed. New York: Wiley, 1996.

[OHE96b]   R. Orfali, D. Harkey, and J. Edwards. *The Essential Distributed Objects Survival Guide*. New York: Wiley, 1996.

[Oke96]   A. Okerson. "Who Owns Digital Works?" *Scientific American*, July 1996.

[Ole98]   D. O'Leary. "Enterprise Knowledge Management." *IEEE Computer*, March 1998.

[OPR96]   R. Otte, P. Patrick, and M. Roy. *Understanding CORBA, The Common Object Request Broker Architecture*. New York: Prentice Hall, 1996.

[OST97]   Office of the President of the United States, Office of Science and Technology Policy, "Cybernation: The American Infrastructure in the Information Age." Washington, D.C., April 1997.

[Oud97]   B. Oudet. "Multilingualism on the Internet." *Scientific American*, March 1997.

[Ous98]   J. Ousterhout. "Scripting: Higher-Level Programming for the 21st Century." *IEEE Computer*, March 1998.

[Pah95]   K. Pahlavan and A. Levesque. *Wireless Information Networks*. New York: Wiley, 1995.

[Pan98]   A. Pang. "General Motor's New Intranet Sets the Pace." *Internet Computing*, March 2, 1998.

[Pen96]   A. Pentland, "Smart Rooms." *Scientific American*, April 1996.

[Per85]   S. Personick. *Fiber Optics: Technology and Applications*. New York: Plenum, 1985.

[Pet96]   L. Peterson and B. Davie. *Computer Networks: A Systems Approach*. San Francisco: Morgan Kaufmann, 1996.

[Pre96]   R. Pressman. *Software Engineering, A Practitioner's Approach*. New York: McGraw-Hill, 1996.

[Ram98]   R. Ramaswami and K. Sivarajan. *Optical Networks: A Practical Perspective*. San Francisco: Morgan Kaufmann, 1998.

[Ran95]   J. Ranade. *CORBA: A Guide to Common Request Broker Architecture*. New York: McGraw-Hill, 1995.

[Rap96]   T. Rappaport. *Wireless Communications: Principles and Practice*. New York: Prentice-Hall, 1996.

[Res97a]   P. Resnick and H. Varian, eds. "Special Section: Recommender Systems." *Communications of the ACM*, March 1997.

[Res97b]   P. Resnick. "Filtering Information on the Internet." *Scientific American*, pages 106–108, March 1997.

[Ros97]   R. Rosenberg. *The Social Impact of Computers*, 2d ed. San Diego: Academic Press, 1997.

[Row92]   L. Rowe and B. Smith. "A Continuous Media Player," *Proceedings of the Third International Workshop on Network and Operating System Support for Digital Audio and Video*, 1992.

[Sam90]   P. Samuelson. "Should Program Algorithms Be Patented?" *Communications of the ACM* 33:(8) (August 1990).

[SAP97]   SAP. "An Integrated Vision for High Performance Supply Chain Management," white paper by Systems, Applications, and Products in Data Processing AG, 1997.

[Sch90]   M. Schroeder. *Number Theory in Science and Communication*, 2d ed. Berlin: Springer-Verlag, 1990.

[Sch95]   B. Schatz. "Information Analysis in the Net: The Interspace of the Twenty-First Century," white paper for *America in the Age of Information: A Forum on Federal Information and Communications R & D*. National Library of Medicine, July 1995.

[Sch96]   B. Schneier. *Applied Cryptography*. New York: Wiley, 1996.

[Sha98]   C. Shapiro and H. Varian. *Information Rules: A Strategic Guide to the Network Economy.* Boston: Harvard Business School Press, 1998.

[Sie96]   J. Siegel. *CORBA: Fundamentals and Programming.* New York: Wiley, 1996.

[Sil97]   A. Silberschatz and P. P. Galvin. *Operating System Concepts.* Reading, Mass.: Addison-Wesley, 1997.

[Ste97]   M. Stefik. "Trusted Systems." *Scientific American*, March 1997.

[Szy98]   C. Szyperski. *Component Software: Beyond Object-Oriented Programming.* Reading, Mass.: Addison-Wesley, 1998.

[Tan97]   A. Tanenbaum and A. Woodhull. *Operating Systems: Design and Implementation.* Upper Saddle River, N.J.: Prentice Hall, 1997.

[Tyg96]   J. Tygar. "Atomicity in Electronic Commerce," in *Proc. ACM Symposium on Principles of Distributed Computing.* New York: ACM, 1996.

[Var87]   H. Varian. *Intermediate Microeconomics.* New York: W. W. Norton, 1987.

[Var95]   ———. "Pricing Information Goods." Research Libraries Group Symposium on Scholarship of the New Information Environment Proceedings, Harvard Law School, May 2–3, 1995.

[Var97]   ———. "Versioning Information Goods." Unpublished paper available at *http://www.sims.berkeley.edu/~hal/Papers/ version.pdf*

[Wal89]   R. Walton. *Up and Running: Integrating Technology and the Organization.* Boston: Harvard Business School Press, 1989.

[Wal96]   J. Walrand and P. Varaiya. *High-Performance Communication Networks.* San Francisco: Morgan Kaufmann, 1996.

[Wat95]   K. Watterson. *Client/Server Technology for Managers.* Reading, Mass: Addison-Wesley, 1995.

[Wei93]   M. Weiser. "Ubiquitous Computing." *Computer*, October 1993.

[WGH98]   J. Ware, J. Gebauer, A. Hartman, and M. Roldan. *The Search for Digital Excellence.* New York: McGraw-Hill, 1998.

[Woo94]   M. Wooldridge and N. Jennings, eds. "Intelligent Agents." *Proceedings of ECAI-94 Workshop on Agent Theories, Architectures, and Languages.* Amsterdam: Springer-Verlag, August 1994.

[You97]   E. Yourdon and P. Becker. *Death March: The Complete Software Developer's Guide to Surviving "Mission Impossible" Projects.* New York: Prentice Hall, 1997.

Index